Birnbaum's

Walt Disney World®

Stephen Birnbaum
Founding Editor

Tom Passavant
Editorial Director

Jill Safro
Editor

Deanna Caron
Managing Editor

Todd Sebastian Williams
Art Director

Isabel Shamlian
Copy Editor

Suzy Goytizolo
Editorial Assistant

Alice Garrard
Contributing Editor

Alexandra Mayes Birnbaum
Consulting Editor

THE OFFICIAL GUIDE

HYPERION AND HEARST BUSINESS PUBLISHING, INC.

Table of

Getting Ready to Go

7

Here is all the practical information you need to organize a Walt Disney World visit, down to the smallest detail: when to go; how to get there; how to save money; plus hints for parents, travelers with disabilities, singles, and older visitors.

Transportation & Accommodations

39

Two big questions about Walt Disney World are where to stay and how to get around. Accommodations range from plush suites to modest campsites, with thousands of rooms, villas—even treehouses—in between. Our guide describes every Disney resort, along with some off-property options. And, we explain the World's vast transportation system.

Magic Kingdom

85

The enchantment of Walt Disney World is most apparent in the wealth of attractions and amusements that fill this, the most famous entertainment zone of all. Our land-by-land guide describes all there is to see and do, where to shop, and how to avoid the crowds, plus plenty of other insider tips.

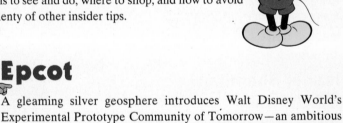

Epcot

115

A gleaming silver geosphere introduces Walt Disney World's Experimental Prototype Community of Tomorrow—an ambitious exploration of the world of the future as well as the present. Future World and World Showcase offer every visitor the opportunity to be a global and cerebral voyager, without setting foot outside Florida. Here's how to make the most of this uniquely fascinating destination.

Disney-MGM Studios

149

Now's your chance to be part of Hollywood's Golden Years. Everything from the magic of animation to the excitement of daring stunts and special effects is waiting to be enjoyed. There are also opportunities to be part of classic TV shows and to create sound effects. We've developed strategies for seeing this Tinseltown, ensuring the most fun and the least time standing around.

Contents

Animal Kingdom

The newest addition to Disney's theme park lineup celebrates the circle of life and all the wonders of the animal world. Amid nature's soothing majesty, you'll experience a heart-pounding hunt for ivory poachers, dodge dastardly dinosaurs, and encounter a fire-breathing dragon. Our exclusive coverage guarantees a fun-filled trip to a place where humans are humbly reminded of their tenuous position in the food chain.

Everything Else in the World

Beyond the theme park boundaries lie countless acres full of just the sorts of wonders for which Walt Disney World is famous: state-of-the-art water parks; a nighttime entertainment, shopping, and dining district; and the Disney Institute among them. So if you want to ride down watery slides, dance the night away, shop at elegant boutiques, or "go to school" behind the scenes, this chapter will help you find your way.

Sports

Walt Disney World has more tennis courts and golf greens than most posh resorts, plus plenty of places for boating, biking, horseback riding, swimming, and fishing. The rest of the sporting bases are covered by Disney's Wide World of Sports, a multi-sport facility that aims to please athlete and spectator alike. Here's how to combine these options with the rest of the fun at Walt Disney World.

Good Meals, Great Times

Restaurants around the Walt Disney World property run the gamut from simple snack shops to bastions of haute cuisine. The choices are nearly endless, so we've organized them all into alphabetical, area-by-area, and meal-by-meal directories that let you know where each restaurant is located and what specialties it offers. We also tell you about the various dinner shows, the best family fare, where to dine with the Disney characters, and where to enjoy an after-dinner drink.

For Steve, who merely made all this possible.

Other 1998 Birnbaum's Official Disney Guides

Disneyland
Walt Disney World For Kids, By Kids
Walt Disney World Without Kids

A WORD FROM THE EDITORS

For some of us, our first Walt Disney World experience dates back to 1971, the year this new "Disneyland in Florida" made its debut. At that time, the Magic Kingdom was the only theme park, and it could be explored easily in a few days. Early visitors will remember, too, that many attractions were still under construction. Nonetheless, for those who came, it was love at first sight, and we've returned again and again.

Never before has there been so much incentive to visit (and revisit) the memory-making capital of the world. The confetti from Walt Disney World's 25th anniversary celebration will hardly have time to settle before it starts flying all over again, marking yet another major milestone in WDW history—the grand opening of

Animal Kingdom, the fourth in an ever-expanding family of theme parks, this May. We are both privileged and proud to provide our readers with an exclusive first look at Animal Kingdom, the newest and largest Disney park to date.

When Steve Birnbaum launched this guide back in 1981, he made it very clear what was expected of anyone who worked on it. The book would be meticulously revised each year, leaving no attraction untested, no snack or meal untasted, no hotel untried. When Steve became curious as to how efficiently the bus system ran at Walt Disney World, he dispatched an editor to spend an entire day riding buses around the resort and report her findings. (The buses did, by the way, run on schedule.)

It is experiences like these, accumulated over the years, that make this book the most authoritative guide to the World. Our expertise, however, was not achieved by being escorted through back doors of attractions or bypassing lines (although we would have thoroughly enjoyed that). Instead, we waited with all the other visitors in hopes of uncovering strategies that would allow readers to avoid the pitfalls many first-timers encounter. In one typical case, an editor waited more than an hour to take a backstage tour at the Studios. Standing in line with notebook and tape recorder in hand, she was asked by the man behind her if there was a quiz at the end. When she explained what she was doing, he expressed surprise to learn that she was waiting with the rest of the hordes. How better, she replied, to help people like you?

After more than a quarter of a century, the World and the number of visitors has expanded—and so has our knowledge of the most popular vacation destination on the planet. On some occasions we've encountered sweltering weather and swelling crowds, times when even the happiest of families or best of friends turn into arch-enemies for a day. At times the lines seemed endless and, in a triumph of bad planning, we managed to take in just a few attractions before dinnertime. Had we known then what we know now, we could have spared ourselves some trying experiences.

We've done our best to keep you from making the same mistakes. We realize that even the most meticulous vacation planner needs detailed, accurate, and objective information to prepare an intelligent itinerary. Anyone who takes the time to read even the outlines of the pages that follow will find an emerging pattern that fits his or her special needs and tastes; for those unwilling to exert even that much effort, we've compiled specific day-by-day itineraries for visits of varying length—in order to protect you from yourself.

This guidebook owes an enormous debt to the extraordinary people who manage and run Walt Disney World. Despite the designation "Official Guide," we want to stress that *the Walt Disney World staff members have exercised no veto power whatsoever over the contents of this book.* What they *have* done is open their files and explain operations to us in the most generous way, so that we could prepare comprehensive appraisals to help visitors understand the complex workings of a very complex enterprise. A special nod goes to all those involved with Animal Kingdom—as much for their cooperation as for their infectious enthusiasm.

We daresay there have been times when the Disney folks are less than delighted with some of our opinions, yet these statements all remain in the guide. This year, we've even sprinkled "Birnbaum's Bests" throughout the book, highlighting our favorite attractions—the crowd-pleasers we believe stand head, shoulders, and ears above the rest.

You, the reader, benefit from the combination of our years of experience and independent voice that, together with our access to accurate, up-to-date inside information from the Disney staff, make this guide unique. We like to think it's indispensable, but we'll let you be the judge of that a few hundred pages from now.

The fact remains that this guide would never have become as useful as it is without the extremely forthcoming cooperation of Walt Disney World personnel at every level. Both in the park and behind the scenes, they've been the source of the most critical factual data. We hope we're not omitting any names in specifically thanking Kim Carlson (Information Management); Robin Domigan (Resorts); Rick Sylvain (Media Relations); Gene Duncan (Photography); and Tim Lewis (Disney Publishing); Tom Elrod, Bo Boyd, Marty Sklar, Charlie Ridgway, Greg Albrecht, Tina Rebstock, Shelly Anderson, Jacqui Cintron, and Todd Crawford. To Linda Warren, Julie Woodward, Laura Simpson, Diane Hancock, Regina Maher, and Valjean Smoley, who do so much to make our job easier (and often possible), more thanks for their extraordinary help.

We'd also like to thank our favorite off-site Disney expert, Wendy Lefkon, who edited these guides for many years and is still instrumental in their publication as executive editor at Hyperion. Hats off to Shari Hartford, who kept our own cast of characters on schedule; Susan Hohl, who provided valuable artistic input; Laura Vitale, for her wondrously uncompromising sense of style; and Louise Collazo for her excellent eye in proofreading the final galleys.

Of course, no list of acknowledgments would be complete without mentioning our founding editor, Steve Birnbaum, whose spirit, wisdom, and humor still infuse these pages, as well as Alexandra Mayes Birnbaum, who continues to be a guiding light—to say nothing of a careful reader of every word.

Finally, it's important to remember that every worthwhile travel guide is a living enterprise; the book you hold in your hands is our best effort at explaining how to enjoy Walt Disney World at this moment, but its text is in no way cast in bronze. Walt Disney World is constantly changing and growing, and in each annual edition we refine and expand our material to serve your needs even better. For this year's edition, though, this must be the final word.

Have a great visit!

The Editors

Don't Forget to Write

No contribution is of greater value to us in preparing the next edition of this book than your comments on what we have written and on your own experiences at Walt Disney World. Please share your insights with us by writing to:

The Editors, Official Disney Guides
Birnbaum's Walt Disney World 1998
1790 Broadway, Sixth Floor
New York, NY 10019

Getting Ready to Go

T he key to a fabulous vacation at Walt Disney World is advance planning. This remarkably varied complex is too vast and diverse to allow a spontaneous visit to be undertaken with much success—especially when you consider the rapid rate at which the World is expanding. That does not mean that even the most casual visitors can't have some significant fun, but they are bound to have regrets about things they missed because of time pressures or a simple lack of information. The main purpose of this guide is to eliminate that potential frustration.

What follows, then, is meant to provide a sensible scheme for planning a satisfying visit to Walt Disney World, one that will offer the most fun and the least amount of disappointment. But how do you know which of the countless activities will be the most enjoyable for you and your family? Do your homework—the best strategy is to make sure you have a clear idea of all that is available *before* you arrive in the Orlando area.

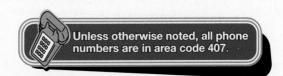

Unless otherwise noted, all phone numbers are in area code 407.

WHEN TO GO

When talk finally turns to the best time to make a trip to Walt Disney World, Christmas and Easter are often mentioned, as well as the weeks that comprise the traditional summer vacation period—especially if there are children in the family. But there is also good reason to avoid these periods, namely the hordes they inevitably attract. And when Walt Disney World is crowded, it can be very crowded indeed. On the busiest days, visitors may wait more than an hour to see some of the more popular attractions. That's at least twice as long as during less crowded times of the year.

Considering seasonal hours, the weather, and the crowd patterns described in the charts that follow, optimal times to visit Walt Disney World are usually mid-January through early February, late April through early June, and September through December (except Thanksgiving and Christmas weeks). However, once Animal Kingdom opens in May, expect crowds throughout the World to swell a bit.

Hot Tip

The period beween the end of Thanksgiving weekend and the week before Christmas is one of least crowded and most festive times of the year. The World is teeming with holiday parties, parades, fireworks, and other special events.

Note that during some of the less crowded times of the year—particularly during January and February—some attractions are typically closed for renovations. In addition, the water parks are often closed for refurbishment during the cooler months.

Late December is an especially festive time of year the world over, and Walt Disney World is no exception. All of the theme parks are decorated to the nines for the holiday season. The Magic Kingdom, Epcot, and the Disney-MGM Studios feature nightly tree-lighting ceremonies. Many other special events are held during this period, including Mickey's Very Merry Christmas Party in the Magic Kingdom (separate admission ticket required). The party brings a dusting of snow to Main Street from 8 P.M. to 1 A.M. for several days during the first three weeks of December. It also features holiday shows around the park, including Mickey's Very Merry Christmas Parade, plus a special finale of Fantasy in the Sky fireworks. Select performances from Mickey's Very Merry Christmas Party are also staged in the park during regular hours throughout the holiday season.

Epcot celebrates the season with Holidays Around the World, including nightly performances of the Candlelight Processional, complete with a 450-voice choir, a 50-piece orchestra, and a reading of the story of Christmas by a celebrity narrator. Dinner packages are available for selected World Showcase restaurants, and the night ends with a holiday version of IllumiNations. The Disney-MGM Studios features the largest family-owned collection of Christmas lights, in a display of about four million twinkling lights depicting holiday scenes and a 65-foot "wall of angels" that together illuminate Residential Street.

One way to take advantage of all there is to see and do at Walt Disney World during this time of year is to book a Jolly Holidays package, offered from late November through late December. The packages are available for two to ten nights and include admission to the Jolly Holidays Dinner Show held at the Contemporary resort. This festive show, available only as part of a package, features an all-you-can-eat old-fashioned holiday feast and a lively performance by a cast of more than 100 singers and dancers. A steady stream of Disney and Christmas characters enchants kids as traditional carols sate adults.

There are holiday receptions at WDW hotels too, including a turn-of-the-century Christmas at the Grand Floridian, a seaside party at the Yacht Club and Beach Club, a Southwestern Christmas at the Contemporary, and a Cajun holiday at Dixie Landings. Transportation is provided to each of the receptions as part of the packages, most of which also include unlimited admission to the theme parks and Pleasure Island. For reservations, contact a travel agent, or call W-DISNEY (934-7639), or the Walt Disney Travel Company at 800-828-0228.

Keeping WDW Hours

Because operating hours fluctuate, we advise calling 824-4321 for up-to-the-minute schedules for the time of your visit.

THEME PARKS: Hours of operation at all four Disney theme parks vary seasonally. For more than a third of the year—in May, September, October, parts of November and December, and all of January—the Magic Kingdom is usually open from 9 A.M. to 7 P.M.; Epcot is open from 9 A.M. to 9 P.M. (Future World opens at 9 A.M., World Showcase at 11 A.M.); the Disney-MGM Studios is open from 9 A.M. to 9 P.M.; and Animal Kingdom is expected to be open from 7:30 A.M. until about one hour after dusk.

The Magic Kingdom keeps later hours through the summer and other high-attendance periods. Epcot and the Disney-MGM Studios stay open till 10 P.M. during Presidents' week and spring school breaks, and till midnight during certain holiday periods (Thanksgiving, Christmas, and Easter). With the exception of Animal Kingdom, the parks stay open until 1 A.M. or 2 A.M. on New Year's Eve. The Disney-MGM Studios often stays open till midnight in the summer, too. On select days,

WDW resort guests can enter Magic Kingdom, Epcot, or the Disney-MGM Studios 1½ hours before the official opening time. Note that only some attractions in a given park open early. For details about early-entry days, see "Park Primer" in each park chapter (pages 88, 118, and 152).

DOWNTOWN DISNEY MARKETPLACE: Shops are open from 9:30 A.M. to 11 P.M. daily. Restaurant hours vary.

DOWNTOWN DISNEY WEST SIDE: At the AMC Theatres cineplex, movies are shown throughout the day, beginning at about 1 P.M. Clubs are open from about 7 P.M. to 2 A.M.

PLEASURE ISLAND: Clubs on the island are open from about 7 P.M. to 2 A.M. daily; shops, from 11 A.M. to 2 A.M.; and restaurants, from about 11:30 A.M. to midnight.

WATER PARKS: Although hours vary, the water parks are generally open from about 10 A.M. to 5 P.M., with extended hours in effect during summer months.

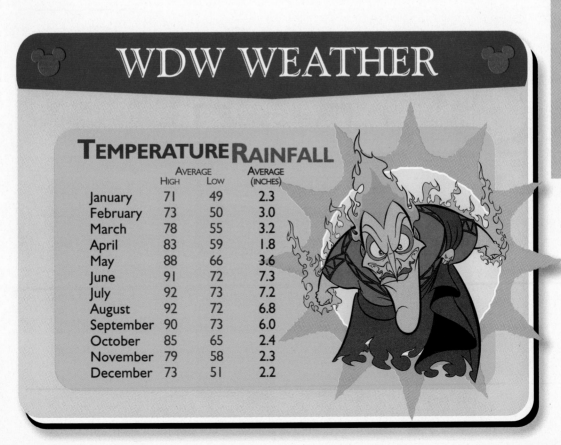

WDW WEATHER

| | TEMPERATURE | | RAINFALL |
	AVERAGE HIGH	AVERAGE LOW	AVERAGE (INCHES)
January	71	49	2.3
February	73	50	3.0
March	78	55	3.2
April	83	59	1.8
May	88	66	3.6
June	91	72	7.3
July	92	73	7.2
August	92	72	6.8
September	90	73	6.0
October	85	65	2.4
November	79	58	2.3
December	73	51	2.2

Crowd Patterns

Day-to-Day Trends

Many visitors to Walt Disney World assume that weekends are by far the busiest days in all of the theme parks. However, with the exception of certain holiday periods, Monday, Thursday, and Saturday tend to be the most crowded days at the Magic Kingdom; Tuesday and Friday generally net the biggest throngs at Epcot; and Wednesday and Sunday draw larger crowds at the Disney-MGM Studios. Keep in mind that as Disney unveils Animal Kingdom in May, the newest and biggest theme park in the World, very large crowds will be drawn to the property on a daily basis. We expect Saturdays and Sundays to be among the busiest days at this park.

When the time comes to plot an itinerary, it's helpful to know about crowd patterns beyond the four theme parks as well. As a rule, Downtown Disney (Pleasure Island, the Marketplace, and the West Side) and Disney's water parks host their largest throngs on weekends. Of course, in these circles, a bigger crowd can often mean a better time. Golfers should note that weekend tee times are typically in the highest demand, while Monday and Tuesday times are the easiest to come by.

Seasonal Shifts

The chart below indicates the density of crowds in the theme parks throughout the year. Though it's tough to generalize about a property as vast and ever-changing as Walt Disney World—special events and package deals can swell park attendance during a period typically marked by smaller crowds— the chart highlights historic trends. Again, the spring addition of Animal Kingdom could bring thicker crowds to all Disney parks.

Least crowded means that there may be lines, but most attractions can be visited without much waiting; average attendance refers to times when there are lots of people around but lines are manageable; and most crowded reflects times when lines at popular attractions can mean a wait of as much as two hours.

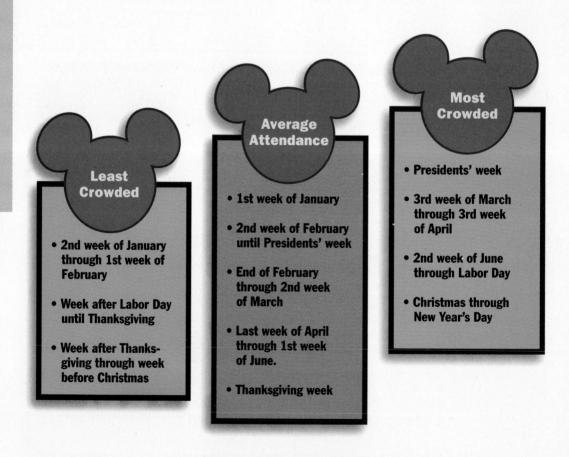

Least Crowded

- 2nd week of January through 1st week of February

- Week after Labor Day until Thanksgiving

- Week after Thanksgiving through week before Christmas

Average Attendance

- 1st week of January

- 2nd week of February until Presidents' week

- End of February through 2nd week of March

- Last week of April through 1st week of June.

- Thanksgiving week

Most Crowded

- Presidents' week

- 3rd week of March through 3rd week of April

- 2nd week of June through Labor Day

- Christmas through New Year's Day

Holidays & Special Events

Inside Walt Disney World

Special affairs are staged throughout the year, not only to mark holidays but also to celebrate other interests. The Magic Kingdom, Epcot, the Disney-MGM Studios, and Downtown Disney host many happenings, from sporting events to festivals geared toward jazz, gardens, technology, and even soap operas. Call 824-4321 for specific dates and additional information about any of the listed events.

JANUARY

Walt Disney World Marathon (January 11): Some 7,000 entrants run through the Magic Kingdom, Epcot, the Disney-MGM Studios, and other scenic areas of the World during this 26.2-mile race. Live bands, hot-air balloons, and Disney characters are on hand to inspire runners. Call 939-7810 for additional information.

LPGA HealthSouth Inaugural (January 17–19): Each year, top women golf pros mark the dawn of a new season with this three-day tournament on the Lake Buena Vista golf course.

Indy 200 (January 22–24): Indy race cars burn rubber in this annual event, held at the Walt Disney World Speedway, a one-mile track just south of the Magic Kingdom.

FEBRUARY

Mardi Gras (February): Jazz bands, Creole food, and street performers toast New Orleans' biggest party at Pleasure Island. At Epcot, visit World Showcase to see how other countries celebrate Mardi Gras.

MARCH

Epcot Sci-Tech Adventure (March): A month-long series of special events that highlight the latest inventions, discoveries, and new ways to have fun with science and technology.

Soap Opera Festival (March): A weekend-long celebration of ABC daytime dramas is held at the Disney-MGM Studios. Guests meet soap stars; learn how dramas are made; talk to the producers and writers; see the sets, props, and costumes from the shows; and even have a shot at an audition.

Saint Patrick's Day (March 17): Everyone is Irish on Saint Patrick's day—especially at Pleasure Ire-land. Don't forget to wear something green to celebrate the Emerald Isle.

APRIL–MAY

Easter (April 12): A nationally televised parade in the Magic Kingdom helps make this holiday celebration special. All of the Disney theme parks stay open late during the two weeks straddling the Easter holiday. This is an extremely busy time to visit.

Epcot International Flower and Garden Festival (April 17–May 31): Epcot is blooming with elaborate gardens (including more than 30 million blossoms) and topiary displays, behind-the-scenes tours, gardening workshops, and guest speakers. Learn from the experts how to create a beautiful garden at home. Call 827-7200 for package information.

JUNE

Black Music Month Celebration (June): Pleasure Island and *Vibe* magazine showcase all genres of black music: gospel, rap, R & B, reggae, jazz, and more.

JULY

Fourth of July Celebration: Double-size fireworks over the Magic Kingdom, the Disney-MGM Studios' spectacular fireworks show, and Epcot's IllumiNations make for a colorful night. This is a very busy time to visit.

SEPTEMBER

Disneyana (September): A veritable heaven for Disney collectors. The 1998 event will be held at Disneyland; Walt Disney World hosts the following year.

Night of Joy (September 12–13): Three nights of musical celebration highlight the best in contemporary Christian music.

OCTOBER

Pleasure Island Jazz Fest (October): Great jazz from today and yesterday is performed for one weekend throughout the island.

Walt Disney World/Oldsmobile Golf Classic (October 22–25): Top PGA Tour players compete alongside amateurs in this big tourney, played on the Palm, Magnolia, and Lake Buena Vista courses.

Epcot International Food and Wine Festival (late October–November): World Showcase celebrates food, beverages, and cultures from around the world (even those not represented around the lagoon). Guests experience the flavors of a variety of countries through tastings, demonstrations, wine and cooking seminars, and special entertainment.

Mickey's Not-So-Scary Halloween Party (October 31): All the lands of the Magic Kingdom get dressed up for the occasion in festive Halloween decor. Activities include a costume contest and parade, special appearances by Disney villains, trick-or-treating, plus fireworks and SpectroMagic.

NOVEMBER–DECEMBER

Festival of the Masters (November): This three-day fine arts show draws over 200 top artists to the Downtown Disney Marketplace to showcase their work.

Teddy Bear & Doll Convention (November): Both longtime collectors and newcomers descend on the Contemporary resort and Epcot to see world-renowned craftspeople's creations. Packages include seminars and workshops, a limited-edition private sale, an auction, parties, and an awards ceremony.

Disney's Magical Holidays (November 27–December 31): Decorations and festivities abound in Walt Disney World's parks and resorts. The Magic Kingdom hosts Mickey's Very Merry Christmas Party on several nights during the first two weeks of December, complete with snow on Main Street and hot cocoa. Entertainment for the special-ticket party includes Mickey's Very Merry Christmas Parade and a holiday edition of Fantasy in the Sky fireworks; select performances are also staged during regular hours throughout the holiday season. Epcot's Holidays Around the World features a special edition of IllumiNations, "The Lights of Winter," and a Candlelight Processional with choral concert. The Osborne Family Spectacle of Lights brightens the Disney-MGM Studios with about four million sparkling lights on Residential Street. A variety of packages include admission to special-ticket holiday shows and parties, including the Jolly Holidays Dinner Show at the Contemporary resort, a feast and musical extravaganza. For information on these events and the Jolly Holidays packages offered during this period, call 934-7639, or call the Walt Disney Travel Company at 800-828-0228.

New Year's Eve Celebration (December 31): There are extra-large fireworks displays over the Magic Kingdom, Epcot, and the Disney-MGM Studios. (The Magic Kingdom and Epcot are open until 2 A.M. and the Studios is open until 1 A.M. for the occasion.) Pleasure Island hosts a grand special-ticket bash. Many of the resorts, as well as the clubs at Downtown Disney West Side, also ring in the new year Disney-style.

Especially for Kids

Epcot's World Showcase supplements its usual multicultural offerings with kids' activity zones that have a playful twist. Past activities have included piñata decorating (in Mexico), macaroni art (in Italy), and watercolor painting (in France). The United Kingdom hosts the popular Alice's Tea Party. All events are free to Epcot guests.

PLANNING AHEAD
Logistics

Organizing a trip properly takes time, but most travelers find the increased enjoyment well worth the effort. The fact is, planning can become a pleasant sort of "armchair" exercise, and kids will enjoy their visit to Walt Disney World all the more if they, too, are involved in the planning process.

To aid in that effort, we immodestly recommend our guide, *Birnbaum's Walt Disney World For Kids, By Kids* ($9.95), a comprehensive look at the World from a young person's perspective, written for kids ages 7 to 14. For adults traveling sans children, our *Birnbaum's Walt Disney World Without Kids* ($11.95), is the definitive source.

Information Sources

For information about Walt Disney World, call WDW Information at 824-4321 or write to the Walt Disney World Company; Box 10000; Lake Buena Vista, FL 32830-1000. Internet users can tap into updates about the World, order tickets, and make Walt Disney World resort reservations, by entering *http://www.disneyworld.com*.

For information and discounts on Orlando area attractions and accommodations, contact the Official Visitor Information Center; 8723 International Dr., Suite 101; Orlando, FL 32819; 363-5872 or 800-551-0181; *http://www.goflorida.com/Orlando*.

For details about other Central Florida attractions, contact the Florida Tourism Industry Marketing Corp.; 661 E. Jefferson St., Suite 300; Tallahassee, FL 32301; 904-487-1462.

To receive a free copy of The Orlando Magicard, call 800-551-0181. Cardholders receive information and discounts at many Orlando-area hotels, restaurants, and theme parks.

Disney/AAA Travel Center: It's best to arrive on-site with a confirmed hotel reservation. Those driving to Walt Disney World from points north can arrange that assurance easily at this full-service visitors center, located at the intersection of I-75 and S.R. 200 in Ocala, Florida, about 90 miles north of Orlando. The facility is equipped to help WDW-bound vacationers plan their time, purchase theme park tickets, make (or confirm) hotel reservations, and even make dining reservations. For departing guests who didn't buy enough pairs of mouse ears, it also stocks character merchandise; 352-854-0770.

On-site resources: A variety of other information sources is available upon arrival. Those staying at WDW resorts should consider their hotel's Guest Services desk the primary resource. WDW resort guests can also turn their room TV to Channel 5 for a preview of attractions (a good orientation for first-time visitors). Fort Wilderness campers are advised to stop at the Pioneer Hall Information and Ticket

What to Pack

While there is hardly a dress code at Walt Disney World, casual clothing is the rule, with few exceptions. Most notably, jackets are required for men at Victoria & Albert's restaurant in the Grand Floridian resort. More generally, T-shirts and shorts are acceptable during the day. For evening, slacks, jeans, or Bermuda shorts are appropriate. Bathing suits are a must, along with the appropriate attire for any sport you want to pursue.

Lightweight sweaters are necessary even in summer—to wear indoors when the air-conditioning gets frigid. From November through March, warmer clothing is a must for evening. Pack for weather extremes so you'll be comfy should it become unseasonably warm or cool. Always bring plenty of sunscreen, since even the winter sun here can be brutal. In summer, pack lightweight rain gear and a compact umbrella. The most important item of all? Comfortable walking shoes.

Window, call extension 2788, or touch 11 on a phone at any comfort station.

Guests at the resorts on Hotel Plaza Blvd. can access a tourist-information program of their own on Channel 7. Some other area hotels also show a version of the orientation, usually aiming to provide an overview of all Central Florida attractions.

For day visitors: All day visitors—that is, those staying off Disney property or living in the Orlando area—receive a useful handout at the Auto Plazas. When purchasing one-day admission to a given theme park, guests receive a guidemap to that park. Multi-day pass holders may receive all four park guides upon request. Extra guides are available at City Hall (in the Magic Kingdom) and at Guest Relations (in Epcot, the Disney-MGM Studios, and Animal Kingdom).

Package Pointers

The sheer number and diversity of packages offering vacations in Central Florida are enough to bewilder even the savviest traveler. Still, such plans are worth exploring. They offer the convenience of a vacation that's completely organized in advance, and that will generally cost less than the sum of the same transportation, accommodations, and admission elements purchased separately.

American Airlines Fly Away Vacations (800-321-2121), Delta Dream Vacations (800-872-7786), TWA Getaway Vacations (800-438-2929), American Express Vacation Travel (800-937-2639), and the Walt Disney Travel Company (800-828-0228) offer packages featuring WDW on-site hotels, as well as off-property accommodations. Some packages offer the added attraction of air transportation. AAA members should inquire about AAA Disney Driveaway Vacation packages, which offer perks for drivers to the World. Also check the travel section of your local newspaper for other possibilities, such as Go Go Tours or Carlson Travel.

Generally, the Walt Disney Travel Company's offerings run the gamut from value to deluxe lodging, with airfare, theme park admission, or meals sometimes incorporated. Some WDW vacation plans are available year-round; others, such as Jolly Holidays, Sunshine Getaway, and Fall Fantasy, are tied to seasonal WDW events. Still others are designed around a specific type of vacation—a golf getaway, a honeymoon—and include special elements, such as unlimited tee times or champagne upon arrival. Finally, add-on escapes allow guests to combine a WDW vacation with a short cruise or a stay at the Disney resort at Vero Beach.

The value of a given package depends entirely on your specific needs. Before considering your options, use the descriptions in this book to help determine which of the plethora of accommodations, activities, and attractions at Walt Disney World most appeal to you. There's real value in some package elements, such as airport transfers and meal discounts. Several packages also include meals with the Disney characters, tennis lessons, golf greens fees, tennis court fees, boat rentals, and the like. But don't choose a package that includes elements you don't want or won't have time for. Remember that while extras such as welcoming cocktails sound attractive, their cash value is negligible. Also beware of any packages that announce as selling points certain services that are available to every Walt Disney World guest.

Cost-Cutting Tips

Lodging: When it comes to saving money on accommodations, timing is almost everything. While off-season dates vary, depending upon the hotel, value season for most Disney resorts generally means January through early February and July through late December.

Also consider how much time you will be spending at your hotel, and don't pay for a place packed with perks you won't have time to enjoy. If swimming pools and other amenities matter, consider all of the establishments that meet your needs—but remember that the cutoff age (above which there is a charge

Lost Adults

Occasionally, traveling companions get separated in the crush of the crowds, or someone may fail to show up at a meeting spot. When this happens, it's good to know that messages can be left for fellow travelers at Guest Relations at City Hall in the Magic Kingdom, or at the Guest Relations buildings in Epcot, the Disney-MGM Studios, and Animal Kingdom.

The Rental Car Dilemma

A car is a must strictly for those planning to visit Orlando-area restaurants and any attractions outside Walt Disney World. If you plan to spend all of your time on WDW turf, you can spare yourself the expense. Shuttle service from the airport to all area hotels is available around the clock, and taxis are in good supply. Within the World, an exhaustive (occasionally exhausting) network of bus, monorail, and boat transportation brings guests from point to point. Visitors lodging off-property can usually get to and from Walt Disney World theme parks via their hotel's own bus service (inquire in advance about schedules and costs, if any). See "From the Airport" on page 26 for airport shuttle information and the *Transportation & Accommodations* chapter for details on WDW internal transportation.

for children sharing their parents' room) does vary. Budget chains such as Days Inn, Econo Lodge, and Holiday Inn Express can prove economical but usually do not offer many frills. A good source of information is the *State by State Guide to Budget Motels*, by Loris G. Bree, revised annually and available in bookstores for $12.95, or for $15.95 from Marlor Press; 4304 Brigadoon Dr.; St. Paul, MN 55126; 612-484-4600 or 800-669-4908.

When considering the cost-effectiveness of off-property lodging, factor in the time, money, and inconvenience of commuting to and from attractions. Realize, too, that the advantages of staying on-property (including access to WDW transportation) also apply to those staying in the least expensive rooms in Disney's brood of hotels. The most important addresses for budget-watching Disney fans, the All-Star Sports and All-Star Music resorts, offer the lowest rates on WDW property. Rooms at Caribbean Beach, Dixie Landings, Port Orleans, and Coronado Springs are slightly higher priced. See the *Transportation & Accommodations* chapter for details.

Food: Eat some quick-service meals instead of going to full-service restaurants. Visit fancier establishments (if you've a yen) at lunchtime rather than at dinner; the same entrées usually cost less then. Carry sandwich fixings and have lunches alfresco whenever possible (keeping in mind that outside food is not welcome inside Disney parks). Look for lodging with kitchen facilities: The savings on food, especially for families at breakfast time, may be more than the extra accommodations expense. Small refrigerators are available for $5 a day at many Disney resorts.

Transportation: Comparison shop for the best airfares and rental car fees. If you decide to fly, factor in the cost of getting to and from the airport. If you travel by train, get off at the Kissimmee station rather than in Orlando—it's much closer to Walt Disney

World, and the cab fare is considerably less; rental cars, on the other hand, are available only at the Orlando station. You can avoid rental car costs altogether by staying at a resort on Disney property. For help weighing the rental car options, see the box above and refer to the "How to Get There" section in this chapter.

Discounts: Membership in the Magic Kingdom Club means discounts on Disney vacation packages, park admission, accommodations (based on availability), car rentals, select theme park restaurant meals, select merchandise at the Downtown Disney Marketplace and in The Disney Store and The Disney Catalog, and more. Many companies offer free membership in the club as an employee benefit. For others, The Gold Card costs $65 for a two-year family membership ($50 for seniors 55 and over). Outside the United States it's $85. For information, call 800-893-4763. Allow at least two weeks to receive membership materials.

Certain discounts are also available to Florida residents, and other seasonal promotions occur. Call 824-4321 for up-to-the-minute details.

At-a-Glance
Reservations Guide

GETTING READY TO GO

Walt Disney World vacations go more smoothly when details are planned ahead of time. Procrastinators may find no room at the inn, or no space left for a show that they wanted to see, particularly during busy seasons. Golf starting times, tennis courts, restaurant priority seating, and other affairs should also be reserved in advance.

Accommodations: It's extremely important to book a room ahead of time to get your first choice, although most requests can be satisfied. Stays during popular summer and holiday periods must be booked well in advance. Would-be guests should contact a travel agent or call Walt Disney World's Central Reservations Operations; the telephone number is W-DISNEY (934-7639). The reservations office is open Monday through Friday from 7 A.M. to 10 P.M.; Saturday and Sunday from 7 A.M. to 6 P.M. Most calls will be answered within one minute. Have pen and paper (and your credit card) close at hand when calling, to jot down dates and the number of your reservation. (Parties in need of ten or more rooms should call 828-3318.)

Packages: An excellent option for the convenience of having all of your vacation arrangements made with a single phone call. For Walt Disney Travel Company package reservations, call 800-828-0228. For more details about Walt Disney World packages, refer to "Package Pointers" on page 14.

Dining: Priority seating has replaced reservations at almost all WDW restaurants except for dinner shows (see page 245 of the *Good Meals, Great Times* chapter for details about the policy). Most dinner show reservations and restaurant priority seating arrangements are handled by one phone number—WDW-DINE (939-3463).

Sports: Reservations for sporting activities are handled by the individual resorts and sports facilities. It's wise to make your plans and reserve your place as far in advance as WDW policy will allow. (See chart below.) For information on Disney's Wide World of Sports, turn to page 206.

Activity	Phone for reservations (area code 407)	Advisability of reservations	How far in advance can reservations be made?
SPORTS			
Golf starting times—all courses	WDW-GOLF (939-4653)	Necessary from January through April; suggested at other times	60 days for guests at WDW resorts or resorts on Hotel Plaza Blvd. 30 days for others (if reserved with credit card; 7 days if not)
Golf lessons Palm and Magnolia courses	WDW-GOLF (939-4653)	Necessary	...................1 year..................
Tennis			
Contemporary	824-3578	Suggested	...................1 year..................
Grand Floridian	824-3578	Necessary	...................1 year..................
Swan and Dolphin	934-4396	Suggested	...................no limit..............
Tennis lessons			
Contemporary	824-3578	Necessary	...................1 year..................
Grand Floridian	824-3578	Necessary	...................1 year..................
Trail rides Fort Wilderness	824-2621	Necessary	...................14 days ....
Fishing trips			
Fort Wilderness	824-2621	Necessary	...................14 days ....
Dixie Landings	934-5409	Necessary	...................14 days ....
Downtown Disney Marketplace	828-2461	Necessary	...................14 days ....
Yacht Club and Beach Club	824-2621	Necessary	...................30 days ....
Waterskiing	824-2621	Necessary	...................14 days ....
Parasailing	824-1000, ext. 3586	Necessary	...................no limit..............

Activity	Phone number	Advisability of priority seating	How far in advance can arrangements be made?
GOOD MEALS			
Polynesian resort	WDW-DINE		...................60 days..................
'Ohana		Suggested	
Coral Isle Café		Available	
Grand Floridian resort	WDW-DINE		...................60 days..................
Victoria & Albert's		Necessary	
Narcoossee's		Suggested	
Cítricos		Suggested	
1900 Park Fare		Suggested	
Grand Floridian Café		Available	
Contemporary resort	WDW-DINE		...................60 days..................
California Grill		Suggested	
Concourse Steakhouse		Suggested	
Chef Mickey's		Suggested	
Wilderness Lodge	WDW-DINE		...................60 days..................
Artist Point		Suggested	
Whispering Canyon Café		Suggested	
BoardWalk resort	WDW-DINE		...................60 days..................
Flying Fish Café		Suggested	
Spoodles		Suggested	
Beach Club resort	WDW-DINE		...................60 days..................
Cape May Café		Available	
Yacht Club resort	WDW-DINE		...................60 days..................
Yachtsman Steakhouse		Suggested	
Yacht Club Galley		Suggested	
Caribbean Beach resort	WDW-DINE		...................60 days..................
Captain's Tavern		Suggested	
Dixie Landings resort	WDW-DINE		...................60 days..................
Boatwright's Dining Hall		Suggested	
Port Orleans resort	WDW-DINE		...................60 days..................
Bonfamille's Café		Suggested	
Coronado Springs resort	WDW-DINE		...................60 days..................
Maya Grill		Suggested	
Old Key West resort	WDW-DINE		...................60 days..................
Olivia's Café		Suggested	
Disney Institute	WDW-DINE		...................60 days..................
Seasons Dining Room		Suggested	
Dolphin resort	934-4884		...................60 days..................
Harry's Safari Bar & Grill		Suggested	
Juan & Only's		Suggested	
Swan resort	934-1609		...................60 days..................
Garden Grove Café		Suggested	
Palio		Suggested	
Fulton's Crab House	WDW-DINE	Suggested	...................60 days..................
Wolfgang Puck Café	WDW-DINE	Suggested	...................60 days..................
In the theme parks	WDW-DINE	Suggested	...................60 days..................
GREAT TIMES			
Hoop-Dee-Doo Musical Revue Fort Wilderness	WDW-DINE	Necessary	...................2 years..................
Polynesian Luau Polynesian resort	WDW-DINE	Necessary	...................2 years..................
Mickey's Tropical Luau Polynesian resort	WDW-DINE	Necessary	...................2 years..................
WDW Character Meals (see page 244 for locations)	WDW-DINE	Suggested	...................60 days..................

All About Theme Park Tickets

The Disney organization defines a ticket as admission for one day only; admission media valid for longer periods are called passes. All passes are nontransferable.

Although Animal Kingdom prices were undetermined at press time, they should be comparable to those at other parks. When the park opens in May, it is likely that the ticket structure and admission prices quoted on this page will change. If you plan to visit WDW after Animal Kingdom opens, call 824-4321 for up-to-the-minute information.

Deciding factors: One-day tickets are valid for admission to one park only—the Magic Kingdom, Epcot, or the Disney-MGM Studios. Four-Day Value Passes may be used for one day in each of these parks, plus one day in a park of your choice (but not at more than one park on the same day). Four-Day Park Hopper Passes and Five-Day World Hopper Passes can be used at three parks on the same day. The Five-Day World Hopper Pass also allows admission to Disney's water parks, Discovery Island, and Pleasure Island for a seven-day period beginning with the first use of the pass.

WDW resort guests can buy a multi-day pass geared to the length of their visit. The Length of Stay Pass offers savings over other passes and unlimited admission to the three theme parks, water parks, Discovery Island, and Pleasure Island for the duration of a guest's stay.

Unlike one-day tickets, all multi-day passes include unlimited use of the WDW transportation system. Multi-day passes need not be used on consecutive days. Unused days on any multi-day pass—with the exception of Length of Stay passes—may be used for a future visit. Guests who have at least one day left on a Four-Day Value Pass or Four-Day Park Hopper Pass can upgrade their pass to a Five-Day World Hopper Pass by paying the difference.

Purchasing tickets and passes: Admission media are sold at park entrances, and at WDW resorts, the resorts on Hotel Plaza Blvd., the Orlando International Airport, the Transportation and Ticket Center (TTC), and The Disney Store. Cash, traveler's checks, personal checks (with ID), American Express, Visa, MasterCard, and The Disney Credit Card are accepted.

Passes by phone: Multi-day passes can be purchased in advance by calling 824-4321. There is a $2 handling fee. Allow two to three weeks for delivery.

Passes by mail: Allow three to four weeks for requests to be processed, and include a return address. Send a check or money order (for the exact amount plus $2 for handling), payable to Walt Disney World Company, to:

Walt Disney World
Box 10030
Lake Buena Vista, FL 32830-0030
Attention: Ticket Mail Order

Admission Prices

ONE-DAY TICKET

(Restricted to use in one park only.)

Adult $42.14
Child* $33.92

FOUR-DAY VALUE PASS

(Valid for one day in Magic Kingdom, Epcot, and the Studios, plus an extra day in one of these parks. Includes use of WDW transportation.)

Adult $142.04
Child* $113.42

FOUR-DAY PARK HOPPER PASS

(Valid in the three theme parks for four days. Includes use of WDW transportation.)

Adult $159.00
Child* $127.20

FIVE-DAY WORLD HOPPER PASS

(Valid in the three theme parks for five days; includes use of WDW transportation, and allows admission to Typhoon Lagoon, Blizzard Beach, River Country, Discovery Island, and Pleasure Island for up to seven days from the first use of the pass.)

Adult $217.30
Child* $173.84

LENGTH OF STAY PASS

(Available to WDW resort guests only. Valid in three parks, Typhoon Lagoon, Blizzard Beach, River Country, Discovery Island, and Pleasure Island for the duration of stay; includes use of WDW transportation system.)

Length of Stay	Adult	Child*
4 days	$175.96	$140.98
5 days	$204.58	$164.30
6 days	$231.08	$185.50
7 days	$255.46	$204.58
8 days	$277.72	$222.18
9 days	$297.86	$238.29
10 days	$315.88	$252.71

The cost of a **THEME PARK ANNUAL PASS** is $285.14 for adults and $242.74 for children; renewals are $256.52 for adults and $218.36 for children. The cost of a **PREMIUM ANNUAL PASS** is $380.54 for adults and $323.30 for children; renewals are $342.38 and $290.44 for children; in addition to the the theme parks, it includes admission to Pleasure Island, and all three water parks.

Prices include sales tax and were correct at press time, but will change during 1998. Information applies to the Magic Kingdom, Epcot, and the Disney-MGM Studios, but not Animal Kingdom.

*3 to 9 years of age; children under 3 free

Step-by-Step Sample Schedules

It's no exaggeration to say that a visitor could spend three weeks in Central Florida and still not have time to see everything that's worthwhile. Walt Disney World alone requires every bit of four days just to visit the theme parks, and that doesn't really allow enough time to take in everything. The basic inventory of attractions—namely, Magic Kingdom, Epcot, the Disney-MGM Studios, Animal Kingdom, Downtown Disney (which includes the Downtown Disney Marketplace, Pleasure Island, and Downtown Disney West Side), Typhoon Lagoon, Blizzard Beach, River Country, Fort Wilderness, and Discovery Island—only begins to suggest the nearly endless entertainment opportunities available. And we haven't even mentioned the pools, the Disney Institute, Disney's Wide World of Sports, 99 holes of golf, and all the other sports facilities. Given the rate at which Walt Disney World is expanding, there's even more reason to allow plenty of time to explore.

The schedules suggested here should help put you on the right track—and maybe even keep you there. In general, good sense and normal human stamina dictate that a first-time visitor should count on spending at least two days at the Magic Kingdom, two days at Epcot, one full day at the Disney-MGM Studios, and a day at Animal Kingdom. That allows some time for shopping, the inevitable lines at certain attractions, and a few unhurried meals.

The one-day schedules listed for each theme park should allow you to hit many of the highlights (albeit at a more harried pace). In addition, consider following the two-day schedules for the Magic Kingdom and Epcot, which really require more time to cover fully. To create a personalized itinerary, mix and match the days to suit your own schedule or to correspond with the least crowded days in the parks (see "Crowd Patterns" in this chapter for tips). Deviations from the programs we describe are best based on our "Hot Tips" (pages 114, 148, and 164, and throughout the theme park chapters) and your own preferences.

Note: These schedules are for periods when extended park hours are in effect. However, you may be able to cover the same area during other seasons, when smaller crowds generally mean shorter lines. Remember, too, that it's crucial to begin days in the theme parks promptly at park opening. (It's wise to recognize that the theme parks frequently open their gates a half hour or more before the officially posted time.) Guests staying at WDW resorts might consider taking advantage of early-bird admission (1½ hours before the park opens to the public) to get an early crack at selected attractions in the designated park. (Keep in mind that others are apt to have the same idea.) When the rest of the park opens, begin following these schedules. See "Park Primer" at the beginning of each theme park chapter (pages 88, 118, and 152) for details about the program.

On the day of your arrival at Walt Disney World, check in as close as possible to 3 P.M. Then spend time by the pool at your resort, have a leisurely dinner in one of the resort's restaurants, and plan to make it an early night. Of course, if the parks are open late and you have a Length of Stay, or a Park or World Hopper Pass, you may prefer to head straight to the Magic Kingdom for an evening of fireworks and the SpectroMagic parade. This is also a good time to get a jump on the more popular attractions.

One to Four Days

This plan is suggested only for the highly energetic, since all the new attractions at Walt Disney World make it barely possible to see even the high points in such a time frame. There's so much else to see and do that we don't really recommend a visit this frustratingly brief. But if that's all the time you've got, first decide which of the four theme parks (the Magic Kingdom, Epcot, the Disney-MGM Studios, or Animal Kingdom) you want to see, depending on how many days you have. Study all available material in advance so that you're as familiar as possible with the park's layout and offerings. Be sure to arrive early and move quickly while there. The following are one-day schedules for each of the theme parks. Keep in mind that the Disney-MGM Studios and Animal Kingdom are more easily covered in this time than the Magic Kingdom or Epcot. On each day, the idea is to make a quick tour of the premises, visiting the major attractions during the least crowded hours of the early morning, then repeating the circuit of the park once again later in the day.

MAGIC KINGDOM

• Arrive in the parking lot at least 45 minutes before the scheduled park opening, so as to be at the Central Plaza end of Main Street before the official opening time. Go to City Hall for a guidemap. If you'd like a full-service meal and you haven't made advance plans, make priority seating arrangements for an early dinner. Try a character meal at Crystal Palace or Liberty Tree Tavern.

• Move rapidly and purposefully from one attraction to the next—first to Space Mountain and Alien Encounter, then to Splash Mountain, Big Thunder Mountain Railroad, The Haunted Mansion, Pirates of the Caribbean, and Jungle Cruise.

• If you are traveling with young children, your best bet is to begin by taking the Walt Disney World Railroad directly to Mickey's Toontown Fair and then visiting the Fantasyland attractions.

• Plan on lunching at around 11 A.M. to avoid mealtime lines (try one of the many fast-food spots wherever you happen to be at the time). After visiting the most popular attractions, see Tom Sawyer Island and the Country Bear Jamboree before or after lunch, as time allows.

• Make a second trip around the park, stopping at The Timekeeper, Legend of the Lion King (check a guidemap or swing by for showtimes), It's A Small World, Peter Pan's Flight, The Hall of Presidents, the shops and entertainment en route, and anything else that catches your eye.

• Eat an early dinner at your chosen full-service dining spot, or try one of the many fast-food options. It's also easy to take the monorail to the Contemporary, Polynesian, or Grand Floridian resorts, each of which offers a variety of dining options (see the *Good Meals, Great Times* chapter for recommendations, and be sure to make priority seating arrangements).

• During busy seasons, when many Walt Disney World attractions are open late, we recommend spending the time after dinner at the Magic Kingdom, where fireworks and the late installment of SpectroMagic combine to make an evening especially memorable. This is also a great time to visit favorite attractions once again, since lines are usually shorter during the parades and before closing.

• Another option for a change of pace is to have dinner at Planet Hollywood or another Downtown Disney restaurant. Spend the rest of the evening exploring the clubs at Downtown Disney West Side or Pleasure Island, and shopping at the Downtown Disney Marketplace. Or head to the BoardWalk resort for dinner and a nostalgic walk on the boards.

EPCOT

• Arrive at the park at least a half hour before the park's official opening. Go immediately to Guest Relations to arrange for dinner priority seating around 7:30 P.M. (if you haven't made advance plans) at one of the many international restaurants in World Showcase. Pick up a guidemap while you're there.

• Test Track is an extremely popular Future World attraction, so stop there first, before the lines build up. Next, go to Honey, I Shrunk the Audience, at Journey Into Imagination. Then see as much as you can of The Land. As soon as World Showcase opens (at 11 A.M.), head there and see *O Canada!* in the Canada pavilion and *Impressions de France* in the France pavilion.

• Pausing to grab a bite at one of the international fast-food spots when hunger calls, travel from country to country, making sure to catch the show at The American Adventure (stop by for showtimes) and the boat ride in Norway. Check out the street entertainment and any shops that catch your eye.

• Try to return to Future World by mid-to late afternoon. Explore Wonders of Life first. Then see Universe of Energy and Spaceship Earth. Spend the remaining time at Innoventions before heading back to World Showcase for dinner.

• Keep an eye on the time so that you can secure a good spot around World Showcase Lagoon to watch IllumiNations. (Although the best view is from Showcase Plaza, we prefer the less congested area between Italy and The American Adventure.)

DISNEY-MGM STUDIOS

• Arrive at the park at least a half hour before the scheduled opening time. Note that some attractions open later in the morning; pick up a guidemap, and consult it for exact times. Also check the guidemap for showtimes throughout the day. If you'd like to try one of the full-service restaurants for lunch or dinner, and you haven't made advance plans, stop at the corner of Holly- wood and Sunset boulevards or at the indi- vidual eatery to arrange for priority seating. Try the 50's Prime Time Café for some old- time television nostalgia or the Hollywood Brown Derby for a touch more elegance.

• If you're ready for a 13-story drop (or two), head directly to the Tower of Terror. Then try to see the next showing of Voyage of The Little Mermaid or Disney's The Hunchback of Notre Dame show. After- ward, head for Muppet*Vision 3-D and Star Tours, since these attractions are very crowded later in the day.

• Plan on grabbing a quick lunch at one of the fast-food eateries around 11 A.M. to avoid mealtime crowds.

• See The Magic of Disney Animation and The Great Movie Ride. Slot in times to see Indiana Jones Epic Stunt Spectacular, Super- Star Television, and The ABC Sound Studio (be sure to volunteer to participate). Note that the Hercules Zero to Hero Victory Parade passes through at 2 P.M.

• If small children are along, spend some time at the Honey, I Shrunk the Kids Movie Set Adventure. Browse through the shops along Hollywood Boulevard and Sunset Boulevard, taking time to notice all the Stu- dios' interesting details.

• At about 5 P.M., head for the Studio Backlot Tour and Backstage Pass to 101 Dalmatians. Also see The Making of... for a behind-the-scenes perspective on the latest Disney live-action release.

• After a leisurely dinner at your chosen spot, catch the last showing of Beauty and the Beast Live on Stage (it's particularly won- derful at night), any attractions you missed, and the scheduled nighttime entertainment.

ANIMAL KINGDOM

• Arrive at the park at least a half hour before the posted opening time. As Walt Disney World's newest theme park, it's sure to draw big crowds.

• Pick up a guidemap at Guest Relations, located in The Oasis. If you haven't made previous arrangements and you'd like a full- service meal, try to secure priority seating for an early dinner at Rainforest Café. As the park's only full-service restaurant, expect it to be quite busy. (Because priority seating is limited, we suggest trying to make arrangements long before leaving home.)

• Pass quickly through The Oasis, and walk straight ahead for the bridge to Safari Village. Your goal is to see the two most thrilling (and popular) rides in Animal Kingdom early in the morning.

• If you're traveling with small children, an alternative plan is to wander through The Oasis and get to know the animals there before moving on to the bigger (and perhaps more frightening) animals. Another option is to spend some time in the character area near Safari Village. All the animal character favorites are in residence, and the stars from The Lion King put on a show (check your guidemap and see the first show if possible).

• As you approach The Tree of Life, gawk if you must, but don't stop. Instead, head directly to DinoLand U.S.A. for a thrilling ride on Countdown to Extinction.

• Next it's on to Africa and the Kiliman- jaro Safaris ride (take the bridge back to Safari Village and bear right around The Tree of Life). Spend time on the Gorilla Falls Exploration Trail before breaking for an early lunch (a quick bite at a fast-food spot in Safari Village or Africa's Harambe).

• When afternoon crowds descend, hop on the Wildlife Express to Conservation Sta- tion—and don't miss all the interactive exhibits when you arrive. Kids will particu- larly enjoy the Affection Section, where they can actually touch the animals.

• Take a relaxing ride on the Discovery River Boats that pass by all the lands in Animal Kingdom (one dock is in Safari Vil- lage; the second is across the river, near what will soon be Asia). Expect to find a few surprises lurking in the river.

• Now see the show "It's Tough to Be a Bug" in The Tree of Life. Take time to notice the animal carvings on the tree and on all the shops of Safari Village; the detail throughout the land is amazing.

• Head back to DinoLand U.S.A. for a leisurely walk on the Cretaceous Trail. While you're here, slot in a time to see the show at the Theater in the Wild (check a guidemap for schedules). Kids will enjoy the huge sandbox known as The Boneyard. Don't miss Chester and Hester's—the shop that's themed as a roadside souvenir stand.

- If there's time before dinner, swing by the character area (by Safari Village) to see the show (check a guidemap for schedules). Then, if you haven't already done so, wander about The Oasis.
- Since there are no nighttime fireworks (the animals must get their beauty rest), we suggest eating at Rainforest Café. (Try to make priority seating arrangements ahead of time.) Consider it dining as entertainment, since thunderstorms, waterfalls, and exotic fish compete with the imaginative fare for your attention. If you have other plans for the evening, or if you'd rather eat at a restaurant in Safari Village, at least stop in for a peek.

Five or Six Days

A stay of this length, while not exactly leisurely, is still the shortest time that can be recommended for families with young children, older visitors, or anyone else who wants to visit all the best of Walt Disney World at a less than breakneck clip. Although the pace is slower than that required during a four-day visit, it's still important not to waste time in order to cover all the high points.

The following are two-day schedules for the Magic Kingdom and Epcot. They can be used in any combination with our one-day schedules to create a personalized itinerary. For example, if you have five days and you're traveling with children, you might use our one-day schedule for Epcot, the Disney-MGM Studios, and Animal Kingdom; and then add our two-day schedule for the Magic Kingdom. If you're not traveling with children, perhaps it's better to swap in a one-day schedule for the Magic Kingdom and follow the two-day schedule for Epcot. If you have six days, use our two-day schedules listed below with one-day schedules for the Disney-MGM Studios and Animal Kingdom.

DAY 1 MAGIC KINGDOM
- Arrive at the Magic Kingdom parking lot at least 45 minutes before the official park opening. Have breakfast at one of the restaurants on Main Street that begin serving early and be at the Central Plaza end of Main Street at the park's official opening time. Then begin circumnavigating the park, taking in just the major attractions described for the first morning of a one-day visit.
- At about noon, consider leaving the park to go to Typhoon Lagoon, Blizzard Beach, or River Country. Have lunch and enjoy the water park's various swimming areas, water slides, and recreational activities. Golfers may want to reserve ahead to sample one of the World's first-rate golf courses instead.
- Return to the Magic Kingdom at about 5 P.M. and grab a quick dinner. Give your stomach time to digest before taking another ride

on Space Mountain and Splash Mountain. By 8 P.M. head for Main Street to stake a claim to a section of curb for the 9 P.M. showing of the SpectroMagic parade. Watch the Fantasy in the Sky fireworks after the parade.

DAY 2 MAGIC KINGDOM
- Try one of the character breakfasts (described in *Good Meals, Great Times*).
- At the Magic Kingdom, spend the rest of the day following our guidelines for the afternoon of a one-day visit, taking time for any other attractions that catch your eye.
- If you'd like to see the afternoon parade, find a good spot on Main Street no later than 2:30 P.M. If you would like to participate, get there at least 45 minutes before the 3 P.M. start; volunteers are chosen randomly from along the parade route. If you don't want to see the parade, now is a good time to hit the more popular attractions or anything in Fantasyland.
- Stop for dinner when hunger strikes. If you have reservations, an alternative plan is to leave the Magic Kingdom at about 4 P.M. for the Hoop-Dee-Doo Musical Revue at Fort Wilderness. (Be sure to call to make 5 P.M. reservations long before leaving home, since they are very hard to come by.)
- In the evening (if you have the energy), go to Pleasure Island for some dancing, comedy, or music. Or, if the Magic Kingdom is open late, return for another round of your favorites in the cooler evening hours. If tired feet prohibit such activity, see a movie at the cinema in Downtown Disney West Side.

DAY 1 EPCOT
- Arrive at least a half hour before the posted opening time. If you haven't had breakfast, grab a quick bite at the Sunshine Season Food Fair in The Land pavilion.
- First ride Test Track. See Honey, I Shrunk the Audience, at Journey Into Imagination, next. Then spend as much time at The Land as possible before 11 A.M.
- Head immediately for World Showcase when it opens (at 11 A.M.), and see the movies in Canada and France. Backtrack and fully explore France, the United Kingdom, and Canada. Perhaps have lunch at Le Cellier.
- Then return to Future World, where you'll spend the remainder of the day. Check the Tip Board (which lets you know the waiting times for the most popular attractions) in Innoventions Plaza before proceeding to The Living Seas, Universe of Energy, Wonders of Life, and any other attractions you have not yet seen.
- See Spaceship Earth late in the day. Spend the evening hours exploring Innoventions. Stop for dinner when hunger calls.
- Plan to be around World Showcase Lagoon for IllumiNations.

Day 2 Epcot

• Arrive at Epcot about half an hour before the park's official opening. If you were unable to make advance plans, go directly to Guest Relations to make priority seating arrangements for lunch and dinner in World Showcase. Secure a 1:30 P.M. seating for lunch and an 8:30 P.M. seating for dinner. (Refer to the *Good Meals, Great Times* chapter for additional guidance and our dining suggestions).

• That done, take in any major attractions in Future World that you missed on your first day. Spend the remaining time before 11 A.M. at Innoventions.

• Next, head for World Showcase as close to its 11 A.M. opening time as possible. Start your route around the promenade with Mexico, making sure to catch the boat ride in Norway and the movie in China before heading to your lunch spot.

• Slot in a time to see the show at The American Adventure pavilion. Even if you hate shopping, browse through Germany's collectibles and toy shops, and Morocco's brass and leather bazaars. Check your guidemap for the best times to look in on the entertainers who perform daily along World Showcase Promenade.

• Stop at one of the many snack stands for a late-afternoon international treat. The hours between 6 P.M. and your scheduled dinner time should be spent seeing any World Showcase attractions that were missed on your previous circuits.

• Remember to allot enough time to walk to your dining spot. Skip dessert at the restaurant and instead head for the Boulangerie Pâtisserie in the France pavilion for pastry and espresso.

• If you couldn't get priority seating in the Epcot restaurant of your choice, or you need a change of pace, head for Downtown Disney or the BoardWalk, where there are plenty of restaurants from which to choose (see *Good Meals, Great Times*).

Making the Most of Longer Visits

In addition to our schedule for six days, an even longer stay allows a chance to sample some of the World's myriad of other offerings. Spend another day in the one park you most enjoyed. Lounge by the pool, play tennis or golf, or bike. Go shopping at the Downtown Disney Marketplace. Cool off at one of Disney's innovative water parks. Have lunch at a WDW resort and try a special dinner at Victoria & Albert's at the Grand Floridian, or at Pleasure Island's Portobello Yacht Club. Check out the clubs at Pleasure Island or Downtown Disney West Side, or spend the evening at the BoardWalk. Take golf or tennis lessons. Go fishing, waterskiing, or parasailing. Visit the spa at the Disney Institute or the Grand Floridian resort. Participate in a behind-the-scenes program. Play miniature golf at Fantasia Gardens. See a game at Disney's Wide World of Sports. Enroll for a stay (or a day) at the Disney Institute; check out the Sports & Fitness Center and plan to catch the evening entertainment. For more ideas, see our *Sports, Everything Else in the World*, and *Good Meals, Great Times* chapters.

HOW TO GET THERE

By Car

These suggested routes, courtesy of the American Automobile Association (AAA), lead from a number of metropolitan areas to Walt Disney World. Figure on driving 350 to 400 miles a day—a reasonable distance that won't wear you down so much that you can't enjoy your trip.

Atlanta: I-75 south, I-475 south around Macon, I-75 south, Florida's Turnpike south, U.S. 27 south, U.S. 192 east to entrance. Total mileage: 428 miles.

Baltimore: I-95 south, I-495 east and south around Washington, I-95 south, I-295 around Jacksonville, I-95 south, I-4 west, U.S. 192 west to entrance. Total mileage: 948 miles.

Boston: I-90 west, I-84 west, I-91 south, I-95 south, I-287 west, Garden State Parkway south, New Jersey Turnpike south to Delaware Memorial Bridge, I-95 south (through Fort McHenry Tunnel in Baltimore), I-495 west and south around Washington, D.C., I-95 south, I-295 around Jacksonville, I-95 south, I-4 west, U.S. 192 west to entrance. Total mileage: 1,366 miles.

Buffalo: I-90 west, I-79 south, U.S. 19 south, West Virginia Turnpike south, I-77 south, I-26 east, I-95 south, I-295 around Jacksonville, I-95 south, I-4 west, U.S. 192 west to entrance. Total mileage: 1,250 miles.

Chicago: I-94 south, I-80 east, I-65 south, I-465 south around Indianapolis, I-65 south to Nashville, I-24 east to Chattanooga, I-75 south, I-285 west and south around Atlanta, I-75 south, I-475 south around Macon, I-75 south, Florida's Turnpike south, U.S. 27 south, U.S. 192 east to entrance. Total mileage: 1,172 miles.

Cincinnati: I-75 south, I-285 west and south around Atlanta, I-475 south around Macon, I-75 south, Florida's Turnpike south, U.S. 27 south, U.S. 192 east to entrance. Total mileage: 885 miles.

Cleveland: I-77 south, West Virginia Turnpike south, I-77 south, I-26 east, I-95 south, I-295 around Jacksonville, I-95 south, I-4 west, U.S. 192 west to entrance. Total mileage: 1,101 miles.

Dallas: I-20 east to Shreveport, S.R. 3132 south, I-49 south, S.R. 1/U.S. 71 south through Alexandria, I-49 south, I-10 east, I-12 east around New Orleans, I-10 east, I-75 south, Florida's Turnpike south, U.S. 27 south, U.S. 192 east to entrance. Total mileage: 1,174 miles.

Detroit: I-75 south, I-285 west and south around Atlanta, I-75 south, I-475 south around Macon, I-75 south, Florida's Turnpike south, U.S. 27 south, U.S. 192 east to entrance. Total mileage: 1,158 miles.

Indianapolis: I-65 south to Nashville, I-24 east to Chattanooga, I-75 south, I-285 west and south around Atlanta, I-75 south, I-475 south around Macon, I-75 south, Florida's Turnpike south, U.S. 27 south, U.S. 192 east to entrance. Total mileage: 977 miles.

Louisville: I-65 south to Nashville, I-24 east to Chattanooga, I-75 south, I-285 west and south around Atlanta, I-75 south, I-475 south around Macon, I-75 south, Florida's Turnpike south, U.S. 27 south, U.S. 192 east to entrance. Total mileage: 877 miles.

Minneapolis: I-94 east to Madison (WI), I-90 east, I-294 south around Chicago, I-80 east, I-65 south, I-465 south around Indianapolis, I-65 south to Nashville, I-24 east to Chattanooga, I-75 south, I-285 west and south around Atlanta, I-75 south, Florida's Turnpike south, U.S. 27 south, U.S. 192 east to entrance. Total mileage: 1,581 miles.

New York City: Lincoln Tunnel west, S.R. 495 west, New Jersey Turnpike south to Delaware Memorial Bridge, I-95 south (through Fort McHenry Tunnel in Baltimore), I-495 west and south around Washington, D.C., I-95 south, I-295 around Jacksonville, I-95 south, I-4 west, U.S. 192 west to entrance. Total mileage: 1,164 miles.

Philadelphia: I-95 south (through Fort McHenry Tunnel in Baltimore), I-495 east and south around Washington, D.C., I-95 south, I-295 around Jacksonville, I-95 south, I-4 west, U.S. 192 west to entrance. Total mileage: 1,015 miles.

Pittsburgh: I-279 south, I-79 south, U.S. 19 south, West Virginia Turnpike south, I-77 south, I-26 east, I-95 south, I-295 around Jacksonville, I-95 south, I-4 west, U.S. 192 west to entrance. Total mileage: 1,072 miles.

Richmond: I-95 south, I-295 around Jacksonville, I-95 south, I-4 west, U.S. 192 west to entrance. Total mileage: 757 miles.

Toronto: Queen Elizabeth Way south, I-190 east, I-90 west, I-79 south, U.S. 19 south, West Virginia Turnpike south, I-77 south, I-26 east, I-95 south, I-295 around Jacksonville, I-95 south, I-4 west, U.S. 192 west to entrance. Total mileage: 1,359 miles.

By Bus

Relatively few vacationers come to Walt Disney World by bus. But it makes sense to consider this means of transportation if you don't drive, if you're traveling only a short distance, if you have plenty of time, or if you don't like to fly. Bus travel can be economical, although the greater the distance involved, the more likely the lowest available airfare will be competitive.

Greyhound provides frequent direct service into Orlando and Kissimmee (the latter is actually closer to Walt Disney World). From either destination, you can hire a taxi to take you to your hotel, but first check to see if your hotel offers shuttle service.

Consider these sample travel times by bus to Orlando: from Jacksonville, Florida, it's about 4 hours; from Tallahassee, Florida, approximately 7 hours; from Atlanta, Georgia, or Mobile or Montgomery, Alabama, about 12 hours.

For further information, contact Greyhound at 800-231-2222.

Resources for Road Trippers

AUTOMOBILE CLUBS: Reputable national automobile clubs can offer help with breakdowns en route; emergency towing; insurance that covers personal injury, accidents, arrest, bail bond, and lawyers' fees for defense of contested traffic cases; and travel-planning services, including free maps and route mapping. Services vary from one club to the next, and membership fees range widely, from $25 to $90 a year.

Among the leading clubs:

Allstate Motor Club; 1500 W. Shure Dr.; Arlington Heights, IL 60004; 800-347-8880

American Automobile Association; 1000 AAA Dr.; Heathrow, FL 32746; 800-564-6222

Amoco Motor Club; Box 9059; Des Moines, IA 50368; 800-334-3300

Ford Auto Club; Box 224688; Dallas, TX 75222; 800-348-5220

Gulf Motor Club; 6001 N. Clark St.; Chicago, IL 60660; 800-633-3224

Montgomery Ward Auto Club; 200 N. Martingale Rd., 3rd Floor–Enrollment; Schaumburg, IL 60173; 800-621-5151

Motor Club of America; Box 20689; Oklahoma City, OK 73156; 800-227-6459

ROAD MAPS: Travelers can also check with state tourist boards about the availability of free maps. Other excellent sources for maps are the *AAA North American Road Atlas* and the *Rand McNally Road Atlas*; they cost $9.95 each and are sold in bookstores.

From the Airport

By car: For the most direct route, take the North Exit to Route 528 (Beeline Expressway), going west toward Tampa. Pick up I-4 west, and follow it until you reach the appropriate WDW exit. The distance is 22 miles, the trip takes about half an hour, and the tolls add up to $1.25. If this route is congested, take the airport's South Exit to the Central Florida Greeneway (Route 417) to Route 536, which leads directly to Walt Disney World. The tolls total $2.

Shuttles: It's also possible, and easy, to get to WDW resorts from Orlando International Airport without a car. Mears Motor Shuttles offers vans about every 15 to 20 minutes around the clock, serving Disney resorts, the resorts on Hotel Plaza Blvd., and other area hotels. The cost to most hotels is $14 one way, $25 round-trip per adult; $10 one way, $17 round-trip per child age 4 to 11; free for children under 4. Fares to International Drive properties are $2 to $3 lower. Call 423-5566 for reservations.

By Train

Amtrak serves the Orlando area twice daily from New York City. The trip takes about 22 hours and costs anywhere from $146 to $408 round-trip. (Book early for lower fares; special discounts are often available, so be sure to ask about them.) On the way to Orlando, the train stops to pick up additional passengers in Philadelphia and Washington, D.C., as well as various cities in Virginia, North Carolina, South Carolina, and Georgia. If you don't plan to rent a car, disembark in Kissimmee. It's closer to Walt Disney World, and cab fare is much cheaper. Note that there are no rental cars available at the Kissimmee station.

Amtrak also offers Auto Train service daily in both directions from Lorton, Virginia, which is 17 miles south of Washington, D.C., direct to Sanford, Florida, just 25 miles northeast of Orlando. Accommodation charges for cars and passengers for the 17½-hour trip vary depending on the time of year and the direction traveled (going south in winter, or north in summer, is pricier). The fare includes two meals and some entertainment.

For reservations and schedule information on these and other routes, send a self-addressed, stamped envelope to Amtrak Distribution Center; 1549 W. Glenlake Ave.; Box 7717; Itasca, IL 60143; or call 800-USA-RAIL (800-872-7245).

By Air

Orlando International Airport is continually upgrading to keep up with the millions of visitors who flock to Central Florida each year. Monorails transport passengers to and from the central terminal, where a well-stocked shop supplies travelers with T-shirts, watches, and other Disney paraphernalia.

Finding the Lowest Airfare: If there's a trick to unearthing the most economical fares, it's this: Shop around. In the process, keep these tips in mind:

• Find out which airlines fly from your point of departure and call them all. Or let your travel agent do this for you—at no charge.

• Watch the newspapers for ads announcing short-term promotional fares.

• The more flexible you can be in your dates and duration of stay, the more money you're likely to save. Fares tend to be lowest on competitive, heavily traveled routes.

• Fly when most other people don't: at night, over weekends on routes that usually serve business travelers, or midweek to and from vacation destinations.

• When it's necessary to change planes en route, it's best to stick with one airline; the airline agent will know his or her own company's routing—and its discounted fares—better than those offered by other carriers.

• Plan ahead so you can take advantage of advance-purchase fares (lower rates that apply if a ticket is bought two to three weeks prior to the date of departure).

• Keep in mind that the lowest airfares usually carry a penalty if you have to revise your flight schedule, and that certain discount fare tickets are nonrefundable.

• When you call to make a reservation, ask about any applicable fare restrictions, including obligatory Saturday night stayover.

• Most carriers guarantee fares, so you won't have to pay more if fares go up after you buy your ticket. On the other hand, if fares come down, you can request a refund.

CUSTOMIZED TRAVEL TIPS
Traveling with Children

Tell youngsters that a Walt Disney World vacation is in the works and the response is apt to be overwhelming. Get them involved in the planning from the outset. Our guide, *Birnbaum's Walt Disney World For Kids, By Kids* ($9.95), written by and for children ages 7 to 14, can be a useful resource. Filled with information about the World from a kid's perspective, it can be used as a reference before and during the trip and as a souvenir.

EN ROUTE: The journey is likely to be fraught with "Are-we-there-yet?" Certain ploys can quiet this refrain, such as setting up a series of intermediate goals to which kids can look forward. Young children can anticipate discovering the contents of a pint-size suitcase packed with familiar games and toys, plus a few surprises. Pre-packed snacks keep things peaceful when stomachs start rumbling and food is miles away. Above all, and especially if the trip is by car, allow time for plenty of breaks.

Those who fly should schedule travel during off-peak hours, when empty seats might be available. During takeoff and landing, babies should be given bottles, pacifiers, or even thumbs to promote swallowing and clear ears. Newborn babies should not be taken aloft, since their lungs may not adjust easily to the altitude. For finicky young eaters, request special meals when reserving seats.

AT WALT DISNEY WORLD: This vacationland ranks among the easiest spots on earth for families with children. Older kids don't need to be driven around, and the general supervision is such that kids are hard pressed to get into trouble. Keep in mind, however, that kids under seven must be accompanied by an adult to enter the theme parks. With teens, it's enough to establish a meeting place and time inside the Magic Kingdom, Epcot, the Studios, or Animal Kingdom.

Theme Park Favorites: Although kids are usually enchanted by all of Walt Disney World, some attractions hold their interest more than others. If you're traveling with very young children, your best bet is the Magic Kingdom. Visit Mickey's Toontown Fair first and then Fantasyland, keeping in mind that some attractions frighten kids who are afraid of the dark. For older kids, thrill rides get the highest rating. Don't miss Space Mountain, Alien Encounter, Splash Mountain, and Big Thunder Mountain Railroad in the Magic Kingdom; Epcot's Test Track; and Tower of Terror at the Disney-MGM Studios. Other favorites include The Haunted Mansion, Legend of the Lion King, Pirates of the Caribbean, and Peter Pan's Flight in the Magic Kingdom; Wonders of Life, Journey Into Imagination, Innoventions, and Norway in Epcot; and Muppet*Vision 3-D, Star Tours, and the Voyage of The Little Mermaid in the Studios. In Animal Kingdom, DinoLand

Parental Perk

Families with small children should know about the "kid switch" policy at the theme parks. At attractions with age or height restrictions, a parent who waits with a young child while the other parent rides the attraction can go right on when the first parent comes off. (Be sure to ask the attendant.)

U.S.A. is a surefire kid-pleaser, as is the park's thrilling Kilimanjaro Safaris attraction.

Restaurant Picks: Fast food, buffet, and food court meals generally win with most kids, but there are a few specifics in the theme parks. In the Magic Kingdom, Pinocchio Village Haus in Fantasyland and Tony's Town Square on Main Street are favorable spots for lunch. Aunt Polly's on Tom Sawyer Island is a good bet for a snack; while adults are sipping lemonade, the kids can explore every nook and cranny on the island. At Epcot, kids prefer the Sunshine Season Food Fair in The Land and the Liberty Inn at The American Adventure. The Sci-Fi Dine-In and the 50's Prime Time Café at the Studios are good choices as well. (Always ask to see the special kids' menu at full-service restaurants.) At Animal Kingdom, Restaurantosaurus is a safe bet for kids. Character meals are hits with kids of all ages (see page 244 in *Good Meals, Great Times* for details).

Resort Fun: All WDW resorts have at least a small room full of video games; the arcades at the Contemporary and All-Star resorts are positively vast. Most of the hotels have playgrounds; the ones located at the Polynesian, Dixie Landings, Caribbean Beach, and All-Star resorts get high marks from children. The best pools for kids are at the Yacht Club and Beach Club, Port Orleans, Contemporary, Caribbean Beach, Coronado Springs, and BoardWalk.

Child Care: The Polynesian, Grand Floridian, Contemporary, Wilderness Lodge, Yacht Club, Beach Club, BoardWalk, Swan, and Dolphin have child care facilities. In-room child care can be summoned to all WDW resort locations; contact the Guest Services desk. There is also a center known as Kinder-Care, which accepts kids ages one to four. For details and availability, phone 827-5444.

Strollers: Available for rent for $5 (plus a $1 deposit) at strollers and wheelchair rental shops at the following locations: on the east side of Main Street, at the entrance to the Magic Kingdom; on the east side of the Entrance Plaza and at the International Gateway, at Epcot; Oscar's Super Service at the Disney-MGM Studios; and Garden Gate Gifts near The Oasis at Animal Kingdom. The deposit is refundable. You'll need to present the receipt when returning the stroller and get a Disney Dollar back.

If the stroller disappears while you're in an attraction, a replacement may be obtained at Merchant of Venus in Tomorrowland, at the Frontier Trading Post in Frontierland, at Tinker Bell's Treasures in Fantasyland, at the World Traveler shop at Epcot's International Gateway and the Germany pavilion in World Showcase, at Oscar's at the Disney-MGM Studios, and at Garden Gate Gifts in Animal Kingdom. Guests have to pay only once a day for a stroller. If you rent one in the morning and plan to spend the afternoon at another park, just present the receipt for a stroller there.

Baby Care Centers: Located at the Magic Kingdom (next to Crystal Palace restaurant on Main Street), Epcot (in the Odyssey Center between Future World and World Showcase), the Disney-MGM Studios (in Guest Relations, just inside the gate), and Animal Kingdom (in Safari Village, behind Creature Comforts), these centers are helpful to parents with young children. There are rooms with rocking chairs and love seats for nursing mothers, and cheery feeding rooms (with high chairs, bibs, and spoons available). Baby centers have facilities for changing infants, preparing formula, and warming bottles. Disposable diapers, nurser bags, rubber pants, bottles, formula (Similac, Isomil, and Enfamil, Carnation, Good Start, and Follow-Up), teethers, pacifiers, prepared cereal, juices, and a small selection of baby food are for sale. The decor is soothing; the atmosphere is such that it seems a million miles away from the parks. Changing areas are available in most women's and some men's restrooms as well. Hours at baby centers vary; check at City Hall or Guest Relations.

Lost Children: The security forces inside Disney theme parks are far more serious than the happy appearance of things indicates. This is a welcome thought on those rare instances when a child suddenly disappears or fails to show up on schedule. If this happens, check the lost children's logbooks at the Baby Care Center or City Hall in the Magic Kingdom; at Guest Relations or the Baby Care Center (behind the Odyssey Center) in Epcot; at Guest Relations at the Disney-MGM Studios; or at Guest Relations, just inside the park entrance, in Animal Kingdom. All Disney employees know what to do if a lost child starts to call for his or her parents. There are no paging systems in the parks, but in serious emergencies an all-points bulletin can be put out among employees. The Guest Relations staffs at the entrances to all theme parks can also assist.

Disney has special name tags for very young children. Guests may pick one up at the Magic Kingdom's City Hall or Baby Care Center, Epcot's Guest Relations or Baby Care Center, or at Guest Relations in the Disney-MGM Studios or Animal Kingdom.

Older Travelers

Walt Disney World may be a cinch for a five-year-old to maneuver, but it can sometimes be overwhelming for older travelers (especially when in the company of a five-year-old). Many first-time visitors don't realize that Epcot encompasses significant distances; and the Magic Kingdom, the Disney-MGM Studios, and Animal Kindgom can be disorienting because of their profusion of sights, sounds, and criss-crossing pathways. And the heat, particularly in summer, can be hard to take. But with the proper planning and precautions, all of Walt Disney World can be just as delightful for older visitors as for kids. Here are just a few suggestions:

- Join a tour to Walt Disney World. Surprisingly few companies offer them specifically designed for older travelers. One that does is Eventures Unlimited Inc.; 7648 Southland Blvd., Suite 101; Orlando, FL 32809; 826-0055 or 800-356-7891.

- Schedule visits for off-peak seasons and hours when the crowds will not be overwhelming and discouraging. Also, note that special values are available to Florida residents during selected nonpeak dates. Call 824-4321 for details.

- Read all WDW literature before arrival so that the parks and resort hotels are familiar, and you are alert to the facilities and services available to you. Consider perusing a copy of *Birnbaum's Walt Disney World Without Kids* ($11.95), our adult-oriented companion guide to this book.

- In the parks, don't be timid about asking for directions or advice. Disney cast members are extremely knowledgeable, friendly, and helpful.

- Don't skip meals. Touring takes energy, and only a hearty meal can provide it.

- Try to eat early or late to avoid the mealtime crowds. In the Magic Kingdom, select more sedate restaurants such as Tony's Town Square on Main Street or Cinderella's Royal Table in Cinderella Castle. Or take the monorail to the still calmer Polynesian, Contemporary, or Grand Floridian resort. It's a quick trip, and pleasant dining options abound (check ahead to find out which restaurants serve lunch). In Epcot, the Coral Reef restaurant in Future World and Le Cellier in World Showcase are especially restful spots for lunch. At the Disney-MGM Studios, the Hollywood Brown Derby offers a relaxing sit-down meal.

- Protect yourself from the sun, which can be hot even in winter. Always wear a hat; don't skimp on the sunscreen; and remember to cover your legs, which are easily sunburned by rays reflected from pavements.

- Don't become overheated. Take frequent rest stops in the shade, and get out of the midafternoon heat by stopping for a snack in an air-conditioned restaurant. Avoid standing in line at attractions where the queue is not wholly protected from the sun and can therefore be very hot, such as the Magic Kingdom's Tom Sawyer Island. In Epcot, spend afternoon hours in Innoventions, Wonders of Life, or the Sea Base Alpha exhibit at The Living Seas in Future World.

- Don't underestimate the distances at Epcot or Animal Kingdom; you may need to walk more than three miles in a day at each park. If taken slowly and in short increments, this is not too onerous. But if you don't think you can cover such a distance, be sure to rent a wheelchair when you first arrive. (Also, Epcot's *FriendShip* water launches, which make regular trips across the lagoon, can also ease the burden on weary feet.)

- Pace yourself. It's smart to head back to your hotel for a swim or a nap in the afternoon, and then return to the parks later on. This is easy enough to do via WDW transportation if you're staying at an on-property hotel, particularly one connected by monorail. Many off-property hotels also offer free shuttle service to and from the theme parks; just be sure to check the pick-up schedule before you disembark.

- Above all, don't push yourself. Half the fun of Walt Disney World—the part that younger travelers often miss out on—is just sitting under a tree on a park bench, watching the people go by.

Travelers with Disabilities

Walt Disney World gets high marks from travelers with disabilities because of the attention paid to special needs. Below is an overview of the services provided.

GETTING AROUND: Special parking is available for guests at all four theme parks; ask for directions at the Auto Plazas upon entering. From the Transportation and Ticket Center (TTC), the Magic Kingdom is accessible by ferry or by monorail (for those using wheelchairs, the former is preferable, since the monorail ramp has a steep slant.) Note that all WDW monorail stations are accessible to wheelchairs except at the Contemporary resort. Valet parking is available at Downtown Disney and is free to guests with disabilities.

Wheelchairs: Wheelchairs can be rented in all theme parks; they cost $5 per day, with a $1 refundable deposit. In the Magic Kingdom, wheelchairs are available at the Stroller and Wheelchair Rental on the right side of the souvenir area, just inside the turnstiles. Epcot's rental area is just inside the turnstiles on the left. Oscar's Super Service rents wheelchairs at the Disney-MGM Studios. At Animal Kingdom, wheelchair rental is available at Garden Gate Gifts near The Oasis.

Electric Convenience Vehicles (ECVs) are available for rent in every park. They cost $30 plus a $10 refundable deposit, per park per day. They usually sell out early.

There are designated areas for guests in wheelchairs to view IllumiNations at Epcot, and to view the parades in the Magic Kingdom and the Disney-MGM Studios. Check a park guidemap for locations.

Accessibility: It's easy to get around the theme parks by wheelchair. Most attractions are accessible to guests who can be lifted from their chairs with assistance from a member of their party, and many can accommodate guests who must remain in wheelchairs at all times.

> ## Theme Park Resource
>
> The *Walt Disney World Guidebook for Guests with Disabilities* describes the accessibility of all WDW attractions. It's available at wheelchair rental locations, City Hall in the Magic Kingdom, and Guest Relations in Epcot, Animal Kingdom, and the Disney-MGM Studios. To receive it by mail, write to: Walt Disney World Guest Communications; Box 10000; Lake Buena Vista, FL 32830.

Consult the *Walt Disney World Guidebook for Guests with Disabilities* (see box) for details about attraction access, or check with the ride host or hostess. At the water parks, life jackets are available for travelers with disabilities.

All WDW hotels have accommodations for guests with disabilities. For assistance in selecting one that best fits your requirements, ask to speak to someone in the Special Requests Department when you call Central Reservations (934-7639).

RESOURCES: Sight-impaired guests can rent a tape recorder and a cassette that describes each theme park, as well as a Braille guidebook. Each requires a $25 refundable deposit. Service animals are permitted in all the parks.

Guests who use telecommunications devices for the deaf (TDDs) can call 827-5141 for WDW information. TDDs are available for no charge at City Hall in the Magic Kingdom; Guest Relations in Epcot, the Disney-MGM Studios, and Animal Kingdom; Guest Services at Downtown Disney Marketplace; and at all resorts. Sign language interpretation is available for select shows. Call at least two weeks in advance to make arrangements. Listening devices that amplify attraction sound tracks are available at City Hall in the Magic Kingdom, and at Guest Relations in Epcot, Animal Kingdom, and the Disney-MGM Studios. A $25 refundable deposit is required. Sites with assistive listening systems are listed on park guidemaps.

Be sure to inquire about the availability of reflective and video captioning devices. The former projects show dialogue onto panels positioned in front of a guest; the latter activates captioning on video monitors. (At press time, The Hall of Presidents was the only attraction with reflective captioning.) Also, written scripts are available at each show and attraction for use by guests with hearing impairments. Contact a park employee for assistance.

Tours: The Society for the Advancement of Travel for the Handicapped (347 Fifth Ave., Suite 610; New York, NY 10016; 212-447-7284) has travel agents with experience in booking tours for travelers with disabilities. Send a check or money order for $5 to receive a listing and other information; membership costs $45. Flying Wheels Travel (143 W. Bridge St.; Owatonna, MN 55060; 800-535-6790) also organizes trips for travelers with disabilities.

Local Assistance: Holiday Assistants (7798 Indian Ridge Trail North; Kissimmee, FL 39749; 397-4845) provides free referrals for many needs, from medical care and barrier-free hotels to hourly helpers.

Single Travelers

Those who travel alone for the freedom and fun of it, or in a small group with singles, can have just as memorable a time at Walt Disney World as they would anywhere else. Meeting people is easy here. Standing in line for an attraction or a meal provides ample opportunity to chat and swap tips and adventures.

WDW employees are fun to engage in conversation, not to mention wonderful sources of information, since many have worked at WDW for a long time. It's a treat, as well, to discuss life abroad with a World Showcase employee who was born and educated in the country his or her pavilion represents. In doing this, the single traveler usually learns more about the ways of the World than any group member ever could.

For singles on the lookout for company, Downtown Disney's clubs and restaurants can prove to be fertile meeting places. The Board-Walk is another lively destination. Sports fans find BoardWalk's ESPN Club particularly inviting. In addition to Walt Disney World guests and employees, lots of folks from the Orlando area patronize these locales, especially on weekends and during holidays.

The bars and lounges at Walt Disney World hotels are relaxed and welcoming. The same atmosphere prevails at the Catwalk Bar at the Disney-MGM Studios, and at the Rose & Crown Pub (in the United Kingdom pavilion) and the Matsu No Ma lounge (Japan) in Epcot's World Showcase. The Biergarten in World Showcase's Germany pavilion and the Teppanyaki Dining Rooms in Japan's Mitsukoshi restaurant are especially convivial, as parties are seated together at large tables.

Another way to meet people is to sign up for a behind-the-scenes tour. The Disney Institute is the best place to meet folks with similar interests. The water parks and the hotel pools are also good places for making friends.

Those in need of a partner should consider the "Tennis Anyone?" program at Disney's Racquet Club.

A Note for Budget Watchers: Rates at all WDW resorts, the resorts on Hotel Plaza Blvd., and most other area accommodations are the same whether one or two persons occupy a room. The Disney Institute, however, does offer single rates.

How to Get the Best Photos

There are so many wonderful images all over the World that just about any camera in working order can capture them for you. Here are some useful hints:

- Flash photography is not permitted inside any WDW attractions.

- Don't shoot closer than 4 feet from your subject, and don't try for a flash picture from more than 15 feet away.

- For more interesting photos, fill the frame with as much of the prime subject as possible.

- Do not shoot directly into the sun. Instead, stand so that sunlight falls directly onto your subject—coming from behind you or from the side.

- To photograph fireworks, your camera must have a manually adjustable shutter speed and aperture. Use color negative film (ASA 400). Set the aperture at f/8 and the shutter speed at B. Hold the lens open for three to five seconds at each burst; cover between explosions.

- Photo spots around the theme parks can help you capture the best photos.

- If your camera isn't working, visit the Camera Center on Main Street in the Magic Kingdom; the Camera Center near Spaceship Earth, Cameras and Film at Journey Into Imagination, or World Traveler at International Gateway in Epcot; The Darkroom on Hollywood Boulevard in the Disney-MGM Studios; or Garden Gate Gifts near The Oasis in Animal Kingdom.

- Film is available at many shops around the Magic Kingdom, Epcot, the Disney-MGM Studios, Animal Kingdom, and the WDW resorts. The best selection can be found at the camera shops in each park.

Film processing: Two-hour processing is available at the Magic Kingdom, Epcot, the Disney-MGM Studios, and Animal Kingdom, WDW resorts, and Downtown Disney Marketplace wherever a Photo Express sign is displayed. Film is processed on site.

Rental Cameras: Video cameras may be rented at the camera shops in all theme parks. Cost is $30 per day, with a $450 refundable deposit. Disposable cameras are available for purchase.

WDW Weddings & Honeymoons

Walt Disney World is the most popular honeymoon destination in the country. The resorts offer some romantic stretches of white-sand beaches for evening strolls, fine restaurants for candlelight dinners, and a host of activities to rival almost any Caribbean or Hawaiian destination. Add to that the fantasy of the Magic Kingdom, the wonder of Epcot, the glamour of the Disney-MGM Studios, and the majesty of Animal Kingdom, plus Downtown Disney and BoardWalk nightlife, and water park thrills, and it's not very hard to see why Walt Disney World is number one with newlyweds. Because honeymooners have been flocking to the WDW resorts for many years, a variety of packages cater specifically to newly married couples. For information, call 827-7200. (You don't have to buy a package to get special treatment; just let the staff know you're on your honeymoon.)

For years, the folks at Walt Disney World received hundreds of requests from couples who wanted to marry at a Walt Disney World theme park. Today, couples can tie the knot in evening ceremonies at many of them during seasons that the parks close early. (The spot in front of Cinderella Castle is one of WDW's wedding hot spots.) The Yacht Club and Beach Club, BoardWalk, Polynesian, Wilderness Lodge, and Contemporary resorts also host their share of weddings, with The Villas at the Disney Institute providing a more rustic option.

The Wedding Pavilion near the Grand Floridian offers a Victorian-style indoor setting with a prime view of Cinderella Castle. A combination of stained glass, sage green and soft pink florals, and benches with heart-shaped cutouts (seating around 250) creates the romantic ambience. Couples can fill their wedding albums with photos taken at Picture Point, under a trellis of climbing white roses, with the faraway castle prominently in the background. Private ceremonies can also be performed at this scenic spot.

Weddings range from elegant affairs, without a hint of Disneyana, to ceremonies in which the bride and groom arrive in Cinderella's coach and Mickey and Minnie are among the guests. At Franck's Bridal Studio, WDW coordinators work with couples to customize each wedding. Unique merchandise is available for purchase. Among the services offered are cakes, invitations, photography, hairstyling, flower arranging, and musical entertainment. Specialists can help arrange accommodations, rehearsal dinners, bachelor parties, and more. For information about a WDW wedding, call 828-3400; honeymoon packages, call 827-7200.

FINGERTIP REFERENCE GUIDE

BARBERS AND SALONS

The most amusing place to get a haircut is the old-fashioned Harmony Barber Shop in the Magic Kingdom. It's tucked away at the end of the flower-filled cul-de-sac just off the west side of Main Street. This is also the place where the Dapper Dans, the park's barbershop quartet, are most likely to be heard throughout the day. Mustache cups and other nostalgic shaving items are for sale, as are special souvenir mousketeer ears.

Haircuts, coloring, manicures, and other services are available at the following resorts: the salon in the Contemporary (824-3411), the Periwig Salon at the Yacht Club and Beach Club (934-3260), Ivy Trellis at the Grand Floridian (824-3000, ext. 2581), the Niki Bryan shop at the Swan and Dolphin (934-4250), and the Casa de Belleza at Coronado Springs (939-1000).

CAR CARE

Several Exxon gas stations with convenience stores are on the property, all of which are open 24 hours a day. One is on Buena Vista Drive across from Pleasure Island; another is on Floridian Way near the Magic Kingdom Auto Plaza. The third, near the BoardWalk resort on Buena Vista Drive, also has a car wash.

Breakdowns sometimes occur, but they don't spell disaster. All WDW roads are patrolled constantly by security vehicles equipped with radios that can be used to call for help. If you need a tow, contact security (824-4777). If your car needs servicing, but does not need to be towed, call the AAA Car Care Center (824-0976). Located in the Magic Kingdom Auto Plaza, the AAA Car Care Center offers full mechanical services, Monday through Saturday.

DISNEY DOLLARS

Dollars bearing Mickey's, Goofy's, or Minnie's image are available at City Hall (Magic Kingdom) and Guest Relations (Epcot, the Disney-MGM Studios, and Animal Kingdom) in $1, $5, and $10 denominations. They are accepted as cash throughout Walt Disney World.

DRINKING LAWS

In Florida, the legal drinking age is 21. There are many bars and lounges all over Walt Disney World; minors are permitted to accompany their parents, but are prohibited from sitting or standing at the bar. No alcohol is served in the Magic Kingdom (where even the piña coladas are nonalcoholic), but alcoholic beverages are sold at restaurants

and bars in Epcot, Disney-MGM Studios, Animal Kingdom, and Downtown Disney.

By the bottle: Alcoholic beverages are sold in at least one shop at most WDW resorts. Liquor may be purchased from room service at the Polynesian, Contemporary, Grand Floridian, Yacht Club, Beach Club, BoardWalk, Swan and Dolphin resorts; beer and wine are usually available for delivery at other resorts.

LOCKERS

Attended lockers can be found in the following theme park locations: underneath Main Street Railroad Station in the Magic Kingdom; on the west side of Spaceship Earth in Epcot; next to Oscar's Super Service near the main entrance at the Disney-MGM Studios; and just inside the entrance and to the right at Animal Kingdom. Lockers are also available at the Transportation and Ticket Center (TTC). Cost is $3 per day (plus a $2 deposit) for unlimited use. Items too big to fit can be checked at the Guest Relations window at the Magic Kingdom entrance and at City Hall, at package pickup in Epcot, and at Guest Relations at the Disney-MGM Studios and Animal Kingdom.

LOST & FOUND

The extensive indexing system maintained by Walt Disney World's Lost and Found department is impressive, especially when a prized possession turns up missing, whether it's false teeth or a camera. (Both have been lost in the past; the dentures were never claimed.)

If you lose (or find) something, report it at any one of these Lost and Found locations: the Ticket and Transportation Center (TTC); City Hall in the Magic Kingdom; the Gift Stop in the entrance plaza at Epcot; Oscar's Super Service just inside the Disney-MGM Studios; Guest Relations near the Animal Kingdom entrance; or Guest Services at any WDW resort. At Fort Wilderness, dial 7-2726 from a comfort station telephone; from outside the campground, phone 824-2726; and from the Downtown Disney Marketplace, phone 828-3058.

Items lost in one of the theme parks can be claimed on the day of the loss at the park's Lost and Found, and thereafter at the main Lost and Found station at the TTC. To report lost items after your visit, call 824-4245. Hats, strollers, and sunglasses are kept one month. Everything else is kept three months. Articles not claimed by the owner may be claimed by the finder.

MAIL

Postage stamps can be purchased at all WDW resorts; at City Hall in the Magic Kingdom; at most shops near the lockers in Epcot, the Disney-MGM Studios, and Animal Kingdom; and at Guest Services in the Downtown Disney Marketplace.

The old-fashioned, olive-drab mailboxes that punctuate the thoroughfares in the theme parks are not official U.S. post boxes, but letters can be mailed from them. Postmarks read "Lake Buena Vista," not "Walt Disney World." A post office is at the Shoppes at Lake Buena Vista shopping center (opposite Summerfield Suites); it's open from 9 A.M. to 4 P.M. weekdays and 9 A.M. to noon on Saturday (238-0223).

Mail may be addressed to guests in care of their hotel; the address for all WDW resorts is Walt Disney World; Box 10000; Lake Buena Vista, FL 32830-1000.

MEDICAL MATTERS

For travelers with chronic health problems, it's a good idea to carry copies of all prescriptions and to get names of local doctors from hometown physicians. However, Walt Disney World is equipped to deal with many types of medical emergencies. In the Magic Kingdom, next to the Crystal Palace, there's a First Aid Center staffed by a registered nurse; there is another at Epcot in the Odyssey Center complex. At the Disney-MGM Studios, the First Aid Center is in the Guest Relations building at the main entrance, accessible from both inside and outside the park. The Animal Kingdom First Aid Center is in Safari Village near the back side of Creature Comforts.

Walt Disney World resort guests and those staying at other area hotels have access to services providing non-emergency medical care. HouseMed can dispatch a physician directly to a guest's room 24 hours a day or have medications delivered (239-1195 or 396-1195). The service also operates a walk-in medical treatment center, MediClinic, just east of I-4 on U.S. 192; open 8 A.M. to 9 P.M. daily. Centra Care Walk-In Medical Care has two locations (call 239-6463 for either): One, at 12500 South Apopka-Vineland Road, is open 8 A.M. to midnight weekdays, 8 A.M. to 7 P.M. weekends; the other, at 12139 South Apopka-Vineland Road, is open 9 A.M. to 5 P.M. weekdays. Courtesy shuttle service is available from most area hotels to all three clinics.

The most common malady? Not sensitive stomachs upset by rides, but simple sunburn. So be forewarned. Wear a hat, and slather on sufficient sunblock or sunscreen, especially during the spring and summer.

Serious emergencies should be reported to nearby Sandlake Hospital (351-8550).

For Diabetics: Walt Disney World resorts provide refrigeration services for insulin. All villa accommodations have their own refrigerators, and small refrigerators are available at other resorts for a nominal per diem.

Prescriptions: For a referral to the closest pharmacy or to have medications delivered, call HouseMed (239-1195 or 396-1195).

MONEY

Cash, traveler's checks, personal checks, American Express, MasterCard, Visa, and The Disney Credit Card are accepted as payment for most charges at Walt Disney World. Checks must bear your name and address, be drawn on a U.S. bank, and be accompanied by proper identification—a valid driver's license and a major credit card. Note that all snack stands accept only cash. WDW resort guests who have left a credit card imprint at check-in may use their hotel IDs to cover purchases in shops, lounge and restaurant charges, and recreational fees incurred inside Walt Disney World. These cards are not valid for charges made past check-out time on the last day of the guest's stay.

Automated Teller Machines: ATMs are scattered throughout Walt Disney World. Theme park locations include three in the Magic Kingdom (under the train station on Main Street, U.S.A., in Adventureland near The Enchanted Tiki Birds, and in the Tomorrowland arcade), three in Epcot (near the main entrance, on the pathway between Future World and World Showcase, and in Germany), one at the Disney-MGM Studios (at the entrance), and one at Animal Kingdom (at the entrance), plus one at the TTC. All WDW resorts have ATMs in the lobby; the Fort Wilderness ATM is outside Pioneer Hall. Three can be found in Downtown Disney: near the Rock 'n' Roll Beach Club at Pleasure Island, next to Cap'n Jack's Oyster Bar in the Marketplace, and at Downtown Disney West Side. Most bank cards and credit cards are accepted; there is a nominal fee for use.

Banking Services: SunTrust, which is located across from the Downtown Disney Marketplace, can:

• Give cash advances on MasterCard and Visa credit cards, with a $25 minimum.

• Cash and sell traveler's checks for American Express and Bank of America.

• Cash personal checks for American Express Gold Card holders for up to $500 upon presentation of their card (payable in cash up to $200, the rest in traveler's checks).

• Provide refunds for lost American Express traveler's checks.

• Assist with incoming wire transfers of up to $5,000 from a guest's bank to the SunTrust branch for a fee of $30; no outgoing wires allowed.

SunTrust is open from 9 A.M. to 4 P.M. weekdays and until 6 P.M. Thursdays; drive-in teller windows are open from 8 A.M. to 6 P.M. weekdays (828-6106).

Traveler's Checks: Even the most careful of vacationers occasionally loses a wallet, and traveler's checks can take the sting out of that loss. Look for promotions by banks at home in the months preceding a vacation to see if one of the major brands—American Express, MasterCard, Visa, Citicorp, and Bank of America—is available free. Stash the receipt bearing the check numbers in a place separate from the checks themselves, along with a piece of identification such as a duplicate driver's license or a spare credit card to speed the refund process should your checks get lost.

Foreign Currency Exchange: Up to $500 per person in foreign currency may be exchanged daily at Guest Relations in the theme parks, and at the Guest Services desk at WDW resorts, or at the SunTrust across from Downtown Disney Marketplace at other times.

PETS

No pets (other than service dogs) are allowed in the Magic Kingdom, Epcot, the Disney-MGM Studios, Animal Kingdom, or the WDW resorts, except at certain campsites at Fort Wilderness (request a pet site for $3 extra per day). Travelers who bring pets along can lodge them in one of the five air-conditioned Pet Care Kennels: near the Transportation and Ticket Center (TTC); to the left of the Epcot Entrance Plaza; at the Disney-MGM Studios entrance; at the Animal Kingdom entrance; and at the Fort Wilderness campground entrance, next to a huge field where pet owners can take their animals out for a run. During the busy seasons, it is best to arrive before the 9 A.M. morning rush hour. Note that the kennels close one hour after the theme parks close.

Animals such as bears, cougars, and ocelots have all been accommodated by the kennels, and exotic pets may be accepted—if a bit reluctantly. However, owners themselves must put the more unusual animals into the kennel's cages; and snakes, rabbits, birds, turtles, hamsters, and other animals unsuited (because of their size) to cat- and dog-size cages must have their own escape-proof accommodations.

Guests may board their pets overnight in any Walt Disney World kennel. Cost is $11, including Friskies dry food (WDW resort guests pay $9 per night to leave pets overnight); a day stay is $6, with one feeding. Guests who board pets overnight are encouraged to stop by to walk them at least twice a day, as the animals are not otherwise let out of their cages. Pets will be fed special food, if provided.

Be sure to bring along your pet's certificate of vaccinations, since Florida law requires proof of immunization for animals involved in biting incidents. And never leave pets in your car. It is extremely dangerous for the animal and is against the law in the state of Florida.

For more information and reservations (accepted, not required), call 824-6568.

Outside Walt Disney World: A number of hotels in the Orlando area permit pets to stay with guests, including the Holiday Inn Hotel & Suites in Kissimmee (396-4488), which has a P.A.W. (Pets Are Welcome) Program and a Paw Park. For other possibilities, contact the Orlando/Orange County Convention & Visitors Bureau (363-5872 or 800-551-0181).

POCKET PAGERS

Two types of devices are available to signal a telephone call or message. They can be rented at nearly all WDW hotels; inquire at the front desk.

RELIGIOUS SERVICES

A number of services are held at Walt Disney World and in the surrounding area. For more information on nearby Catholic and Protestant services, call the Christian Service Center at 425-2523.

Protestant: 9 A.M. on Sunday at Luau Cove at the Polynesian resort.

Muslim: Muslim services are held at Jama Masijid; 11543 Ruby Lake Rd. Call 238-2700 for information.

Catholic: 8 A.M. and 10:15 A.M. on Sunday at Luau Cove at the Polynesian resort. For more information, check with Guest Services at any WDW hotel or call 239-6600. The closest Catholic church off the property is Mary, Queen of the Universe Shrine, 2½ miles north of Lake Buena Vista on the I-4 service road. This enormous church seats 3,000 people, and has beautiful gardens and fountains. Call 239-6600 for mass times.

Jewish: Conservative services are held at 8 P.M. on Friday and 9:30 A.M. on Saturday at Temple Ohalei Rivka, also known as the Southwest Orlando Jewish Congregation (11200 Apopka-Vineland Road; 239-5444), located about three miles from Downtown Disney. Reform services are held at 10:30 A.M. on Saturday and Shabbat services at 7:30 P.M. the first Friday of the month and 8:15 P.M. the remaining Fridays, at the Congregation of Liberal Judaism (928 Malone Dr., Orlando; 645-0444), near Winter Park about 20 miles from WDW.

SMOKING

Disney is committed to providing guests with a smoke-free environment. All buildings and attraction waiting areas are designated no-smoking areas. All Walt Disney World–owned restaurants are included, with the exception of outdoor seating areas. However, most clubs at BoardWalk and Downtown Disney (except Adventurers Club and Comedy Warehouse at Pleasure Island), as well as many of the Walt Disney World resort lounges, allow smoking in certain areas.

SHOPPING FOR NECESSITIES

Almost any everyday item can be purchased right on the property. The following resort shops stock toiletries: Concourse Sundries &

is the best source for books. Another possibility is the Emporium in the Magic Kingdom, which carries children's books. In World Showcase, the United Kingdom's The Toy Soldier and Germany's Der Bücherwurm also stock kid's books. Books related to themes of Epcot's Future World pavilions are sold at Centorium. At the Disney-MGM Studios, adult and children's books are sold at Legends of Hollywood; Animation Gallery stocks books about animation; and Ellen's Buy the Book has a far-reaching selection.

TELEPHONE NUMBERS

The folks at home can reach Walt Disney World resort guests at the following phone numbers (all are in area code 407):

All-Star Music:	939-6000
All-Star Sports:	939-5000
Beach Club:	934-8000
BoardWalk Inn:	939-5100
BoardWalk Villas:	939-6200
Caribbean Beach:	934-3400
Contemporary:	824-1000
Coronado Springs:	939-1000
Dixie Landings:	934-6000
Dolphin:	934-4000
Fort Wilderness:	824-2900
Grand Floridian:	824-3000
Old Key West:	827-7700
Polynesian:	824-2000
Port Orleans:	934-5000
Swan:	934-3000
Villas at the Disney Institute:	827-1100
Wilderness Lodge:	824-3200
Yacht Club:	934-7000

Weather: Call Walt Disney World Weather Information at 824-4104.

TIPPING

Walt Disney World is not a place where bellmen stick out their hands even before they put down your luggage. Instead, they seem genuinely glad to help. Oddly enough, this pleasant attitude seems to discourage tipping at the same time it arouses sentiments that make most travelers reach for their wallets.

Tips are no less valued at WDW resorts than at any other hotel—$1 per bag is appropriate for lugging luggage; $1 to $2 per night for housekeeping service. Gratuities of 15% to 18% are customary at full-service restaurants. (As always, if service is exceptional, gratuities should be adjusted accordingly.)

Gratuities are not required in fast-food restaurants, but in the salons, it's customary to leave a tip of about 15% of the total bill.

Cab drivers in the Orlando area expect a 15% tip. Baggage handlers at the train station and airport expect about $1 per bag.

Spirits in the Contemporary, the Grog Hut at the Polynesian, Sandy Cove at the Grand Floridian, Calypso Trading Post at Caribbean Beach, Fittings & Fairings at the Yacht Club, Atlantic Wear and Wardrobe Emporium at the Beach Club, Dundy's Sundries at the BoardWalk, Jackson Square Gifts & Desires at Port Orleans, Fulton's General Store at Dixie Landings, Conch Flats General Store at Old Key West, Wilderness Lodge Mercantile at the Wilderness Lodge, Maestro Mickey's at the All-Star Music, Sport Goofy's Gifts and Sundries at the All-Star Sports, Panchito's Gifts & Sundries at Coronado Springs, Daisy's Garden at the Dolphin, Disney Cabana at the Swan, and the Meadow and Settlement Trading Posts at Fort Wilderness.

In addition, a number of over-the-counter health aids, plus many other useful items, can be purchased at the Emporium on Main Street in the Magic Kingdom; they're kept behind the counter, so ask for what you want. Aspirin and sunscreen are also available at Island Supply in Adventureland, and Mickey's Star Traders in Tomorrowland. In Epcot, sundries are sold in at least one shop in each World Showcase pavilion and at all Future World stores. At the Disney-MGM Studios, stop by the Crossroads of the World and Movieland Memorabilia shops. At Animal Kingdom, you can pick up bare necessities at Island Mercantile.

Gooding's supermarket, at the Crossroads of Lake Buena Vista shopping center near Downtown Disney, has a large pharmacy.

Reading Matter: Newspapers, magazines, best-sellers, and paperbacks are available at the resort shops mentioned above, with one exception: at the Polynesian, News from Civilization is the place to go. Most of these shops carry the daily papers from Orlando and Miami, *The Wall Street Journal*, and, on Sunday, *The New York Times* and *The Chicago Tribune*. By far, 2R's Reading and Riting at the Downtown Disney Marketplace

Magical Milestones

Even frequent visitors have trouble keeping up with all the changes at Walt Disney World. The time line below will help you determine which major attractions have opened since your last visit.

GETTING READY TO GO

1971—Magic Kingdom; Polynesian resort; Contemporary resort; Fort Wilderness

1972—Carousel of Progress and If You Had Wings (now Take Flight) at Magic Kingdom

1973—Pirates of the Caribbean, Tom Sawyer Island at Magic Kingdom; Golf Resort (now Shades of Green)

1974—Star Jets (now Astro Orbiter) at Magic Kingdom; Treasure Island (now Discovery Island)

1975—Space Mountain and WEDway PeopleMover (now Tomorrowland Transit Authority) at Magic Kingdom

1976—River Country

1977—Empress Lilly Riverboat (now Fulton's Crab House)

1980—Big Thunder Mountain Railroad at Magic Kingdom

1982—Epcot

1983—Journey Into Imagination and Horizons at Epcot

1984—Morocco pavilion at Epcot

1986—Captain EO, The Living Seas at Epcot

1988—Wonders of Life, Norway, and IllumiNations at Epcot; Grand Floridian and Caribbean Beach resorts

1989—The Disney-MGM Studios; Mickey's Starland at Magic Kingdom; Body Wars and Cranium Command at Epcot; Typhoon Lagoon; Pleasure Island

1990—Star Tours and Honey, I Shrunk the Audience Movie Set Adventure at Disney-MGM Studios; Yacht Club and Beach Club resorts; Swan and Dolphin resorts

1991—SpectroMagic (replaced Main Street Electrical Parade) at Magic Kingdom; Jim Henson's Muppet*Vision 3-D at Disney-MGM Studios; Port Orleans resort

1992—Splash Mountain at Magic Kingdom; Voyage of The Little Mermaid at the Studios; Disney's Old Key West and Dixie Landings resorts

1993—New productions of The Hall of Presidents and Carousel of Progress at Magic Kingdom; new production of The American Adventure at Epcot

1994—Legend of the Lion King and The Timekeeper opened (20,000 Leagues Under the Sea closed) at Magic Kingdom; Innoventions (replaced Communicore), Honey, I Shrunk the Audience (replaced Captain EO), Food Rocks (replaced the Kitchen Kabaret), and The Circle of Life at Epcot; The Twilight Zone Tower of Terror at Disney-MGM Studios; Blizzard Beach; All-Star Sports and Music resorts; Wilderness Lodge resort

1995—Alien Encounter at Magic Kingdom; Disney's Wedding Pavilion

1996—Mickey's Toontown Fair (replaced Starland) at Magic Kingdom; Ellen's Energy Adventure at Epcot; Backstage Pass to 101 Dalmatians and Disney's The Hunchback of Notre Dame—A Musical Adventure at Disney-MGM Studios; Disney Institute; Fantasia Gardens Miniature Golf; Celebration; BoardWalk

1997—Test Track at Epcot; Disney's Wide World of Sports; Coronado Springs resort

WHAT'S NEW IN 1998?

Any year that welcomes a whole new Walt Disney World theme park is already a momentous one, but several other debuts make 1998 even more so! To spotlight these auspicious openings, some listings are marked with our special stamp, shown at right. Look for this symbol throughout the book. Here are a few highlights:

- **Disney's Animal Kingdom** (page 165)
- **Downtown Disney West Side** (page 185)
- **Disney Cruise Line** (page 71)

Transportation& Accommodations

The popularity of Walt Disney World has made the region around Orlando one of the world's major tourism and commercial centers, and transportation facilities from a state-of-the-art airport to an efficient network of highways bring visitors to the area by the millions.

There's no doubt that getting to and around the Walt Disney World region can be very confusing. The only more perplexing dilemma may be choosing the best accommodations for your family from among the huge assortment of hotels and motels.

The accommodations operated by Walt Disney World itself range from futuristic high-rise towers to treehouses buried deep in piney woods. In between are resorts that evoke striking images of the South Pacific, old Florida, the Pacific Northwest, the Caribbean, New England, early Atlantic City, Louisiana, northern Mexico, and the sports and music worlds, plus efficient trailer-type facilities and cabins in a sprawling, beautifully maintained campground. And that list doesn't include the many villas that provide extraordinary space and luxury, or the studios and homes with one, two, and three bedrooms that can be purchased through a special vacation-ownership system. What follows should help travelers sort out all the lodging options on Walt Disney World property, as well as shed light on the broad range of possibilities that exist outside the WDW gates.

Unless otherwise noted, all phone numbers are in area code 407.

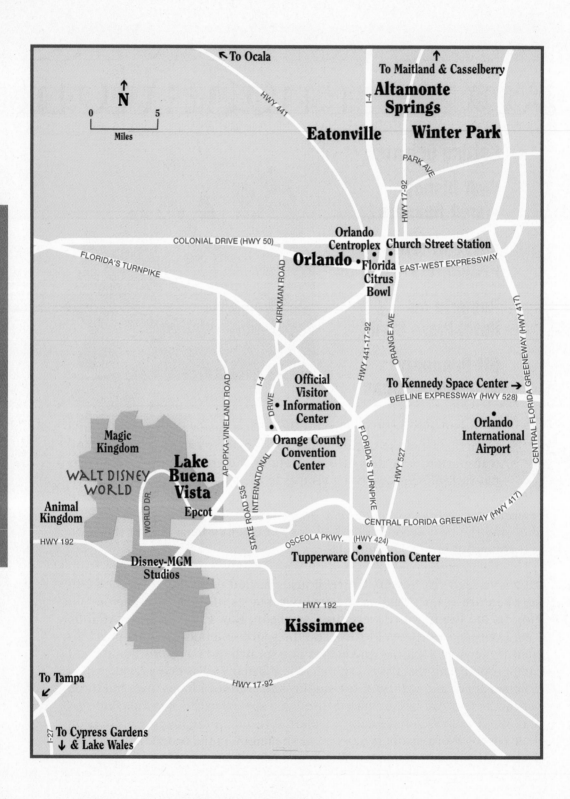

To Ocala

To Maitland & Casselberry

N

0   5
Miles

Altamonte
Springs

Eatonville   Winter Park

HWY 441

I-4

PARK AVE

HWY 17-92

COLONIAL DRIVE (HWY 50)

Orlando
Centroplex   Church Street Station
Orlando   • Florida   EAST-WEST EXPRESSWAY
Citrus
Bowl

FLORIDA'S TURNPIKE

KIRKMAN ROAD

HWY 441-17-92

ORANGE AVE

CENTRAL FLORIDA GREENEWAY (HWY 417)

Official
Visitor
Information
Center

To Kennedy Space Center →
BEELINE EXPRESSWAY (HWY 528)

Orange County
Convention
Center

Orlando
International
Airport

APOPKA-VINELAND ROAD

I-4 DRIVE

FLORIDA'S TURNPIKE

HWY 527

Magic
Kingdom

WALT DISNEY
WORLD

Lake
Buena
Vista

Epcot

Animal
Kingdom

WORLD DR.

STATE ROAD 535

INTERNATIONAL

CENTRAL FLORIDA GREENEWAY (HWY 417)

HWY 192

Disney-MGM
Studios

OSCEOLA PKWY.   (HWY 424)
Tupperware Convention Center

I-4

HWY 192

Kissimmee

To Tampa

HWY 17-92

I-27   To Cypress Gardens
& Lake Wales

40

GETTING ORIENTED

Orlando, the Central Florida city of more than one million residents, is the municipality with which Walt Disney World is most closely associated. Walt Disney World, however, is in a far smaller community called Lake Buena Vista, 15 miles from Orlando's business center. Many hotels and restaurants are located here, though there are many more in Orlando. Among the other compelling adjacent communities are Winter Park (northeast of Orlando), Maitland (northwest of Winter Park), and Altamonte Springs (near Maitland).

ORLANDO-AREA HIGHWAYS: The most important Orlando traffic artery is I-4, which runs diagonally through the area from southwest to northeast, cutting through the southern half of Walt Disney World. It then angles on toward Orlando and Winter Park, ending near Daytona Beach at I-95, which runs north and south along the coast.

All the city's other important highways intersect I-4. From south to north, these include U.S. 192 (a.k.a. Irlo Bronson Memorial Highway), which takes an east–west course that crosses the WDW entrance road and leads into downtown Kissimmee on the east; S.R. 528 (a.k.a. the Beeline Expressway), which shoots eastward from I-4; S.R. 435, also known as Kirkman Road, which runs north and south and intersects International Drive, where many motels catering to WDW visitors are located; U.S. 17-92-441 (a.k.a. Orange Blossom Trail), which runs due north and south, paralleling Kirkman Road on the east; and S.R. 50 (a.k.a. Colonial Drive), which runs due east and west.

WALT DISNEY WORLD EXITS: The 45-square-mile tract that is Walt Disney World is roughly rectangular. I-4 runs through its southern half from southwest to northeast. The major WDW destinations are most efficiently reached by taking the I-4 exits suggested below; off the highway, clear signage makes it easy for visitors to get anywhere in the World. Keep in mind that special events will often require rerouting of traffic patterns, so it's best to follow signs as directed.

- **Exit 27**, marked "S.R. 535/Lake Buena Vista," is the route taken to the resorts on Hotel Plaza Blvd. and the Crossroads of Lake Buena Vista shopping center.
- **Exit 26B**, marked "Epcot/Downtown Disney" leads to Epcot, Animal Kingdom, Typhoon Lagoon, Downtown Disney, Lake Buena Vista golf course, the Disney Institute, Bonnet Creek Golf Club, and the BoardWalk, Caribbean Beach, Swan, Dolphin, Yacht Club, Beach Club, Port Orleans, Dixie Landings, and

Old Key West resorts. It is also a good alternate route to the Disney-MGM Studios.
- **Exit 25**, marked "192/Magic Kingdom," leads to the Magic Kingdom, Disney-MGM Studios, Blizzard Beach, Fort Wilderness, River Country, Palm and Magnolia golf courses, Disney's Wide World of Sports, and the All-Star Music, All-Star Sports, Coronado Springs, Contemporary, Polynesian, Grand Floridian, and Wilderness Lodge resorts.

WDW TRANSPORTATION: The internal transportation system at Walt Disney World is quite extensive, with boats, buses, and the famed monorail all doing their part to shuttle guests around property. The system is always being revised to serve the ever-increasing number of attractions and accommodations. Visitors staying at WDW hotels receive detailed information about transportation options upon checking in. For up-to-the-minute information about WDW transportation, call 824-4321.

The system's central link is a hub called the Transportation and Ticket Center (TTC), located near the Magic Kingdom. Monorail, bus, and ferry service connect the TTC to points throughout the World. Day visitors must park here before taking a monorail or ferry to the Magic Kingdom. (Most Disney resort guests can bypass the TTC via direct buses.)

WDW's monorail train runs along a circular route near the Magic Kingdom, stopping at the TTC, Polynesian, Grand Floridian, Contemporary, and Magic Kingdom. A separate extension of the monorail system connects the TTC to Epcot. Monorails run from 7 A.M. until about two hours after park closing.

Bus service is the cornerstone of the Walt Disney World transportation system. It is efficient, if occasionally confusing. With a few exceptions, buses circulate every 15 to 20 minutes, from one hour prior to park opening until about one hour after closing; bus stops are clearly marked. Travel times vary, depending on the route. Build in extra time for travel, especially if you have made priority seating arrangements at a restaurant.

From several Walt Disney World locales, water launches usher guests to the Magic Kingdom, Epcot, the Disney-MGM Studios, Downtown Disney, or between resorts. Boats generally depart every 20 to 30 minutes.

Transportation ID Requirements

Guests wishing to use the Walt Disney World transportation system must present proof of their riding privileges, usually a park ticket or WDW resort ID card. The various accepted IDs afford different degrees of access. Specific requirements and limitations are noted below.

• WDW resort ID cards allow guests unlimited use of any WDW buses, monorails, and boats.

• Four-Day Value Passes, Four-Day Park Hopper Passes, Five-Day World Hopper Passes, Length of Stay Passes, and Annual Passes allow guests use of any WDW transportation.

• Valid one-day theme park tickets permit guests to use all monorails and the ferries running between the TTC and the Magic Kingdom. They do not allow use of WDW buses.

• River Country and Hoop-Dee-Doo Musical Revue dinner show tickets allow guests use of buses from the TTC, water launches from the Contemporary, Wilderness Lodge, and the Magic Kingdom to River Country and Pioneer Hall in Fort Wilderness.

ACCOMMODATIONS

When it comes to securing accommodations for a Walt Disney World vacation, there are two major categories to consider: those on Walt Disney World property and those off-property, or outside Disney boundaries. Both offer a wide selection of rooms, usually with two standard double beds, a television set, and a private bathroom. The biggest differences among accommodations, on- and off-property, seem to be in the dimensions of the rooms and bathrooms, attention to decor, level of service, variety of dining options, recreational facilities, landscaping, and location.

In choosing a place to stay, first decide how much you want to spend. If you choose to stay outside the World, select accommodations based on your budget, location (proximity to Walt Disney World and other area attractions), the availability of transportation to and from Walt Disney World, as well as restaurants and other amenities.

Several off-property options are described in the latter part of this chapter. Those closest to Walt Disney World are located on or just off S.R. 535 in Lake Buena Vista. Others are located in Kissimmee, along U.S. 192 (which runs east and west) intersecting the WDW entrance road, and along International Drive (off S.R. 435 at the Orlando city limits). Note that the U.S. 192 establishments are closer to the WDW main entrance—many only a few miles away—while those on International Drive are some ten miles from the WDW theme park gates. The latter area, however, presents an extensive array of accommodations, restaurants, and other attractions. Its proximity to still more of the same in Orlando, just a few miles north, constitutes an additional lure.

Although rates are generally higher at WDW addresses than at most others in the area, there are Disney accommodations starting as low as $74 per night. We highly recommend staying on Walt Disney World property. Why? For starters, most Disney resorts offer guests early admission to the Magic Kingdom, Epcot, and the Disney-MGM Studios on designated days; use of the WDW transportation system; rooms equipped with the Disney Channel and a closed-circuit TV station announcing WDW events; free delivery of purchases back to the resort; and excellent access to Guest Services personnel. Guests can also reserve tee-off times on the golf courses up to 60 days in advance.

In addition to the aforementioned perks, there is another important, if less tangible factor to consider: atmosphere. At the end (or in the middle) of a day, when you leave the parks behind, you take the "magic" with you: every Disney resort offers top-notch service, a full battery of whimsical diversions, and a never-ending supply of festive ambience. Add to that the sheer convenience of staying in the heart of all the action and it's clear why an on-property stay makes for a less harried vacation. Be wary of anyone who encourages you to stay elsewhere for reasons other than a major difference in price.

Remember, when examining rate sheets for the best buy for your family, always check the cutoff age at which children accompanying you (and staying in the same room) will be billed as extra adults. Those with large families should note that the Disney villa-type accommodations, which may seem more expensive at first, could prove less costly in the long run—by eliminating the necessity of an additional room and by providing cooking facilities that can mean big savings on meals.

It's helpful to think of accommodations on the WDW grounds in terms of their location. Therefore, the Walt Disney World properties described in this chapter are divided into the following sections: Magic Kingdom, Epcot, Animal Kingdom, and Downtown Disney areas, as well as the Disney Cruise Line and the resorts on Hotel Plaza Boulevard.

WALT DISNEY WORLD RESORTS

With the addition of moderately priced resort rooms at Caribbean Beach, Port Orleans, Dixie Landings, and Coronado Springs, and the even more economical rooms at the All-Star Sports and All-Star Music resorts, we find it difficult to recommend staying off the property. And reservations are generally easy to obtain, since there are more than 25,000 rooms available.

In general, rooms at the Contemporary, Polynesian, Grand Floridian, Yacht Club and Beach Club, BoardWalk Inn, and the Swan and Dolphin are quite large and can accommodate up to five guests in a single room without difficulty. Rooms at the Wilderness Lodge, Caribbean Beach, Port Orleans, Dixie Landings, Coronado Springs, All-Star Sports, and All-Star Music resorts accommodate up to four people. Many rooms have

patios or balconies. And considering the incredibly high occupancy rate, it's astonishing that things look so fresh. Even the rooms without dramatic views often have pleasant vistas, if only across gardens.

The Villas at the Disney Institute, which can accommodate larger groups, makes particularly good sense for families, especially those who want to cook some of their own meals "at home." The vacation villas at Old Key West and BoardWalk are also popular with families. At Fort Wilderness there are campsites and fully equipped Wilderness Homes and Cabins set on 700 acres of peaceful woods.

The Walt Disney World hotels in this section are broken into four geographic groups: Magic Kingdom Area, Epcot Area, Downtown Disney Area, and the Animal Kingdom Area. The hotels, rooms, and facilities are described in detail. All WDW resorts offer laundry facilities and dry-cleaning services, and rooms feature clock radios, safes, and voice-mail messaging. Restaurants listed here are described at length in the *Good Meals, Great Times* chapter. Note that all restaurants at WDW resorts are nonsmoking, as are all public spaces, with the exception of lounges.

Disney Rates the Resorts

The Walt Disney World rating system helps you choose the resort, hotel, villa, or campsite that best suits your needs. Here's a breakdown of the core amenities, room rates, and resorts in each category. For specific pricing, see the chart on pages 74 and 75.

Deluxe ($175 to $395)
- Full-service restaurants
- Room service
- Bellman luggage service, valet parking
- Swimming pools, beach access
- On-site recreation, such as boat rental
- Most rooms sleep five
- On-site child care programs
- Monorail, boat, or bus transportation to all theme parks

Resorts
- BoardWalk Inn (page 61)
- Contemporary (page 46)
- Grand Floridian (page 49)
- Polynesian (page 47)
- Swan and Dolphin (page 58)
- Wilderness Lodge (page 51)
- Yacht Club and Beach Club (page 57)

Home Away From Home ($185 to $1,295)
- Kitchen facilities, pizza delivery
- Luggage service
- Swimming pools
- Front-door parking for your vehicle
- Flexible room arrangements accommodating 4 to 12 guests
- Full-service restaurants
- Bus transportation to all theme parks

Resorts
- Disney's BoardWalk Villas Resort (page 61)
- Disney's Old Key West Resort (page 67)
- Fort Wilderness Homes and Fort Wilderness Cabins (page 53)
- The Villas at the Disney Institute (page 65)

Moderate ($119 to $154)
- Full-service restaurants, food courts, limited room service
- Bellman luggage service
- Swimming pools with slides
- On-site recreation, such as playgrounds and bike rental
- Rooms sleep four
- Bus transportation to all theme parks

Resorts
- Caribbean Beach (page 55)
- Coronado Springs (page 70)
- Dixie Landings (page 64)
- Port Orleans (page 63)

Value ($74 to $89)
- Food courts, pizza delivery
- Hourly luggage service
- Swimming pools
- Bus transportation to all theme parks

Resorts
- All-Star Music (page 69)
- All-Star Sports (page 69)

Campground ($35 to $64)
- Received perfect ratings from *Trailer Life* magazine and from Woodall's

- Fort Wilderness Campground (page 53)

TRANSPORTATION & ACCOMMODATIONS

Magic Kingdom Area

Contemporary

Watching the monorail trains disappear into this hotel's enormous 15-story A-frame tower never fails to amaze first-timers. The sleek trains look like long spaceships docking as they slide inside. (Note that guests with non-collapsible strollers or those who use wheelchairs cannot board the monorail here, but they can at the Polynesian and Grand Floridian, whose platforms are accessible.)

Passengers, for their part, are impressed by the cavernous lobby, with its tiers of balconies and, at its center, designer Mary Blair's huge 90-foot-high, floor-to-ceiling tile mural depicting Native American children, stylized flowers, birds, trees, and other scenes from the Southwest. (Look carefully and you may be able to spot the five-legged goat.)

This imposing structure has 1,041 rooms in its tower and the garden buildings that flank it on either side. There are six shops, three restaurants, two snack bars, two lounges, a marina, a beach, a health club, and more. The recently renovated pool area incorporates two whirlpools, a water slide, and water jets. The lively Food and Fun Center—a vast area with an arcade and snack bar—is open 24 hours a day. The large convention center offers access to business services.

A concierge package is available for guests who stay in the hotel's 14th-floor suites. Amenities include express check-in and check-out, complimentary continental breakfast, hors d'oeuvres and refreshments at night, and nightly turndown service. To contact the Contemporary resort, call 824-1000.

ROOMS: Modern-art designs accented by bold colors drive the decor of rooms evenly apportioned among the tower and two garden buildings. Rooms in the tower boast private balconies and fantastic views of Bay Lake or the Magic Kingdom. Most rooms can accommodate five guests (plus one child under three). Typical units have a day bed and two queen-size beds; some rooms have a king-size bed and a daybed. Connecting rooms may be requested. Rooms equipped for guests with disabilities and nonsmoking rooms are available. Bathrooms in the Contemporary resort are large and well laid out. A variety of elegant suites, consisting of a living room and one or two bedrooms, can accommodate 7 to 12 people.

WHERE TO EAT: In addition to the many restaurants and snack spots, 24-hour room service provides a wide range of offerings.

California Grill: On the 15th floor. The specialty is California fare, including pizza baked in wood-burning ovens, grilled meats, seafood, and market vegetables. An added treat: the spectacular view of the Magic Kingdom fireworks, and sensational sunsets.

Chef Mickey's: Located on the fourth-floor concourse. Mickey and his friends cook up daily buffets. Breakfast features Mickey Mouse waffles as well as more traditional items. Dinner offers two carved meats, prime rib, nightly specials, peel-and-eat shrimp and a variety of entrées, plus a sundae and dessert bar.

Concourse Steakhouse: On the fourth-floor concourse. A full breakfast; burgers, salads, and sandwiches for lunch; steaks, seafood, and pasta for dinner.

Food and Fun Center: On the first floor. Serves light fare 24 hours a day.

WHERE TO DRINK: The Magic Kingdom's no-alcohol policy doesn't trickle over to its nearest neighbor.

California Grill Lounge: On the resort's 15th floor, adjoining the California Grill. Prime views provide a dramatic backdrop for sipping California wines and other drinks, and nibbling on appetizers.

Contemporary Grounds: A lobby coffee bar, near the escalators. Serves cappuccino, espresso, lattes, and other gourmet coffees, as well as biscotti.

Outer Rim: On the fourth-floor concourse, overlooking Bay Lake. Serves appetizers, cocktails, and specialty drinks.

Sand Bar: This poolside spot offers drinks and light snacks seasonally.

WHAT TO DO: The Contemporary boasts more activities and recreational facilities than many large resorts. Volleyball nets are set up on the beach. Waterskiing, basketball, fishing, and parasailing excursions are available (see *Sports* for details).

Boating: Sailboats (including catamarans), canopy boats, Water Sprites, and Seariders are available for rent at the marina, near the pool.

Children's Program: The Mouseketeer Clubhouse is open from 4:30 P.M. to midnight for children ages 4 to 12 (four-hour maximum stay). Cost is $4 per hour per child. Reservations are necessary; call 824-1000, ext. 3897.

Health Club: The Contemporary Fitness Center has modern Nautilus equipment, stair climbers, rowing machines, bicycles, sauna, lockers, and massage (by appointment).

Salon: Contemporary Resort Salon on the third floor of the tower provides haircuts, facials, manicures, and other services.

Shopping: The fourth-floor concourse is home to several first-class shops. Fantasia sells an array of Disney character merchandise, including plush animals and clothing, for both children and adults. The Contemporary Woman offers a range of quality women's clothing (and plenty of bathing suits) in all price ranges, and the adjoining Contemporary Man stocks casual clothes and beachwear. The adjacent Kingdom Jewels Ltd. specializes in jewelry, including Disney character jewelry. Bayview Gifts carries souvenirs, gifts, and fresh flowers. Concourse Sundries & Spirits has a selection of newspapers, magazines, books, snack foods, and liquor—just what's needed for a cocktail party on the terrace.

Swimming: In addition to a round quiet pool that is practically on top of Bay Lake, the free-form pool features a 17-foot-high curving slide. Two large whirlpools have been added, one on a peninsula protruding into the pool. Water jets shoot unexpectedly while smaller fountains spout randomly, delighting older and younger kids alike. A toddler's pool is located near the hotel's north wing. Wading is also permitted in the roped-off area of Bay Lake beside the beach.

Tennis: Disney's Racquet Club, Walt Disney World's premier tennis center, is located near the north wing. It features six state-of-the-art hydrogrid clay courts. Private lessons are available (see *Sports* for details). The shop here has tennis equipment, fashions, and shoes. Racquet restringing is also available.

Video Arcades: On the first floor, the Food and Fun Center boasts everything from Skee-Ball to air hockey, and all the favorites of the pinball-and-electronic-games-playing set. A much smaller arcade is near the pool.

TRANSPORTATION: The resort is connected to the TTC and the Magic Kingdom by monorail. Board just above the fourth-floor concourse, inside the atrium area of the tower. From the TTC, Epcot can be reached via monorail, and Typhoon Lagoon and Downtown Disney can be reached by bus. Direct buses go to the Disney-MGM Studios, Animal Kingdom, and Blizzard Beach. Watercraft travel from the marina to Fort Wilderness, Wilderness Lodge, and River Country.

Polynesian

The Polynesian resort is as close an approximation of the real thing as Walt Disney World's designers could create. The vegetation is as lush as anywhere else in the World, and the architecture summons the tropics.

The mood is set by a three-story garden that occupies most of the lobby. To call the construction at the center a fountain is to do it a grave injustice; it's more like a waterfall. The water cascades over craggy volcanic rocks. Coconut palms tower over about 75 different species of tropical and subtropical plants—anthuriums, banana trees, gardenias, orchids, ferns, and other greens. The climatic conditions are nearly perfect, so that everything blooms year-round.

The structure that contains this mass of greenery, the Great Ceremonial House, is the central building in the Polynesian resort complex. The front desk, the shops, and most of the restaurants are located here. Flanking the Great Ceremonial House on either side are 11 two- and three-story village longhouses named for various Pacific islands. These structures house the resort's 853 guestrooms. The monorail stops at this hotel, making it an especially convenient place to stay; in fact, it's just a few minutes' ride to the Magic Kingdom. But because the accommodations are scattered around the property, things seldom feel as hectic as at some other resorts.

The Polynesian offers a concierge service called King Kamehameha. Special amenities with the service include express check-in and check-out, continental breakfast each morning, soft drinks and hors d'oeuvres every afternoon, and access to a peaceful lounge with a prime fireworks view. A concierge is on duty from 7 A.M. to 11 P.M. Concierge rooms and suites are located in the Tonga and Bali Hai buildings, and are the most expensive in the hotel. The telephone number for the Polynesian resort is 824-2000.

ROOMS: Many rooms have balconies, and most have a view of the gardens, Seven Seas Lagoon, or one of the resort's swimming pools; rooms in the Oahu, Moorea, and Pago Pago buildings are the largest. All rooms have two queen-size beds and a daybed, and can accommodate five guests (plus a sixth under age three). Connecting or adjoining rooms may be requested. The Oahu and Pago Pago buildings have rooms specially equipped for guests with disabilities. Non-smoking rooms are available.

The resort's suites—located exclusively in the Bali Hai building—can accommodate four to six guests. Some have a king-size bed in the bedroom and two queen-size beds in the parlor.

WHERE TO EAT: A variety of specialties are available from room service between 6:30 A.M. and midnight. Also, some interesting eating spots are located here.

Captain Cook's Snack Company: On the lobby level of the Great Ceremonial House. This is a good spot for continental breakfast. Sandwiches and snacks are available 24 hours a day.

Coral Isle Café: On the second floor of the Great Ceremonial House. This restaurant with South Seas decor serves the usual assortment of breakfast items, plus a WDW specialty, banana-stuffed french toast; it also does a booming business in steaks and seafood at lunch and dinner. A good bet for a no-fuss meal.

'Ohana: On the second floor of the Great Ceremonial House. 'Ohana serves family-style dinners roasted in the World's largest fire pit. Minnie's Menehune character breakfast is held daily. The room is large and open, and offers fine views across Seven Seas Lagoon to Cinderella Castle. Specialty desserts and gourmet coffees are available.

WHERE TO DRINK: The Polynesian theme has inspired a whole raft of deceptively potent potables. As might be expected, both the drink offerings and the settings in which they are served are decidedly tropical.

Barefoot Bar: Adjoining the Swimming Pool Lagoon, and open seasonally.

Tambu: There's a tropical air about this lounge adjoining 'Ohana. The bar serves appetizers and exotic specialty drinks while guests wait to be seated.

WHAT TO DO: A wide range of activities are available at the Polynesian resort. Waterskiing and fishing excursions can also be arranged (see *Sports* for details).

Boating: Several types of sailboats (including catamarans), speedy little Water Sprites, and pontoon boats are available for rent at the marina.

Children's Program: Kanaka Kids is a supervised evening activity program for children ages 4 to 12. The program operates between 5 P.M. and midnight, with a kids' buffet from 6 P.M. to 8 P.M. The cost is $8 per hour and there is a three-hour minimum. Reservations are necessary and can be made by calling 939-3463.

Playground: The playground near the Swimming Pool Lagoon features apparatuses for climbing, swinging, and sliding.

Shopping: News from Civilization, on the first floor of the Great Ceremonial House, is the locale for hotel and Florida logo items, as well as newspapers, magazines, film, sun care products, and gifts. Robinson Crusoe, Esq.

sells casual sportswear and swimwear for men; the Polynesian Princess stocks brightly colored resort fashions, bathing suits, and accessories for women. Upstairs, Trader Jack's sells a variety of Disney souvenirs, toys, fashions, and other items; the Grog Hut has food, liquor, wine, beer, soft drinks, and other fixings for an impromptu party.

Swimming: There are two main pools here: the elliptical East Pool, in the shadow of the Oahu, Tonga, Hawaii, Bora Bora, and Moorea buildings, and the larger free-form Swimming Pool Lagoon, found closer to the marina and main beach. The latter is framed by a large cluster of boulders that forms a water slide much beloved by youngsters; to get to the ladder they must duck underneath a waterfall. Toddlers have their own shallow wading pool. Wading is also permitted in the roped-off areas of Seven Seas Lagoon.

Video Arcade: Moana Mickey's Arcade has a small assortment of video games. It is located on the eastern edge of the property near the Oahu guest building.

TRANSPORTATION: The resort is on the monorail line to the Magic Kingdom and the TTC; the platform is on the second floor of the Great Ceremonial House. From the TTC, Epcot is accessible by another monorail, and Typhoon Lagoon and Downtown Disney can be reached by bus. Direct buses go to the Disney-MGM Studios, Animal Kingdom, and Blizzard Beach. Launches leave from the Polynesian dock for the Magic Kingdom and the Grand Floridian.

Grand Floridian

At the turn of the century, Standard Oil magnate Henry M. Flagler saw the realization of his dream: The railroad he had built to "civilize" Florida had spawned along its right-of-way an empire of grand hotels, lavish estates, prominent families, and opulent lifestyles. High society blossomed in winter,

as the likes of John D. Rockefeller and Teddy Roosevelt checked into the Royal Poinciana in Palm Beach, enjoying the sea breezes from the oceanside suites.

The hotel later burned to the ground, and Florida's golden era faded with the Depression. But nearly a century after Flagler first made Florida a fashionable resort destination, Walt Disney World opened a grand hotel—a 900-room Victorian structure with gabled roofs and carved moldings—on 40 acres of Seven Seas Lagoon shorefront, between the Magic Kingdom and the Polynesian resort.

Like its late-19th-century predecessors, the Grand Floridian resort boasts abundant verandas, ceiling fans, intricate latticework and balustrades, turrets, towers, and red-shingle roofs. And yet, it offers all the advantages of 20th-century living—including monorail service. With five restaurants, two lounges, five shops, and an arcade, plus a child care facility, a convention center offering access to business services, a swimming pool, marina, and health club and spa, the Grand Floridian is not only a grand hotel but a complete resort.

The main building houses the Grand Lobby, a palatial space soaring five stories to a ceiling of stained-glass domes and glittering chandeliers. Potted palms and an aviary decorate the sitting area; an open-cage elevator carries guests to the shops and restaurants on the second floor. The turn-of-the-century theme is everywhere, from the Edwardian

Shades of Green

This resort (formerly The Disney Inn) is a recreational retreat for active and retired military personnel and their families, members of the reserves and the National Guard, and Department of Defense employees. The 288-room resort features two tennis courts, two pools, a small health club, restaurant, bar and lounge, gift shop, arcade, laundry facilities, and free transportation around Walt Disney World. Room rates are based on military or civilian grade. Discounted Length of Stay Passes are also available. The property's three golf courses—the Palm, the Magnolia, and Oak Trail—are open to all WDW guests (See *Sports* for details). All other activities are for hotel guests and their families only. The telephone number for Shades of Green is 824-3400.

costumes worn by the employees to the shop displays, restaurants, and the room decor. The telephone number for the Grand Floridian resort is 824-3000.

ROOMS: The accommodations are quite luxurious, with rooms decorated as they might have been a century ago—in soft colors, with printed wall coverings, armoires and light-wood furnishings, marble-topped sinks, ceiling fans, and Victorian woodwork. The resort's main building houses 65 concierge rooms and 9 suites; five lodge buildings, each four and five stories high, contain 623 standard rooms, 161 slightly smaller "attic" chambers, and 16 suites. Most rooms measure about 400 square feet and include two queen-size beds, plus a daybed, to accommodate five people. Many rooms have terraces. Suites include a parlor, plus one, two, or three bedrooms; there are king-size or queen-size beds in the bedrooms. Most of the 15 honeymoon rooms, located on the second, third, fourth, and fifth floors, enjoy wonderful views. In the main building, access to the upper three concierge-suite levels is restricted by private elevator to guests occupying rooms on those floors.

On the third floor, the concierge desks offer such personalized services as reservations and information. The fourth floor features a quiet seating area where continental breakfast and evening refreshments are served. There are rooms equipped for guests with disabilities; nonsmoking rooms are also available.

WHERE TO EAT: Most of the restaurants and lounges are located on the first two floors of the main building. Room service offers a wide assortment of items 24 hours a day.

Cítricos: On the Alcazar Level (second floor). The largest of the hotel's restaurants is also the newest (it replaced Flagler's). It features market fresh, Mediterranean fare with Floridian influences that changes with the seasons. Open for dinner.

Gasparilla Grill & Games: This 24-hour snack bar on the first floor offers light items for all-day dining and snacking, plus a selection of video games.

Grand Floridian Café: Located on the first floor. Its peaches-and-cream color scheme and veranda-like feel make this the best place to get a quick, sit-down breakfast. Lunch and dinner are also available.

Narcoossee's: This octagonal restaurant and bar has a romantic shoreline location. Steaks, seafood, and chicken cooked in an open kitchen characterize the lunch and dinner menu. Beer is served in yard-tall glasses.

1900 Park Fare: A buffet restaurant on the Windsor Level (first floor), festively decorated with carousel horses, plenty of plants, and Big Bertha—the carnival organ. Breakfast and dinner with the characters are served daily.

Victoria & Albert's: On the second floor. The hotel's finest dining establishment, it is named after the former queen and prince consort of England. Elegant meals are served to no more than 90 guests; service is refined and diligent. Jackets are required for men and priority seating is a must.

WHERE TO DRINK: Guests will find the refined lounges here to be nice escapes.

Garden View: This pleasant spot on the first floor offers a view of the hotel's lush, landscaped garden and pool area. Afternoon tea is served.

Mizner's: Named after the eccentric, wildly prolific architect who defined much of the flavor of Palm Beach County, this bar is on the second floor.

Summerhouse: The only bar serving the pool and beach, this spot features a variety of snacks and beverages.

WHAT TO DO: The Grand Floridian offers all the recreational facilities of a typical beachside resort—and much more. Waterskiing and fishing excursions can be arranged (see the *Sports* chapter for details). Volleyball equipment is available.

Boating: Sailboats (including catamarans), canopy boats, and Water Sprites are rented at Captain's Shipyard Marina.

Children's Program: The Mouseketer Club is a supervised program for kids ages 4 to 12. It's open from 4:30 P.M. to midnight; the cost is $4 per hour for each child. There is a four-hour maximum. Reservations are required; phone 824-2985.

Health Club: The spa within the 9,000-square-foot Grand Floridian Spa & Health Club offers 17 treatment rooms for massage, herbal wraps, and aromatherapy. The health club has exercise equipment, plus men's and women's saunas, whirlpools, and steamrooms.

Playground: Adjacent to the Mouseketeer Clubhouse, the play area includes swings and a climbing apparatus.

Salon: The Ivy Trellis salon offers a full line of hair care services.

Shopping: On the first floor (Windsor Level) of the main building is Summer Lace, a women's apparel shop, and Sandy Cove, where guests may purchase gifts and sundries. One floor up at the Alcazar Level is the M. Mouse Mercantile character shop, a Bally leather-goods store, and Commander Porter's, a men's shop.

Swimming: In addition to the 275,000-gallon swimming pool just outside the main building, the hotel has a whirlpool and its own white-sand beach along Seven Seas Lagoon.

Tennis: There are two clay courts for play. Reservations are required; phone 824-3578. Private lessons are available.

Video Arcade: Gasparilla Grill & Games, located on the first floor of the main building, features video games.

TRANSPORTATION: The Grand Floridian is connected to the TTC and the Magic Kingdom by monorail. The platform is located outside the hotel under an awning on the second floor. From the TTC, Epcot is accessible by another monorail, and Typhoon Lagoon

and Downtown Disney can be reached by bus. Direct buses go to the Disney-MGM Studios, Animal Kingdom, and Blizzard Beach. Launches leave from Tocoi Landing for the Magic Kingdom and the Polynesian.

Wilderness Lodge

This resort recalls both the spirit of the early American West and the feeling of the National Park Service lodges built during the early 1900s. These grand structures architecturally unified the elements of the unspoiled wilderness parks, kept harmony with nature, and incorporated the culture of Native Americans. The Wilderness Lodge artfully recaptures this rustic charm.

The resort is situated between the Contemporary resort and Fort Wilderness on Bay Lake. Guests arrive along a winding road shaded by pines. The lobby is in an impressive

eight-story, log-structured building. Massive bundled log columns support a series of trusses. Four large chandeliers featuring silhouettes of Indians and buffalo are topped with glowing tepees. Two authentic Pacific Northwest totem poles soar 55 feet on each side of the lobby. Both the grand stone fireplace and the intricately detailed, multicolored floor recall Northwest Indian designs. Four levels of corridors surround the lobby, providing access to guestrooms, sitting nooks, and terraces. There are 38 rooms equipped for guests with disabilities, and nonsmoking rooms are available. The telephone number for the Wilderness Lodge is 824-3200.

ROOMS: The 728 guestrooms are located in a U-shaped building. Most rooms have two queen-size beds, a table and chairs, and a balcony. Some rooms have a queen-size bed and a bunk bed. The bathrooms have separate vanity areas with double sinks. The wallpaper has a Native American–motif border, and the colorful bedspreads and plaid curtains add to the decor. Images of wildlife complete the theme.

WHERE TO EAT: The American West theme is carried out with flair in the hotel's eateries. Room service is served from 7 A.M. to 11 A.M.; dinner selections are available through room service from 4 P.M. to midnight.

Artist Point: Decorated with artwork representing the painters who first chronicled the Northwest landscape, this fine dining spot features wild salmon, game, steaks, seafood, and wines from the Pacific Northwest. Pocahontas hosts breakfast here daily.

Lobby Coffee Bar: Continental breakfast is served here, and evenings bring coffee and hot chocolate to this fireside spot.

Roaring Fork: Light snacks are available here, in the hotel's arcade, 24 hours a day.

Whispering Canyon Café: A casual, family-style restaurant with all-day dining.

WHERE TO DRINK: Two spots are available for a relaxing break.

Territory: Located between the Whispering Canyon Café and Artist Point, this spot honors the survey parties who led the move westward. In addition to a light lunch and appetizers, specialty drinks, microbrewed beer, and espresso are served.

Trout Pass: The poolside bar features a variety of specialty drinks and snacks.

WHAT TO DO: A resort unto itself, it offers a plethora of activities. Teton Boat & Bike Rental is located in the Colonel's Cabin by the lake. Volleyball equipment is available. Waterskiing and fishing excursions on Bay Lake may also be arranged (see *Sports* for details). Or consider taking one of the two daily guided tours of the lodge.

Biking: Bicycles can be rented for a ride around the resort. A three-quarter-mile path leads to Fort Wilderness and River Country.

Boating: A variety of watercraft, including Water Sprites, canopy boats, sailboats, and pontoon boats can be rented for a trip around Bay Lake.

Children's Program: The Cubs Den is a supervised dining and entertainment club for kids ages 4 to 12. Supervised activities, including Disney movies and western-themed arts and crafts, occupy kids from 5 P.M. to midnight. Cost is $7 per hour per child, including dinner. Call 939-3463 for reservations, which are required.

Playground: The playground is near the Teton Boat & Bike Rental.

Shopping: Wilderness Lodge Mercantile stocks necessities and sundries as well as a line of clothing with the Wilderness Lodge logo. A selection of Disney character merchandise is also featured.

Swimming: The pool begins as a hot spring in the hotel lobby. From there, water flows out of the building into Silver Creek, a quiet setting in the upper courtyard. The creek develops first into a roaring waterfall and then into a swimming area that looks as if it were carved from the rockscape. A beach, a kiddie pool, two whirlpools, and a geyser complete the design. Fire Rock Geyser erupts on the hour from early morning until 10 P.M.; those nearby should be prepared for quite a splash.

Video Arcade: The Roaring Fork Arcade features about 30 of the latest games to keep kids occupied.

TRANSPORTATION: Boats go to the Magic Kingdom, Contemporary, and Fort Wilderness. Buses go to Epcot, the Disney-MGM Studios, Animal Kingdom, Blizzard Beach, and the TTC. From the TTC, transfer to buses for Typhoon Lagoon and Downtown Disney. It's possible to ride a bike to Fort Wilderness and River Country.

Fort Wilderness Resort & Campground

The very existence of this canal-crossed expanse—with more than 700 acres of cypress and pine laced with pleasant blacktop roadways—always surprises visitors who come to Walt Disney World expecting to find the theme parks and nothing more. If they've heard about Fort Wilderness at all, they often confuse it with the Magic Kingdom's Frontierland section.

But the Fort Wilderness atmosphere is not at all frenetic. In one corner, a group of kids may be battling it out at tetherball, and on the playing fields there are often a couple of energetic touch football games in progress. In the morning, the campground smells sweetly of dew-dampened pines, then of frying bacon. In the evening, the warmth and stillness of the afternoon give way to dinnertime bustle, and fish and steaks are tossed onto grills as next-door neighbors organize get-togethers. Later on, groups of kids gather alongside the trading posts or at the arcade at Pioneer Hall.

The recreational possibilities make Fort Wilderness one of the livelier places to be at Walt Disney World. There's a marina and a beach, a nature trail, and waterways where fishing, canoeing, and pedal boating are popular. The Meadow Recreation Complex, located behind the Meadow Trading Post, features two lighted tennis courts, a swimming pool, an arcade, and a snack bar.

You can enjoy the Fort Wilderness experience even if you don't have your own camping gear. Among the campsites there are 408 air-conditioned Wilderness Homes and Cabins available for rent, complete with daily maid service and enough other amenities that the woods are the only reminders of the fact that you're camping out. The cost is comparable to that of some of the more expensive rooms at the hotels. (But those don't have kitchens and so don't offer the money-saving option of cooking some of your vacation meals "at home.") The telephone number for the Fort Wilderness resort is 824-2900.

CAMPSITES: Fort Wilderness has 784 traditional campsites, ranging in length from 25 to 65 feet, spaced throughout 20 camping loops. All types of camping can be accommodated—RV, travel trailer, and tent. Preferred campsites feature cable-TV connections as well as electricity hookups (30/50–amp), water, and sanitary disposal. Partial-hookup campsites supply electricity and water hookups only. All campsites are bordered by lush wilderness and feature a paved driveway pad, picnic table, and charcoal grill. Most loops have at least one air-conditioned comfort station equipped with restrooms, private showers, an ice machine, telephones, and a laundry room.

A site allows for occupancy by up to ten people. Each site has room for parking one car (in addition to the camping vehicle). Additional cars can be parked in the main parking lot.

The various campground areas are designated by numbers. The 100, 200, 300, 400, and 500 loops are closest to the beach, the Settlement Trading Post, and Pioneer Hall. The 1500, 1600, 1700, 1800, 1900, and 2000 loops are farthest away from the beach and many other Fort Wilderness activities, but they are quieter and more private. Pets are welcome at certain campsites for a nightly charge of $3.

WILDERNESS HOMES: The 159 Wilderness Homes here provide all the advantages of villa accommodations—with woodsy surroundings to boot. There are two types of homes. One model sleeps four adults and two children; it has a bedroom with a double bed, a bunk bed, plus a separate vanity area and a spacious living room with a pull-down double bed and a ceiling fan. The other trailers sleep four, with a double bed in the bedroom and a pull-down double bed in the living room. Both types come equipped with pots and pans, dishes, and all basic kitchen equipment, plus a color TV set and a complete bathroom. The bathroom is not the sort of makeshift setup you might expect; in fact, it's comparable to a bathroom in a standard hotel room. There are Wilderness Homes equipped for travelers with disabilities, and nonsmoking trailers are available.

WILDERNESS CABINS: Walt Disney World's newest woodland dwellings offer a quaint rustic vacation escape. The interiors of the cozy six-person log-cabinlike buildings, with their vaulted ceilings and exposed beams, are decorated with richly-colored wilderness accents. In addition to all the comforts of the Wilderness Homes, each of the 249 cabins has a private deck, shaded by a lush pine canopy.

Note: No extra camping equipment is permitted on the site; all guests must be accommodated in a Wilderness Home or Cabin. (For complete price information, see the chart "Rates at Walt Disney World Properties" on pages 74–75.)

WHERE TO EAT: There are a couple of options here, but most people cook their own meals. Groceries and supplies are available at the Meadow Trading Post and the Settlement Trading Post (open from 8 A.M. to 10 P.M. in winter, to 11 P.M. in summer). Sandwiches, fruit, ice cream, and chips are available there for takeout. Also, Gooding's supermarket is located at the Crossroads of Lake Buena Vista shopping center across from the resorts on Hotel Plaza Blvd.

Trail's End Buffet: An informal, log-walled, beam-ceilinged cafeteria inside Pioneer Hall, where home-style fare is served for breakfast, lunch, and dinner. Pizza is an option from 9:30 P.M. to 11 P.M. nightly. Beer and wine are also available.

WHERE TO DRINK: Beer, wine, and cocktails are served at **Crockett's Tavern** in Pioneer Hall. It's also a short ride to Downtown Disney, where a plethora of imbibing opportunities are available.

FAMILY ENTERTAINMENT AFTER DARK: The Hoop-Dee-Doo Musical Revue is presented three times nightly at 5 P.M., 7:15 P.M., and 9:30 P.M.; reservations are required and are so hard to come by that they need to be made well in advance by calling WDW-DINE (939-3463). Cancellations do occur, however. WDW resort guests who can't get a reservation can go to the Pioneer Hall Ticket Window 45 minutes before showtime and place their names on the waiting list.

There's also a nightly campfire program held at the center of the campground, near the Meadow Trading Post. A sing-along (featuring Chip 'n' Dale) and free screenings of Disney movies and cartoons are the main goings-on. At 9:45 P.M., catch the Electrical Water Pageant—a procession of waterborne floats. This can be viewed from the Fort Wilderness beach. (For details, see *Everything Else in the World* and *Good Meals, Great Times*.)

WHAT TO DO: More on-site activities are available at Fort Wilderness than at almost any other area in the World. There are two tennis courts in the campground, and the Osprey Ridge and Eagle Pines golf courses play from the nearby Bonnet Creek Golf Club.

There are two heated swimming pools and an ample beach for swimming in Bay Lake. You can rent tandems and other bicycles at the Bike Barn for afternoon excursions or as transportation around the campground. Visits to the Petting Farm and the horse barn near Fort Wilderness are amusing. Boating is popular; rentals are available at the marina. Canoes and pedal boats can be hired at the Bike Barn. Pony rides are available from 9 A.M. to 5 P.M. Basketball, checkers, electric cart rentals, fishing (on your own in the canals or on organized morning or afternoon angling

excursions), horseback riding (on guided trail outings), horseshoes, tetherball, volleyball, and waterskiing are also available. Or you can just stroll along the three-quarter-mile trail leading to the Wilderness Lodge. All of these activities are described in detail in the *Everything Else in the World* and *Sports* chapters. Video game fans have two hangouts: Davy Crockett's Arcade in Pioneer Hall and Daniel Boone's Arcade at the Meadow Trading Post. The Tri-Circle-D Ranch Museum invites guests to learn about the history of the horse, Disney-style. The walls are lined with cels of animated horses from classic Disney films, as well as some other horsey memorabilia.

River Country, an attraction in its own right with a separate admission charge, is also located at Fort Wilderness. The features of this watery playground are discussed in detail in *Everything Else in the World*.

TRANSPORTATION: Buses circulating at 20-minute intervals provide transportation within the campground, while buses and watercraft connect Fort Wilderness to the rest of the World. The Magic Kingdom, the Contemporary, and the Wilderness Lodge are most efficiently reached via watercraft that depart regularly from the marina. Buses make the trip from the Settlement Depot to Blizzard Beach. To get to other WDW points, take a bus from the Fort Wilderness visitor parking lot to the TTC. Here, change to a monorail for Epcot or take another bus for the Disney-MGM Studios, Animal Kingdom, Typhoon Lagoon, and Downtown Disney.

Electric golf carts can be rented at the Bike Barn as an alternative means of getting around within the campground. Call 824-2742 for reservations.

Epcot Area

Caribbean Beach

This colorful hotel is set on 200 acres southeast of Epcot and near the Disney-MGM Studios. It is composed of five brightly colored "villages" surrounding a 45-acre lake called Barefoot Bay. Each village is identified with a different Caribbean island—Martinique, Barbados, Trinidad, Aruba, and Jamaica—and features pastel walls, white railings, and vividly colored metal roofs. There are 2,112 rooms in all, making Caribbean Beach one of the largest hotels in the United States.

The villages consist of a cluster of two-story buildings, a swimming pool, a guest laundry, and a lakefront stretch of white-sand beach. Guests check in at the Custom House, a reception building that immediately projects the feeling of a tropical resort. Decor, furnishings, and staff costumes all reflect the Caribbean theme. Old Port Royale, a complex located near the center of the property, evokes images of an island market. Stone walls, pirates' cannons, and tropical birds and flowers add to the atmosphere. The area houses the resort's food court, restaurant and lounge, two shops, and an arcade. The port opens onto a lakeside recreation area that includes a pool with waterfalls and a slide; the main beach; the Barefoot Bay Boat Yard and Bike Works, where boats and bicycles may be rented; a 1.4-mile promenade around the lake that's perfect for biking, walking, or jogging; and Parrot Cay Island, an area in the middle of Barefoot Bay with a playground and wildlife trail. The telephone number for the Caribbean Beach resort is 934-3400.

ROOMS: Rooms are located in two-story buildings in each island village. A typical 340-square-foot room has two double beds and can sleep up to four. The rooms here are a bit larger than the standard rooms at Disney's other moderately priced resorts, and the bathrooms are amply sized. The rooms are decorated in tones softer than the colors found on the exterior, with furniture made of white oak. Each room has a minibar and coffeemaker. Rooms equipped for travelers with disabilities and nonsmoking rooms are available.

One note for the budget-conscious: All the rooms here are identical in terms of size and comfort, and the only difference between the most and least expensive is the view.

WHERE TO EAT: A full-service eatery called Captain's Tavern and a food court with six counter-service restaurants are located in Old Port Royale. Limited room service (pizza, chicken in a basket, and sandwiches) is available from 4 P.M. to midnight.

Bridgetown Broiler: Spit-roasted chicken and home-style meals are menu highlights.

Captain's Tavern: The menu at this 200-seat restaurant at Old Port Royale includes prime rib, baked chicken, and a catch of the day. Tropical drinks, wine, beer, and traditional cocktails are also served.

Cinnamon Bay Bakery: Freshly baked rolls, croissants, and pastries are available in addition to ice cream and other treats.

Kingston Pasta Shop: A variety of pasta dishes is served.

Montego's Deli: Soups, salads, and cold sandwiches are offered.

Port Royale Hamburger Shop: Hot sandwiches and burgers are on the menu.

Royale Pizza Shop: Very good pizza is available by the slice or the pie, along with a variety of hot and cold pasta dishes.

Meetings & Conventions

With the addition of Coronado Springs, convention-goers have yet another resort to choose from within the ranks of WDW hotels. Coronado Springs, the first moderately priced Disney resort to offer convention facilities, boasts the largest ballroom in the Southeast.

Convention centers at Walt Disney World range in size from 20,000 to over 200,000 square feet. The Dolphin's center, featuring an exhibit hall and an executive boardroom, is the largest; the Swan provides additional space. The Contemporary has three ballrooms and a spacious pre-function area with lots of natural light. The convention center at the Yacht Club and Beach Club is reminiscent of a grand turn-of-the-century New England town meeting hall. The Grand Floridian has a lavish center with silk brocade walls. The BoardWalk offers a smaller conference area with a lakeside gazebo for outdoor events.

Among the unique services available to Disney conventioneers is the use of Disney characters and performers for events. Special events can even be held in the parks. Resort business centers have clerical staffs and computers, in addition to faxing and photocopying equipment. (These services are available to all resort guests.)

Those interested in scheduling a convention should call 828-3200 for reservations or information. Organizers are advised to book their events six months in advance, especially for large groups. Keep in mind that the busiest times are January, May, September, and October.

WHERE TO DRINK: The tropical Caribbean theme is carried out in the specialty drinks found at **Banana Cabana**. Snacks are also available at this poolside spot.

WHAT TO DO: There are many recreational opportunities. The 1.4-mile promenade around the lake is perfect for walking, biking, or a morning jog. Nature walks are conducted at Parrot Cay Island.

Biking: Bikes can be rented at the Barefoot Bay Boat Yard and Bike Works.

Boating: Sailboats, Water Sprites, canopy boats, canoes, and pedal boats are available for rent at the Barefoot Bay Boat Yard and Bike Works for use on the resort's scenic 45-acre lake.

Playgrounds: A lovely playground is on Parrot Cay Island, across the footbridge from the Barefoot Bay Boat Yard and Bike Works. Playgrounds are also located on the Barbados, Jamaica, and Trinidad beaches.

Shopping: At Old Port Royale, there's the Calypso Straw Market, which carries items with the Caribbean Beach resort logo and a variety of island-themed goods. Calypso Trading Post stocks a large selection of character merchandise and sundries.

Swimming: Each village has its own pool, and the main pool features waterfalls and a slide in a Caribbean-themed setting.

Video Arcade: Goombay Games at Old Port Royale offers a selection of games.

TRANSPORTATION: Direct buses go to the Magic Kingdom, Epcot, the Disney-MGM Studios, Animal Kingdom, and Blizzard Beach. Other bus routes lead to Downtown Disney and Typhoon Lagoon.

Yacht Club & Beach Club

The New England seaside exists at Walt Disney World in the form of the Yacht Club and its sister next door, the Beach Club. Situated just west of Epcot, the hotels, designed by noted architect Robert A. M. Stern, are set around a 25-acre lake. The adjacent properties share most facilities—including a convention center offering access to business services—and transportation options.

The Yacht Club's design evokes images of the New England seashore hotels of the 1880s. Guests enter the five-story oyster-gray clapboard building along a wooden-planked bridge. Hardwood floors, millwork, and brass enhance the nautical theme. A lighthouse on the pier serves as a beacon to welcome guests back to the hotel from WDW attractions. To reach the Yacht Club by telephone, call 934-7000.

Distance from the ocean is irrelevant at the sand- and surf-focused Beach Club resort, approached along an entrance drive flanked by oak trees. A patterned walkway leads past a croquet court to beachside cabanas on the white-sand shore. Guests are met by hosts and hostesses dressed in colorful beach resort costumes of the 1870s. The telephone number for the Beach Club resort is 934-8000.

ROOMS: The 630 rooms at the Yacht Club are spacious and decorated in a nautical motif. Concierge rooms are available. In each room the furniture is white, and the headboard design on the one king-size bed or two queen-size beds incorporates small ship's wheels. Some rooms also have daybeds. Most of the suites have a king-size bed as well as two sleeper sofas. The carpeting is blue; drapes and bedspreads are blue and dusty

rose. In the large bathrooms there is a separate vanity with double sinks and silver mirrors trimmed with brass. Each room has a ceiling fan, minibar, table (complete with checkerboard top), and two chairs. Chess and checkers sets are provided. There are rooms equipped for guests with disabilities, and nonsmoking rooms are available.

The Beach Club's 583 rooms are spacious and, naturally, reflect a beach motif. The wallpaper is seafoam green, and the curtains and bedspreads are white and green with a border of mauve beach umbrellas. The room layouts are similar to those at the Yacht Club; each unit features a ceiling fan, two queen-size beds (some rooms have a king-size bed and a daybed), double sinks, and a wall-mounted makeup mirror. There are rooms equipped for guests with disabilities, and nonsmoking rooms are available.

WHERE TO EAT: The themes of yachting and the sea play an important role in the restaurants that are found at their respective resorts. A wide variety of menu items are available from room service 24 hours a day.

Beaches & Cream Soda Shop: A classic American soda fountain where shakes, malts, and oversize sundaes are the prime lures. The other specialty is the Fenway Park Burger, served as a single, double, triple, or home run. (It is located between the two resorts.)

Cape May Café: An indoor clambake is held here at the Beach Club each night. The varied buffet features several types of clams and mussels, plus pasta and chicken. Lobster is available for an extra charge. A character breakfast is presented daily.

Hurricane Hanna's Grill: Burgers, hot dogs, sausages, and other snacks are served at this spot on the shores of Stormalong Bay. A full bar is also located here, and poolside beverage service is available.

Yacht Club Galley: The buffet breakfast is bountiful. Breakfast, lunch, and dinner are available from an à la carte menu.

Yachtsman Steakhouse: Select cuts of aged beef are the specialty of the house. Fresh seafood and poultry are also offered.

WHERE TO DRINK: The lounges in both resorts offer a variety of specialty drinks in relaxing seaside settings.

Ale and Compass: This Yacht Club lobby lounge features specialty coffees and drinks, a nice respite after a long day in the parks.

Crew's Cup: The place to try a wide assortment of beers shipped in from the world's seaports before dining at Yachtsman Steakhouse next door.

Martha's Vineyard: This lounge at the Beach Club offers selections from American and international vineyards, served in sample sizes and by the glass or bottle.

Rip Tide: The Beach Club lobby lounge features a variety of California wines, wine coolers, and frosty concoctions.

WHAT TO DO: There is enough to do here to fill an entire vacation. A sand volleyball court and a croquet court may be found on the Beach Club side of the property. Equipment for both pursuits is available at no cost at the Ship Shape health club. The Fantasia Gardens Miniature Golf complex is close at hand, and guided fishing excursions can be arranged (see *Sports* for details). And last, but not least, the BoardWalk entertainment district is just a short trip around the lake.

Boating: Pedal boats, Hydro Bikes, canopy boats, and Water Sprites are available for rent at the Bayside Marina.

Children's Program: The Sandcastle Club, for children 4 to 12, is available from 4:30 P.M. to midnight. Cost is $4 per hour for each child. Reservations are required; call 939-3463. A variety of toys, videos, games, and Apple computers are on hand to keep children entertained. Milk and snacks are also served.

Health Club: The Ship Shape health club is located in the area between the two resorts, and features Nautilus and cardiovascular machines, sauna, whirlpool, steamroom, personal trainers, and massage (by appointment). The health club is open only to Yacht Club and Beach Club guests, who must be over 13 to use the facilities.

Playground: A small play area with a slide and climbing apparatus is located by the pool.

Salon: The Periwig salon for men and women is located in the central area.

Shopping: At the Yacht Club, Fittings & Fairings Clothes and Notions is an all-purpose shop offering nautical fashions, character merchandise, and sundries. At the Beach Club, Atlantic Wear and Wardrobe Emporium features a similar selection of goods (albeit with a beach theme).

Swimming: Between the marina and the beach is the centerpiece of the dual resort—Stormalong Bay, a 750,000-gallon pool that's really a mini water park. There is a lagoon expressly for relaxed bathing, and another "active" lagoon with currents, jets, and sand-bottomed areas. Several whirlpools are scattered throughout the area. Adjacent to the main pool is a shipwreck, where guests can enjoy a variety of unique water slides. There is also a quiet pool and a whirlpool at the far end of each hotel.

Tennis: There are two lighted tennis courts on the Beach Club side of the property. Rental equipment is available at the Ship Shape health club.

Video Arcade: Lafferty Place Arcade, located in the central area, has about 60 video games and pinball machines.

TRANSPORTATION: Guests ride boats or walk to the nearby Epcot entrance (beside the France pavilion). Watercraft go to the Disney-MGM Studios. Buses go to the Magic Kingdom, Animal Kingdom, Downtown Disney, Typhoon Lagoon, and Blizzard Beach.

Swan & Dolphin

These massive sister resorts, situated on the shores of Crescent Lake, can easily be distinguished by the 46-foot swan and 56-foot dolphin statues that top them. The waterfalls, lush rows of palm trees, and beachfront location all reflect the tropical Florida landscape that was their inspiration. Both hotels were designed by noted architect Michael Graves as prime examples of "entertainment architecture." The rolling turquoise waves on the colored facade of the Swan's 12-story main building and two 7-story wings are clearly evidence of this design, as is the Dolphin's exterior mural, which features a playful banana-leaf pattern. The soaring 27-story triangular tower at the center of the Dolphin, once honored by *Progressive Architecture* magazine, is flanked by four 9-story guestroom wings.

The resorts share extensive convention facilities, many recreational options, and a host of restaurants. The Swan and Dolphin are operated by Westin and ITT Sheraton, respectively, but are treated as Walt Disney World resorts; guests here enjoy most WDW resort benefits.

The phone number for the Swan is 934-3000; for the Dolphin it's 934-4000. Reservations can be made by calling 800-227-1000 or by visiting the Swan and Dolphin Web site at *http://www.swandolphin.com*.

ROOMS: The corridors outside the Swan guestrooms feature patterned carpets and murals on the walls that extend the wave theme from the exterior design. Inside, the rooms are decorated in shades of coral and turquoise, and they feature such whimsical touches as lamps in the shape of birds and pineapples painted on the dressers. Each has one king-size or two queen-size beds; safes and minibars are among the amenities. There are 45 concierge rooms on the 11th and 12th floors, and 64 suites.

The 1,509 rooms at the Dolphin, including 136 suites, are decorated in a lighthearted fashion, with lamps in the shape of palm trees and colorful bedspreads and curtains. All feature two double beds or a king-size bed, as well as minibars, vanity dressing areas, irons and ironing boards, and coffee-makers. Concierge rooms are located in the main building. There are rooms equipped for guests with disabilities, and nonsmoking rooms are available at both resorts.

WHERE TO EAT: In addition to many restaurant choices, 24-hour room service provides an extensive all-day dining menu.

Cabana Bar & Grill: This full-service pool-side spot near the Dolphin serves burgers, sandwiches, yogurt, and fruit. The full bar serves specialty drinks.

Coral Café: Buffets, as well as à la carte selections, are served during breakfast, lunch, and dinner in a casual setting at the Dolphin.

Dolphin Fountain: Homemade ice cream is the specialty here. Huge sundaes, shakes, malts, and burgers are also offered.

Garden Grove Café: This Swan eatery features a greenhouse atmosphere, and serves breakfast and lunch daily. At dinner, the restaurant transforms into Gulliver's Grill. The theme is played out with exaggerated serving utensils, and steak and seafood entrées with imaginative names like Blushklooshen (red snapper). A buffet breakfast with the characters is held on Saturday, while a character dinner takes place three nights a week.

Harry's Safari Bar & Grille: This festive Dolphin eatery features grilled beef, poultry, and seafood; a character brunch takes place on Sundays.

Juan & Only's: Authentic Mexican food is served at this Dolphin hot spot. The atmosphere is festive, filled with warm hues and rich fabrics of old Mexico.

Palio: A pleasant Italian bistro, located at the Swan, featuring veal specialties, home-made pasta, and brick-oven pizza. There are tasty daily specials and live entertainment.

Splash Grill: A poolside café near the Swan serving breakfast, lunch, dinner, and snacks. A full-service bar is also located here.

Tubbi's: A cafeteria with a little flair. The checkerboard design makes this a pleasant place for a quick meal at the Dolphin resort. The 24-hour convenience store here sells snacks and sundries.

WHERE TO DRINK: Between the two resorts, it's easy to find an interesting spot for a drink.

Copa Banana: The tabletops are shaped like slices of fruit, and the tropical atmosphere makes this a lively place for a drink. Deejay music, a dance floor, karaoke, and eight large-screen televisions provide the entertainment at this Dolphin fun spot.

Harry's Safari Bar: Pull up a stool and enjoy the jungle-like atmosphere and frosty drinks. Located at the Dolphin.

Lobby Court: This spot at the Swan offers a respite from the hubbub. Enjoy gourmet coffees with fresh pastries in the morning and wine and specialty drinks at night in a European-style bistro setting.

Kimono's: The Asian decor helps make this Swan lounge an inviting place for sake, sushi, and other Japanese specialties.

Special Room Requests

Central Reservations accepts requests for rooms with particular views or in certain locations. Agents will do their best to accommodate such requests, but cannot guarantee they will be able to fulfill every wish. Call W-DISNEY (934-7639).

Only's Bar & Jail: Patrons at the companion lounge to the Dolphin's Juan & Only's restaurant can enjoy the warm atmosphere here while sampling margaritas, sangria, rare tequilas, and beers from every region of Mexico.

WHAT TO DO: The Swan and Dolphin share a multitude of recreation options. Volleyball nets and a few hammocks are set up on the beach. The Fantasia Gardens Miniature Golf complex and BoardWalk entertainment district are nearby.

Boating: Pedal boats and Hydro Bikes are available for rent on the white-sand beach between the Swan and Dolphin.

Children's Program: Camp Dolphin, open to children 3 to 12, offers supervised activities from 4 P.M. to midnight. The cost is $5 per hour for the first child and $3 per hour for each extra child. Dinner, ordered through room service, is extra.

Health Clubs: A branch of Body By Jake (run by famous fitness guru Jake Steinfeld) is near the pool area at the Dolphin. State-of-the-art equipment is available, as are personal trainers. There are aerobics classes (including water aerobics), a sauna, steam room, large whirlpool, and massage therapists. There's also a smaller health club with basic exercise equipment near Splash Grill.

Playground: An extensive play area with a slide, swings, wooden chain bridge, sandbox, and three jungle gyms, is located next to the grotto pool.

Salon: The Nikki Bryan shop at the Dolphin provides a full line of services, including haircuts, manicures, and pedicures.

Shopping: Disney Cabanas, located in the lobby of the Swan, features men's and women's fashions, character merchandise, and sundries. Four specialty shops are located at the Dolphin. A large selection of Cartier and other brand-name watches can be found at Brittany Jewels. Indulgences allows chocolate lovers the chance to sample some tasty concoctions. Statements of Fashion offers resortwear for men and women. Daisy's Garden is the place to find character goods at the Dolphin.

Swimming: A large rectangular pool near the Dolphin is perfect for swimming laps; a themed grotto pool with a slide lies between the Swan and Dolphin; a small rectangular pool is situated near the Swan; and several whirlpools are scattered around the area.

Tennis: Four hard-surface tennis courts are located behind the pool area closest to the Dolphin. They are lighted for night play and are open 24 hours a day.

Video Arcades: A room full of video games is located near Tubbi's. Another can be found adjacent to the Swan pool.

TRANSPORTATION: Guests ride boats or walk to Epcot's entrance near the France pavilion. Boats make the trip to the Disney-MGM Studios. Buses go to the Magic Kingdom, Animal Kingdom, Downtown Disney, Typhoon Lagoon, and Blizzard Beach.

BoardWalk

The enchantment of a bygone era is recaptured in the BoardWalk. The resort combines a waterside entertainment complex with deluxe hotel accommodations and vacation villas. Dining, recreation, shopping, and entertainment venues line the boardwalk, and twinkling lights trim the buildings. The boardwalk ambience continues throughout, with intricately detailed architecture featuring sherbet-colored facades, deep colonnades, flagged turrets, and striped awnings, all reminiscent of the turn of the century. The BoardWalk resort is adjacent to Epcot's International Gateway and connected via walkway. The telephone number for Board-Walk is 939-5100.

ROOMS: Accommodations evoke the charm of early eastern seaboard inns. All have private balconies or patios. The BoardWalk Inn has 378 deluxe hotel rooms decorated with cherry wood furniture, boardwalk postcard–print curtains, and light green accents. Guestrooms at the Inn sleep up to five, and feature two queen-size beds (or one king-size bed) and a child's daybed. Romantic two-story garden suites each have a private

garden enclosed by a white picket fence. They sleep four and feature a living room on the first floor and a king-size bed in the bedroom loft. The Inn also has several one-story concierge suites.

The 517 vacation villas are collectively called Disney's BoardWalk Villas Resort. These are Disney Vacation Club villas, available when not occupied by members. Each

studio features a queen-size bed and double sleeper sofa, plus a wet bar with microwave, coffeemaker, and small refrigerator. Larger (one-, two-, and three-bedroom) villas sleep 4 to 12 people, and feature dining rooms, fully equipped kitchens, laundry facilities, master baths with whirlpool tubs, and VCRs. They also include king-size beds in the master bedroom, living rooms with queen sleeper sofas, and two queen-size beds (or one plus a double sleeper sofa) in any additional bedrooms.

WHERE TO EAT: By virtue of its entertainment district status (see page 187 of the *Everything Else in the World* chapter), the resort has a wealth of dining and snacking options. A variety of vendors along the boardwalk tempt with hot dogs, crêpes on a stick, gourmet coffee, and more. For those looking to eat in, 24-hour room service is available.

Big River Grille & Brewing Works: This working brewpub features a full menu, complemented with fresh specialty ales. View the on-site brewmaster through floor-to-ceiling glass walls.

BoardWalk Bakery: A popular stop that offers baked goods, ice cream, espresso, and cappuccino. Huge display windows allow passersby to watch bakers at work. Bun rises are held here every morning.

ESPN Club: A serious sports bar for serious sports fans, it provides interactive sports video entertainment and all-day dining.

Flying Fish Café: This restaurant has a show kitchen and its menu emphasizes seafood, steak, and fresh seasonal items.

Seashore Sweets': An old-fashioned sweetshop serves candies, saltwater taffy, ice cream, frozen yogurt, and specialty coffees.

Spoodles: Mediterranean cuisine is the focus of this establishment geared toward families; the appetizers are meant for sharing.

WHERE TO DRINK: Guests of this resort have a multitude of options right in their backyard, with the BoardWalk's clubs and lounges on hand. The variety ensures that even the undecided needn't wander far.

Atlantic Dance: Dance or sip champagne while listening to the band play retro-swing—a style of music based on 1940s swing. Enjoy hors d'oeuvres or dessert on the balcony. The cover charge varies, depending on the performers.

Belle Vue Room: Listen to old-time tunes on antique radios and play board games in this cocktail lounge near the lobby. Appetizers are served.

Jellyrolls: Dueling pianos provide live entertainment in a casual warehouse atmosphere. Popcorn is served. There is a $3 cover charge on weekends (none on weekdays).

Leaping Horse Libations: The carousel-themed pool bar at Luna Park serves a variety of cocktails, as well as tuna sandwiches, salads, hot dogs, fruit, and ice cream.

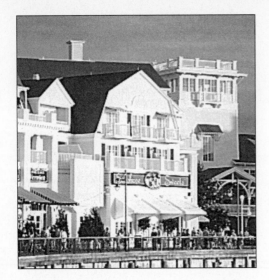

WHAT TO DO: The three-quarter-mile pathway encircling Crescent Lake (en route to Epcot) provides a ready venue for walkers and joggers. BoardWalk guests may rent boats from a neighboring resort's marina. The Fantasia Gardens Miniature Golf complex is nearby. At the resort itself, Ferris W. Eahlers Community Hall rents out equipment for just about any recreational pursuit imaginable, including croquet, shuffleboard, table tennis, Frisbee, badminton, in-line skating—even books and videos.

Biking: Community Hall offers a variety of bicycles for rental. In addition, surreys (canopied quadracycles for four) can be rented along the boardwalk.

Children's Program: The Harbour Club provides supervised activities for children age 4 to 12 from 4 P.M. to midnight. Cost is $4 per child per hour; dinner is available for an additional charge. Call 939-3463 for necessary reservations.

Health Club: Muscles & Bustles health club offers steam rooms, Nautilus machines, and circuit-training equipment, as well as massages (by appointment).

Midway Games: This area on the Board-Walk's Wildwood Landing features games of luck and skill similar to those found along traditional boardwalks.

Playground: Luna Park Crazy House and an elephant-studded play area offer kids water pranks and other fun activities.

Rolling Chair Ride: A trip along the boardwalk in a special rolling cart is available for a fee.

Shopping: Dundy's Sundries in the lobby is the source for film and basic necessities. Character Carnival on the boardwalk features children's apparel as well as a large selection of Disney character merchandise. Screen Door General Store stocks groceries, dry goods, snacks, and beverages. Thimbles & Threads, located on the boardwalk, carries resortwear, swimwear, and accessories for

men and women. Wyland Galleries features marine and environmental art and collectibles (stop in for a peek even if you don't plan to make a purchase).

Swimming: The BoardWalk's amusement park–themed swimming area, Luna Park, features a large pool with a 200-foot water slide, "Keister Coaster," patterned after a wooden roller coaster. A family of elephants is found posed throughout the area; their trunks act as a shower for adults on the pool deck or children in the wading pool. The resort's two quiet pools are heated; one is located within the Inn's courtyard, the other, adjacent to Community Hall in the Villas area. Tubes may be rented. There are three whirlpools.

Tennis: Two lighted soft-surface tennis courts are available for play.

Video Arcades: Side Show Games Arcade has poolside video games, and a sports-themed arcade called The Yard Arcade entertains at the ESPN Club.

TRANSPORTATION: Guests get to Epcot via boats or walkways, and to the Disney-MGM Studios by boats. Buses go to the Magic Kingdom, Animal Kingdom, Typhoon Lagoon, Blizzard Beach, and Downtown Disney.

A Room with a View

There's a lot to be said for throwing back the curtains and taking in a breathtaking view, provided you have the time to really appreciate it and that your view is on a par with your price range. The following is a breakdown of all the different "views" you have to select from at the various Walt Disney World resorts. Refer to it before booking accommodations—it will help you determine the best view for your budget. Although the categories vary, depending on the resort type, the "standard view" is always the lowest rate available. Call W-DISNEY (934-7639) for current rate information.

- **Value Resorts:**
  Standard View = Parking lot, pool, garden, and everything else

- **Moderate Resorts:**
  Standard View = Parking lot or landscaping
  Water View = Pool, marina, lake, river

- **Deluxe Resorts:**
  Standard View = Parking lot
  Garden View = Landscaping
  Water View = Pool, lake, or other water
  Lagoon = Seven Seas Lagoon

Downtown Disney Area

Port Orleans

This 1,008-room resort invites comparisons to the historic French Quarter of New Orleans. Starting at the entrance gate, with its wrought-iron portal and overgrown landscape, the appeal of the Delta City surrounds arriving guests. The entry drive leads to the heart of the city, which is Port Orleans Square. The central building, The Mint, was based on an original turn-of-the-century mint where farmers would go to trade their harvest for "dixes." A dix was a ten-dollar bill, and when the farmers said they were going to get their dixes, they probably didn't know they had coined a phrase. The Mint houses the hotel's check-in facilities, the Guest Services desk, a shop, the food court, an arcade, and the restaurant. It has a vaulted ceiling, and the check-in desks are designed as old-fashioned bank-teller windows. The mural behind the check-in counter, featuring a Mardi Gras street scene, was painted by an artist in three parts; each piece was shipped here separately. The musical notes in the mural are the notes to "When the Saints Go Marching In." The telephone number for Port Orleans is 934-5000.

ROOMS: The guestrooms are located in seven three-story buildings (with elevators). Each room has two double beds; some king-size beds are available. The rooms are a bit smaller than the standard rooms at the more expensive Disney hotels, but they are comfortable for a family of four. The photographs on the walls were donated by Disney employees, and the captions explain their history.

The buildings are painted cream, pink, blue, purple, and yellow, and feature wrought-iron railings of varying designs. About half of the rooms have doors that connect to a neighboring room. Connecting rooms can be requested, but can't be guaranteed. The rates are based on the room's view. The least expensive rooms overlook parking areas, the midrange units overlook gardens, and the most expensive room options offer water views. Rooms equipped for guests with disabilities and non-smoking rooms are available.

WHERE TO EAT: Options here include one restaurant with table service and a food court with counter-service stands. Also, the Sassagoula Pizza Express delivers to guestrooms from 4 P.M. to midnight.

Bonfamille's Café: The name of this table-service eatery comes from the Disney movie *The Aristocats*. Steaks, seafood, and Creole cooking highlight the dinner menu. Breakfast is also served.

Sassagoula Floatworks & Food Factory: This food court has a 300-seat dining area. A variety of specialty foods are available, including gumbo, spit-roasted chicken with red beans and rice, fresh beignets, and other traditional Creole dishes. Burgers, pizza, ice cream, and baked goods are also served.

WHERE TO DRINK: The New Orleans theme is carried through in the hotel's watering holes.

Mardi Grogs: The poolside bar serves specialty drinks, popcorn, hot dogs, and ice cream during pool hours.

Scat Cat's Club: A traditional bar featuring nightly entertainment and a light menu of hors d'oeuvres.

WHAT TO DO: A special pool is the highlight of the recreational opportunities here.

Biking: Bicycles are available for rent at Port Orleans Landing.

Boating: Pedal boats, canoes, rowboats, canopy boats, and pontoon boats are available for rent at Port Orleans Landing.

Playground: A small play area with slides is located across from the food court.

Shopping: Jackson Square Gifts & Desires, located at Port Orleans Square, features Disney character merchandise, clothing bearing the Port Orleans logo, and sundries.

Swimming: Doubloon Lagoon is a pool built around a sea serpent that, as the legend goes, is still lingering underground. Its tail can be seen jutting up in spots along walkways, and the water slide is actually the serpent's tongue. The shower at the pool has an alligator's head, and there is a large clamshell where an alligator band serves as the centerpiece of a fountain. A whirlpool is located nearby. Port Orleans guests may also swim at Dixie Landings' Ol' Man Island.

Video Arcade: South Quarter Games is located at Port Orleans Square. It features state-of-the-art video and arcade games.

TRANSPORTATION: Buses go to the Magic Kingdom, TTC, Epcot, Animal Kingdom, the Disney-MGM Studios, Typhoon Lagoon, Blizzard Beach, Downtown Disney. The Sassagoula River Cruise makes the trip to Dixie Landings and Downtown Disney.

Dixie Landings

The city feel of Port Orleans gives way to the rural South upriver at Dixie Landings. The resort is divided into "parishes." Closest to the "city," guestrooms are found in Mansion homes; farther upriver are the Bayou rooms, with a more rustic feel. The guest registration area is located in a building designed to resemble a steamship. When guests check in, they are booking passage on the steamboat. The food court, restaurant, lounge, and Fulton's General Store are all located in the same building. The telephone number for Dixie Landings is 934-6000.

ROOMS: The 2,048 Mansion and Bayou guestrooms are of the same size, and each room features two double beds (some king-size beds are available); 963 of the Bayou rooms have trundle beds (designed to sleep one child) as well. There is an additional fee of $15 per night for a trundle bed. The Magnolia Bend Mansion rooms are situated in sprawling, elegant manor homes with stately columns and grand staircases. The Alligator Bayou rooms are in rustic, weathered-wood tin-roofed buildings that are tucked among trees and bushes native to the area. These rooms surround Ol' Man Island, a 3½-acre recreational area with a pool, playground, and fishing hole. Decorative touches in the rooms include wood and tin armoires and pedestal sinks with brass fittings. The beds have hickory bedposts. The rooms are a bit smaller than the standard rooms at the more

expensive Disney hotels, but they are comfortable for a family of four. Rooms equipped for guests with disabilities and nonsmoking rooms are available.

WHERE TO EAT: In addition to a full-service restaurant and themed food court, the hotel offers limited room service via Sassagoula Pizza Express, which delivers from 4 P.M. until midnight.

Boatwright's Dining Hall: This 200-seat table-service eatery, next to Colonel's Cotton Mill, serves Cajun specialties and traditional American specialties for dinner. The restaurant is modeled after a boatmaking warehouse. Breakfast is also served.

Colonel's Cotton Mill: The hotel's food court resembles an old-fashioned cotton mill with a 30-foot working waterwheel that powers a real cotton press inside.

The five counter-service stands here offer all sorts of choices. Basic selections are available for breakfast. Acadian Pizza 'n' Pasta has pasta dishes, fresh pizza with a variety of toppings, as well as calzones. Bleu Bayou Burgers and Chicken offers fried and grilled chicken and an assortment of burgers. Cajun Broiler serves spit-roasted chicken and barbecued ribs. Riverside Market and Deli is a convenience store that stocks snack foods, soda, salads, sandwiches, beer, and wine. Southern Trace Bakery specializes in pastries, freshly baked pies, and sticky buns. Soft drinks can be refilled at no extra charge on a meal-by-meal basis.

WHERE TO DRINK: Two lounges possess a certain degree of charm.

Cotton Co-Op: Situated in a room designed as a cotton exchange, this lounge features specialty drinks, some light hors d'oeuvres, and live entertainment.

Muddy Rivers: The poolside bar serves specialty and traditional drinks plus hot dogs, popcorn, and ice cream during pool hours.

WHAT TO DO: Many of the resort activities are found at Ol' Man Island, a 3½-acre recreation center featuring a themed pool, whirlpool, children's wading pool, playground, and fishing hole stocked with a variety of fish for catch and release.

Biking: Bicycles of all types can be rented at the Dixie Levee.

Boating: Pedal boats, canoes, rowboats, canopy boats, and pontoon boats are available for rent at the Dixie Levee.

Fishing: Two-hour guided fishing excursions are available, and guests may fish on their own at the Ol' Fishin' Hole.

Playground: A fun play area is located on Ol' Man Island next to the pool.

Shopping: Fulton's General Store in the Dixie Landings building stocks Disney character merchandise, clothing with the Dixie Landings logo, and sundries.

Swimming: In addition to the themed pool and children's wading pool at Ol' Man Island, there are five pools set among the parishes of the resort. Dixie Landings guests may also swim at Port Orleans' Doubloon Lagoon next door.

Video Arcade: The Medicine Show Arcade, located in the Dixie Landings building, features a small selection of games.

TRANSPORTATION: Buses go to the Magic Kingdom, Epcot, the Disney-MGM Studios, Animal Kingdom, Typhoon Lagoon, Blizzard Beach, and Downtown Disney. Port Orleans and Downtown Disney can also be reached aboard the Sassagoula River Cruise.

The Villas at the Disney Institute

The area near the Downtown Disney Marketplace and the Lake Buena Vista golf course is dotted with villa-type accommodations (formerly known as Disney's Village Resort), many fitted out with fully equipped kitchens and other extras and amenities. Some may cost more than individual guestrooms at the conventional Disney hotels, but they accommodate more people as well. For families of more than five (who might otherwise need an extra hotel room), this is the most economical way to stay on-property. Smaller families can often break even by cooking some of their own meals (especially breakfast) in their villa. Accommodations for guests with disabilities are available in the Fairway Villas. Nonsmoking accommodations are available in the Bungalows and selected villas.

The resort serves as headquarters for the Disney Institute (see the *Everything Else in the World* chapter for details). Guests participating in the Disney Institute's enrichment programs are housed in the Bungalows and

Town Houses. Recreational facilities are available to all guests when not in use for programming (additional charges apply for use of the Sports & Fitness Center and The Spa).

The villas are exceptionally spacious, quiet, and secluded—albeit decorated on the dull side, at least as Disney accommodations go. The resort's pace is relaxed and the atmosphere is low-key (except at the Town Houses near Pleasure Island, which can be lively until late in the evening). The Villas are conveniently located with respect to the Disney-MGM Studios, Epcot, Animal Kingdom, Downtown Disney, and Typhoon Lagoon, although a few are a bit of a walk from the Disney Institute campus. The telephone number for The Villas at the Disney Institute is 827-1100.

TYPES OF ACCOMMODATIONS: There are five major types of villas. All have either full kitchens or wet bars with small refrigerators. Check-in and check-out for all guests take place at the Welcome Center near the Bungalows and the Fairway Villas.

One-Bedroom Bungalows: The 316 Bungalows are slightly northeast of the Town Houses. The smallest one-bedroom units are roughly L-shaped, with a sitting area (equipped with a daybed, wet bar, refrigerator, microwave, and coffeemaker) that's pleasantly removed from the sleeping area, with its two queen-size beds. The layout provides families with a bit more privacy and space than they would get in the standard rooms at the WDW hotels. (The single disadvantage for families: small bathrooms.) All have a balcony or a patio.

One- and Two-Bedroom Town Houses: These accommodations are about a five minutes' walk from Downtown Disney. They are simple in feeling and decor; living rooms have cathedral ceilings. A one-bedroom unit can

accommodate four; there's a queen-size bed in the bedroom and a queen-size sleeper sofa in the living room. A two-bedroom unit, which can accommodate six, features a queen-size bed in the master bedroom, two twin-size beds in the loft bedroom, and a queen-size sleeper sofa in the living room.

Fairway Villas: These cedar-sided, slant-roofed units, located near the first, second, eighth, and ninth fairways of the Lake Buena Vista golf course, are among the World's most spacious and attractive accommodations, with cathedral ceilings, rough-hewn walls, large windows, contemporary-styled furniture, and an overall feeling that there's lots of elbow room. There is a queen-size bed in one bedroom, two double beds in the other, and either a pull-out bed or a double sleeper sofa in the living room. Each villa can sleep eight, plus there's room for a crib.

Treehouse Villas: Guests who lodge in one of these octagonal houses-on-stilts, scattered along a barbell-shaped roadway, go to sleep to a cacophony of crickets and wake up to a chorus of birds. You're literally in the woods, alongside some of the winding WDW canals, and you feel a million miles from the rest of the World. Upstairs are the small (but modern) kitchen, the living room (where the television set is located), two bedrooms (each with a queen-size bed), and two bathrooms; the entire floor is surrounded by a deck. Downstairs, there's a bedroom with a double bed and television, and a utility room equipped with a washer and dryer. The canals offer some of the World's best fishing, mainly for bass, and the roadways—shady, flat, and generally untrafficked—are great for jogging.

Grand Vista Homes: Four ultraluxurious homes—each with two or three bedrooms and a fully equipped kitchen—are available for rent. Each features a master bedroom with a king-size bed, and most of the other bedrooms have two queen-size beds (some have two twins). Bed turndown service and daily newspaper delivery are provided, refrigerators are stocked with staples, and furnishings are all first-class. Use of golf carts and bicycles is included in the price. (For complete price information, see the chart "Rates at Walt Disney World Properties" starting on page 74.)

WHERE TO EAT: The **Seasons Dining Room** features four dining areas, each with a different seasonal decor. There's also **Reflections Coffee & Pastries** at the Disney Institute, as well as many other options at nearby Downtown Disney and the resorts on Hotel Plaza Blvd. (See *Good Meals, Great Times.*)

Groceries: In these parts, many guests cook their own meals. Dabblers, located in the Welcome Center, has a limited selection of groceries. The Gourmet Pantry at the Downtown Disney Marketplace stocks staples of all sorts. Purchases can be delivered to your villa; if you won't be there to receive them, arrangements may be made for the delivery person to be let in so that perishables can be stashed in the refrigerator. It's also possible to order by phone; call 828-3886 for the Gourmet Pantry, or 827-4453 for Dabblers. A Gooding's supermarket is located at the Crossroads of Lake Buena Vista shopping center nearby.

WHERE TO DRINK: For liquid refreshment, head for the **Seasons Terrace Lounge**, located on a terrace by Seasons Dining Room. At the Downtown Disney Marketplace, nearby, you'll find Cap'n Jack's Oyster Bar, or try one of the clubs at Pleasure Island or the West Side (for details, see *Everything Else in the World*).

WHAT TO DO: In addition to boating, fishing, and shopping at the Downtown Disney Marketplace (discussed in more detail in *Sports* and *Everything Else in the World*), you can also enjoy a variety of activities around the villas themselves. Two sand volleyball courts are situated among the villas.

Lagoon, and Downtown Disney. These circulate through the villa areas, making pickups at bus stops located at regular intervals along the roadways.

Another option: transport to the Downtown Disney Marketplace via an electric golf cart or bike. Both are rented at the health club.

Disney's Old Key West Resort

Escape to the spirit of the Florida Keys. Disney's Old Key West Resort is the flagship Disney Vacation Club property (see the box on the next page for details), but villas not occupied by members are available for nightly rental. It has the laid-back feel of a resort community and all the amenities that go with resort life. Conch Flats Community Hall provides a wide range of activities, from board games and movie rentals to basketball and table tennis, plus an activities director to schedule events. The homey accommodations have lots of space and the convenience of kitchen facilities, making the resort especially comfortable for longer stays. The villas are designed in a Key West theme, with soothing color schemes of seafoam green and mauve. The telephone number for Disney's Old Key West Resort is 827-7700.

Biking: The rustic pathways and meandering roads around the villas can make for an enjoyable hour of pedaling. Bicycles are rented at the health club.

Boating: Canoes are available for hourly and daily rental from the health club.

Golf: Fairways of the Lake Buena Vista course based here nudge right up to the Fairway and Treehouse villas. Practice greens and a driving range are available, along with top-quality rental clubs and shoes. (For fees and starting information, see the *Sports* chapter.)

Health Club: The large Sports & Fitness Center features aerobics, a gymnasium, and Cybex equipment (complimentary to guests participating in programs; available to any WDW resort guest for a fee). A full-service spa is within the center (use of facilities included with purchase of treatments).

Playground: A play area is located near the main pool.

Shopping: Dabblers in the Welcome Center offers a mix of merchandise related to Disney Institute programs. Browse through books, gardening and cooking accessories, and spa-at-home inspirations.

Swimming: There are six pools and several whirlpools dotted about the grounds.

Tennis: The four lighted clay courts are often given over to Disney Institute programs, but are available to any guest (with a fitness center pass) at other times.

Video Arcade: A small arcade with electronic games and pinball machines is located near the Town Houses.

TRANSPORTATION: Buses go to the Magic Kingdom, Epcot, the Disney-MGM Studios, Animal Kingdom, Blizzard Beach, Typhoon

VILLAS: There are studios and villas with one, two, and three bedrooms. A studio consists of a large bedroom with two queen-size beds, a table and chairs, and a kitchenette with a refrigerator, coffeemaker, microwave, and sink. The bathrooms are spacious. Each one-bedroom villa has a king-size bed in the master bedroom and a queen-size sleeper sofa in the living room; the master bath has a whirlpool tub, sink, and shower. The two-bedroom villa features a king-size bed in the master bedroom, two queen-size beds in the second bedroom, a living room with a queen-size sleeper sofa and a VCR, a dining

Disney Vacation Club

Imagine a club that gives members the convenience of ready-made vacations from year to year, with the flexibility of choosing when and where to visit, how long to stay, and the type of accommodations. It starts with the purchase of a real estate interest in a Disney Vacation Club property. For a one-time price and annual dues, members garner vacation stays that can be enjoyed at any of four destinations: Disney's Old Key West Resort and Disney's BoardWalk Villas Resort at Walt Disney World, Disney's Vero Beach Resort, and Disney's Hilton Head Island Resort in South Carolina.

Disney's Vero Beach Resort is a two-hour drive from Walt Disney World. It has villa-type accommodations comparable to those at Disney's Old Key West Resort—with lush surroundings, an endless uncrowded beach, and lots of local sights. The proximity makes it easy to tack a beach vacation onto a WDW visit (for the vacation needed *after* the vacation). Members can also elect to stay at their choice of more than 100 other resorts worldwide. Accommodations are subject to availability.

room, and a spacious kitchen with a refrigerator, dishwasher, toaster, and coffeemaker, plus dishes, silverware, cooking utensils, and more. The master bathroom is split into two separate rooms with an extra-large whirlpool tub and a sink in one and an oversize shower, sink and vanity, and toilet in the other. There's a terrace off the living room and bedroom, and ceiling fans in each room. The configuration of the three-bedroom Grand Villas is similar to that of the two-bedroom models, but adds a third bedroom with two double beds. As for capacity, the studios and one-bedroom villas sleep 4 people, the two-bedroom villas sleep 8, and three-bedroom villas accommodate 12. Some units are equipped for guests with disabilities. Non-smoking villas are available.

WHERE TO EAT: In addition to the restaurant and snack bar here, there are grills and picnic tables available for meals outdoors. Guests can also make a short boat journey to the Downtown Disney Marketplace. Pizza delivery is available from Dixie Landings from 4 P.M. to midnight.

Good's Food to Go: Pick up continental breakfast or burgers, conch fritters, salads, sandwiches, and snacks at this casual spot by the main pool.

Olivia's Café: This casual full-service restaurant serves an assortment of Key West favorites plus more traditional items for breakfast, lunch, and dinner. Menus change seasonally. A Winnie the Pooh character breakfast is held on Wednesday and Sunday.

WHERE TO DRINK: The watering holes at Old Key West are as laid-back as they come.

Gurgling Suitcase: Near the main pool area, this bar serves specialty drinks, cocktails, wine, beer, and soft drinks. Sit at outdoor tables or on stools inside.

Turtle Shack: In the recreation area located off Turtle Pond Road, a poolside spot serves pizza, salads, sandwiches, and snacks (seasonal).

WHAT TO DO: An activities director is on hand to schedule events for guests and members alike. At Conch Flats Community Hall, table tennis, board games, playing cards, a large-screen television set, video rentals, and planned activities all are on hand. Basketball, shuffleboard, and volleyball courts are located throughout the resort, and equipment is available from Hank's Rent 'N Return.

Biking: A variety of bicycles may be rented from Hank's.

Boating: Pedal boats, rowboats, and pontoon boats are available for rent at Hank's.

Health Club: The R.E.S.T. health club features Nautilus and cardiovascular machines, a sauna, and massage (by appointment).

Playground: The kids' play area is located between the main swimming pool and the tennis courts.

Shopping: Conch Flats General Store stocks groceries, books, magazines, sun care products, and Disney character merchandise.

Swimming: The sprawling main pool, with a large whirlpool nearby, is located behind the Hospitality House. The children's pool and play area resembles a giant sand castle. Additional pools are found around the resort.

Tennis: There are two lighted courts located near the main pool. A third court, located in a more removed area, is not equipped for night play.

Video Arcade: The Electric Eel Arcade is located in the Hospitality House.

TRANSPORTATION: Buses go to the Magic Kingdom, Epcot, the Disney-MGM Studios, Animal Kingdom, Blizzard Beach, Typhoon Lagoon, and Downtown Disney. Water launches also make the trip between the resort and Downtown Disney.

Animal Kingdom Area

All-Star Sports & All-Star Music

The first Disney entries into the value-priced hotel market, the All-Star Sports and All-Star Music resorts are the most startlingly themed at Walt Disney World. Each resort has 1,920 rooms housed in ten buildings, devoted to five sports and five types of music, respectively. (A new All-Star resort is scheduled to open in early 1999.)

Sports fans will find themselves in a world of baseball, football, tennis, surfing, or basketball at the All-Star Sports resort. Brightly colored larger-than-life football helmets, surfboards, tennis balls, basketball hoops, and baseball bats adorn the buildings. Stairwells in the shape of three-story soda cups, lifeguard shacks, and tennis ball cans lead guests to the second and third floors.

At the All-Star Music resort, Broadway, country, jazz, rock, and calypso are the themes. A walk-through, neon-lit jukebox, a three-story pair of cowboy boots, and a Broadway theater marquee are among the giant icons.

Guests check in at Stadium Hall for All-Star Sports or at Melody Hall for All-Star Music. Each building houses a food court, arcade, shop, and Guest Services. To reach the All-Star Sports resort, call 939-5000; to contact the All-Star Music resort, call 939-6000.

ROOMS: The guestrooms, measuring 260 square feet, are rather small compared with the rooms at Port Orleans and Dixie Landings, which are 314 square feet. Each room has two double beds (with the exception of rooms designed for travelers with disabilities, which have one king-size bed and a small refrigerator), a vanity area with a single sink, a separate bathroom, a closet bar and shelf, a small dresser, and a small table with two chairs. Nonsmoking rooms are available.

WHERE TO EAT: The **End Zone** food court in Stadium Hall and the **Intermission** food court in Melody Hall each feature a bakery, convenience market, and several stands geared to barbecue, pizza and pasta, and burgers. Each food court has a common seating area with a central beverage bar.

For entertainment, the End Zone offers children's movies during the day and showcases big games on its large-screen TV; Intermission features Tuesday night karaoke. Both All-Star Sports and All-Star Music deliver pizza, salads, beer, and wine to rooms from 5 P.M. to midnight.

WHERE TO DRINK: There are no lounges at the All-Star resorts; however, the **Team Spirits** pool bar and the **Singing Spirits** pool bar serve drinks throughout the day and evening. These bars are located at the main pool areas.

WHAT TO DO: Swimming gets top priority here. Guests may pay a fee for unlimited boat rentals at the nearby Caribbean Beach resort.

Playground: A playground is located in each hotel's courtyard area.

Shopping: Sport Goofy Gifts and Sundries in Stadium Hall and Maestro Mickey's in Melody Hall feature magazines, books, sun care products, character merchandise, and sundries.

Swimming: Each hotel has two pools and one kiddie pool. At the All-Star Sports resort, Surfboard Bay has a soothing ocean motif. The smaller Grand Slam Pool pays tribute to our national pastime—it's shaped like a baseball diamond (Goofy is on the mound). At the All-Star Music resort, the Calypso Pool is in the form of a giant guitar, while the Piano Pool is designed to look like—you guessed it.

TRANSPORTATION: Buses make regular pickups at Stadium Hall and Melody Hall for trips to the Magic Kingdom, Epcot, the Disney-MGM Studios, Animal Kingdom, Blizzard Beach, Typhoon Lagoon, and Downtown Disney.

Coronado Springs

This resort, which opened in August 1997, has the mystical feel of a lost kingdom of riches that's only recently been unearthed. Inspired by explorer Francisco de Coronado's unsuccessful search for the fabled realm of Cibola, it reveals its theme in such elements as an intricately tiled stucco lobby with a fountain, and a stepped pyramid with water tumbling down from it that appears to have created the Mayan ruin–themed pool. The hotel's 1,967 rooms are found in three distinct guest areas that stretch around Lago Dorado, a 15-acre lake, reflecting urban, rural, and coastal regions from the American Southwest to northern Mexico. The food court, restaurant, and lounge are centrally located near the rotunda lobby. A convention center offers access to business services. The telephone number for Coronado Springs is 939-1000.

ROOMS: Standard rooms are smaller than those at Disney's deluxe hotels, but perfectly adequate for a family of four; each has two double beds (some king-size beds are available). In-room amenities include a coffeemaker and extra phone jack. Decor varies in each section, but is characterized by vibrant yellow, blue, and scarlet accents, and Mexican and southwestern touches. In the Casitas area, where most of the hotel's suites are located, terra-cotta guest buildings occupy a citylike landscape interspersed with colorful plazas and palm-shaded courtyards; rooms are awash in autumnal tones. In the pueblo-style Ranchos, scattered along a dry stream bed amid cacti, rooms have a rustic feel. Cabanas, located along the rocky palm-lined beach, reflect the fun, casual feel of their namesake inside and

out; more than half have water views. Walkways link guestroom areas with the recreational facilities. Rooms equipped for guests with disabilities and nonsmoking rooms are available.

WHERE TO EAT: In addition to a full-service restaurant and food court, limited room service is available 24 hours a day.

Maya Grill: A casually elegant specialty restaurant, the Maya Grill offers traditional Mayan cuisine—seafood, steak, lamb, and pork cooked over an open-pit wood-fired grill.

Pepper Market: High ceilings and huge windows make this food court feel like an open-air market. The fare includes tacos, tostadas, pizza, pasta, and omelettes made to order. The Pepper Market has both indoor and outdoor seating.

WHERE TO DRINK: There are two places to wet your whistle at Coronado Springs.

Francisco's: A colorful lounge providing cocktails and evening entertainment is located in the main building.

Siesta's: In the Dig Site area, this poolside bar lets swimmers and archaeologists enjoy a variety of cocktails and light snacks.

WHAT TO DO: The resort's main recreation area is the Dig Site, a stepped pyramid with a water slide that spills into a large pool. There is an array of water sports in which to participate, as well as volleyball, and hiking along the many nature paths. For more information, see *Sports*.

Biking: Bikes may be rented at La Marina.

Boating: A variety of boating equipment is available for rental at La Marina.

Health Club: La Vida health club offers a full range of fitness equipment.

Salon: The Casa de Belleza salon is located near La Vida health club.

Playgrounds: There are two playgrounds. The more elaborate one is part of the Dig Site area, and includes a sandbox stocked with Mayan trinkets waiting to be excavated.

Shopping: Panchitos Gifts & Sundries is the place to pick up pottery, jewelry, and other items with a Southwest flavor, Disney character merchandise, film, and basic necessities.

Swimming: The main pool can be found in the Dig Site area. It surrounds a Mayan pyramid and features a towering water slide. There is a 22-person whirlpool and a kiddie pool nearby. Each of the guestroom areas features a quiet pool.

Video Arcades: The Jumping Bean Arcade is found in the main building and the Iguana Arcade is in the Dig Site area.

TRANSPORTATION: Buses take guests to the Magic Kingdom, Epcot, the Disney-MGM Studios, Animal Kingdom, Typhoon Lagoon, Blizzard Beach, and Downtown Disney.

Disney Cruise Line

In March 1998, the *Disney Magic* officially joins the ranks of the world's finest ocean-going vessels. Weighing in at 85,000 tons, the custom-built cruise ship is the first in Disney history. (Its sister ship, the *Disney Wonder*, makes its debut in December 1998.)

A Disney Cruise Line vacation begins with a three- or four-day stay at a WDW resort. After that, guests simply retain the same room keys for their staterooms. Disney staffers remove luggage from the resort and move it into the appropriate shipboard stateroom. There is no second check-in on the ship, ensuring a seamless land-sea vacation. (Staterooms closely match the category of the resort accommodations, from Moderate to Deluxe.)

After transferring to Port Canaveral, the departure point for all Disney cruises, guests board the 1,750-passenger *Disney Magic* for a three- or four-day journey. The weeklong adventure reinvents the cruise experience in distinctly Disney fashion. From the innovative ship design to entertainment options, families, teens, and adults without kids will all have their own comfort zones afloat—without ever having to say bon voyage to Mickey. (In addition to the big cheese, the usual cast of characters is on hand to meet, greet, and entertain guests of all ages.) The itinerary includes a stop at the port of Nassau in the Bahamas, plus a daylong stay on Disney's private Bahamian island, Castaway Cay, which will offer a slew of recreational interests.

Back at Port Canaveral, guests are transported directly to Orlando International Airport. The ship's classic exterior recalls the majesty of early ocean liners. Guests enter a three-story atrium, where traditional definitions of elegance expand to include a demure bronze statue of Mickey as helmsman and subtle cutout Disney character silhouettes along the grand staircase. Disney's touch is evident throughout, as even the elevators have entertainment value (guests see different scenes as they travel). There's even a 15-foot, topsy-turvy statue of a decidedly "goofy" painter hanging off the ship's stern.

Disney Cruise Line vacations can be booked through travel agents, or by calling Disney Cruise Line reservations at 566-7000.

ROOMS: All 875 staterooms aboard the *Disney Magic* are a cut above the standard cruising cabin. Overall, each offers about 25% more space; most have a bath and a half; and 73% are outside rooms with ocean vistas—many with verandas. All feature telephones with "land lines," minibars, televisions, hair dryers, and safes. There are rooms equipped for guests with disabilities, and nonsmoking rooms are available.

There are 12 stateroom categories that correspond to WDW resorts with comparable room rates. The seven-day vacations range from $1,229 to $3,539 per person, double occupancy. Package prices include airfare to Orlando from major U.S. cities, transfers, accommodations, unlimited admission to the theme parks, meals, recreation, and more. Depending on availability, guests may opt for a three- or four-day sea-only vacation. Note: Be sure to pack a passport, or a birth certificate—proper ID is required to visit the Bahamas.

WHERE TO EAT: There are three themed dining rooms (and one picturesque adults-only alternative dining room), in addition to 24-hour room service; guests rotate, spending a night in each of the three main rooms, enjoying a refreshingly different dining experience each time.

Animator's Palate: Here the restaurant and the food—California cuisine—are works of art. As in the movie *The Wizard of Oz,* everything begins in black and white—from the checked floors and giant paintbrushes to the waiters' attire and even the appetizers. The artwork on the television monitors starts out color-deprived, too. As the meal progresses, color slowly begins to creep into the picture. By the time dessert arrives, the room is awash in a sea of brilliant hues.

Islands: A colorful Caribbean setting complete with Sebastian wall sconces, Islands features tasty tropical cuisine.

Lido Café: An indoor-outdoor café serving breakfast, lunch, snacks, and a buffet dinner for kids.

Lumière's: French food, chandeliers, and *Beauty and the Beast* trompe l'oeil effects characterize this, the most formal dining room on the ship. An abundance of roses completes the theme.

Palo: A dining room reserved strictly for adults, Palo is a romantic restaurant perched atop the *Disney Magic*. Chefs prepare contemporary Mediterannean cuisine in an exhibition kitchen. Picture windows provide ocean views.

WHERE TO DRINK: Among the options are a variety of lounges, including a sports bar, and a number of clubs. Beat Street, like Pleasure Island, is an adults-only cluster of nighttime entertainment venues:

Offbeat: An anything goes, improvisational comedy club.

Rockin' Bar "D": A dance club with a split personality—one night it's rock 'n' roll, the next it's country.

Sessions: An intimate piano bar lounge.

WHAT TO DO: In addition to shuffleboard, basketball, and paddleball, there are many sporting activities to enjoy aboard the *Disney Magic*. Recreational areas on the ship, as well as at its ports of call, are strategically located to attract families, teens, and adults to different areas, with nearly an entire deck devoted exclusively to kids.

Biking: Bikes are available for rent at Castaway Cay.

Buena Vista Theater: A 270-seat cinema, this theater features a variety of first-run movies and classic Disney films.

Common Ground: Here teens can hang out, watch movies, and listen to music in a lounge that was designed specifically with them in mind.

Golf: Golfers can practice their swings in a safely netted area aboard the ship.

Health Club: Guests get in shipshape at the Vista Spa, a modern salon and spa offering exercise equipment and spa treatments, educational and enrichment programs, a sauna, steam room, whirlpool, and massage.

Oceaneer's Adventure: This huge area, dedicated to kids, offers supervised, age-specific programs for kids ages 3 to 12 from 9 A.M. until 1 A.M. The Oceaneer's Club provides engaging activities for the 3- to 8-year-old set. The Oceaneer's Lab, designed for children 9 to 12, is a science-based interactive play area. This state-of-the-art amusement center is sure to keep older kids entertained for hours at a time.

Salon: The Vista Spa provides a full line of services, including haircuts, manicures, and pedicures (for an extra fee).

Shopping: In addition to the colorful shipboard shops—Radar Trap, Mickey's Mates, Treasure Ketch, Shutters, and ESPN Gear—guests can indulge their shopping fantasies while exploring Nassau.

Studio Sea: A family lounge with a soundstage theme. Guests participate in live entertainment, such as cabaret acts, and a family game show in a setting that looks like a television studio.

Swimming: There are several whirlpools and three swimming pools on the ship: a family pool, a sports-activity pool, and an adults-only pool. Guests may also swim off the white-sand shores of Castaway Cay.

Volleyball: Guests can play water volleyball in the *Disney Magic* pool and sand volleyball at Castaway Cay.

Walt Disney Theatre: A tribute to the grand theatrical palaces of long ago. Guests can see a different musical production each night, featuring Broadway-style staging and special effects.

Anchors Aweigh!

Every Disney Cruise Line trip culminates with a visit to Castaway Cay (pronounced *key*). Disney has allowed the island to retain its natural beauty while accommodating a host of outdoor activities, including scuba diving, sand volleyball, snorkeling, biking, and hiking. The island features a beach area for families, as well as a mile-long stretch of secluded sand for adults seeking less action and more privacy.

As guests awaken on the final day of their Disney Cruise Line vacation, they find their ship already docked at Castaway Cay's private pier. The pier allows for easy access to and from the ship.

Castaway Cay, a 1,000-acre tropical island, is located in the Bahamas, due east of Fort Lauderdale. Trams and other transportation are available for guests who wish to explore the island. All of the architecture, including a bar, restaurant, shop, and even a post office, is in true Bahamian style.

WDW Resort Primer

The Walt Disney World hotels and villas have some important operating procedures that first-time guests don't always take seriously—much to their later dismay.

Deposit Requirements: Deposits equal to one night's lodging (or campsite rental) are required within 21 days of the time that a reservation is made. Personal checks, traveler's checks, cashier's checks, and money orders are acceptable forms of payment. To have deposit charges billed to an American Express, Visa, MasterCard, or The Disney Credit Card account, you'll need to provide the reservation agent with your credit card number and its expiration date. Deposits will be fully refunded if you cancel your reservation at least 48 hours before your scheduled arrival. Reservations are canceled if deposits are not received by the 21-day deadline. (Reservations booked less than 30 days prior to arrival will receive special instructions for deposits.)

Check-In and Check-Out Times: While not unique to the Orlando area, the early check-out time (11 A.M. at all WDW lodging places) and the late check-in times (1 P.M. at the campsites, 3 P.M. in the hotels, 4 P.M. in the villas) often surprise. They need not be an inconvenience, however. When checking in, guests should pre-register, purchase passes, and head for the parks. Luggage can be stored at the resorts.

Payment Methods: Hotel bills may be paid with credit cards (American Express, Visa, MasterCard, or The Disney Credit Card), traveler's checks, cash, or personal checks. Checks must bear the guest's name and address, be drawn on a U.S. bank, and be accompanied by proper identification—that is, a valid driver's license or a government-issued passport.

Additional Per-Person Charges: Certain charges apply when more than two adults (over 17 years of age) occupy a standard room. The fee is $5 per extra adult per day at Fort Wilderness homes and cabins; $2 per extra adult per day at Fort Wilderness campsites; $10 per extra adult per day at the All-Star resorts; $15 per extra adult per day at Caribbean Beach, Port Orleans, Dixie Landings, and Coronado Springs; and $25 per extra adult per day at all other WDW resorts and at the Swan and Dolphin.

WDW ID Cards: Issued on arrival at WDW-owned resorts, these cards are among resort guests' most valuable possessions while in Walt Disney World. They entitle you to:

• Theme park admission if you've purchased a Length of Stay Pass.

• Unlimited transportation by bus, monorail, and watercraft.

• Use of many of the roadways within Walt Disney World.

• Charge privileges: If you've left a credit card imprint with your hotel, ID cards may be used (up to certain account limits) to cover purchases in shops, lounges, and restaurants, and recreational fees incurred anywhere in the World. At the Magic Kingdom, Epcot, the Disney-MGM Studios, and Animal Kingdom, guests may use their IDs to charge meals at full-service restaurants, shops, and fast-food locations, but not at any food carts.

Note: ID cards are valid for use of transportation facilities through the end of the last day of your stay, but are not valid for charging past check-out time. Swan and Dolphin guests may not use their IDs to charge meals at restaurants outside the two hotels or have purchases delivered to their rooms. Other restrictions may apply. Read the information on the cards carefully when checking in.

Rates at Walt Disney World Properties

	CHARGE FOR SINGLE OR DOUBLE OCCUPANCY		
	Value	Regular	Peak
DELUXE			
BoardWalk Inn			
Rooms (5)	$249–$305	$264–$325	$279–$340
Rooms–Concierge (4)	$385–$455	$405–$475	$420–$490
Suites (6)		Call 934-7639 for prices	
Contemporary			
Rooms–Garden Buildings (5)	$209–$265	$229–$285	$244–$299
Rooms–Tower (5)	$290–$350	$310–$375	$325–$390
Suites (7 to 12)		Call 934-7639 for prices	
Grand Floridian			
Rooms (5)	$294–$360	$314–$380	$329–$395
Rooms–Concierge (5)	$495–$510	$425–$530	$440–$545
Suites (4 to 10)		Call 934-7639 for prices	
Polynesian			
Rooms (5)	$269–$325	$289–$340	$305–$355
Rooms–Concierge (5)	$335–$410	$355–$430	$370–$445
Suites (4 to 6)		Call 934-7639 for prices	
Swan and Dolphin			
Rooms (5)	$265–$315	$295–$380	not applicable
Rooms–Club Level (5)	$385	$410	not applicable
Suites (5 to 10)	$610–$2,850	$610–$2,850	not applicable
Wilderness Lodge			
Rooms (4)	$175–$290	$195–$315	$210–$330
Suites (4 to 6)		Call 934-7639 for prices	
Yacht Club and Beach Club			
Rooms (5)	$260–$305	$280–$325	$295–$340
Rooms–Concierge* (5)	$385–$420	$405–$440	$420–$455
Suites (5 to 10)		Call 934-7639 for prices	
*Yacht Club only			
HOME AWAY FROM HOME			
Disney's BoardWalk Villas Resort			
Studios (4)	$249–$260	$264–$280	$279–$295
1-BR Villas (4)	$305–$345	$325–$365	$340–$380
2-BR Villas (8)	$410–$460	$499–$560	$520–$580
Grand Villas (12)	$1,100	$1,200	$1,300
Disney's Old Key West Resort			
Studios (4)	$224	$239	$254
1-BR Vacation Home (4)	$295	$315	$330
2-BR Vacation Home (8)	$410	$430	$450
3-BR Grand Villas (12)	$850	$870	$885
Fort Wilderness			
Cabins (6)	$199	$219	$234
Homes (6)	$179	$199	$214

	CHARGE FOR SINGLE OR DOUBLE OCCUPANCY		
	Value	Regular	Peak

HOME AWAY FROM HOME

The Villas at the Disney Institute

	Value	Regular	Peak
Bungalows (4)	$199	$219	$234
1-BR Town Houses (4)	$245	$265	$280
2-BR Town Houses (6)	$330	$350	$365
Treehouse Villas (6)	$365	$385	$399
Fairway Villas (6 to 8)	$385	$415	$430
Grand Vista Homes (6 to 8)	$995–$1,185	$995–$1,185	$1,045–$1,245

MODERATE

Caribbean Beach

	Value	Regular	Peak
Rooms (4)	$119–$134	$129–$144	$139–$154

Coronado Springs

	Value	Regular	Peak
Rooms (4)	$119–$134	$129–$144	$139–$154
Suites (4 to 6)	Call 934-7639 for prices		

Dixie Landings

	Value	Regular	Peak
Rooms (4)	$119–$134	$129–$144	$139–$154

Port Orleans

	Value	Regular	Peak
Rooms (4)	$119–$134	$129–$144	$139–$154

VALUE

All-Star Sports and All-Star Music

	Value	Regular	Peak
Rooms (4)	$74	$84	$89

CAMPGROUND

Fort Wilderness Campsites

	Value	Regular	Peak
Sites w/partial hookup (10)	$35	$45	$49
Sites w/full hookup (10)	$39	$54	$59
Preferred Sites (10)	$49	$59	$64

Check-in time: 3 P.M. except at The Villas at the Disney Institute and Old Key West, where check-in is at 4 P.M. and at Fort Wilderness, where it's 1 P.M. **Check-out time:** 11 A.M. for Fort Wilderness and all hotels.

Value rates apply: January 1, 1998, through February 12, 1998, and August 23, 1998, through December 22, 1998, for all properties except the Swan and Dolphin; they are July 5, 1998, through December 22, 1998, for all Home Away From Home and Deluxe properties except the Swan and Dolphin. Value rates at the Swan and Dolphin are January 6–31 and May 1 through December 17. **Regular rates apply:** April 26, 1998, through July 4, 1998, for all properties except the Swan and Dolphin; they are April 26, 1998, through August 22, 1998, for all Moderate and Value resorts. Swan and Dolphin regular rates are February 1 through April 30 and December 18 through January 5. **Peak rates apply:** February 13, 1998, through April 25, 1998, and December 23, 1998 through December 31, 1998. These designations in no way reflect park attendance.

Room capacity: Numbers provided in parentheses reflect maximum occupancy based on existing beds. Trundles and cribs usually may be requested. A trundle bed (which sleeps one) can be rented for $12 a day. Cribs are free.

Note: The prices provided here were correct at press time, but the rates do change, so be sure to double-check with the hotels before setting your final budget.

CALL W-DISNEY (934-7639) FOR RESERVATIONS

Resorts on Hotel Plaza Boulevard

These seven hotels—the Hilton, Buena Vista Palace, Travelodge, Grosvenor, Doubletree Guest Suites, Royal Plaza, and Courtyard by Marriott—occupy a unique position among Orlando-area accommodations not owned by Disney: They are located inside the boundaries of Walt Disney World, several of them within walking distance of the Downtown Disney Marketplace.

Guests at the resorts on Hotel Plaza Blvd. receive preferred access to the five Disney golf courses and preferred admission at Planet Hollywood before 5 P.M. Three of the properties offer meals with Disney characters.

All the hotels offer complimentary bus service every 30 minutes to the Magic Kingdom, Epcot, the Disney-MGM Studios, and Animal Kingdom, with limited service to Downtown Disney and the WDW water parks. All sell park tickets, have Disney gift shops, and offer car rental and meeting facilities. The Hilton, Buena Vista Palace, and Grosvenor are directly across the street from the Marketplace, and the other properties are within a half mile. All are near Goodings 24-hour grocery and a number of restaurants, at the Crossroads of Lake Buena Vista.

To book, contact the individual hotel or WDW Central Reservations at W-DISNEY (934-7639). The resorts on Hotel Plaza Blvd. are included in several Walt Disney Travel Company packages as well.

The following listings are arranged according to standard room rates, from highest to lowest starting price. All offer nonsmoking rooms and accommodations for travelers with disabilities. Internet users can access information about the resorts on Hotel Plaza Blvd.: *http://www.ten-io.com/disney-vha.*

HILTON: This hotel, with a splashy beige, salmon, and aqua facade, is a good choice for its 23 well-groomed acres, its laid-back resort ambience, its impressive pool area, and its upscale shops. The 814 rooms are tastefully decorated and feature minibars and phones with voice mail and computer hookups.

Among the hotel's seven restaurants and lounges, Finn's Grill offers dinners of seafood and steaks in an old Key West atmosphere; County Fair serves breakfast (with characters in attendance on Sunday), lunch, and dinner; and the Rum Largo Pool Bar & Café offers hamburgers, salads, sandwiches, and tropical drinks. The Old-Fashioned Soda Shoppe serves ice cream, pizza, and more; you can eat outside at the County Fair Terrace. A Benihana Japanese steak house, with sushi bar, is also on the premises. For light meals, snacks, or cocktails, drop by John T's Plantation Bar in the lobby.

Recreational facilities include two whirlpools and heated swimming pools, a children's pool with a fountain at the center, and a spa and health club with Nautilus equipment. The Vacation Station Kid's Hotel, designed for children 4 to 12 years old, has a video room, play area, and scheduled recreational activities supervised by a trained staff. The cost is $4 for the first child, with a $1 discount for each additional child. Rates range from $195 to $255; suites are $459 to $759. Hilton; 1751 Hotel Plaza Blvd.; Lake Buena Vista, FL 32830; 827-4000 or 800-782-4414.

BUENA VISTA PALACE: The largest of the Hotel Plaza Blvd. resorts (it's actually at the intersection of Buena Vista Drive and

Hotel Plaza Blvd.), it is a cluster of towers, one of them 27 stories high, set on 27 acres beside Lake Buena Vista. The lobby has several intimate nooks with overstuffed chairs and couches; the staff is helpful; and guest requests are handled efficiently with a touch of the telephone. Each of the 1,014 newly renovated, classically elegant rooms has a ceiling fan and two phones (one with voice mail and speakerphone), and most have a balcony or patio.

The concierge rooms offer special amenities. The hotel's European-style spa (the first luxury hotel in Central Florida to have one) opened in 1996 with 14 treatment rooms, a full-service salon, a fitness center with personal trainers, and a lap pool. Recreation Island features two swimming pools, a kiddie pool, a whirlpool, sauna, three lighted tennis courts, a sand volleyball court, a marina with boat and bike rentals, and a new children's playground. Kids' Stuff is a year-round recreational program for children 4 to 12.

The hotel also provides 24-hour room service, a Disney-run gift shop, a boutique with men's and women's fashions, a guest laundry, and the Family Calling Center (a large booth with a speakerphone). Eating spots include the lakeside Watercress Café, which serves breakfast, lunch, and dinner, with a buffet available for breakfast and dinner (characters are in attendance on Sunday morning); the adjacent Watercress Pastry Shop, open 24 hours for counter-service baked goods and sandwiches; Arthur's 27, with an international menu and a gorgeous view; the Outback restaurant, which serves hefty portions of fresh seafood and Black Angus steaks; and the pleasant Spa Courtyard for relaxed snacking or nibbling on spa fare around a fountain.

The Laughing Kookaburra Good Time Bar, nicknamed "The Kook," has live bands

and dancing. Noise from the restaurants can flow through the atriums and penetrate the solid oak doors, so if silence matters, choose accommodations in the poolside Island Suite resort building (also good for families) or the 27-story tower.

The Top of the Palace lounge provides the perfect perch to gaze at the sunset or fireworks and sip fine wines. For the allergy prone, 65 EverGreen Rooms provide filtered air and water. Rooms range from $165 to $270 per night (no charge for kids under 18); suites are $270 to $505. Buena Vista Palace Resort & Spa; 1900 Buena Vista Dr.; Lake Buena Vista, FL 32830; 827-2727 or 800-327-2990.

DOUBLETREE GUEST SUITES: Striking outside and in, this 229-unit property has a low-slung futuristic facade, public areas with bright colors and whimsical patterns, and an aviary in the lobby, where a child's check-in desk stands next to the "grown-up" one. Young guests receive a bag of gifts, and adults get oversize cookies when they register. The only all-suite hotel at Walt Disney World, it features 640-square-foot units, each with a living room (and sleeper sofa), a large dressing area, and a separate bedroom. Each can sleep up to six persons; there are some two-bedroom suites as well. Most bedrooms have two double beds, though some kings are available. Room amenities include two remote control televisions, a small TV in the bathroom, a wet bar, a refrigerator, a coffeemaker with daily coffee and tea refills, a microwave oven, a hair dryer, and a safe.

Recreational facilities include a heated pool, whirlpool, arcade, children's play area, sand volleyball court, and two lighted tennis courts (with pro instruction available). The children's playroom has a big-screen television, toys, games, and seasonal children's activities. The menu at festive Streamers restaurant features American classics. Streamers Market sells snacks items and groceries. Rates range from $129 to $239. Doubletree Guest Suites; 2305 Hotel Plaza Blvd.; Lake Buena Vista, FL 32830; 934-1000 or 800-222-8733.

GROSVENOR: The 626 rooms are located in a mauve 19-story tower and two wings on formal grounds. Each room has voice mail, coffeemaker, and a VCR; movie rentals are available. An exercise room, two lighted tennis courts, shuffleboard courts, a basketball court, a volleyball court, two heated pools, a children's pool, a large play area, and an arcade are available. Baskervilles, the hotel's main restaurant, incorporates a Sherlock Holmes museum, and serves breakfast and dinner buffets; characters are in attendance for breakfast on Tuesday,

Thursday, and Saturday, and for dinner on Wednesday. Baskervilles is also the scene, during dinner on Saturday, for the Murder Watch Mystery Theatre. Continental breakfast, snacks, and lighter fare are available 24 hours a day at Crumpets Café. Crickets lounge offers occasional entertainment. The Grosvenor (pronounced GROVE-nor) is affiliated with Best Western. Rates range from $115 to $175 for two, year-round; suites are $195 to $495. Grosvenor; 1850 Hotel Plaza Blvd.; Lake Buena Vista, FL 32830; 828-4444 or 800-624-4109.

TRAVELODGE: This 18-story tower, surrounded by pines and located just minutes from the Crossroads of Lake Buena Vista shopping center, has 325 newly refurbished, spacious rooms and suites. All rooms have either one king-size or two queen-size beds, voice mail, minibars, coffeemakers, safes, hair dryers, and private balconies (floors 7 through 16 provide a WDW view). Two rooms, called Sleepy Bear Dens, are specially themed for children. The four suites on the 18th floor offer a fine view of the other resorts on Hotel Plaza Blvd. and the fireworks at the Disney theme parks.

The hotel also has an arcade, small heated pool, kiddie pool, landscaped playground, and coin-operated laundry. Traders restaurant serves breakfast and dinner. The Parakeet Café offers light entrées for breakfast, lunch, and dinner, as well as snacks and made-to-order pizza. Besides views of Pleasure Island and Epcot, Toppers lounge, on the 18th floor, has dart machines, pool tables, and music videos. Flamingo Cove is the lobby-level cocktail lounge. EverGreen Rooms feature filtered air and water. Rates range from $99 to $169 for guestrooms; $199 to $299 for suites. Travelodge; 2000 Hotel Plaza Blvd.; Box 22205; Lake Buena Vista, FL 32830; 828-2424 or 800-348-3765.

COURTYARD BY MARRIOTT: This pleasant 323-room hotel, the country's second-largest Courtyard, has some of the most spacious guestrooms on Hotel Plaza Blvd. Situated in a 14-story tower and a 6-story annex, rooms feature sitting areas, computer-data ports, clock radios, marble vanities, voice mail, coffeemakers with china mugs, irons and ironing boards. The bathrooms tend to be on the small side.

A breakfast bar, tables topped with colorful umbrellas, and the Tipsy Parrot lounge fill the atrium lobby. The Courtyard Café & Grille is a full-service restaurant with a breakfast buffet, and the Village Deli serves snacks, muffins, fruit, sandwiches, TCBY yogurt, and Pizza Hut pizza. There are three heated pools, including one for children; a whirlpool; a playground; an arcade; and an exercise room. The pool bar is open seasonally. Rates range from $109 to $169 year-round. Courtyard by Marriott; Box 22204; 1805 Hotel Plaza Blvd.; Lake Buena Vista, FL 32830; 828-8888 or 800-223-9930.

ROYAL PLAZA: The 394 guest units here are divided between a 17-story high-rise and 2-story lanai wings with gated patios or small balconies. Each tower room has a sitting area, desk, dresser, double armoire with closet space, safe, and minibar. The baths have marble counters and corner tubs (whirlpools on the concierge level). All rooms have VCRs, hair dryers, and coffeemakers. There are also 22 suites available.

Recreation facilities include a heated pool, a spa, two saunas, an arcade, and four lighted tennis courts. The hotel has two restaurants, a lounge, and a poolside bar. Depending on the season and the view, room rates range from $109 to $859 for up to five in a room; suites are $169 to $209. Royal Plaza; Box 22203; 1905 Hotel Plaza Blvd.; Lake Buena Vista, FL 32830; 828-2828 or 800-248-7890.

OFF-PROPERTY ACCOMMODATIONS In Lake Buena Vista

A full lineup of accommodations, from laid-back to luxurious, abuts the crossroads at I-4 and S.R. 535 in the heart of Lake Buena Vista. Most offer free transportation to the four main Disney parks. Prices are highly competitive, so shop around before making a reservation. The following listings are arranged according to standard room rates, from highest to lowest starting price. All offer nonsmoking rooms and accommodations for guests with disabilities unless otherwise indicated.

GRAND CYPRESS: Adjacent to the resorts on Hotel Plaza Blvd. and just three miles from Epcot, the Hyatt Regency Grand Cypress has a dramatic 18-story atrium lobby and 750 Florida-inspired guestrooms and suites with wicker furniture, ceiling fans, and shutters. The hotel has four bars and five restaurants, including the ever-popular Hemingway's, which serves game, seafood, and steaks. Four concierges are kept very busy.

The secluded Villas of Grand Cypress house the resort's exquisite Mediterranean-style accommodations. Each club suite consists of a spacious bedroom with a separate sitting area, a large luxury bath with a separate shower and tub, and a sundeck or a patio or a veranda. The villas proper each contain a large living room, a dining room, and a fully equipped kitchen. The Villas area has three dining possibilities, including the sophisticated Black Swan restaurant. Fairways and the Poolside Snack Shop are casual eateries.

The Hyatt Regency Grand Cypress and the Villas of Grand Cypress share a half-acre free-form swimming pool with 12 waterfalls, 2 water slides, and 3 whirlpools (the Villas also has its own pool and whirlpool); a 21-acre lake with rental boats; and a tennis complex with 12 courts. Also offered are racquetball and volleyball courts, a playground, bicycling, a 4.7-mile jogging trail, a 45-acre nature area, and a health club. Forty-five holes of Jack Nicklaus–designed golf separate the Hyatt Regency from the Villas (which are actually 1½ miles apart; a 24-hour shuttle connects the two). The superb North South course features two Scottish-style shared greens, grassy dunes, elevated tees, and a greens fee that will set you back $140 ($100 in the summer). Sports buffs may sign up for activities at the Grand Cypress Academy of Golf, Equestrian Center, or Racquet Club.

Shuttle service to the four Disney theme parks costs $7 round-trip. Rates at the Hyatt Regency range from $195 to $380; suites start at $650. Rates at the Villas range from $210 to $425 for a club suite, $310 to $525 for a one-bedroom villa, and $420 to $850 for a two-bedroom villa. Hyatt Regency Grand Cypress; One Grand Cypress Blvd.; Orlando, FL 32836; 239-1234 or 800-233-1234; Villas of Grand Cypress; One N. Jacaranda; Orlando, FL 32836; 239-4700 or 800-835-7377.

SUMMERFIELD SUITES LAKE BUENA VISTA: A bit off the beaten track but still close to everything, this popular all-suite hotel has 150 units, most of which feature two separate bedrooms with a king-size bed in the master bedroom, each with a private bath, three televisions, VCR, living room, and good-size, fully equipped kitchen with full-size refrigerator. A guest laundry and a deli–convenience store are on the property. The staff will even do your grocery shopping for you if you provide a list early in the day. Nearby restaurants offer takeout. Scheduled complimentary shuttle service to the Disney theme parks is provided. Rates range from $169 to $209 for a one-bedroom unit (for up to four guests), and $209 to $269 for a two-bedroom trio unit (for up to eight guests). Prices include a continental breakfast buffet. (Another Summerfield Suites property is at 8480 I-Drive; 352-2400). Summerfield Suites Lake Buena Vista; 8751 Suiteside Dr.; Orlando, FL 32836; 238-0777 or 800-830-4964.

VISTANA: This sprawling complex of more than 1,100 two-bedroom, two-bath units is only a mile from the Downtown Disney Marketplace, near the intersection of I-4 and S.R. 535. One of the area's earliest time-share resorts—it still is one—it also operates as a luxury resort behind its controlled-entry gate. Each of the stylishly decorated 1,200-square-foot villas sleeps six to eight people and has a living room with a queen-size sleeper sofa and VCR, and a fully equipped kitchen, complete with a clothes washer and dryer. The housekeepers do the dishes daily. Facilities include 13 lighted tennis courts with instruction available, 6 outdoor swimming pools, 5 children's pools, volleyball, a miniature golf course, and a video library. There are three recreational centers with steam rooms, saunas, exercise rooms, and arcades. A number of adult and children's activity programs are available for a nominal charge. Two restaurants are on the property, along with a general store and a Pizza Hut. Complimentary bus service to the four Disney theme parks is provided. Nonsmoking villas are not available. Rates range from $159 to $350 per villa per night. Vistana; 8800 Vistana Centre Dr.; Orlando, FL 32821; 239-3100 or 800-877-8787.

HOLIDAY INN SUNSPREE–LAKE BUENA VISTA: Pretty and pink, this 507-unit property, about 1½ miles from the Downtown Disney Marketplace, has an innovative children's program and a most obliging staff. Its unique Kidsuites provide privacy for adults and kids, who get a soundproof, themed room within a room. Among the options are Sesame Street, Noah's Ark, an igloo, a circus tent, or a space capsule—complete with three beds, TV, VCR, Nintendo, and cassette player. Kids' Corner rooms are similar, only semiprivate. Teen Suites have movie, music,

and sports theming, full-size twin bunk beds, a desk, and a vanity with a makeup mirror. Each standard guestroom has a refrigerator, microwave, coffeemaker (with free coffee packet daily), hair dryer, electronic safe, and VCR. Most of the rooms have two queen-size beds, although some have king-size beds and sleeper sofas.

Camp Holiday, an activity program for children 3 to 12, is open every evening at no charge—a real bargain. Parents can rent a beeper for $5 so they can be reached at any time. Children receive a special surprise when they register at the Kids' Check-In Desk, and a free bedtime tuck-in from Max, the hotel's mascot, on request. A child under 13 eats breakfast, lunch, and dinner free from a special menu when accompanied by a paying adult.

Recreational facilities include a heated pool, two whirlpools, a basketball court, playground, fitness center, and the Cyber-Arcade, a family entertainment center. Maxine's Food Emporium serves a buffet breakfast and features outlets of national fast-food chains. Pinky's Convenience Court, self-service for microwavable and refrigerated items, also carries baby supplies and diapers. Free scheduled transportation to the four Disney theme parks is provided. Rates run $89 to $129, depending on the season; add an additional $39 for Kidsuites or $25 for king family rooms. Anyone who's 100 years old (or older) stays free. Holiday Inn SunSpree–Lake Buena Vista; 13351 S.R. 535; Lake Buena Vista, FL 32821; 239-4500 or 800-366-6299.

HOWARD JOHNSON PARK SQUARE INN & SUITES: A top-rated property within the chain, it works hard to maintain that status. Located in the Vista Centre shopping and dining complex off S.R. 535, it is less than a five-minute drive from the Downtown Disney Marketplace, and is popular with families. The 222 guestrooms and 86 suites all offer lake or courtyard settings. The rooms have two double beds, and the bathrooms are a decent size for the price. Each suite has a microwave oven–refrigerator unit and a coffeemaker, as well as a sleeper sofa. Recreational facilities include two large heated pools, a whirlpool, a children's pool, a small playground, and an arcade. The Courtyard Café serves a buffet breakfast and an à la carte dinner. One child under 18 eats free with one paying adult. The comfortable lobby lounge has a big-screen television. Complimentary shuttles carry guests to the four Disney theme parks. Room rates range from $75 to $125; suites are $90 to $140, depending on the season. Howard Johnson Park Square Inn & Suites; 8501 Palm Pkwy.; Box 22818; Lake Buena Vista, FL 32830; 239-6900 or 800-635-8684.

Along U.S. 192

The properties along this multilane highway (also known as Irlo Bronson Memorial Highway), which intersects I-4 in the community of Kissimmee, are closer to Disney's theme parks than those accommodations along Orlando's International Drive. The area itself is less attractive and tends to be cluttered, but the motels west of I-4, near the so-called main gate to Walt Disney World, are well maintained. (The term main gate, by the way, is now fairly meaningless, since it originated when there was just one park, the Magic Kingdom.)

Most of the hostelries described here are within two miles of Walt Disney World and just minutes from a shopping center with a 24-hour grocery, a large drugstore, a one-hour dry cleaner, numerous eateries, and a tourist information kiosk. All are recommended for their value and convenience.

Room Service

In this country's largest hotel market, with more than 82,000 rooms, rarely is is there no room at the inn. Almost every type of accommodation, from the all-suite hotel to the bed-and-breakfast to the budget motel, is represented in the area—as is almost every major U.S. chain. But these categories (and even the number of rooms) do not include the profusion of rental condominiums, apartments, and single-family houses that are also available. By shopping around, you can find just what you need.

For more information, contact the Orlando/Orange County Convention & Visitors Bureau at 7208 Sand Lake Rd., Suite 300; Orlando, FL 32819; or call 363-5871. If you arrive in the area without secured lodging, go in person to the Official Visitor Information Center (8723 International Dr., Suite 101; 383-5872), and ask a staffer to check the "black book" for the day's best rates on available rooms. You have to show up in person for this service, but it can save you time and money.

For information about the properties along U.S. 192, you can also contact the Kissimmee–St. Cloud Convention and Visitors Bureau, Box 422007; Kissimmee, FL 34742-2007; 800-327-9159.

The following listings are arranged by standard room rates, from highest to lowest starting price. All offer nonsmoking rooms and accommodations for guests with disabilities.

HOLIDAY INN MAIN GATE EAST: Like its sister property, the Holiday Inn SunSpree in Lake Buena Vista, this 614-unit property, three miles from the World, was designed with families in mind. Each guestroom has a refrigerator, microwave, coffeemaker, ironing board, safe, and VCR. Kids have free use of sleeping bags. The whimsical Kidsuites give kids and their parents plenty of privacy, while the suites with a Murphy bed, sofa bed, and roomy kitchen and bar are also impressive. There are two large swimming

pools, a kiddie pool, two playgrounds, two lighted tennis courts, and an arcade, as well as a P.A.W. (Pets are Welcome) Program and even a Paw Park.

Camp Holiday, a supervised activity program for children 3 to 12, is a bargain at $2 per hour for the first child and $1 per hour for each additional child. It runs from 2 P.M. to 10 P.M. daily. For $5, parents can rent a beeper so they can always be reached. Kids receive free gifts and can be tucked into bed by the property's Holiday Hound mascots. Children under 12 eat free when accompanied by a paying adult. The Vineyard Café serves a breakfast buffet; snacks and light fare are available in the People's Choice Food Court; and the General Store sells groceries and snacks. Pizza delivery is available until midnight.

Free scheduled transportation to the four Disney theme parks is provided. Rooms are $65 to $130, depending on the season; add an additional $39 for Kidsuites or $75 for standard suites. Holiday Inn Hotel & Suites Main Gate East; 5678 Irlo Bronson Memorial Hwy.; Kissimmee, FL 34746; 396-4488 or 800-366-5437.

Marriott Maingate; 7675 W. Irlo Bronson Memorial Hwy.; Kissimmee, FL 34747; 396-4000 or 800-568-3352.

KNIGHTS INN MAINGATE: This revamped 121-room property is one of the best bargains along the U.S. 192 strip. The refurbished rooms, all on the ground floor, are spartan but functional, and the facilities include a heated pool, guest laundry, an attraction ticket sales counter, and an arcade. Complimentary shuttle service is provided to the four Disney theme parks. Rates are $32 to $64. Knights Inn Maingate; 7475 W. Irlo Bronson Memorial Hwy.; Kissimmee, FL 34746; 396-4200 or 800-944-0062.

ORLANDO/KISSIMMEE HOSTEL: The area's newest hostel opened in 1995 in a renovated motel on 2½ acres beside Lake Cecile, five miles from Walt Disney World. Besides dormitory rooms, it has rooms for families and couples, each with a private bath. The hostel also has a kitchen, laundry, common room, outdoor pool, tiled fountain, and picnic area, and provides pedal boats free for guests' enjoyment. Dorm rates are $13 to $16; private rooms are $29 to $49. Hostelling International Orlando/Kissimmee Resort Hostel; 4840 W. Irlo Bronson Memorial Hwy.; Kissimmee, FL 34746; 396-8282.

RAMADA PLAZA GATEWAY: This well-appointed 500-unit hotel (a Hilton property prior to December 1996) does a brisk meetings business, but it has not forgotten its leisure visitors. Each room has a small refrigerator, and the 147 luxury high-rise rooms feature microwaves. There are two outdoor pools (one heated), an exercise room, a guest laundry, an 18-hole putting green, and an arcade, as well as basketball and shuffleboard courts.

The Palms restaurant is open for breakfast and dinner (buffets are offered seasonally). Children under 13 eat free when accompanied by a paying adult. A self-service deli–snack bar offers a good variety of items for eating in or taking out, and free coffee and tea from 6 A.M. to 10 A.M. Entertainment takes place nightly in the Ficus lounge. The hotel boasts 24-hour security and is entered through a staffed gate. Complimentary shuttle service is provided to Walt Disney World. Rates range from $60 to $145 a night; suites start at $300. Ramada Plaza Hotel & Inn Gateway; 7470 W. Irlo Bronson Memorial Hwy.; Kissimmee, FL 34747; 396-4400 or 800-327-9170.

COURTYARD BY MARRIOTT MAINGATE: A major renovation in 1994 turned this 198-room motel into a sleek hostelry with an Art Deco–style lobby. Rooms feature electronic locks, safes, clock radios, and coffeemakers and supplies for tea making. Rooms with a king-size bed also have a small refrigerator and microwave. An outdoor pool, kiddie pool, small exercise room, arcade, gift shop, and guest laundry are available. The property's restaurant serves only breakfast, but the Tiki Bar at the pool offers sandwiches and light fare for lunch and dinner (children under 12 eat free). Pizza delivery is also available to all rooms. Free shuttle service is provided to the four Disney theme parks. Rates run from $59 to $109. Courtyard by

Gone Camping

The lush, cypress-hung woods of WDW's Fort Wilderness are unrivaled by any other Orlando-area campground. But not everyone can get a reservation or afford to stay there. As an alternative, consider the Kissimmee/Orlando KOA campground; 4771 W. Irlo Bronson Memorial Hwy. (U.S. 192 west); Kissimmee, FL 34746; 396-2400 or 800-562-7791. Only five miles east of I-4 and convenient to Walt Disney World, it has a heated pool, tennis court, miniature golf, shuffleboard, playground, arcade, laundry, hot showers, and a convenience store. Some good, inexpensive eateries are nearby. Besides tent and RV sites, there are 33 air-conditioned cabins that sleep four or six people. Free shuttle service to the Magic Kingdom is provided. Rates are $18 for tent sites; $28 to $33.50 for RV hookups. Rates are for two adults and any children under 18; $5 more for each additional adult.

On International Drive

Many well-known hotel, motel, and restaurant chains—and one of Orlando's finest hotels—are located on International Drive, or I-Drive, as it is known locally. Many more are clustered nearby on Sand Lake and Kirkman roads close to where they intersect I-Drive. This famous thoroughfare has two distinct sectors: the more orderly south end, which stretches from Sea World to the Orange County Convention Center and beyond it to Sand Lake Road, and the more cluttered north end, jammed with restaurants, T-shirt shops, and outlet stores.

Convenient I-Ride buses traverse I-Drive, stopping at most of the properties listed here. The fare is 85 cents (plus 10 cents for a transfer), with exact change required; children under 12 ride free.

The following listings are arranged by standard room rates, from the highest to the lowest starting price.

PEABODY ORLANDO: The sister property to the famed Peabody in Memphis, this 27-story, 891-room hotel is International Drive's most luxurious establishment. And, of course, there are the famous Peabody ducks, which every day at 11 A.M. waddle into the lobby, down a red carpet, then settle into a marble fountain—a spectacle that continues to attract visitors. They waddle back at about 5 P.M. Each of the Peabody's guestrooms has a hair dryer, two telephones, two televisions (including one in the bathroom), and turndown service on request. Facilities include a heated pool, four lighted tennis courts (lessons available), a pro shop, arcade, and health club with aerobics and personal trainers. Baby-sitting services are available.

Dux (where no duck is served) is the hotel's signature restaurant. Capriccio showcases northern Italian cuisine and mesquite-grilled specialties in an exhibition kitchen, and offers a champagne brunch on Sunday; and the B-Line Diner, the perfect re-creation of a fifties-style diner, serves entrées, sandwiches, and homemade confections 24 hours a day. Afternoon tea is served Monday through Friday in the Dux foyer. There are also four bars.

The Peabody hosts many of the groups attending meetings at the Orange County Convention Center, which is right across the street. The hotel's whimsical Double-Ducker bus provides shuttle service to the four Disney theme parks (for guests and the general public) for $7 round-trip. Rates range from $240 to $300 for standard rooms; $450 to $1,350 for suites. Peabody Orlando; 9801 International Dr.; Orlando, FL 32819; 352-4000 or 800-732-2639.

CLARION PLAZA: A good choice for its lively ambience, large outdoor heated pool, spacious rooms, and proximity to a shopping center and Orlando's Official Tourist Information Center, this 810-unit hotel is adjacent to the Orange County Convention Center. Each of the brightly colored rooms has a safe, and a separate vanity area; in-room movies are available. The property also has a whirlpool, an arcade, guest laundry, two restaurants, a baby-sitting service, and a business center.

Jack's Place serves steaks, seafood, and memorable desserts. Café Matisse provides buffet and à la carte meals, and Lite Bite is a convenient (24-hour) bakery-deli. Backstage, a 400-person capacity nightclub, stays open until 2 A.M. and features a deejay and a generously long happy hour daily. Shuttle service to Walt Disney World costs $11 round-trip. Rates for up to four people range from $135 to $155 for doubles, although special-value rates as low as $79 are usually available during select periods of the spring and fall; suites are $310 to $680. There's no charge for children under 18. Clarion Plaza; 9700 International Dr.; Orlando, FL 32819; 352-9700 or 800-627-8258.

EMBASSY SUITES INTERNATIONAL DRIVE SOUTH: Popular with families, this hotel has a lobby lined with gleaming marble, and a tropical atrium with waterfalls and a pond. The eight-floor property contains 143 king suites, 94 suites with two double beds, and 4 conference suites, and 1 two-bedroom suite. Each suite offers a private bedroom with a separate living/dining room, as well as a wet bar, coffeemaker, microwave, refrigerator, and sleeper sofa.

Facilities include indoor and outdoor swimming pools, and a whirlpool, sauna, steam room, health club, arcade, laundry, and gift shop. The hotel offers room service, car rental, and laundry and valet service. Its staff can arrange for baby-sitting and tickets for attractions and entertainment. The hotel has a restaurant and lounge; guests receive a full cooked-to-order breakfast and are invited to a complimentary cocktail reception daily. Free shuttle service to the four Disney theme parks is provided. Rates range from $119 to $179. Embassy Suites International Drive South; 8978 International Dr.; Orlando, FL 32819; 352-1400 or 800-433-7275; *http://www.embassy-suites.com.*

COUNTRY HEARTH INN: The rocking chairs on the porch make this the closest thing to a quaint inn you'll find on International Drive. The beautifully maintained property across the street from the convention center (though you'd hardly know it) *does* attract conventioneers, but it also maintains a loyal following among vacationers and wedding parties. A patterned tin ceiling, hardwood floors, and half a dozen chandeliers grace the lobby.

Each of the 150 renovated guestrooms has French doors, polished cherry furniture, colorful drapes and bedspreads, a veranda, cable television, a refrigerator, and a coffeemaker. Most have two double beds, although a few rooms have king-size beds. Movie rental is available. A good-size heated pool is nestled in a lush, landscaped courtyard, complete with gazebo (ask them how they got it).

The Country Parlor restaurant serves a complimentary continental breakfast, a Sunday champagne brunch, and an à la carte dinner. The inn also has room service and a popular cocktail lounge, the Front Porch. Rates range from $49 to $109. Country Hearth Inn; 9861 International Dr.; Orlando, FL 32819; 352-0008 or 800-447-1890.

WYNFIELD INN WESTWOOD: Weatherbeaten shutters give this three-story motel, which is right off International Drive, the look of an inn, and the landscaped grounds make it even more appealing. Each of the 300 rooms is pleasantly decorated and features two double beds, voice mail messaging, a separate vanity, a safe (for a nominal fee), and free local and 800-number calls. Request a poolside room to avoid expressway noise. An arcade is situated off the lobby and guests also enjoy a heated swimming pool. The pool bar serves beer, wine, soft drinks, and snacks. Although there is no restaurant on the premises, nearby restaurants offer a 10% discount. Complimentary shuttle to the four theme parks is provided. There are rooms specially equipped for travelers with disabilities. Nonsmoking rooms are available. Rates run from $68 to $98 and include coffee, tea, and fruit in the lobby each morning. Wynfield Inn Westwood; 6263 Westwood Blvd.; Orlando, FL 32821; 345-8000 or 800-346-1551.

Magic Kingdom

The Magic Kingdom is the most enchanting part of the World. Few who have visited it are disappointed, and even the most blasé travelers manage a smile. The sight of the soaring spires of Cinderella Castle, the gleaming woodwork of the Main Street shops, and the crescendo of music that follows the parades never fail to have their effect. Even when the crowds are large and the weather is hot, a visitor who has toured this wonderland dozens of times can still look around and think how satisfying this place is for the spirit.

What makes the Magic Kingdom timeless is its combination of the classic and the futuristic. Both childhood favorites and space-age creatures have a home here. Every "land" has a theme, carried through from the costumes worn by the hosts and hostesses and the food served in the restaurants to the merchandise sold in the shops, and even the design of the trash cans. Thousands of details contribute to the overall effect, and recognizing these touches makes any visit more enjoyable.

But the delight most guests experience upon first glimpse of the Magic Kingdom can disappear when disorientation sets in. There are so many bends to every pathway, so many sights and sounds clamoring for attention, it's too easy to wander aimlessly and miss the best the Magic Kingdom has to offer. So we earnestly suggest that you study this chapter before your visit.

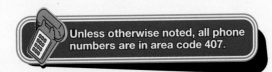

Unless otherwise noted, all phone numbers are in area code 407.

MAGIC KINGDOM

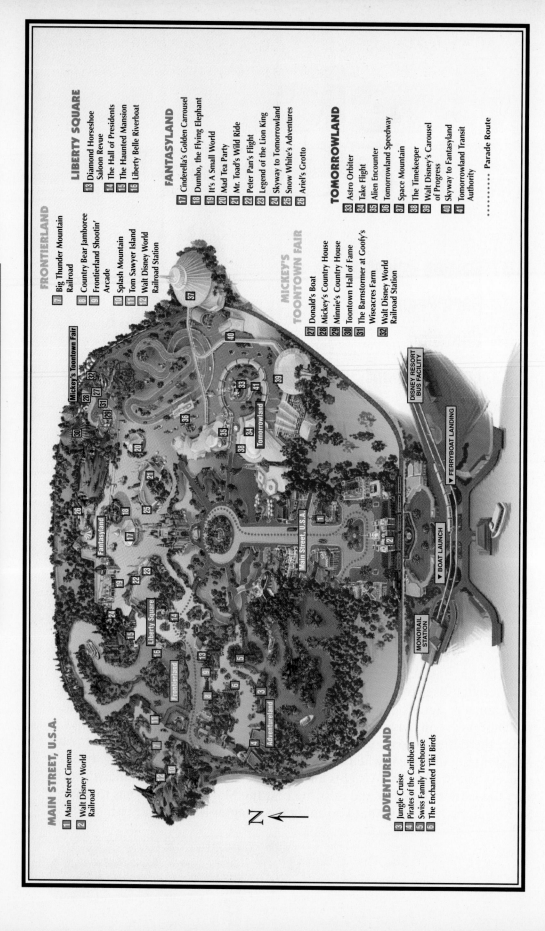

MAIN STREET, U.S.A.

1 Main Street Cinema
2 Walt Disney World Railroad

ADVENTURELAND

3 Jungle Cruise
4 Pirates of the Caribbean
5 Swiss Family Treehouse
6 The Enchanted Tiki Birds

FRONTIERLAND

7 Big Thunder Mountain Railroad
8 Country Bear Jamboree
9 Frontierland Shootin' Arcade
10 Splash Mountain
11 Tom Sawyer Island
12 Walt Disney World Railroad Station

LIBERTY SQUARE

13 Diamond Horseshoe Saloon Revue
14 The Hall of Presidents
15 The Haunted Mansion
16 Liberty Belle Riverboat

FANTASYLAND

17 Cinderella's Golden Carrousel
18 Dumbo, the Flying Elephant
19 It's A Small World
20 Mad Tea Party
21 Mr. Toad's Wild Ride
22 Peter Pan's Flight
23 Legend of the Lion King
24 Skyway to Tomorrowland
25 Snow White's Adventures
26 Ariel's Grotto

MICKEY'S TOONTOWN FAIR

27 Donald's Boat
28 Mickey's Country House
29 Minnie's Country House
30 Toontown Hall of Fame
31 The Barnstormer at Goofy's Wiseacres Farm
32 Walt Disney World Railroad Station

TOMORROWLAND

33 Astro Orbiter
34 Take Flight
35 Alien Encounter
36 Tomorrowland Speedway
37 Space Mountain
38 The Timekeeper
39 Walt Disney's Carousel of Progress
40 Skyway to Fantasyland
41 Tomorrowland Transit Authority

·········· Parade Route

86

GETTING ORIENTED

When you visit Walt Disney World's original theme park, it's vital to know the lay of the lands. The Magic Kingdom has seven "lands"—Main Street, U.S.A.; Adventureland; Frontierland; Liberty Square; Fantasyland; Mickey's Toontown Fair; and Tomorrowland. Main Street begins at Town Square, located just inside the park gates, and runs directly to Cinderella Castle. The area in front of the castle is known as the Central Plaza, or, more aptly, the Hub. Bridges over the several narrow waterways here serve as passages to each of the lands.

As you enter the park, the first bridge on your left goes to Adventureland; the next, to Liberty Square and Frontierland. On your right, the first bridge heads to Tomorrowland, the second to Fantasyland and Mickey's Toontown Fair. The end points of the pathways leading to the lands are linked by a street that is roughly circular, so that the layout of the Magic Kingdom resembles a wheel. All attractions, restaurants, and shops are found along the wheel's rim and spokes.

A note on north, south, east, and west: When you stand at the Magic Kingdom entrance and face Cinderella Castle, you're looking north. Main Street, U.S.A., is straight ahead, with Fantasyland and Mickey's Toontown Fair beyond the castle. Adventureland, Liberty Square, and Frontierland are to the west. Tomorrowland flanks the Hub on the east.

HOW TO GET THERE

Take Exit 25 off I-4. Continue about four miles to the Auto Plaza and park; walk or take a tram to the main entrance complex, known as the Transportation and Ticket Center (TTC). Choose a five-minute ferry ride or a slightly shorter trip by monorail for the last leg of an anticipation-filled journey.
By WDW Transportation: From the Grand Floridian, Contemporary, and Polynesian: monorail (Contemporary also has a walkway).

From Epcot: monorail to the TTC, then transfer to the Magic Kingdom monorail or ferry. From the Disney-MGM Studios, Animal Kingdom, Downtown Disney, and the resorts on Hotel Plaza Blvd.: buses to the TTC, then transfer to ferry or monorail. From Fort Wilderness and the Wilderness Lodge: boats. From all other WDW resorts: buses.

PARKING

All-day parking at the Magic Kingdom is $5 for day visitors (free to WDW resort guests with presentation of resort ID). Simply bear left shortly after passing through the Auto Plaza; attendants will direct you into one of a dozen lots, all named after Disney characters. Minnie, Sleepy, and Dopey are within walking distance of the TTC; other lots are served by trams. Be sure to note the section and aisle in which you park. Also, know that the parking ticket allows for reentry to the parking area throughout the day.

HOURS

The Magic Kingdom is generally open from 9 A.M. to 7 P.M. However, during busy seasons, it is open later than usual. It's best to plan on reaching the park entrance at least half an hour before the posted opening time. Another way to avoid the morning crush is to put off your visit until 1 P.M. or later. Call 824-4321 for up-to-the-minute schedules.

GETTING AROUND

Walt Disney World Railroad steam trains make a 21-minute loop of the park, stopping to pick up and discharge passengers at stations on the edge of Main Street, Frontierland, and Mickey's Toontown Fair. Horseless carriages, a fire engine, and horse-drawn trolleys take turns offering one-way trips down Main Street. And while the Skyway aerial tram is not necessarily the quickest commute between Tomorrowland and Fantasyland, the five-minute ride nets a fine bird's-eye view of the park.

Early Sunday morning ranks as the most peaceful time to visit the Magic Kingdom.

PARK PRIMER

BABY FACILITIES

The best place in the Magic Kingdom to take care of little ones' needs is the Baby Care Center. This center, equipped with changing tables and facilities for nursing mothers, is located at the Hub end of Main Street next to the Crystal Palace restaurant. Disposable diapers are kept behind the counter at many Magic Kingdom shops; just ask. Restrooms are also equipped with baby facilities.

CAMERA NEEDS

The Kodak Camera Center on Main Street proffers disposable cameras as well as the requisite film and batteries. It also rents camcorders ($30 per day, with a $450 refundable deposit). Two-hour film processing is available here and wherever you see a Photo Express sign. Film is also sold in most Magic Kingdom shops.

DISABILITY INFORMATION

Most shops and restaurants, and many attractions, are accessible to guests in wheelchairs. Convenient parking is reserved for guests with disabilities. Special provisions have been made to enhance sight- and hearing-impaired guests' enjoyment of the park. The *Walt Disney World Guidebook for Guests with Disabilities* is available at City Hall. For more information, refer to the "Travelers with Disabilities" section of the *Getting Ready to Go* chapter.

EARLY-ENTRY DAYS

On Monday, Thursday, and Saturday, guests staying at WDW resorts may enter the Magic Kingdom 1½ hours before the official opening time to enjoy Space Mountain and Fantasyland attractions. Early-entry days and attractions are subject to change.

FERRY VS. MONORAIL

For guests arriving by car or bus, it's necessary to decide whether to travel to the Magic Kingdom by ferry or monorail. The monorail makes the trip from the Transportation and Ticket Center (TTC) to the Magic Kingdom in a bit less than the five minutes required by the ferries. However, the ferry will often get you there more quickly during the busier seasons, because long lines can form at the monorail; most people simply don't make the short extra walk to the ferry landing. When the lines are short, the monorail is your best choice. Vacationers who use wheelchairs should note that while the monorail platforms are accessible, the ramp leading to the boarding area is a bit steep.

FIRST AID

A registered nurse tends to minor medical problems at the First Aid Center, located near the Crystal Palace restaurant at the Hub end of Main Street.

INFORMATION

City Hall, located just inside the park entrance in the cul-de-sac known as Town Square, serves as the park's informal information headquarters. Guest Relations representatives here can answer any questions about the Magic Kingdom. Park guidemaps, updated weekly, (including details about the day's entertainment, as well as character greeting times and locations) are available here, and all kinds of arrangements can be made, including priority seating for full-service restaurants.

LOCKERS

Attended lockers are conveniently located underneath the Main Street Railroad Station just inside the park entrance. Lockers are also available on the west side of the TTC and beside the bus parking lot on the TTC's east side. Cost is $3 per day (plus a $2 refundable deposit) for unlimited use. Items too big to fit into the larger units can be checked at the Guest Relations windows at the main entrance to the Magic Kingdom.

LOST & FOUND

On the day of your visit, report lost articles at City Hall or at the TTC. Recovered items can also be claimed at these locations. After your visit, call 824-4245.

LOST CHILDREN

Report lost children at City Hall or the Baby Care Center, or alert a Disney employee to the problem.

MONEY MATTERS

The Magic Kingdom has three ATMs: one under the train station on Main Street, another near The Enchanted Tiki Birds in Adventureland, and a third at the Tomorrowland Light & Power Co. (the arcade at Space Mountain's exit). Foreign currency exchange is available at City Hall from 9 A.M. to 4 P.M.

Credit cards (American Express, Visa, Master-Card, and The Disney Credit Card) are accepted as payment for admission, merchandise, and meals at all full restaurants and fast-food locations. Traveler's checks and WDW resort ID cards are also accepted. Only cash is accepted at food carts.

Disney Dollars are available at City Hall in colorful $1, $5, and $10 denominations. They are accepted for dining and merchandise throughout Walt Disney World. They can be exchanged at any time for U.S. currency; however, many visitors opt to keep some as inexpensive souvenirs.

PACKAGE PICKUP

Individual shops can arrange for large or heavy purchases to be transported to a location next to Main Street's Emporium for pickup after noon and until two hours before the Magic Kingdom closes. The service is available free of charge. (Disney resort guests may have packages delivered to their rooms at no extra charge.)

SAME-DAY REENTRY

Be sure to have your hand stamped and to retain your ticket upon exiting the park if you plan to return later the same day.

STROLLERS & WHEELCHAIRS

Stroller and Wheelchair Rental, on the right, inside the Magic Kingdom entrance, offers one-day rentals of strollers, wheelchairs, and Electric Convenience Vehicles (ECVs). The cost for strollers and wheelchairs is $5, with a $1 refundable deposit; $30 for ECVs, with a $10 refundable deposit. Quantities are limited. Remember to keep your rental receipt; it can be used on the same day to obtain a replacement stroller or wheelchair at Epcot, the Disney-MGM Studios, Animal Kingdom, or here at the Magic Kingdom.

TIP BOARD

Located at the end of Main Street, U.S.A., closest to Cinderella Castle, the "Main Street Gazette" Tip Board is an excellent source of information on waiting times for the most popular attractions, as well as showtimes and other entertainment information. Check here throughout the day and make your plans accordingly.

Admission Prices

ONE-DAY TICKET

(Restricted to use only in the Magic Kingdom. Prices include sales tax and are subject to change.)

Adult..$42.14
Child*.......................................$33.92

*3 to 9 years of age; children under 3 free

MAIN STREET, U.S.A.

This is the Disney version of turn-of-the-century small-town Main Streets all over the country—freshly painted, full of curlicued gingerbread moldings and pretty details—and, with its baskets of hanging plants and genuine-looking gaslights, a showplace both in the bright light of high noon and after nightfall, when the tiny lights edging all of Main Street's rooflines are flicked on.

The street represents an ideal American town. Although such a town never really existed, many towns claim to have served as the inspiration for it. Chances are Walt Disney got the idea from Marceline, Missouri, the tiny rural town that was his boyhood home.

What's particularly amazing about Main Street, U.S.A., is that the full variety of furbelows and frills that a real, growing Main Street might have enjoyed has been assimilated into the Disney version. Most of the structures along the thoroughfare are given over to shops, and each one is different, from the wallpaper and layout of displays to style of chandelier, even lighting level. Some emporiums are big and bustling, others are relatively quiet and orderly; some are spacious and airy, others are cozy and dark. Inside and out, maintenance and housekeeping are superb. White-suited sanitation workers patrol the street to pick up litter and quickly shovel up any droppings from the horses that pull the trolley cars from Town Square to the Hub. As in the rest of the Magic Kingdom, the pavement here is washed down every night with fire hoses. There's one crew of maintenance workers whose sole job is to change the little white lights around the roofs; another crew devotes itself to keeping the woodwork painted. As soon as these people have worked their way as far as the Hub, they start all over again at Town Square. The greenish, horse-shaped cast-iron hitching posts are repainted 20 times a year on average—and totally scraped down each time. It's no wonder that professional painters who visit marvel at the quality of work they see.

Some visitors find these details so fascinating it takes them a good deal longer than the 40 minutes spent by the average guest to get from one end of Main Street to the other. There are only three real "attractions" along Main Street, U.S.A., and they are relatively minor compared to the really big deals such as Tomorrowland's Space Mountain, Frontierland's Splash Mountain, or the Haunted Mansion in Liberty Square. But each and every shop has its own quota of merchandise that is meant as much for show as for sale. It's almost as entertaining to watch the cooks stir up batches of peanut brittle at the Main Street Confectionery as it is to actually savor a sweet sample. The shop windows, particularly at the Emporium, are also worth a look.

Before heading toward Cinderella Castle, stop at City Hall for a guidemap listing the times and places where live entertainment is scheduled to take place that day.

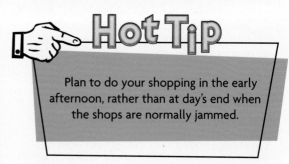

Plan to do your shopping in the early afternoon, rather than at day's end when the shops are normally jammed.

Once you start to meander along Main Street, note the names on the second-story windows. Above Crystal Arts are the names of Roy Disney, Walt's brother, and, Patty Disney, Roy's wife; above The Shadow Box, that of Dick Nunis, chairman of Walt Disney Attractions. And you'll see Walt's name above the ice cream parlor. Other names are also those of people connected with the Walt Disney Company.

Note: Attractions in Main Street, U.S.A., are described in the order that they are encountered upon entering the park.

WALT DISNEY WORLD RAILROAD: The best introduction to the layout of the Magic Kingdom, the 1½-mile, 21-minute journey on this rail line is as much a must for the first-time visitor as it is for railroad buffs. For the former, it offers an excellent orientation, as it passes through Adventureland and Frontierland and skirts Fantasyland, Mickey's Toontown Fair, and Tomorrowland. The trains make stops here on Main Street and at the Frontierland and Mickey's Toontown Fair stations.

The 1928 steam engine happens to be exactly the same age as Mickey Mouse. Aficionados of railroadiana may remember that Disney himself was among their number—and perhaps, during the early years of television, saw films of him circling his own backyard in a one-eighth-scale train, the *Lilly Belle*, named for his wife. The Walt Disney World Railroad also has a *Lilly Belle* among its quartet of locomotives. The others

are named *Roy O. Disney*, *Walter E. Disney*, and *Roger E. Broggie* (a Disney Imagineer who shared Walt Disney's enthusiasm for antique trains). All of them were built in the United States around the turn of the century and later taken to Mexico to haul freight and passengers in the Yucatán, where Disney scouts found them in 1969. The United Railways of Yucatán was using them to carry sugarcane. Brought north once again, they were completely overhauled, and even the smallest parts were reworked or replaced.

MAIN STREET VEHICLES: A number of these can be seen traveling up and down Main Street—horseless carriages and jitneys patterned after turn-of-the-century vehicles (but fitted out with Jeep transmissions and special mufflers that make the putt-putt-putting sound); a spiffy scarlet fire engine, which is on display near the Firehouse adjoining City Hall when not in operation; and a troop of trolleys drawn by Belgians

and Percherons, two strong breeds of horse that once pulled plows in Europe. These animals—between six and ten years old, weighing in at about a ton each, and shod with plastic (easier on their hooves)—pull the trolley the length of Main Street about two dozen times during each of their three to four working days; afterward, they're sent back to their homes at the barn at the Fort Wilderness campground.

MAIN STREET CINEMA: The beauty of this prominent Main Street attraction is that most vacationers bypass it in their rush to get to Space Mountain in Tomorrowland, Pirates of the Caribbean in Adventureland, or other thrill-a-minute attractions. Yet on a steamy summer afternoon—when everyone else is standing in line for these blockbusters—this air-conditioned theater is a fine place to cool off. The feature attraction is *Mickey's Big Break*, a ten-minute film that shows how Mickey is chosen for his first starring role. As the story goes, Mickey is one of many actors auditioning for a part in *Steamboat Willie*, the first sound cartoon. Talent agents make their choice—and the rest is history. A vintage Disney cartoon follows the film. There are so many Mickey classics that it's impossible to predict what will be airing and when. But rest assured, *Steamboat Willie* is on the list of those shown. The groundbreaking cartoon was first released on November 18, 1928, a date that has since become known as Mickey Mouse's birthday. (By the way, Mickey was originally going to be named Mortimer, but Lillian Disney convinced her husband to make the change.)

ADVENTURELAND

Adventureland seems to have even more atmosphere than the other lands. That may be a result of its neat separation from the rest of the Magic Kingdom by the bridge over Main Street on one end and by a gallerylike structure (where it merges with Frontierland) on the other; or possibly it's because of the abundance of landscaping. There are Canary Island date palms, small Cape Sable palms, as well as pygmy date palms, and more. On the Adventureland bridge alone, visitors see Cape honeysuckle from South Africa, flame vines from Mexico, bougainvillea from Brazil, and hibiscus from China, to name just some of the flora.

As for the architecture, although it derives from areas as diverse as the Caribbean, Polynesia, and Southeast Asia, it gives one the sense of being in a single place, a nowhere-in-particular that is both familiar and distinctly foreign, smacking of island idylls and tropical splendor. Shops offer imports from India, Thailand, Hong Kong, Africa, and the Caribbean islands.

As guests stroll away from Main Street, they hear the sound of beating drums, the squawks of parrots, the regular boom of a cannon. Paces quicken. And the wonders soon to be encountered do not disappoint.

Note: The Adventureland attractions are described in the order that they are encountered upon entering the land from the Hub and heading away from Cinderella Castle.

SWISS FAMILY TREEHOUSE: "Everything we need right at our fingertips," said the father in Disney's 1960 rendition of the classic story *Swiss Family Robinson*. He was describing the treehouse that he and his kids built for the family after their ship was wrecked in a storm. When given a chance—several adventures later—to leave the island, all but one son decided to stay on. That decision is not hard to understand after a tour of the Magic Kingdom's version of the Robinsons' banyan-tree home. This is everybody's idea of the perfect treehouse, with its many levels and many comforts—patchwork quilts, lovely mahogany furniture, candles stuck in abalone shells, even running water in every room. (The system is ingenious.)

The Spanish moss draping the branches is real; the tree itself—unofficially christened *Disneyodendron eximus*, a genus that is translated roughly as "out-of-the-ordinary Disney tree"—was constructed entirely by the props department. Some statistics: The roots, which are of concrete, poke 42 feet into the ground; and some 300,000 lifelike polyethylene leaves "grow" on 1,400 branches, which stretch some 90 feet in diameter. "Boy, Dad sure went out on a limb for that one," quipped a Disney prop worker's son on hearing of his father's task.

JUNGLE CRUISE: Inspired in part by the 1955 documentary *The African Lion*, this ten-minute adventure is one of the crowning achievements of Magic Kingdom landscape artists for the way it takes guests through surroundings as diverse as a Southeast Asian jungle, the Nile Valley, and an Amazon rain forest. Along the way, passengers encounter zebras, giraffes, lions, impalas, vultures, and headhunters (all of the Audio-Animatronics variety); they also see elephants bathing, and tour a Cambodian temple—all while listening to an amusing, though corny, spiel delivered by the skipper. (Bet you didn't know that Schweitzer Falls was named after the famous doctor Albert . . . Falls.)

For most passengers, this is all just in fun. Gardeners, however, are always especially impressed by the variety of species coexisting in such a small area. To keep some of the more sensitive of subtropical specimens alive, gas-fired heaters and electric fans concealed in the rocks pump hot air into the jungle when temperatures fall to 36 degrees (a rarity). This adventure, which is best enjoyed by daylight, is one of the Magic Kingdom's more popular attractions, and it tends to be crowded from late morning until late afternoon.

As you exit the attraction, consider trying your hand at navigating your own miniature jungle boat at Shrunken Ned's Junior Jungle Boats. Note that park admission passes do not include use of the boats; there is an additional charge here.

THE ENCHANTED TIKI BIRDS: The first of the Audio-Animatronics attractions, this one laid the foundation for others such as Great Moments with Mr. Lincoln at the 1964–65 New York World's Fair. Introduced at Disneyland in 1963, the 17-minute show features four emcees—José, Michael, Pierre, and Fritz—plus some 225 birds, flowers, and tiki statues singing and whistling up a tropical storm. The attraction, which has been showing signs of age, is undergoing extensive refurbishment. When it reopens in spring 1998, it will have a spiffy new look, zippy new tunes, and a couple of new faces—Iago (Jafar's partner-in-crime in *Aladdin*) and Zazu (from the *The Lion King*).

PIRATES OF THE CARIBBEAN: One of the very best of the Magic Kingdom's classic adventures, this ten-minute cruise is a Disneyland original, added to Walt Disney World's Magic Kingdom (in revised form) due to popular demand. Here guests board a simple boat and set sail for a series of scenes depicting a pirate raid on a Caribbean island town, dodging cannon fire and weathering one small, though legitimate, watery dip along the way.

There are exploding flowerpots, drunken pigs whose legs actually twitch in the porkers' soporific contentment, and kittens and chickens that look for all the world like the real thing (even when seen at close range); the observant will note that the leg of one resident swashbuckler, dangled over the edge of a bridge, is hairy. Each pirate's face has remarkable personality. While it's not the most politically correct attraction on property, the rendition of "Yo Ho, Yo Ho; a Pirate's Life for Me"—the attraction's theme song—makes what is actually a rather brutal scenario into something that comes across as good fun. Before entering the queue area, stop and give a nod to the parrot dressed in the pirate costume, near the Pirates of the Caribbean sign.

FRONTIERLAND

With the Rivers of America lapping at its borders and Big Thunder Mountain rising up in the rear, this re-creation of the American Frontier encompasses the area from New England to the Southwest, from the 1770s to the 1880s. Hosts and hostesses wear denim, calf-length cutoffs, long skirts, or similar garb. Additionally, the shops, restaurants, and attractions have unpainted barn siding or stone or clapboard walls, and outside there are several wooden sidewalks of the sort Marshal Matt Dillon used to stride along. Near Pecos Bill Café, the landscape seems desert-like, with mesquite trees providing a pleasant respite from the sun.

Note: Attractions are described as they are encountered upon entering the land from the Hub, heading away from Cinderella Castle.

DIAMOND HORSESHOE SALOON REVUE: This hour-long show, presented in an elaborate re-creation of a western dance hall saloon, is the kind of gig that makes sophisticated folk laugh in spite of themselves. The jokes range from silly to absolutely preposterous, yet seldom fall flat, thanks to the enthusiastic efforts of the talented crew of singers and dancers who perform here several times each day. Reservations are not required and guests may drop in at any point during the performance. For those who want to snack between laughs, there is also a fast-food counter here. See *Good Meals, Great Times* for more details.

FRONTIERLAND SHOOTIN' ARCADE: This arcade is set in an 1850s town in the Southwest Territory. Gun positions overlook Boothill, a town complete with bank, jail, hotel, and cemetery. But silver bullets have given way to infrared beams at the completely electronic shooting arcade. Genuine Hawkins .54-caliber buffalo rifles have been refitted, and when an infrared beam strikes any of the 97 reactive targets, a humorous result is triggered. Struck tombstones rise, sink, spin, or change their epitaphs; hit the cloud and a ghost rider gallops across the sky; a bull's-eye on a gravedigger's shovel causes a skull to pop out of the grave. Sound effects—howling coyotes, creaking bridges, and shooting guns—are created by a digital audio system. Note that admission passes do not include use of Frontierland Shootin' Arcade; there is an additional charge here.

COUNTRY BEAR JAMBOREE: An occasional determined sophisticate will remain impervious to the charms of this country-and-western hoedown in the big stone-walled Grizzly Hall. But for many guests, with the exception of the 10-to-18 crowd, it's an old favorite. Ostensibly concocted by one Ursus H. Bear after an especially inspiring hibernation season, it is performed by a cast of life-size Audio-Animatronics bruins.

Here, Henry, the debonair seven-foot-tall master of ceremonies, introduces the Five Bear Rugs (a country-and-western plinking group made up of Zeke, Zeb, Ted, Fred, and Tennessee). A big-bodied, tiny-headed pianist named Gomer plays while the girthy Trixie sings "Tears Will Be the Chaser for Your Wine." Teddi Barra floats down from the ceiling crooning "He Doesn't Know the Heart He's Breakin.'" Bubbles, Bunny, and Beulah, in sweet harmony, sing "All the Guys That Turn Me On Turn Me Down." Assorted other bruins entertain, including Liver Lips McGrowl and Big Al, one of the few Audio-Animatronics figures with a fan following.

Because the 17-minute Country Bear Jamboree is a popular attraction, lines can get long during busy periods. It's worth noting, however, that huge groups of people are admitted together so that once a line starts moving, it dwindles fast. Seats in the rear of the house are just as good as seats toward the front, if not a little better.

TOM SAWYER ISLAND: This small patch of land in the middle of the Rivers of America has hills to scramble up, a working windmill, Harper's Mill, with an owl in the rafters and a perpetually creaky waterwheel, and a pitch-black (and scary) cave. To get to the island, guests take a raft across the river.

Dirt paths wind this way and that, and it's easy to get disoriented, especially the first time around. There are also two bridges—an old-fashioned suspension bridge and a so-called barrel bridge, which floats atop some lashed-together wooden barrels. When

one person bounces, everybody lurches—and all but the most chickenhearted laugh. Both bridges are easy to miss, so keep your eyes peeled and ask an employee for directions if the path eludes you.

Across the suspension bridge is Fort Longhorn, where there is a guardhouse in which the Audio-Animatronics figure of a ratty-looking drunk is snoring off his last bender, accompanied by a mangy dog, chickens, and horses. On the second floor of the fort, there are about a dozen air guns for youngsters to fire in a ceaseless cacophony. This area offers a fine view across the Rivers of America to Big Thunder Mountain Railroad. Keep poking around and you'll find the twisting, dark, and occasionally scary escape tunnel out of the fort. Walk along the pathway on the banks of the Rivers of America and you're back at the bridges.

The whole island seems as rugged as backwoods Missouri, and, probably as a result, it actually feels a lot more remote than it is—enough to be able to provide some welcome respite from the bustle.

One particularly pleasant way to pass an hour here is over lemonade and a snack on the porch at Aunt Polly's Dockside Inn. While adults in the party are giving their feet some rest, watching the stern-wheelers plying the Rivers of America, kids can go out and burn up some more energy. Restrooms are located at the main raft landing and inside Fort Longhorn. Note that this attraction closes at dusk.

SPLASH MOUNTAIN: On the day this attraction made its official 1992 Walt Disney World debut, *everyone* got soaked—thanks in part to a particularly potent Florida rain cloud. But the rain wasn't entirely responsible for the sea of soggy Magic Kingdom guests. The five-story drop into an aqueous briar patch was. And a steady stream of thrill seekers have been taking the plunge ever since.

In this guaranteed smile-inducer, guests are escorted on a waterborne journey through brightly colored swamps and bayous, down waterfalls, and finally, over the top of a steep spillway, hurtling them from the peak of the mountain to a briar-laced pond five stories below. Splash Mountain is based on the animated sequences in Walt Disney's 1946 film *Song of the South*. The scenery entertains as the story line follows Brer Rabbit through a variety of exploits as he tries to reach his "laughin' place." It's tough for a first-time rider to take in all the details, since the tension of waiting for the big drop is all-consuming.

There are three relatively tame drops during the 11-minute trip, all leading up to the big fall—a 52-foot drop at a 45-degree angle at a top speed of 40 miles per hour—the steepest flume in the world. It is a bit terrifying at the top, but once back on the ground, it seems most riders can't wait for another trip—even though they may get drenched! (Water-wary guests are often seen wearing rain ponchos on this attraction. On the other hand, if you *want* to get wet, try to sit up front; seats in the back provide a smaller splash.)

By the second or third time around, it's possible to relax a bit, enjoy the interior scenes, and take in the spectacular views of the Magic Kingdom from the top of the mountain. At this point you may even manage to keep your eyes open for the duration of the final fall—or at least part of it.

Splash Mountain's designers not only borrowed characters and color-saturated settings from *Song of the South* but also used quite a bit of the film's Academy Award–winning music in this attraction. As a matter of fact, the song in Splash Mountain's final scene, "Zip-A-Dee-Doo-Dah," has become something of a Disney anthem over the years.

Note: You must be at least 40 inches tall to ride Splash Mountain.

Birnbaum's Best

BIG THUNDER MOUNTAIN RAILROAD:
This attraction, located partly inside the
redstone mountain that pokes into the sky
behind the Tom Sawyer Island rafts landing,
is something of a cross between the Pirates
of the Caribbean (a tame but visually exciting boat tour) and Space Mountain (an
honest-to-goodness roller coaster). As any
true coaster buff could tell you, this four-
minute ride is relatively mild despite the
posted warnings; the thrills are there, but
the experience is unlikely to scare the living
daylights out of you. The swoops and curves
along the 2,780 feet of track provide a rush
of adrenaline that's more pleasant than
heart-pounding.

As with Pirates of the Caribbean, every
trip through Big Thunder yields new sights.
Don't miss the bats, waterfalls, and best of
all, Tumbleweed, the flooded mining town.
Look for about 20 Audio-Animatronics figures here—including chickens, donkeys,
possums, a goat, a long john–clad resident
spinning through the flood in a bathtub,
and a rainmaker whose name is Professor
Cumulus Isobar. Careful observers will
note a party going on in a not-yet-
swamped second-story room of a saloon,
whose weathered look (like that of some
other sections of the Magic Kingdom)
comes from a judicious mixture of plant
food and paint.

The $300,000 worth of real antique mining
equipment sprinkled around the attraction's
2½ acres—including an ore-hauling wagon,
a double-stamp ore crusher, and an old ball
mill used to extract gold from ore—were
picked up at auctions all over the Southwest,
at less than bargain prices, since the high
price of gold and the resulting profitability of
small-scale mining operations had boosted
demand by miners themselves.

The summit of the mountain is entirely
Disney-made. It was in the planning for
some 15 years and under construction for 2.
Hundreds of rock makers contributed,
applying multiple coats of cement and paint,
throwing stones and kicking dirt on it, and
banging on it with sticks and picks to make
it resemble the rocks of Monument Valley,
Utah—that is, as if Mother Nature had created it. The area inside the mountain that
does not house the tunnels of the ride itself
is occupied by machinery—pumps, electronic equipment, and part of the computer
that runs the show. The total cost was about
$17 million, which, give or take a few mil-
lion, was as much as it cost to build all of
California's Disneyland in 1955. You must
be at least 40 inches tall to ride.

Note on Timing: Some aspects of the ride
are more convincing after dark. Try to experience it first at night, then have a second
go-round by the light of day. The trip is
extremely popular, so plan to take it in during the 9 P.M. running of SpectroMagic (in
season), or just before park closing, when
lines are generally shorter. By day, go during
the early-morning hours.

LIBERTY SQUARE

The transition between Frontierland on one side and Fantasyland on the other is so smooth that it's hard to say just when you arrive at Liberty Square, yet ultimately there's no mistaking the location. The small buildings are clapboard or brick and topped with weather vanes; the decorative moldings are Federal or Georgian in style; the glass is sometimes wavy, and there are flower boxes in shop windows, brightly colored gardens, neatly trimmed borders of Japanese yew, and masses of azaleas in a number of varieties and shades of white, pink, and red. There are a number of good shops, most notably The Yankee Trader and Ye Olde Christmas Shoppe; plus two of the park's most popular attractions, The Haunted Mansion and The Hall of Presidents; and the Liberty Tree Tavern, one of the most charming full-service restaurants in the Magic Kingdom.

Liberty Square is also home to one of the most delightful nooks in all the Magic Kingdom—the small, secluded area just behind Ye Olde Christmas Shoppe. There are tables with umbrellas, plenty of benches, and big trees to provide shade—and the sound of the crowds seems a million miles away.

Note: Liberty Square attractions are described in the order they are encountered upon entering the land from the Hub and heading away from Cinderella Castle.

THE LIBERTY TREE: This live oak (*Quercus virginiana*), not an attraction per se, recalls the trees on which the Sons of Liberty hung lanterns after the Boston Tea Party of 1773. It was found on the southern edge of the Walt Disney World property, and then moved to its present site in one of the more complex of the Magic Kingdom's landscaping operations.

Since the tree was so large, lifting it by cable was out of the question—the cable would have sliced through the bark and injured the tree. Instead, two holes were drilled through the sturdiest section of the trunk; the holes were fitted with dowels, and a 100-ton crane lifted the tree by these rods, which were then replaced with the original wood plugs. Unfortunately, the wood plugs had become contaminated. To save the tree, the plugs were again removed, the diseased areas were cleaned out, the holes were filled with cement, and a young oak was grafted onto the tree at its base, where it grows even today. Careful observers will be able to spot the plugs and the portions of the trunk that were damaged. The 13 lanterns hanging on the branches represent the 13 original states.

THE HALL OF PRESIDENTS: This is not one of those laugh-a-minute attractions, like Pirates of the Caribbean or the Country Bear Jamboree; it's long on patriotism and short on humor. But the detail of this 20-minute show certainly is fascinating. After a film (presented on a sweeping 70 mm screen) discusses the importance of the Constitution from the time of its framing through the dawn of the space age, the curtain goes up on what some guests have mistakenly called the "Hall of Haunted Presidents." A portion of today's Hall of Presidents presentation derives from the Disney-designed Illinois Pavilion's exhibition Great Moments with Mr. Lincoln, from New York's 1964–65 World's Fair.

At the Magic Kingdom show, Bill Clinton and Abraham Lincoln have speaking roles. All 42 chief executives are announced in a roll call and each responds with a nod; careful observers will note the others swaying and nodding, fidgeting, and even whispering to each other during the proceedings.

Costumes were created by two famous film tailors coaxed out of retirement. Not only are the styles those of the period in which each president lived, but so are the tailoring techniques and the fabrics. Some had to be specially woven for the purpose. Each of the Audio-Animatronics figures has at least one change of clothes; jewelry, shoes, hair texture, and even George Washington's chair are all re-created exactly as indicated by careful research of paintings, diaries, newspapers, and government archives. Perceptive viewers should be able to see the braces on Franklin Delano Roosevelt's legs. The effect is so lifelike that the figures look almost real, even at very close range.

LIBERTY BELLE RIVERBOAT: The *Liberty Belle*, built in dry dock at Walt Disney World, is a real steamboat. Its boiler turns water into steam, which is then piped to the engine, which drives the paddle wheel that propels the boat. It is not the real article in one respect, however: It moves through the half-mile-long, nine-foot-deep Rivers of America on an underwater rail. The pleasant 17-minute ride is a good way to beat the heat on steamy afternoons. En route, a variety of props create a sort of Wild West effect: moose, deer, cabins on fire, and the like. From park opening until 3:30 P.M., the *Liberty Belle* offers opportunities to cruise the Rivers of America with Disney characters. Check a guidemap for details.

THE HAUNTED MANSION: This eight-minute experience is among the Magic Kingdom's most enjoyable. However, guests who expect to be scared silly when they enter the big old house, modeled after those built by the Dutch in the Hudson River Valley in the 18th century, will be a tad unfulfilled. In deference to the small children and other easily frightened souls who tour the Magic Kingdom every day, The Haunted Mansion steers clear of anything too terrifying, and a pleasant voice-over—your ghost host—keeps the mood light. Once inside the portrait hall, which you enter after passing through the front doors, it's amusing to speculate: Is the ceiling moving up—or is the floor dropping? (It's one way here, and the other way at The Haunted Mansion in California's Disneyland.)

You begin the spooky journey through the mansion by settling into a "doom buggy." The attraction is full of tricks and treats for the eyes; just when you think you've seen it all, there's something new: bats' eyes on the wallpaper; a plaque that reads "Tomb, Sweet Tomb"; a suit of armor that comes alive; a terrified cemetery watchman and his mangy mutt; and the image of a creepy lady in a crystal ball.

One of the biggest jobs of the maintenance crews here is not cleaning up, but keeping things dirty. Since the mansion is littered with some 200 trunks, chairs, dress forms, harps, rugs, and assorted other knickknacks, it requires a lot of dust. This is purchased by the five-pound bagful and distributed by a device that looks as if it were meant to spread grass seed—sort of a vacuum cleaner in reverse. Local legend has it that enough dust has been used since the park's 1971 opening to bury the mansion. (Which begs the question: Where did it all go?) Cobwebs are bought in liquid form and strung up by a secret process.

When waiting to enter, take note of the amusing inscriptions on the tombstones in the overgrown cemetery.

FANTASYLAND

Walt Disney called this a "timeless land of enchantment," and his successors term it "the happiest land of all"—and it is, for some. Although it's not precisely a kiddieland, it is the home of a number of rides that are particularly well liked by children. The nursery rhyme cadences of "It's A Small World" appeals to them, as do the bright colors of the trash baskets, the flowers, and the tentlike rooftops; and they delight in the fairy-tale architecture and ambience, reminiscent of a king's castle courtyard during a particularly lively fair. Fantasyland is also one of the most heavily trafficked areas of the park. Parents of young children should note that many attractions are dark, and in some cases the special effects may be too intense.

Note: Fantasyland attractions are described in the order that they are encountered upon entering the land via Cinderella Castle and proceeding roughly clockwise through the land.

CINDERELLA CASTLE: Just as the amiable mouse named Mickey stands for all the merriment in Walt Disney World, this storybook castle represents the hopes and dreams of childhood—a time in life when anything seems possible.

At a height of about 180 feet, Cinderella Castle is nearly twice the height of Disneyland's Sleeping Beauty Castle. It was inspired by the architecture of 12th- and 13th-century France, the country where the classic fairy tale originated, as well as the Bavarian King Ludwig's fortress and designs prepared for Disney's 1950 classic, *Cinderella*.

Unlike real European castles, this one is made of steel and fiberglass; in lieu of dungeons, it has service tunnels. Its upper reaches contain security rooms; there's even an apartment originally meant for members of the Disney family (but never occupied). From any vantage point, Cinderella Castle looks as if it came straight from the land of make-believe.

Mosaic Murals: The elaborate murals beneath the castle's archway rank among the true wonders of the World. They tell the story of the little cinder girl and one of childhood's happiest happily-ever-afters, using a million bits of glass in some 500 different colors, plus real silver and 14-karat gold.

Cinderella Wishing Well: This pleasant alcove, nestled along the pathway that leads to Tomorrowland, is the perfect spot to gaze at the castle. Any coins tossed into the water are donated to children's charities.

CINDERELLA'S GOLDEN CARROUSEL: Not everything in the Magic Kingdom is a Disney version of the real article. This carousel, discovered at the now-defunct Olympic Park in Maplewood, New Jersey, was built back in 1917. That was the end of the golden century of carousel building that began around 1825 (when the Common Council of Manhattan Island, New York, granted one John Sears a permit to "establish a covered circus for a Flying Horse Establishment"). During the Disney refurbishing, many of the original horses were replaced with horses made of fiberglass.

While waiting for the two-minute ride, it's worthwhile to take the time to study the animals carefully. No two are exactly alike. The band organ, which plays favorite music from Disney Studios (such as the Oscar winners "When You Wish Upon a Star," "Zip-A-Dee-Doo-Dah," and "Chim-Chim-Cheree"), was made in one of Italy's most famous factories.

LEGEND OF THE LION KING: Based on the animated film *The Lion King*, this Fantasyland show combines 25 minutes of animation, puppetry, special effects, and music to make guests

feel as if they walked into a cel from the film. In the pre-show area guests meet Rafiki, the wise baboon who serves as the narrator. His voice is provided by stage and television actor Robert Guillaume. A clip from the film is shown and Rafiki recounts the legend that is about to unfold.

Once inside the 500-seat theater, visitors see the movie's Circle of Life scene presented on a stage. As the sun rises over Pride Rock, Mufasa assures his son, Simba, that he will always be with him. The characters are depicted by fully articulated puppets—when they speak, their mouths move accordingly. Some of the puppets require up to four people to coordinate their head, feet, ear, and mouth movements. The story advances to other scenes, introducing the assorted characters. Some of the more familiar voices you hear are those of Jeremy Irons as the evil Scar, James Earl Jones as Mufasa, Cheech Marin as Banzai, and Whoopi Goldberg as Shenzi.

Guests experience environmental effects, including warm winds during scenes in the Serengeti Plain, and mists of rain and cold winds during the jungle nights. The climactic stampede scene begins on the screen; the noise builds and the theater shakes as smoke gives way to darkness. Note that small children may become frightened when the room goes dark. Presented by Kodak.

PETER PAN'S FLIGHT: The inspiration for this three-minute attraction was the Scottish writer Sir James M. Barrie's novel about the boy who wouldn't grow up, which appeared as a Disney movie in 1953. Riding in flying versions of Captain Hook's ornate ship—which are suspended from an overhead rail once they leave the boarding area—visitors swoop and soar through a short but sweet reprisal of the tale.

A series of scenes tells the story of how Wendy, Michael, and John get sprinkled with pixie dust and, heading for "the second star to the right and straight on till morning," fly off to Never Land with Tinker Bell. There, they meet Princess Tiger Lily, the evil Captain Hook, his jolly-looking sidekick Mr. Smee, and the crocodile—who has already made off with one of Hook's hands and is on the verge of getting the rest of him as you sail out into daylight.

As in the movie, one of the most beautiful scenes—one that makes this attraction a treat for adults as well as smaller folk—is the sight of nighttime London, dark blue and speckled with twinkling yellow lights, complete with the Thames, Big Ben, London

Bridge, and vehicles that really move on the streets. The song that accompanies the trip is "You Can Fly, You Can Fly, You Can Fly," by Sammy Cahn and Sammy Fain.

SKYWAY TO TOMORROWLAND: This aerial tram transports guests one-way to Tomorrowland in about five minutes. En route it's possible to see the striped tent tops of Cinderella's Golden Carrousel, Tomorrowland Speedway, and the not-so-wonderful rooftops of the buildings where many Magic Kingdom adventures take place. This attraction is best boarded at its Tomorrowland station, where the lines are usually slightly shorter. Guests with disabilities who are able to leave their wheelchairs can take a round-trip ride from Fantasyland station.

IT'S A SMALL WORLD: Originally created for New York's 1964–65 World's Fair with a tunefully singsong melody (written by the Academy Award–winning composers of the music for *Mary Poppins*, among other Disney films), this favorite of young children and seniors is a boat trip through several large rooms where Audio-Animatronics dolls—wooden soldiers, cancan dancers, balloonists, Tower of London guards in scarlet beefeater uniforms, bagpipers and leprechauns, goose herds, little Dutch children in wooden shoes, Don Quixote and a goatherd, yodelers and gondoliers, dancers from Greece and Thailand, snake charmers, Japanese kite flyers, hippos, giraffes, frogs, hyenas, monkeys, elephants, hip-twitching

Polynesians, surfers, clowns, and even flying fish—sing and dance to a melody that runs throughout the journey and continues to run through many guests' heads long after their ten-minute trip around the small, small world.

DUMBO, THE FLYING ELEPHANT: This is purely and simply a kiddie ride—though such noted grown-ups as gymnast Nadia Comaneci and Muhammad Ali have loved it. A beloved symbol of Fantasyland, the ride is most popular with the 2- to 7-year-old set. Inspired by the 1941 film classic *Dumbo*, the attraction lasts two memorable minutes. Consider stopping here during the afternoon parade, when the line—which is often prohibitively long—thins out a bit. Incidently, the mouse that sits atop the mirrored ball at the center of the circle of flying elephants is Dumbo's faithful sidekick, Timothy Mouse.

MAD TEA PARTY: The theme of this two-minute ride—in a group of oversize pastel-colored teacups that whirl and spin wildly—derives from a scene in the Disney Studios 1951 movie production of Lewis Carroll's novel *Alice in Wonderland*. During the sequence in question, the Mad Hatter hosts a tea party for his un-birthday.

Unlike many rides in Fantasyland, this is not just for younger kids; the 9-to-20 crowd seems to like it best. Keep in mind that when the cups stop spinning, your head may continue to do so. Skip this ride if you suffer from motion sickness, or if you've recently enjoyed a snack. Don't miss the woozy mouse that pops out of the teapot at the center of the platform full of teacups—he ignored our advice.

MR. TOAD'S WILD RIDE: Wild in name only, this three-minute attraction is based on the 1949 Disney release *The Adventures of Ichabod and Mr. Toad*, which itself derives from Kenneth Grahame's classic novel *The Wind in the Willows*. It seems that a gang of weasels have tricked Mr. J. Thaddeus Toad into trading the deed to his mansion for a motorcar that turns out to have been stolen.

In the attraction, flivvers modeled on this very car take guests zigging and zagging along the road to Nowhere in Particular, through dark rooms painted in neon colors and lit by black lights, where you witness Mr. Toad trying to get out of the scrape. In the process, you crash through a fireplace, narrowly miss being struck by a falling suit of armor, hurtle through haystacks and a barn door and into a coop full of squawking chickens, then ride down a railroad track on a collision course with a train. Some of this is scary enough for some younger children to end up momentarily frightened. By and large, though, this is a ride to be enjoyed with kids.

SNOW WHITE'S ADVENTURES: This three-minute attraction takes guests on a twisting, turning journey through a few happy moments and several scary scenes from the Grimm brothers' fairy tale, which Walt Disney made into the world's first full-length animated feature in 1937. Snow White makes several appearances, as do the seven Audio-Animatronics dwarfs. But the wicked witch—evil, long-nosed, and practically toothless—appears more than once with a suddenness that startles some youngsters. The adventure ends happily, as the dwarfs wave goodbye to Snow White and the prince.

Ariel's Grotto

The Little Mermaid's Ariel doesn't greet Magic Kingdom guests in the traditional way, since mermaids, like most fish, find it difficult to walk around theme parks. Instead, she invites folks of all ages to stop by her Fantasyland home away from home—a colorful grotto surrounded by starfish, coral, and waterfalls. Here guests can meet and pose for a picture with the popular Disney heroine (don't forget your camera). The area, which is especially popular with little ones, also features a soft-surface play zone filled with squirting fountains. Note that the line here is often long enough to scare Ursula herself.

MICKEY'S TOONTOWN FAIR

The Magic Kingdom's newest land invites guests to wander through Mickey and friends' new neighborhood—a totally interactive setting that's akin to Disneyland's Toontown. Unlike the characters' old stomping ground here at Walt Disney World, Mickey's Toontown Fair is out in the countryside, far removed from all the pressures of toon stardom. The area, completed in fall 1996, is as imaginative and adorable as its predecessor, Mickey's Starland, and even more fun. The best way to get here is aboard the Walt Disney World Railroad, but you can also arrive by walking through Fantasyland.

Upon entering Mickey's Toontown Fair, it's immediately apparent why Mickey and the gang chose to build country houses here—because the county fair is always in town!

Mickey's Country House, an "open mouse house," is always available to visitors. Inside, guests discover that Mickey, whose judge's sash and coat are neatly pressed and hung on the coatrack, is head judge for the county fair. As guests peer into the kitchen, living room, and gameroom, they see that Donald and Goofy have left their marks throughout the house, most obviously with their botched attempts to help remodel Mickey's kitchen.

To meet Mickey, use the back door and head for the **Judge's Tent** (others should exit through the garage, which packs some surprises of its own). It's fun to check out the backyard, where Mickey's award-winning garden is bursting with giant vegetables, all of which have Mickey ears. This is also the spot to take a peek at Pluto's doghouse. Before meeting Mickey in the tent, guests see a pre-show video that highlights all of his county fair successes.

To reach one of the best character scenes going, head for the **Toontown Hall of Fame**, a tent filled with champion pumpkins, lima beans, and more—all winning entries from the fair. Beyond this area, three different rooms offer guests a chance to meet any number of Disney characters. Stop in one of the rooms to meet the classic characters, including Goofy, Chip 'n' Dale, and Pluto. Other rooms provide the opportunity to meet either princesses or villains (not in the same room, of course). Note that there is a separate line for each room, and characters vary throughout the day.

Since Minnie and Mickey are next-door neighbors here in the country, **Minnie's Country House** is merely a hop, skip, and a jump from Mickey's. Young kids will love visiting Minnie because her special toon furniture is made of foam, and meant for climbing. As they explore, guests can push a button to listen to her answering-machine messages; open the refrigerator to see many kinds of cheese and feel a blast of cold air; and try in vain to snatch some fresh-baked cookies (it's a clever mirror effect). Minnie has been known to make occasional appearances in the garden gazebo behind her house.

At **The Barnstormer at Goofy's Wiseacres Farm**, nearby, a small roller coaster lets little pilots "fly" crop-duster planes on a track that goes around the farm and then, causing quite a ruckus among the hens, crashes right through his barn! Guests can see by the shape of the holes through which the coaster enters (and departs) the barn that Goofy himself was the first one to try it. The queue for the ride winds through an adjacent section of the barn that's filled with strange gizmos and whirligigs. The ride is a brief one, but definitely thrill-filled.

If you're looking to cool off a bit, stop at **Donald's Boat**, the *Miss Daisy*. It has sprung so many leaks it looks more like a fountain. Anchored in a "duck pond" that's easy to walk across, it's filled with wet surprises; pull the whistle and water shoots out the top.

Other areas across the land include **Toon Park**, a playground of foam animal sculptures for young kids to climb; **Pete's Garage**, housing the restrooms; and **Mickey's Toontown Fair Station**, where the Walt Disney World Railroad makes regular stops.

TOMORROWLAND

The original Tomorrowland attempted a serious look at the future. But as Disney planners discovered, it isn't easy to portray a future that persists in becoming the present. So the old Tomorrowland has given way to a friendlier, space-age town whose neighborhood atmosphere is more in keeping with the other lands in the Magic Kingdom. This is the future that never was, the fantasy world imagined by the science fiction writers and moviemakers of the 1920s and '30s. It's a land of sky-piercing beacons and glistening metal, where shiny robots do the work, whisper-quiet conveyances glide along an elevated highway, and even time travel is possible.

Note: All Tomorrowland attractions are described in the order that they are encountered upon entering the land from the Hub and heading (roughly counterclockwise) away from Cinderella Castle.

THE TIMEKEEPER: A fantastic 20-minute multimedia presentation combining a Circle-Vision 360 film with Audio-Animatronics characters and special in-theater effects is hosted by Timekeeper, a wacky, mad scientist robot. Inspired by the likes of Jules Verne and H. G. Wells, who wrote about fantastic visions of the future, Timekeeper has created the world's first and only working time machine (at least as far as we know). Assisting Timekeeper in his time voyage demonstration is 9-Eye, a flying robot camera who is the test pilot for Timekeeper's invention. She has volunteered to fly through history and transmit pictures back to guests in the 360-degree time chamber. Guests are able to experience what it was like to hear the young Mozart play his first composition; to fly down a mountain on a bobsled; to see Leonardo da Vinci working on a masterpiece; and to float in a hot-air balloon above Moscow's Red Square, among many other exciting stops on this whirlwind trip through time and space. In a sweep of the 1900 Paris Exposition, guests even see Jules Verne and H. G. Wells themselves. When Verne hitches a ride with 9-Eye to the present and beyond, he gets to see some of his visions realized. Guests may recognize the voice of Timekeeper as that of Robin Williams. Other stars featured are Rhea Perlman as 9-Eye, Jeremy Irons as H. G. Wells, and Michel Piccoli as Jules Verne.

ALIEN ENCOUNTER: The centerpiece of Tomorrowland is the Tomorrowland Interplanetary Convention Center, home of the Magic Kingdom's scariest attraction. Created by Disney Imagineers and director George Lucas, Alien Encounter features some of the most elaborate special effects ever employed by a theme park.

The attraction's premise is this: The Convention Center is hosting X-S Tech, a mysterious corporation from a distant planet. X-S Tech's objective is to impress earthlings, particularly Magic Kingdom guests, with its

to their side. Ultimately, the X-S technicians regain control, but not before guests have been startled enough to jump in their seats.

Note: This 20-minute attraction may be too intense for young children. You must be at least seven years old and 44 inches tall to enter Alien Encounter.

TAKE FLIGHT: A whimsical look at the adventure and romance of flight—as seen through the eyes of a child—awaits guests at this 4½-minute attraction.

Three-dimensional aircraft are used in a variety of scenes showing the early days of flight. A barnstorming flying circus segment features a man and woman, each standing on a wing and keeping up a tennis match.

Guests glide past part of an M-130 Flying Boat, a plane from the 1930s, as monitors show faraway places that the plane made accessible.

Another stop on the journey is the jet age, in its purest form—guests ride through a real engine. Special effects re-create the rotation of the turbine in a realistic fashion.

In a film segment, visitors get that "you are there" feeling as they seem to speed down a runway and fly off toward space. The moon provides lighting for spectacular views of canyons, valleys, and flat terrain, where the suggestions of cities of the future are depicted.

Note: Take Flight will soon be doing just that. The attraction, which is scheduled to undergo extensive refurbishment, will close in the spring and reopen in the fall of 1998.

TOMORROWLAND TRANSIT AUTHORITY: Boarded near Astro Orbiter, these five-car trains (which used to be known as the WED-way PeopleMover) move at a speed of about ten miles per hour along almost a mile of track, alongside or through most of the attractions in Tomorrowland. It is operated by a linear induction motor that has no moving parts, uses little power, and emits no pollution. The peaceful excursion takes about ten minutes.

ASTRO ORBITER: Here, passengers fly around for two minutes in machine-age rockets, designed to look more like oversize Buck Rogers toys than 1990s space shuttles. Riders are surrounded by whirling planets as they get an astronaut's-eye view of Tomorrowland.

high-tech products. Visitors are led into another room for a demonstration of the company's premier product: a teleporter that "beams" people or objects from place to place.

At the podium is a robot named S.I.R. To his left and right are bell jars, one of which holds a fuzzy character named Skippy. S.I.R. tries to teleport Skippy from one jar to the next, but the demonstration doesn't go well—and poor Skippy is seriously singed in the process.

Despite the setback, the folks from X-S Tech continue with their presentation. Guests are shown to a circular auditorium with a large teleporter in the center. Screens around the theater display a live transmission from Planet X. Restraints are suddenly lowered onto guests' shoulders. (Don't panic—this is not rough, just scary.) Just then, X-S Tech's Chairman Clench volunteers to be teleported to Earth, to meet this Magic Kingdom audience.

Hot Tip

If you have doubts about riding Space Mountain, or would like to assess the wait time, take a trip on the Tomorrowland Transit Authority. It travels through the queue area inside Space Mountain and offers a view of the rockets as they hurtle through the darkness.

Special effects abound as the teleporter is fired up and guests await the arrival of Chairman Clench. But something goes terribly wrong, and, instead of Clench, an angry alien is transported into their midst as the theater goes black. Next comes a series of creepy sensations designed to convince members of the audience that the monster has found its way

**WALT DISNEY'S CAROUSEL OF PROG-
RESS:** First seen at New York's 1964–65
World's Fair and moved here in 1975, this
20-minute show features a number of
tableaux starring an Audio-Animatronics
family, and demonstrates the improvements
in American life that have resulted from the
use of electricity. The audience moves around
the scenes as on a carousel. An updated final
scene has been added, in which guests see
what life might be like in the near future: A
grandmother plays a virtual reality game and
the oven talks. (Some of the technologically
advanced products are on display for hands-
on inspection at Epcot's Innoventions.)

SKYWAY TO FANTASYLAND: An aerial
cable car, this attraction transports guests
from Tomorrowland to a point near Peter
Pan's Flight in Fantasyland in five minutes.
The cable car, built in Bern, Switzerland, is
notable for being the nation's first con-
veyance of its type able to make a 90-degree
turn. If you're going to ride the Skyway, this
is the place to get on: The lines at the Fantasyland end are usually slightly longer.

SPACE MOUNTAIN: This attraction, which
blasted onto the Magic Kingdom scene in
1974, is a can't-miss crowd pleaser for throngs
of thrill seekers. Rising to a height of over 180
feet and extending some 300 feet in diameter,
this gleaming steel and concrete cone houses
an attraction that most people call a
roller coaster. It's the Disney version—a roller
coaster and then some. While the 2-minute
38-second ride doesn't quite duplicate a trip
into space, there are impressive effects—
shooting stars and flashing lights among
them—and the ride takes place in an outer
space–like darkness that gets progressively
inkier and scarier as the journey progresses.

The six-passenger rockets that roar
through this blackness attain a maximum
speed of just over 28 miles per hour. Just how
terrifying this actually is to any given passenger depends on his or her level of tolerance.
The Space Mountain experience is wild
enough to send eyeglasses, purses, wallets,
and even an occasional set of false teeth
plummeting to the bottom of the track, so be
sure to find a safe place for your possessions
before the ride starts. It's also turbulent
enough to upset the stomachs of those so
unwise as to ride it immediately after eating—but not so harrowing that passengers'
shaking and weakened knees persist for more
than a minute or two after "touchdown."
(Those who chicken out at the last minute
have their own exit from the queue area.)

With the work lights on, the interior of
Space Mountain looks humdrum and almost
commercially common. The ride is controlled by a computer, monitored on a board
full of dials and a battery of closed-circuit TV
screens by Disney hosts and hostesses in a control room (whose eerie blue glow is another
striking feature of the queue area). As a result,
any guest acting in an unsafe manner can be
warned, and the ride stopped, if necessary.

Note: Children under seven must be accompanied by an adult; guests under 44 inches are
not permitted to ride; and as the signs at the
attraction warn, you must be in good health,
and free from heart conditions, motion sickness, back or neck problems, or other physical
limitations to ride. Expectant mothers should
pass up the trip. Presented by FedEx.

The Tomorrowland Light & Power Co., an
arcade by Space Mountain's exit, is a great
place to wait for your party if you skip the
ride. An ATM is available.

TOMORROWLAND SPEEDWAY: Little cars
that *vroom* down the tracks at this attraction
opposite Cosmic Ray's Starlight Café provide
most of the background noise in Tomorrowland. Kids love the ride and will spend as many
hours driving the Mark VII–model gas-pow-
ered cars as they can. Like true sports cars, the
vehicles have rack-and-pinion steering and disc
brakes; but unlike most sports cars, these run
on a track. Nonetheless, even expert drivers
have a hard time keeping them going in a
straight line. (Don't panic when you notice the
lack of a brake pedal—when you take your
foot off the gas, the car comes to a quick, if not
screeching, halt.) The one-lap trip takes about
five minutes. Presented by Goodyear.

Note: You must be at least 52 inches tall to
drive the cars by yourself.

SHOPPING

No one travels all the way to the Magic Kingdom just to go shopping. But as many a first-time visitor has learned with some surprise, shopping is one of the most enjoyable pastimes here.

The Magic Kingdom's boutiques and stores stock much more than just Disneyana. Along with the more predictable items in Main Street shops, it's possible to find cookbooks and stoneware dishes, pirate hats and toy frontier rifles, 14-karat gold charms and filigreed costume jewelry. In Adventureland, you can buy imported items from around the world—hand-carved elephant statues from Africa, inlaid marble boxes from India, batik dresses from Indonesia, and more. Shops generally stock items that complement the themes of the various lands.

In some shops, you can watch people at work—a candy maker pouring peanut brittle in the Main Street Confectionery, a glassblower crafting wares in Main Street's Crystal Arts, and the like. And every store offers a selection of items from the inexpensive to the somewhat costly.

Finally, some advice. We recommend shopping in the early afternoon, rather than at day's end, when the shops are normally jammed. However, keep in mind that Main Street shops do stay open a half hour after park closing, in case you need any last-minute gifts on the way out of the park. Also note that purchases can be stored for the day in lockers under the Walt Disney World Railroad's depot or, in the case of very large items, sent to package pickup. WDW resort guests may arrange for purchases to be delivered to their hotel rooms free of charge.

Main Street

THE CHAPEAU: This Town Square shop is the place to buy Mouseketeer ears and have them monogrammed, and to shop for visors, straw hats, baseball caps, and assorted other headgear. The hats are fun to try on, even if you don't plan on buying.

CRYSTAL ARTS: Pretty cut-glass bowls, vases, urns, glasses, and plates glitter in the mirror-backed glass cases of this high-ceilinged, brass-chandeliered emporium. An engraver or a glassblower is always at work by the bright light that floods through the big windows. Presented by the Arribas Brothers.

DISNEY & CO.: The wallpaper at this lovely shop on Center Street (the cul-de-sac just off Main) is Victorian and the woodwork elaborate; old-fashioned ceiling fans twirl slowly overhead. This shop specializes in children's clothing, but also stocks an assortment of dolls and stuffed toys. The selection is not as vast as that at the Emporium, but Disney & Co. isn't quite so overwhelming.

DISNEY CLOTHIERS: Character merchandise has always been popular, as evidenced by the number of T-shirts, Mouseketeer ears, watches, and sweatshirts sold each year. This shop caters to the fashion-conscious shoppers with a love for Disney gear. There is a vast array of clothing and accessories, all of which incorporate Disney characters in some way. Hats, ties, and dress shirts round out the selection.

Where to Eat in the Magic Kingdom

A complete listing of all eateries—full-service restaurants, fast-food emporiums, and snack shops—can be found in the *Good Meals, Great Times* chapter. See the Magic Kingdom section beginning on page 214.

DISNEY'S WALK AROUND THE WORLD:
This outdoor booth, located near the entrance
to the Magic Kingdom, answers questions and
processes applications for sponsorship of the
personalized bricks used to build the walkway surrounding the Seven Seas Lagoon. For
information, call 800-272-6201.

EMPORIUM: Framed by a two-story-high
portico, this Town Square landmark, the
Magic Kingdom's largest gift shop, stocks
a little bit of everything—stuffed animals
and toys, an array of dolls, sundries, film, and
more. Every customer seems to have an arm-
load of WDW T-shirts and sweatshirts, towels
and handbags, Mouseketeer ears and other
hats, and various items emblazoned with

Mickey, Minnie, or Walt Disney World logos.
The cash registers always seem to be busy,
especially toward the end of the afternoon
and before park closing. It's a good place to
shop, though, since it's only a few steps from
lockers (under the train station) where packages can be stowed. Don't forget to peer into
the windows, which usually feature elaborate
Audio-Animatronics displays ranging from
spirited seasonal themes to character
tableaux from the latest Disney movie.

FIREHOUSE GIFT STATION: Authentic firefighting paraphernalia provides the backdrop for a variety of *101 Dalmatians* products, Mickey Mouse firefighter apparel and
souvenirs, and reproductions of historical
firefighting objects.

HARMONY BARBER SHOP: The quaint,
old-fashioned setting for this working shop
(complete with harmonizing quartet) merits
a peek even if you have no need for a trim.
Nostalgic shaving items are also for sale.

Let It Rain

The show doesn't stop just because of
a storm. Instead, shops all over the
Magic Kingdom stock inexpensive bright
yellow Mickey ponchos to outfit guests
who have left their own rain gear back
home, at their hotel, or in the car.

KODAK CAMERA CENTER: This high-
ceilinged shop near Town Square is the spot
for film, batteries, photo albums, disposable
cameras, two-hour film processing, and very
minor camera repairs. Video cameras are
available for rent at a cost of $30 a day, with
a $450 refundable deposit.

MAIN STREET ATHLETIC CLUB: Sports-
related gifts and apparel are the hallmarks
of this shop. The merchandise features logos
of popular collegiate and professional
teams, along with the images of Disney
characters gamely pursuing their favorite
sports. The shop also stocks men's golf shirts
with a small Mickey Mouse embroidered on
the pocket.

MAIN STREET CONFECTIONERY: Tasty
chocolates are sold in this old-fashioned
pink-and-white paradise. A delight at any
time of day, but especially when the cooks in
the shop's glass-walled kitchen are pouring
peanut brittle onto a table to cool. Then, the
candy sends up clouds of aroma that you
could swear were being fanned out onto the
street. Several batches are made each day;
the sweet product is for sale in small bags,
along with jelly beans, marshmallow crispies,
nougats, mints, and dozens of other ways to
satisfy a sweet tooth.

MAIN STREET GALLERY: The focus here
is on Disneyana—including limited-edition
Disney plates, cels from Disney movies, and
a variety of other collectibles.

MARKET HOUSE: An old-fashioned spot,
with preserves, syrups, and all kinds of tea and
snack items arranged in oak cases. The floors
are pegged oak, the lighting emanates in part
from brass lanterns, and in one corner there's
a real old-fashioned hand-crank telephone.

NEWSSTAND: No newspapers are sold in
the Magic Kingdom—even at its newsstand,
which is opposite the stroller and wheelchair rental shop near the park entrance. It's
to the left, just inside the turnstiles. The
stand sells a small selection of character
merchandise and souvenirs.

THE SHADOW BOX: Watching Rubio Artist Co. silhouette cutters snip black paper into the likenesses of children is one of Main Street's more fascinating diversions. There's always a crowd on hand.

UPTOWN JEWELERS: Modeled after a turn-of-the-century collectibles shop, this store specializes in fine china and other gift items. China figurines and flowers, and Disney character figurines, priced from $3.50 to $3,500, are the stock-in-trade of this airy establishment. There's also a selection of good-quality and costume jewelry. One counter stocks wonderful souvenir charms in 14-karat gold and sterling silver: among them Tinker Bell, Cinderella Castle, and the Walt Disney World logo (a globe with mouse ears). Clocks and watches in all shapes and sizes are available here, including Mickey Mouse watches in a variety of configurations. There are even a few pocket watches to consider adding to your timepiece collection. Purchases can be shipped on request.

STROLLER AND WHEELCHAIR RENTAL: Inside the turnstiles on the right as you enter the park, this rental concession offers a limited number of strollers and wheelchairs (available on a first-come, first-served basis). Souvenirs may also be purchased here.

Adventureland

BWANA BOB'S: A whimsical and colorful hut full of the critters you may have just observed on the Jungle Cruise or at The Enchanted Tiki Birds.

ELEPHANT TALES: A variety of women's and men's clothing with a safari theme are featured at this shop. Women's accessories and safari plush toys are also available.

ISLAND SUPPLY: This tropical surf shop features a vast assortment of surfing clothing and accessories.

TIKI TROPICS: Discover nature at its finest through apparel and gifts representing gardening and the great outdoors. The merchandise here has an environmental theme: You'll find wind chimes, herb-garden kits, natural lotions, and a selection of T-shirts made of unbleached cotton.

TRADERS OF TIMBUKTU: Located in a marketlike complex in the plaza opposite The Enchanted Tiki Birds, this shop displays a selection of the sort of handsome (but inexpensive) trinkets that travelers find in parts of Africa—carved wooden giraffes and antelope, ethnic jewelry (including carved bangles and malachite-and-elephant-hair baubles), dashikis, and khaki shirts.

Caribbean Plaza

HOUSE OF TREASURE: A good spot to pick up pirates' hats, this swashbuckler's delight adjoins Pirates of the Caribbean on the west and stocks piratical merchandise—toy rifles and brass dolphins, a Pirate's Creed of Ethics printed on parchment, Jolly Roger flags, rings, pirate dolls, sailing-ship models, ships in a bottle, and eye patches. Nautical apparel is available, as are fine nautical gifts, such as lamps and brass items.

PLAZA DEL SOL CARIBE BAZAAR: Located next to the Pirates of the Caribbean, this market sells candy and snacks, a variety of straw hats (including colorful oversize sombreros), piñatas, pottery, straw bags, clothing, and artificial flowers.

Frontierland

BIG AL'S: Named for the most popular (and least talented) member of the Country Bear Jamboree, this riverfront shop is the place to acquire a variety of leather goods, harmonicas, rock candy, and assorted six-shooters.

BRIAR PATCH: Cuddly creatures from the movie *Song of the South* are featured at this shop, located near the exit to Splash Mountain. Country crafts and a selection of Disney character merchandise spotlighting Winnie the Pooh and friends round out the offerings here.

FRONTIER TRADING POST: Outfit a child like a true youngster of the Great Frontier. Cowboy hats or feathered headdresses and moccasins, hefty brass belt buckles, sleeve garters, sheriff's badges, gold nugget and turquoise jewelry, and reproduction pistols and rifles should do the trick.

FRONTIER WOOD CARVING: The spot for wooden gifts with personalized carvings.

PRAIRIE OUTPOST & SUPPLY: Stop by this turn-of-the-century general store for candy and some unusual food, including elk jerky and alligator meat. Decorative items such as candles are also for sale.

TRAIL CREEK HAT SHOP: Hats of all descriptions, plus feathered hatbands and leather goods are on sale at this small emporium tucked away near the Frontierland Shootin' Arcade and the Diamond Horseshoe Saloon Revue.

Liberty Square

HERITAGE HOUSE: Early American reproductions predominate in the stock of this store next to The Hall of Presidents. Parchment copies of famous American documents are popular with youngsters. Homeowners and collectors might be tempted to snap up pewter plates and candlesticks, creweled items, wooden pepper mills, busts of the presidents, souvenir spoons, mugs in Early-American motifs, wrought-iron knickknacks, or lovely enameled paintings of clipper ships.

ICHABOD'S LANDING: This small Liberty Square shop gives guests on their way to The Haunted Mansion a taste of things to come, with a stock of horrific monster masks and assorted ghoulish goodies.

LIBERTY SQUARE PORTRAIT GALLERY: In the midst of Liberty Square, next to The Hall of Presidents, guests can sit to have their portraits drawn in this open-air studio.

THE YANKEE TRADER: No first-time Magic Kingdom visitor would expect to find cast-iron muffin tins and stoneware soufflé dishes for sale in the park. But all you need do is stop by this quaint little shop, immediately to the right after turning into the lane leading to The Haunted Mansion. It is crammed like a too-small kitchen cabinet with the above-mentioned kitchen items, and more. There's a great Mickey Mouse waffle iron, among other Disney-themed goods. The shop also has a wealth of countrified cookware and more varieties of jams and jellies than any supermarket shopper would have imagined existed. Gourmands will be pleased to find a cookbook selection that not only includes old favorites, but also unusual volumes of historic recipes.

YE OLDE CHRISTMAS SHOPPE: A wide selection of Christmas items, including treetop dolls and souvenir ornaments—both Disney-themed and traditional—is available here year-round.

Fantasyland

FANTASY FAIRE: It's difficult to miss this shop upon leaving the Legend of the Lion King show. It has every item imaginable featuring your favorite characters from *The Lion King*, as well an assortment of classic Disney characters.

THE KING'S GALLERY: This shop, inside Cinderella Castle and featuring cuckoo clocks, and other German-inspired wares, may be closed for part of 1998, as it undergoes refurbishment and, quite possibly, a name change.

KODAK KIOSK: A convenient location to buy film and other photo supplies.

SEVEN DWARFS MINING CO.: This souvenir stand next to Snow White's Adventures sells assorted Disney-motif key chains, candies, and stuffed animals, plus a colorful collection of Snow White merchandise.

SIR MICKEY'S: Expect to find all sorts of Disney souvenirs, from T-shirts to more sophisticated fashions and accessories in this shop with a "Brave Little Tailor" theme—the cartoon in which Mickey defeats an evil giant to win the hand of Princess Minnie. (It was one of the most elaborate and expensive Mickey Mouse cartoons ever made.)

TINKER BELL'S TREASURES: One of the more wonderful boutiques in the Magic Kingdom, and a fine toy store by any standard. For sale are stuffed animals, character clothing patches, windup and wooden toys, Mickey and Minnie toys and clothing, and a marvelous array of Madame Alexander dolls. A must.

Shopping Away from the Parks

THE DISNEY CATALOG: T-shirts, stuffed animals, and other souvenir items can be ordered through The Disney Catalog. Phone 800-237-5751 to receive one.

THE DISNEY STORES: Call 818-265-4660 to find a location near you, or visit The Disney Store Web site at *http://www.disneystore.com*.

WDW MAIL ORDER: Merchandise found in shops at Walt Disney World is also available by calling 407-363-6200.

MAGIC KINGDOM

Mickey's Toontown Fair

COUNTY BOUNTY: Disney character memorabilia, featuring all the favorites, can be found in this merchandise location under the big tent. Look for costumes, autograph books, key chains, candy, and more. Don't miss the doll-making exhibit, or the winning entries from previous fairs, including the "most upside-down cake," baked by Daisy Duck.

Tomorrowland

MICKEY'S STAR TRADERS: This is one of the best places to go in the Magic Kingdom for Disney-themed items. Sunglasses and sun care products are also available.

MERCHANT OF VENUS: The kinds of contemporary decorative gifts that teens and preteens love can be found here: futuristic toys, games, jewelry, clothing, and other such items. This is also the only shop that carries Skippy, as well as other Alien Encounter merchandise.

GEIGER'S COUNTER: This small shop near the Tomorrowland Speedway features a variety of souvenir hats, pins, and neon glow jewelry. It also monograms Mouseketeer ears.

URSA'S MAJOR MINOR MART: A small spot tucked away near the Tomorrowland terminus of the Skyway to Fantasyland that's great for Disney souvenirs.

ENTERTAINMENT

In this most magical corner of the World, a tempting slate of live performances ranks among the more serendipitous discoveries. The Magic Kingdom's entertainment mix includes dazzling high-tech shows and old-fashioned numbers alike. To keep apprised of the offerings on any given day, stop at City Hall upon arrival at the park to pick up a current guidemap.

While the specifics are subject to change, the following listing is a good indication of the Magic Kingdom's extensive repertoire. As always, we advise calling 824-4321 to confirm entertainment schedules. For information on special events at the Magic Kingdom, see the "Holidays & Special Events" section of *Getting Ready to Go*.

ALL-AMERICAN COLLEGE MARCHING BAND: During weekdays in summer, this band, which features college students from around the country, performs throughout the Magic Kingdom in the afternoon and early evening.

CASEY'S CORNER PIANO: A pianist tickles the ivories of a snow-white upright daily at the centrally located Casey's Corner restaurant on Main Street.

DAPPER DANS: A barbershop quartet likely to be encountered while strolling down Main Street. Conspicuously clad in straw hats and striped vests, the Dapper Dans tap dance and let one-liners fly during their short four-part harmonic performances.

DIAMOND HORSESHOE SALOON REVUE: A dance hall such as might have been found in 19th-century Missouri hosts this lively old-time show with cancan dancers several times daily. Guests may drop in at any time during the hour-long performances.

FANTASY IN THE SKY: This pyrotechnic extravaganza is presented during peak seasons and select weekends. The program opens (often at 10 P.M.) with Tinker Bell's Flight, a dramatic sprinkling of pyrotechnic pixie dust over Cinderella Castle. The six-minute fireworks presentation is ideally viewed from Main Street, but there are good viewing locations in Fantasyland, Liberty Square, and other areas of the park.

FLAG RETREAT: At about 5:10 P.M., patriotic music fills the air as a color guard marches to Town Square, takes down the American flag that flies from the flagpole, and releases a flock of snow-white homing pigeons symbolic of the dove of peace. Watch carefully: They flap away toward their home (behind the castle) practically before you can say "Cinderella." The entire flight takes 20 seconds.

GALAXY SEARCH: The outdoor Galaxy Palace Theater in Tomorrowland hosts this talent show in search of unique entertainment, starring Mickey and his pals.

J. P. AND THE SILVER STARS: This group surfaces from time to time to play familiar tunes on steel drums, bringing a bit of the Caribbean islands to the area near Adventureland's Pirates of the Caribbean.

KIDS OF THE KINGDOM: Performing often in front of Cinderella Castle, this group puts on a lively show, featuring singing and dancing to Disney tunes—plus appearances by such characters as the portly Winnie the Pooh and Mickey Mouse himself.

REMEMBER THE MAGIC PARADE: This 25-minute dazzler has an interactive twist: cameo appearances by about 1,400 randomly selected Magic Kingdom visitors.

(Guests are tapped for participation by cast members walking along the parade route, beginning about 45 minutes before starting time.) The parade, which has six floats inspired by Disney films, as well as every character imaginable, begins at 3 P.M. in Frontierland and winds its way to Main Street, stopping eight times en route for special participatory sequences.

RHYTHM RASCALS: Specialty songs and comic ditties from the Roaring Twenties on washboards and banjos are their trademark; they usually perform on Main Street.

SWORD IN THE STONE CEREMONY: Several times each day, a child is appointed temporary ruler of the realm by pulling the magical sword, Excalibur, from the stone in front of Cinderella's Golden Carrousel. Merlin the Magician presides over the ceremony.

WALT DISNEY WORLD BAND: This traditional concert band often performs during the flag retreat in Town Square and in front of the castle on select mornings and afternoons.

Holiday Happenings

It's a rare holiday that passes quietly in the Magic Kingdom. During certain holidays, such as Christmas, New Year's Eve, and the Fourth of July, this Kingdom usually breaks curfew, staying open extra late and stepping up its nighttime entertainment. On these occasions, special performances of SpectroMagic and the Fantasy in the Sky fireworks are often in store. Of course, entertainment plans are subject to change, so it's important to call 824-4321 for current schedules.

EASTER: A nationally televised holiday parade on Main Street makes Easter an especially delightful, if a bit crowded, time to visit the Magic Kingdom.

FOURTH OF JULY: The busiest day of the summer—and with reason: There's a double-size fireworks display, whose explosions light up the skies not only above Cinderella Castle, but also over Seven Seas Lagoon.

CHRISTMAS: A towering Christmas tree goes up in Town Square, and the entire Magic Kingdom is decked out as only Disney can do it. On select evenings, the Magic Kingdom hosts a special-admission nighttime celebration called Mickey's Very Merry Christmas Party. The festivities, complete with hot chocolate and snow, include Mickey's Very Merry Christmas Parade and other holiday shows. There are also special holiday performances during the day.

NEW YEAR'S EVE: It has always been true that on December 31, the throngs are practically body to body. For a celebration of this nature, that can be a lot of fun. There is a double-size fireworks display, and the Main Street holiday decorations are still up. There's plenty of nip in the air as the evening wears on, so dress accordingly.

Where to Find the Characters

Mickey and pals appear near City Hall on Main Street throughout the day. Adventureland is a good spot to find Rafiki and Timon from *The Lion King*. Alice and her Wonderland friends show up in Fantasyland, as does Ariel. The Fantasyland Character Festival is an excellent spot to see characters. (Be sure to check the nearby character greeting information board, too.) The Riverboat Character Cruise and the character meals at Crystal Palace, Cinderella's Royal Table, and Liberty Tree Tavern offer guests a chance to meet their favorites. But the best character place is at Mickey's Toontown Fair, where guests can meet Mickey, Minnie, and others. Check a guidemap for updated information.

The Night Sparkles with SpectroMagic

Since its premiere during Walt Disney World's 20th anniversary celebration, this parade has gotten rave reviews and taken its place among WDW's must-sees. Even avid fans of the Main Street Electrical Parade (which, by the way, was shipped to Disneyland Paris) won't be disappointed with this display.

Fiber-optic cable and threads are conduits for shimmering lights that create everything from the strands of "hair" on King Triton's beard on one float to the giant hibiscus blooms and daisy petals on another. Some 600,000 miniature bulbs light in wild, changing patterns, moving in perfect concert with sound effects. Goofy's xylophone keys dance with light at his touch. Mickey's cape becomes a cascade of color sweeping from his shoulders to the base of the float and upward 17 feet above his head. The wonderful spectacle is choreographed to music composed just for the parade.

SpectroMagic borrows its dazzling illusions from the prismatic holographic industry, military lighting developments, electroluminescent and fiber-optic technologies, plus light-spreading thermoplastics, clouds of underlit liquid nitrogen, smoke, and some old-fashioned twinkling lights.

A marvel of the computer age, SpectroMagic is controlled by compact computers, with the audio stored digitally on state-of-the-art microchips. A sequence of electronic triggers activates and coordinates all of the visual and audio effects.

SpectroMagic follows the traditional WDW parade route (although it heads in one direction at 9 P.M. and the opposite at 11 P.M.); of all the spots along the way, the single best vantage point is the very center of the platform of the Walt Disney World Railroad depot. From there, it's possible to see the parade circling Town Square, and then follow it as it makes its way down Main Street.

The next-best viewing points are the curbs on either side along Main Street. It's very crowded here, and you must claim your foot of curb as much as 1½ hours before the parade (particularly for the busier 9 P.M. running). If you hate crowds, head for Pecos Bill Café; park yourself on one of the restaurant's stools right next to the parade route.

The parade lights up the Magic Kingdom during peak seasons and select weekends. If there are two shows, the 9 P.M. parade is always more crowded than the one at 11 P.M.

HOT TIPS

- Study this chapter before you arrive in the Magic Kingdom so that you're familiar with the park's layout and attractions.
- Allow plenty of time to sample the Magic Kingdom in small bites. Trying to see it all in a day (or even two) is like eating a rich ice cream sundae too quickly.
- Consider taking advantage of early-bird admissions to the parks. Each day, sections of one park are open 1½ hours early for WDW resort guests only. But keep in mind that the parks can get crowded on these days—that's when a park hopper pass comes in handy.
- If you are not staying at a Walt Disney World resort, still plan to start out early. Most people arrive between 9:30 A.M. and 11:30 A.M., and the roads and parking lots are jammed. If you're coming at Easter, Christmas, or in summer, plan to arrive before 8:30 A.M., or wait until late afternoon, when things are less hectic. Be at the gates to the Magic Kingdom when they open, and then be at the end of Main Street when the rest of the park opens.
- Wear very comfortable shoes: You'll be spending a lot of time on your feet. (Note that no bare feet are permitted in the park.)
- Shop on Main Street in the early afternoon, not at day's end, when everybody else does (since shops here are open a half hour after park closing). Besides, the stores are good places to escape the afternoon heat.
- WDW resort guests can have packages delivered to their hotels free of charge.

- Check out the Tip Board at the end of Main Street for information on the waiting times for the most popular attractions.
- Organize your visit so that you don't hop around from area to area, for that wastes time. Plan to eat early or late: before 11 A.M. or after 2 P.M., and before 5 P.M. or after 8 P.M.
- At busy times, take in these not-so-packed attractions: Walt Disney World Railroad, Main Street Cinema, Liberty Belle Riverboat, Carousel of Progress, Take Flight, and Tomorrowland Transit Authority.
- Break up your day. Go to one of the water parks, or head back to your hotel (if it's not too far) for some swimming. Be sure to have your hand stamped and hold on to your admission pass and your parking stub.
- If your party decides to split up, set a meeting place and time. Avoid meeting in front of Cinderella Castle, since this area can become quite congested.
- Many Magic Kingdom attractions have two lines. The one on the left usually will be shorter, since most visitors automatically head for the one on the right.
- For a full-service meal in the Magic Kingdom, make advance priority seating arrangements by calling WDW-DINE (939-3463).
- Don't take food into the park. (There are picnic facilities and lockers at the TTC.)
- If you want to be a part of the Remember the Magic Parade, choose your spot at least 45 minutes prior. Guests are randomly picked to participate from the parade route.

Epcot

magine a place whose entertainment inventory includes both a rich sampling of world cultures and a fun, enlightening journey to the technological frontier. You now have an inkling of the eye-opening and mind-broadening potential of Epcot.

Walt Disney suggested the idea back in October 1966: "Epcot will be an experimental prototype community of tomorrow that will take its cue from the new ideas and new technologies that are now emerging from the creative center of American industry." It would never be completed, he said, but would "always be introducing and testing and demonstrating new materials and systems." Now, more than ever, Walt Disney's dream is a reality. Innoventions, an ever-evolving showplace of the near future, is continually bounding into new territory in its mission to close gaps with technological destiny. A transformed Universe of Energy has emerged. And with the recent addition of Test Track, Epcot guests have a (thrilling) inside track on the fast and perilous world of automobile testing.

The theme park, which opened in 1982, consists of two distinct areas of exploration: Future World and World Showcase. The former examines the newest and most intriguing ideas in science and technology in ways that make them seem not only comprehensible but downright irresistible. The latter celebrates the diversity of the world's peoples, portraying a stunning array of nations with extraordinary devotion to detail.

Think of Epcot as Disney's playground for the curious and the thoughtful. The experiences it delivers—all of them wonders of the real world—never fail to amaze, delight, inspire, and (rest assured) entertain.

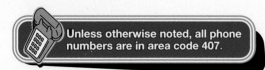
Unless otherwise noted, all phone numbers are in area code 407.

WORLD SHOWCASE LAGOON

MOROCCO

FRANCE

JAPAN

INTERNATIONAL GATEWAY

THE AMERICAN ADVENTURE

AMERICA GARDENS THEATRE

UNITED KINGDOM

ITALY

CANADA

GERMANY

JOURNEY INTO IMAGINATION

THE LAND

SHOWCASE PLAZA

CHINA

INNOVENTIONS WEST SIDE

THE LIVING SEAS

NORWAY

INNOVENTIONS EAST SIDE

MEXICO

TEST TRACK

SPACESHIP EARTH

To Buses

HORIZONS (closed for rehab)

UNIVERSE OF ENERGY

Entrance Plaza

WONDERS OF LIFE

N

GETTING ORIENTED

Double the Magic Kingdom and you have an idea of the size of Epcot. As for layout, the park is shaped something like a giant hourglass. The nine pavilions of Future World fill the northern bulb, while the international potpourri known as World Showcase occupies the southern bulb. Future World is anchored on the north by the imposing silver "geosphere" known as Spaceship Earth.

As you pass through Epcot's main Entrance Plaza, Spaceship Earth looms straight ahead. Pathways curve around either side of the 180-foot-tall geosphere, winding up at Future World's Innoventions Plaza. Here, in addition to a huge show fountain, you see signposts for Innoventions, whose two buildings cradle the east and west sides of the plaza. Beyond this central area, there are two roughly symmetrical north–south avenues; these are dotted with the seven pavilions that form Future World's outer perimeter. Test Track, Horizons (which is currently closed for renovation), Wonders of Life, and Universe of Energy flank Spaceship Earth on the east, while Journey Into Imagination, The Land, and The Living Seas lie to the west.

In World Showcase, the 11 international pavilions are arranged around the edge of sparkling World Showcase Lagoon, with The American Adventure directly south of Spaceship Earth on the lake's southernmost shore. A walkway from Future World leads to Showcase Plaza and the World Showcase Promenade, a 1.3-mile thoroughfare that wraps all the way around the lagoon, winding past each World Showcase pavilion in the process. Proceeding counterclockwise around World Showcase, countries are encountered in the following order: Canada, the United Kingdom, France, Morocco, Japan, the United States (the host pavilion is called The American Adventure), Italy, Germany, China, Norway, and Mexico.

HOW TO GET THERE

Take Exit 26B off I-4. Continue along to the Epcot Auto Plaza; take a tram from the parking lot to the park's main entrance.

By WDW Transportation: From the Grand Floridian, Contemporary, and Polynesian: hotel monorail to the Transportation and Ticket Center (TTC), then switch for the TTC-Epcot monorail. From the Magic Kingdom: express monorail to the TTC, then switch for the TTC-Epcot monorail. From Fort Wilderness and the Downtown Disney Marketplace: buses to the TTC, then change

for the TTC-Epcot monorail. From the Disney-MGM Studios, Animal Kingdom, and all other WDW resorts, and the resorts on Hotel Plaza Blvd.: buses.

Note: A second Epcot entrance, called the International Gateway, provides entry directly to World Showcase. This gateway, which may be reached via walkways and water launches from the Swan, Dolphin, Yacht Club, Beach Club, and BoardWalk resorts, deposits guests between the France and United Kingdom pavilions.

PARKING

All-day parking at Epcot is $5 for day visitors (free to WDW resort guests with presentation of resort ID). Attendants will direct you to park in one of several lots named in honor of Future World pavilions. Trams circulate regularly, providing transportation between the lots and the main entrance. Be sure to note the section and aisle in which you park. Also, know that the parking ticket allows for reentry to the area throughout the day.

HOURS

Future World is usually open from 9 A.M. to 9 P.M. World Showcase hours are 11 A.M. to 9 P.M. During certain holiday periods and the summer months, hours are extended. It's best to arrive at the park at least a half hour before the posted opening time, particularly during these busy seasons. Call 824-4321 for up-to-the-minute schedules.

GETTING AROUND

Water taxis, called *FriendShip* launches, ferry guests across the World Showcase Lagoon. Docks are located near Mexico, Canada, Germany, and Morocco. (The only other way to traverse the area is on foot.)

Admission Prices

ONE-DAY TICKET

(Restricted to use only in Epcot. Prices include sales tax and are subject to change.)

Adult..$42.14
Child*...$33.92

*3 to 9 years of age; children under 3 free

PARK PRIMER

EPCOT

BABY FACILITIES

Changing tables and facilities for nursing mothers can be found at the Baby Care Center in the Odyssey Center, between Test Track and Mexico. Also, disposable diapers are kept behind the counter at many Epcot shops; just ask.

CAMERA NEEDS

The Camera Center on the west side of the Entrance Plaza and World Traveler in International Gateway stock film, batteries, and disposable cameras; they also rent camcorders ($30 per day with a $450 refundable deposit). Two-hour film processing is available here and wherever you see a Photo Express sign. A third camera shop is found in Journey Into Imagination. Film is sold in most Epcot shops.

DISABILITY INFORMATION

Nearly all attractions, shops, and restaurants are barrier-free. Parking for guests with disabilities is available. Special provisions have been made to enhance sight- and hearing-impaired guests' enjoyment of the park. The *Walt Disney World Guide for Guests with Disabilities* is available at Guest Relations. For more information, turn to *Getting Ready to Go*.

EARLY-ENTRY DAYS

On Tuesday and Friday, WDW resort guests may enter Epcot 1½ hours prior to the posted opening time and enjoy selected Future World attractions and pavilions—usually Honey, I Shrunk the Audience, The Living Seas, The Land, Spaceship Earth, and Test Track. Days and attractions are subject to change.

FIRST AID

Minor medical problems can be handled at the First Aid Center, located in the Odyssey Center, between Test Track and Mexico.

INFORMATION

Guest Relations, next to Spaceship Earth, is equipped with guidemaps, a helpful staff, and WorldKey Information Service terminals. Other terminals are near Germany and on the pathway between Epcot's two worlds.

LOCKERS

Attended lockers are found immediately west of Spaceship Earth. Cost is $3 plus a $2 refundable deposit for unlimited use all day.

LOST & FOUND

The Lost and Found department is on the west side of Epcot's main Entrance Plaza at the Gift Stop. To report lost items after your visit call 824-4245.

LOST CHILDREN

Report lost children at Guest Relations, the Baby Care Center, or alert a Disney employee.

MONEY MATTERS

There are ATMs on the east side of the Entrance Plaza, on the path between Future World and World Showcase, and near Germany. Currency exchange is handled at Guest Relations or at the American Express Travel Office on the west side of the Entrance Plaza. Credit cards (American Express, Visa, MasterCard, and The Disney Credit Card), traveler's checks, and WDW resort IDs are accepted for admission, merchandise, and meals at all full-service and fast-food restaurants.

PACKAGE PICKUP

Epcot shops can arrange for bulky purchases to be transported to the Gift Stop on the west side of the Entrance Plaza for later pickup. There is no charge for this service.

SAME-DAY REENTRY

Be sure to have your hand stamped upon exiting the park and to retain your ticket if you plan to return later in the same day.

STROLLERS & WHEELCHAIRS

Strollers, wheelchairs, and Electric Convenience Vehicles (ECVs) may be rented from venues on the east side of the Entrance Plaza and at the International Gateway entrance. Wheelchairs are also available at the Gift Stop. Cost is $5 for strollers and wheelchairs, with a $1 refundable deposit; and $30 for ECVs, with a $10 refundable deposit. Quantities are limited. Keep your rental receipt; it can be used that same day to obtain a replacement at Epcot or at any of the other three theme parks.

TIP BOARD

Check this digital board in Innoventions Plaza throughout the day to learn current waiting times for the most popular attractions.

FUTURE WORLD

A wise alternative is to choose two or three pavilions from those described in this section, and then to head for World Showcase as soon as it opens at 11 A.M., moving clockwise around the lagoon on the first day of your visit and counterclockwise on the next. Then, in the afternoon, when many guests have shifted over to World Showcase, return to Future World. Innoventions is not only a fascinating spot to pass the exceptionally busy hours after lunch, but also a cool refuge when high temperatures prevail outdoors. And although queues can be found during peak seasons at Journey Into Imagination, The Land, Wonders of Life, and Test Track throughout most of the late morning and afternoon, the period from late afternoon until park closing is usually less hectic. But don't forget to make it back to World Showcase in time for the evening's presentation of IllumiNations.

Future World pavilions are described here as a visitor encounters them while moving counterclockwise (from right to left, which is west to east, around the area).

A mere listing of the basic themes covered by the Future World pavilions—agriculture, communications, car safety, the ocean, energy, health, and imagination—tends to sound a tad academic, and perhaps even a little forbidding. But when these serious topics are presented with that special Disney flair, they become part of an experience that ranks among Walt Disney World's most exciting and entertaining.

Some of these subjects are explored in the course of lively and unusual Disney "adventures," involving a whole arsenal of remarkable motion pictures, special effects, and Audio-Animatronics figures so lifelike that it is hard to remain unmoved. And Innoventions offers an invitation to sample cutting-edge technology. The basic elements of Future World are also appealing in their own right, from the palm-dotted Entrance Plaza and the massive buildings of Innoventions to the stupendous fountain just past Spaceship Earth and the many-faceted "geosphere" that has become the universal symbol of Epcot.

There is so much to see and enjoy that it's hard to know just what to do first. Many guests simply stop at Spaceship Earth on their way into Epcot and proceed to wander at random from one pavilion to the next through the morning. As a result, many of the pavilions are frustratingly crowded early in the day—especially Spaceship Earth.

Guest Relations

Located adjacent to Spaceship Earth, this is not only the principal source of Epcot information, but the spot to make restaurant priority seating arrangement via the easy-to-use touch-sensitive screens. (For more information, turn to page 245 in the *Good Meals, Great Times* chapter.)

When the terminals are not being used to arrange tables, they can be used to get an overall picture of Epcot, to learn about each pavilion in considerable detail, and to discover nearly everything else that a guest could conceivably want to know about Epcot. If the system's electronic A-to-Z index of shops, restaurants, attractions, and services does not answer a question, it's possible to communicate with a specially trained host or hostess (who is able to hear and see the querying guest with the aid of a microphone and video camera adjacent to the screen). Hosts and hostesses also manage the message service for Epcot guests and keep records of any lost children who may be at the Baby Care Center or Guest Relations.

Spaceship Earth

As it looms impressively just above the earth, this great faceted silver geosphere—visible on a clear day from an airplane flying along either Florida coast—looks a little bit like the gigantic spaceship in *Close Encounters of the Third Kind* ready to blast off. It appears large from a distance, and it seems even more immense when viewed from directly underneath. It's no surprise that some visitors simply stop beneath it and gawk. The show inside, which explores the continuing search by human beings for ever more efficient means of communication, remains one of Epcot's most visually compelling.

Weighing 16 million pounds, measuring 165 feet in diameter and 180 feet in height, and encompassing 2.2 million cubic feet of space, this geosphere is held aloft by six legs supported by pylons sunk 100 feet into the ground. Its covering derives from a quarter-inch-thick sandwich of two anodized aluminum faces and a polyethylene core. This sheath is made up of 954 triangular panels, not all of equal size or shape.

A common misconception about Spaceship Earth is that it is a geodesic dome. Not so. It's a *geosphere*. A geodesic dome is only half a sphere, while Spaceship Earth is almost completely round. Presented by AT&T.

SPACESHIP EARTH RIDE: The noted science fiction writer Ray Bradbury, together with a number of consultants and advisers from the Smithsonian Institution, the Los Angeles area's prestigious Huntington Library, the University of Southern California, and the University of Chicago (among others), collaborated with Disney designers in developing this memorable 14-minute journey. It begins in an inky black time tunnel complete with a musty smell that suggests the dust of ages, and continues through history from the days of Cro-Magnon man (30,000 or 40,000 years ago) to the future.

The attraction features remarkable special effects, such as the flickering candles in the scene where a monk (himself crafted with such precision and authenticity as to appear to be breathing) has nodded off, and the smell of smoke coming from the fall of Rome.

Every scene is executed in exquisite detail. The symbols on the wall of that Egyptian temple really are hieroglyphics, and the content of the letter being dictated by the pharaoh was excerpted from a missive actually received by an agent of a ruler of the period. The actor in the Greek theater scene is delivering lines from Sophocles' *Oedipus Rex*.

Some visitors wonder as to the identity of the excerpts from the radio and television shows broadcast in this attraction. Take note: The former include "The Lone Ranger," "The Shadow," a commentary by Walter Winchell, and the Joe Louis–Max Schmeling 1938 boxing rematch. Among the television segments featured are Walter Cronkite's reports from the March 10, 1964, New Hampshire Republican primary; Walt Disney introducing "The Wonderful World of Color"; Ed Sullivan and the Harlem Globetrotters; and "Ozzie and Harriet." Film buffs may recognize clips from the movies *Girl Shy* with Harold Lloyd (1924), *Top Hat* with Fred Astaire and Ginger Rogers (1935), and *20,000 Leagues Under the Sea* (1954).

All these sights are enough to keep necks craning and heads turning as the "time machines" wend their way upward. The

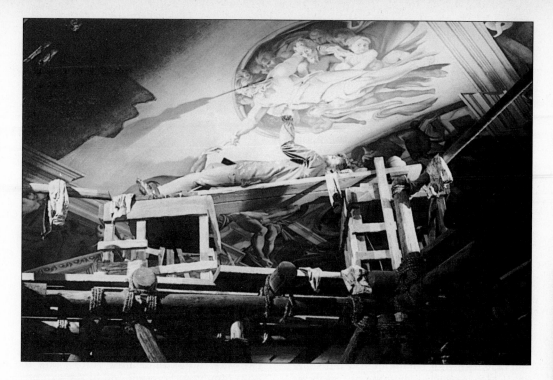

most dazzling scene is the ride's finale, when the audience is placed in the heart of a communications revolution amid interactive global networks that tie all the peoples of the world together. Magical special effects, animated sets, and audience-enclosing laser

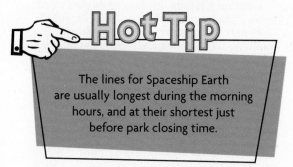

Hot Tip

The lines for Spaceship Earth are usually longest during the morning hours, and at their shortest just before park closing time.

beams are used to create exciting visual sensations. Highlights include glimpses of high-definition TV and virtual reality classrooms of the future.

In the Global Neighborhood exhibit at the end of the journey, guests interact with emerging technologies such as voice recognition, video telephones, and the Internet.

GATEWAY GIFTS AND CAMERA CENTER: These two shops are located near the entrance to Spaceship Earth. The former sells Epcot souvenirs—shirts, mugs, toys, etc.—as well as sunscreen, tissues, and the like. Film and various other Kodak products, including disposable cameras, are sold at the Camera Center. Video cameras may be rented here, and same-day film processing is available.

Innoventions

Imagine being able to get your hands on technological goodies fresh off the drawing board—gadgets that will one day change the way you live and work. At Innoventions, you can see, touch, and test products, some of them so new that many people don't even know they exist! The pavilion is one of Future World's most experiential areas. Equally important, it offers a fun, unintimidating environment where you needn't know how to program a VCR to be able to try out supercomputers, experiment with virtual reality, and see a fully automated home in action.

Within the 100,000-square-foot area, diverse exhibits are presented by major manufacturers. Computers, games, telephones, and appliances are among the wide variety of products on display. Exhibits change constantly, making one of Walt Disney's original dreams for Epcot a reality. Well-informed employees are on hand to answer questions from curious—or even skeptical—visitors. It's also possible to register via computer terminals around the area to receive information about many new products at home.

Innoventions is separated into two buildings, often referred to as Innoventions East and West. The entire area between the pavilions is filled with color, light, an assortment of spinning mobiles, and sidewalks glistening with fiber-optic lighting effects. Inside, areas are divided by company (a sampling is described below). Since exhibits change often, there may be many different technologies available when you visit. Above all, count on spending quite a while exploring the exhibit areas (at least a couple of hours). There's so much to see and do that curiosity will often get the better of any schedule here.

Although the exhibits are all different, two themes emerge, no matter where guests spend their time. Innoventions offers many opportunities to experience virtual reality in its various applications, from education to games. The other focus throughout, the Internet, ensures that everyone leaving Innoventions understands the technology and how to use it.

Exhibitors on the west side of Innoventions include **Sega**, which occupies a very large space. Kids love to try out the numerous new and proposed video games here. Also included is an area just for younger kids, with pint-size games and educational computer programs.

At the **AT&T** area, interactive exhibits deliver a straightforward introduction to the Internet as well as direct TV, a wireless satellite system now accessible through AT&T.

IBM features new ways to think, work, and play with your computer. Try out some of IBM's newest technologies, such as speech recognition and face morphing, plus ThinkPad and Aptiva computers loaded with a host of multimedia software.

Discover magazine holds an annual awards program at Epcot to honor the most innovative minds in science. Guests can learn about the technologies developed by finalists and winners in a permanent display area.

Silicon Graphics has several computers on which guests can try out simulation software, redecorate a room instantly with the click of a mouse via design software, and explore the World Wide Web. This space also presents three virtual reality experiences, including an exhilarating (and, at times, disorienting) *Aladdin*-themed magic carpet ride demonstration, a virtual tour of an Egyptian tomb, and hands-on virtual skiing.

The popular **Enel** exhibit takes guests through a computer-based version of St. Peter's Basilica in Rome, to demonstrate how we can "travel" without leaving home.

Some of the exhibits shown on the east side of Innoventions include the entertaining **House of Innoventions**, presented by Honeywell. In a sample kitchen, living room, bathroom, and bedroom, representatives demonstrate the latest ideas to help make home life a little easier and more relaxing by automating some of our daily tasks. Some of the products highlighted include home security systems, Robochef, breakfast express, flash-bake ovens, and remote control toilets (with heated seats). But our favorite is the Total Home—a computer that fully automates all of the above, plus the lighting, heating, and cooling systems, most appliances, and more.

At **Motorola**, an Audio-Animatronics figure named Sky Cyberguy hosts an amusing show, inviting guests to choose one of three paths for a trip on Motorola's Information Skyway. It's also possible to try out wireless two-way radios that allow you to talk to your family at the other end of the exhibit, personal digital assistants, handwriting recognition software, and pagers. But the big attraction here is the popular virtual reality exhibit, where guests line up to be immersed in a virtual game world while others watch on monitors.

General Electric displays its newest products, from home appliances to jet engines.

Family PC sponsors an exhibit showcasing multimedia technologies. Here, families get a chance to try the latest computer hardware and software. Among the highlights for kids are interactive animated storybooks, including CD-ROMs reprising the latest Disney animated features. **Apple** also has plenty of its latest computers and software on hand for the curious to try.

The **General Motors** display allows guests to "test drive" a new electric vehicle called EV1, enhanced by surround sound and scenery, and see the inner workings of the technology in a cutaway model.

There are also several restaurants and an espresso bar and bakery in the Innoventions complex. See the *Good Meals, Great Times* chapter for details.

CENTORIUM: This large, sleek shop stocks a vast selection of Epcot and Disney character memorabilia and souvenirs—watches, books, candy, key chains, T-shirts, pencils, hats, and much more—making this the number one source for character merchandise in Epcot. There are also many items related to other areas of Future World, such as Figment dolls, along with a large selection of Disney-themed sports apparel and children's clothing.

THE ART OF DISNEY EPCOT GALLERY:
Upstairs from Centorium is Epcot's spot for a unique assortment of Disney collectibles. The shop showcases a wide variety of Disney animation art, including production cels, hand-painted limited-edition cels, sericels, maquettes (character models), fine-art serigraphs, and lithographs. In addition, a large selection of decorative items include renditions of Disney characters by such well-known companies as Lladró.

The Living Seas

A trip four fathoms deep into the Caribbean Sea awaits. The Living Seas is the largest facility ever dedicated to humanity's relationship with the ocean, and was designed by the Disney Imagineers, in cooperation with a board of some of the world's most distinguished oceanographic experts and scientists.

At the entrance is a stylized rockwork marquee that suggests a natural coastline, with waves cascading into tide pools. A 2½-minute multimedia presentation provides an introduction, saluting the pioneers of ocean research, beginning with early ships, diving bells, submarines, and Aqua-Lungs. The show also features a seven-minute film that attempts to demonstrate the critical role of the ocean as a source of energy, minerals, and protein.

From there, a ride through a simulated Caribbean coral reef environment and the hands-on activities of Sea Base Alpha combine to prolong a visitor's stay. The Coral Reef restaurant offers fresh seafood in a setting where diners look out at the reef through acrylic windows 18 feet high and 8 inches thick. Tables are arranged on tiers so that all patrons have an unobstructed view. Presented by United Technologies.

Under the Sea

Two behind-the-scenes tours offer guests a closer look at life in The Living Seas underwater environs. DiveQuest gives certified scuba divers the opportunity to explore one of the world's largest aquariums. A dolphin exploration program offers guests the chance to learn about dolphin behavior as they closely observe researchers and trainers interacting with dolphins. Reservations for either tour can be made by calling WDW-TOUR (939-8687). For more information on both of these programs, turn to page 198 of the *Everything Else in the World* chapter.

CARIBBEAN CORAL REEF RIDE: To reach the two-passenger sea cabs that make the trip to the coral reef, visitors enter "hydrolators," elevator-like capsules that create the illusion of diving deep under the sea, while actually descending only about an inch. The man-made reef exists in an enormous 6-million-gallon tank (203 feet in diameter and 27 feet deep), where more than 65 species of sea life coexist in a simulated environment that accurately re-creates the chemistry and life-support ecosystems of the Caribbean Sea.

Among the 5,000 or so inhabitants are sea turtles, parrot fish, puffers, barracuda, butterfly fish, angelfish, sharks, croakers, dolphins, and diamond rays.

In addition to the vast array of sea life and vegetation, guests also get to see scuba divers testing and demonstrating the newest diving gear and underwater monitoring equipment as they carry on training experiments with dolphins. Wireless radios allow the divers to talk to onlookers and explain their work. Other undersea attractions include a diver in a JIM suit, the latest in atmospheric diving-wear technology (at Sea Base Alpha, guests have the chance to try one on personally), two one-person submarines, and two mini-robotic submersibles. Following the three-minute ride, guests are conveniently deposited at Sea Base Alpha.

SEA BASE ALPHA: This prototype undersea research facility, spread over two levels, includes a visitors' center and six modules, each dedicated to a specific subject. One focuses on ocean ecosystems and shows various forms of adaptation, including camouflage, symbiosis, and bioluminescence. A 6,000-gallon tank displays another coral reef where Bermuda morays, barracuda, and bonnethead sharks swim about. Another module is dedicated to the study of porpoises and manatees. A tank features a step-in port, where guests can see the mammals up close.

At another station, a show stars an Audio-Animatronics submersible named Jason who describes for visitors the history of robotics and its use in underwater exploration. Guests can try on a cutaway JIM suit, and test its maneuverability by doing tasks as part of a game. There are also video screens to test and expand your knowledge of oceanography.

SEA BASE CONCOURSE: Adjacent to the six modules, the concourse features three displays. The floor-to-ceiling diver lockout chamber is where the crew enters and exits the ocean environment. Visitors can see divers enter the chamber, ascend, and disappear through the ceiling. A full-size mock-up of the latest one-person submersible vehicle, the Deep Rover, is suspended from the mezzanine of the concourse.

The Land

Occupying six acres, this enormous sky-lighted pavilion examines the nature of one of everybody's favorite topics—food. A film, *The Circle of Life,* uses characters from *The Lion King* to deliver an entertaining yet inspirational message about humanity and the environment. A boat ride explores farming in the past and future.

Guided tours give visitors the chance to learn more about the experimental agricultural techniques being practiced in the pavilion and nearby greenhouses. In addition, the subject of nutrition is touched upon in one of Future World's wackiest attractions, a musical show called Food Rocks.

Since this is also the home of two of Epcot's most interesting eating spots—the Garden Grill and the Sunshine Season Food Fair—The Land is understandably popular. During peak seasons, lengthy queues build up for both the boat ride and *The Circle of Life.* The best plan is to visit early in the morning and have a quick breakfast at the food court. Or wait until later in the afternoon, when many people have left Future World for World Showcase. Presented by Nestlé USA.

Birnbaum's *Best*

CELEBRATE THE LAND: The 13½-minute boat ride through the rain forest and greenhouses in this pavilion opens with a dramatic storm scene. Guests sail through tropical rain forests, prairie grain fields, and a family farm. As the boat passes through each amazingly realistic setting, the guide offers commentary on mankind's ongoing struggle to cultivate and live in harmony with the land. Note some of the details that make each setting so convincing, such as water dripping from leaves in the rain forest, sand blowing over the desert, and light flickering from the television set in the farmhouse window.

In the next segment, guests enter a living-plant research laboratory-solarium. Here, the earth's major food crops, fruits, and vegetables are being grown in high-tech research projects along with rare new crops that may someday help meet the earth's ever-growing dietary needs. The guide on each boat offers interesting information on the crops being grown. Also of interest are the experiments being conducted to explore the possibilities of raising fish like other farm products, and the desert farm area, where plants receive nutrients through a drip irrigation system that delivers just the right amount of water, and no more—important in an arid climate.

As fantastic and unreal as they appear, all the plants on view in the experimental greenhouses are living. In contrast, those in the biomes (ecological communities) were made in Disney studios out of flexible, lightweight plastic that simulates the cellulose found in real trees. The trunks and branches were molded from live specimens; the majestic sycamore in the farmhouse's front yard, for example, duplicates one that stands outside a Burbank, California, car wash. Hundreds of thousands of polyethylene leaves, made in Hong Kong, were then snapped on. These are fire-retardant, as are the blades of grass, which are made of glass fibers implanted into rubber mats.

THE CIRCLE OF LIFE: This 20-minute film uses animation and live footage to illustrate some of the dangers to our environment, as well as potential solutions. Presented as a fable featuring *The Lion King* favorites Simba, Timon, and Pumbaa, the film takes an optimistic approach to a serious subject. *The Circle of Life* is shown in the 428-seat Harvest Theater (near The Land's entrance) on a 23- by 60-foot screen. To set the mood, the movie opens with a stunning live-action animal sequence that recalls the animated "Circle of Life" scene from *The Lion King*.

As the animated part of the film begins, Simba is startled by the shout of "Timber!" and is drenched by the splash of a fallen tree in the water. The culprits are none other than his friends Timon and Pumbaa, who are clearing the savanna for the development of the Hakuna Matata Lakeside Village. Simba seizes the opportunity to tell the tale, passed on to him by his father, of creatures who sometimes forget that everything is connected in the great Circle of Life: humans. Simba demonstrates to Timon and Pumbaa the consequences of progress, as his lessons are driven home by motion-picture views of humans' mistreatment of the air, water, and land. (Timon: "And everybody was *okay* with this?") The overall effect is a compelling mix of entertainment and a valuable message about environmental responsibility.

FOOD ROCKS: Classic rock 'n' roll songs have been humorously altered to deliver a nutritional message at this 15-minute mock rock concert. The introduction, presented by a "heavy metal" group—giant kitchen utensils atop a cartoon stove—is Queen's "Bohemian Rhapsody" with new lyrics. The show is set in a kitchen of cartoonish proportion, and life-size characters make this an entertaining show. The show is hosted by Füd Wrapper, inspired by rapper Tone Loc.

Musical guests include the Peach Boys, who harmonize a rendition of "Good Vibrations" called "Good Nutrition"; Pita Gabriel singing to the tune of "Sledgehammer;" and The Sole of Rock 'n' Roll, a fish inspired by Cher, singing a new version of the "Shoop Shoop Song." Neil Moussaka, Chubby Cheddar, the Get-the-Point-Sisters, and (Little) Richard also make humorous appearances.

It's interesting to note that Tone Loc, Chubby Checker, Neil Sedaka, Little Richard, and The Pointer Sisters actually recorded the parodies of their music. In the pre-show area, there are murals featuring fun food facts, three-dimensional food pyramids, and interactive "meal kebabs" where guests can create their own nutritional menus. Six giant "smell boxes" open to reveal the aromas of garlic, chocolate, coffee, bacon, orange, and seafood.

BEHIND THE SEEDS: For guests who are interested in a more detailed look at the growing areas at The Land, one-hour guided tours take place throughout the day. The tour travels through four themed greenhouses where plants are grown hydroponically (without soil). Different areas of the greenhouses showcase pioneering research projects undertaken in cooperation with NASA and the U.S. Department of Agriculture. Because this walking tour is an expanded version of the Celebrate the Land boat ride, the ride is a suggested prerequisite. Reservations, which are required, must be made in person early on the day of the tour, at the podium at the Green Thumb Emporium. Cost is $6 for adults and $4 for children ages three to nine.

GREEN THUMB EMPORIUM: This little shop between the Sunshine Season Food Fair and Food Rocks stocks merchandise such as hydroponic plants, seeds, books, topiaries, and kitchen accessories.

Journey Into Imagination

The oddly shaped glass pyramids that house Journey Into Imagination (immediately to your right as you face World Showcase Lagoon) are striking. But they pale in comparison with the experiences inside, which are easily among the most whimsical at Epcot. Dreamfinder, a jolly, red-headed professorial figure—sporting a carrot-colored beard and accompanied by a purple baby dragon called Figment—is only one of the pavilion's delights. He appears in person outside and again inside when he escorts guests through the world of imagination during a 14-minute ride.

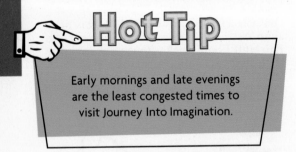

Early mornings and late evenings are the least congested times to visit Journey Into Imagination.

There's also a dazzling 3-D movie, called Honey, I Shrunk the Audience. Not to mention the electronic fun house known as Image Works. Or the quirky fountains outside—the Jellyfish Fountains, which spurt streams of water that spread out at the top, looking for an instant like their namesake sea creature; or the Leap Frog Fountains, which send out smooth streams of water that arc from one garden plot to another in the most astonishing fashion. Kids love them.

Count on spending an hour and 15 minutes at the very least at this pavilion—two hours

wouldn't be too long at all. During peak seasons, the queue outside seems to be longest from about 10 A.M. to noon and remains fairly lengthy throughout most of the day. Presented by Kodak.

JOURNEY INTO IMAGINATION RIDE: It is here that Dreamfinder creates Figment out of a lizard's body, a crocodile's nose, a steer's horns, two big yellow eyes, two small wings, and a pinch of childish delight—and commences the visitor's journey into the world of imagination.

First-timers may perceive the 14-minute ride as a random assortment of scenes that are handsome and scary by turns, but it is actually an organized exploration of how the imagination works and the areas of life in which it functions.

First there is a visit to the Dreamport, the area of the human mind to which the senses are constantly sending data to be stored for later use by the imagination. Subsequent scenes depict the way imagination suffuses the worlds of the visual and performing arts, literature, and science and technology. In the course of all this, laser beams dance, lightning crackles, and letters come pouring out of a gigantic typewriter like notes from an organ. The images are as fanciful as the imagination itself.

When you see flashing lights (about three-quarters of the way through the ride), be sure to sit up straight and smile—your picture is being taken. You'll see your photo toward the end of the ride.

IMAGE WORKS: It's a rare Image Works visitor who doesn't experience at least some of the emotion felt by one four-year-old girl who cried every time her parents tried to take her home. That's not surprising, because Image Works is literally crammed with activities that give every visitor the chance to use his or her imagination.

For instance, at Dreamfinder's School of Drama, near the entrance to Image Works, visitors have the opportunity to be in a TV show. Guests step onto a small stage and,

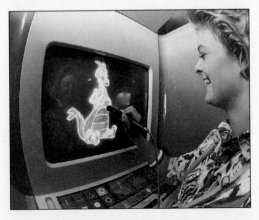

thanks to a Chroma-Key video-effects technique involving foreground and background matting, perform in short video stories. Spectators and performers alike see the results as they happen via video screens. It's always fun to watch the groups of people jumping crazily around on stage following on-screen instructions from Dreamfinder. (And, in fact, having the leisure to spend more than just a few seconds watching these goings-on is sufficient reason to allot more time to your overall Epcot visit.)

Another exhibit here is Figment's Coloring Book, where guests use computer technology to paint giant coloring-book images. The Sensor is a sort of electronic maze whose various elements react to a visitor's presence by producing lights and sounds. Upon entering the Rainbow Corridor, you'll find a tunnel of neon tubes in all the hues of the rainbow. Image Warp's pneumatically powered Mylar mirrors produce moving versions of old-style fun house reflections in a room wackily illuminated by strobe lights. Then there's the Lumia—a plastic ball seven feet in diameter inside of which swirling patterns of light and color appear in response to sounds of different frequencies and intensities. Another feature is Making Faces, a set of screens that allow you to electronically capture your own image and then apply different noses, hairstyles, ears, eyes, even accessories.

At Stepping Tones, hexagonal splotches of colored light on the floor correspond to sounds—a drumroll, a flourish on the harp, a couple of chords sung by a men's chorus, a snippet of hoedown fiddling, and such—emitted when the area is trod upon. The floor was "orchestrated" so that all possible combinations sound interesting at the very least—and the more the merrier.

Other activities include Light Writer, which involves drawing geometric patterns with laser beams, and the Magic Palette, where a special stylus and a touch-sensitive control surface can be used to create all kinds of images, mostly in Day-Glo colors. People often queue up to try these, while the huge kaleidoscopes and the unusual pin screens nearby are practically overlooked. Manufacturing the latter involved putting thousands of straight pins through a screen illuminated with colored lights from below (visitors run their hands across the bottom, thereby creating sweeping patterns of color).

The Electronic Philharmonic, one of the most amusing sections of the Image Works, allows guests to take turns conducting an orchestra. Here's how this works: Each patch of light on the console represents a group of instruments (strings, woodwinds, brass, percussion). Raising and lowering one's hand above that patch of light increases and decreases the volume of the

sound produced by that section of the "orchestra." The faster the movement, the louder they play.

Just outside Image Works, note the terrific photography display. The images are winners of Kodak's International Newspaper Snapshot Awards, and well worth a look.

Birnbaum's Best

HONEY, I SHRUNK THE AUDIENCE:
Welcome to the Imagination Institute, workplace of Professor Wayne Szalinski, the featured character in the three hit "Honey" movies, *Honey, I Shrunk the Kids*, *Honey, I Blew Up the Kid*, and *Honey, We Shrunk Ourselves*. Rick Moranis, Marcia Strassman, and the kids reprise their film roles at this 25-minute attraction.

In the pre-show area, guests see a movie about the imagination. Then they are welcomed to the Imagination Institute and given an overview of what they will see inside the theater. Szalinski is to be presented with the Inventor of the Year Award, and will demonstrate several of his inventions. On the way into the theater, guests are given "protective goggles" (3-D glasses), to shield their eyes from flying debris that can come loose during new-product demonstrations.

Once the audience is seated, Szalinski is nowhere to be found. Then he zooms off the screen in his new HoverPod, out of control and miniaturized by his shrinking machine. Szalinski's son Nick steps in to demonstrate the "Dimensional Duplicator," a machine that can make exact copies of anything. As Nick switches on the machine, his little brother Adam drops his pet mouse into the duplicating chamber, hits the number 999, and suddenly hundreds of mice pour out of the screen in an almost 4-D effect that leaves guests squirming.

Nick quickly gets rid of the mice with Professor Szalinski's No-Mess Holographic Pet System, which projects a 3-D cat out into the

audience to scare away the mice. The cat morphs into a lynx and finally into a ferocious lion before overheating and exploding. Just then, Szalinski returns, blows himself up to normal size, and demonstrates his new, more powerful, shrinking machine. The machine spins out of control and accidentally shrinks the audience and Nick. While the audience is miniaturized the theater shakes with every on-screen footstep. When apparent giants crouch down to ogle guests in the theater, it's a rare person who doesn't feel diminished to ant proportions. The effects are very believable, particularly when Adam picks up the theater and shows it to his mom. Motion effects in the theater add to the realism, as does the full-size pet snake that gets loose. (This effect may frighten younger children.) The audience is eventually brought back to normal size, of course, although not without incident. The attraction has one last surprise in store that we won't divulge.

CAMERAS AND FILM: A good selection of film is for sale here, along with disposable cameras, and other photographic essentials.

Test Track

This groundbreaking General Motors pavilion was among the most keenly anticipated in Epcot history. For while its predecessor, World of Motion, did justice to its mission—regaling guests with a trip through the past, present, and future of transportation—Test Track has greater aspirations. The attraction, which opened recently, is not just a thrill ride in a theme park where such things are conspicuous. It is a thrill ride of the highest order, a blockbuster pushing Epcot to the fore of visitors' attention. Equally important, Test Track honors the park's larger mission to educate as well as entertain.

More precisely, this new industrial-looking pavilion puts guests through the frenetic motions of automobile testing. As ride vehicles progress along the nearly mile-long track, they whiz down straightaways, hug hairpin turns, accelerate up steep inclines, and face near-collisions—and not always on ideal road conditions. En route, riders learn firsthand how tests are performed in real facilities (called proving grounds) and discover why certain procedures are crucial to automotive safety. Ultimately, they walk away with invaluable insight into cars, not to mention new respect for the complex systems therein.

Before developing the attraction, Disney Imagineers toured GM proving grounds around the country. The result: From the roll-up doors of its steely facade to the rows of

authentic testing equipment inside, Test Track bears more than a passing resemblance to the real thing.

The experience begins with a 20-minute pre-show, a walking tour of the plant that reveals the incredible amount of component testing performed before automakers commit to production. Guests witness 21 true-to-life automotive testing vignettes, with everything from human interface (our courageous, crash-prone counterparts) to tires, brakes, air bags, and even seats being put through their paces. Video monitors explain the purposes of many of the tests.

At the end of this winding queue, visitors are invited 48 at a time into a briefing room. Here, they are directed to climb into their test vehicles, fasten their (standard) seat belts, and prepare to embark on Test Track's five-minute ride segment. Each car seats six. The prototype vehicles, computer designed and controlled, travel completely independent of one another on the automated test track. Equipped with video and audio, but no steering wheels or brake pedals, they are sporty and buggy-like. The roads themselves bear the familiar yellow lines and signage of the real world, adding to the attraction's realism.

The rough-and-tumble ride begins on the building's lowest level with an uphill acceleration test over a 16% grade. Then the suspension gets a workout, as the vehicles descend over a very bumpy surface that puts the wheels at odds with one another. Back on the lower level, guests learn by experience how antilock braking systems (ABS) work, and also—in one of the attraction's more tangible lessons—why they are extremely handy when you need to stop suddenly. There are two brake tests, one with ABS and one with traditional brakes. Vehicles get going up to 25 miles per hour, then brake to make a quick curve. Without antilock brakes, the vehicles can't negotiate the turn. During environmental testing, riders feel the heat and get the shivers as vehicles pass first through a radiant heat chamber, then a cold chamber. Roadside robots pitch

BIRNBAUM'S Best

in by spraying the fenders and door panels with water to test for corrosion.

During the road-handling segment, the ride takes a dramatic turn. Vehicles course along a winding road, complete with simulated mountain scenery, and into a darkened tunnel. Passengers hear a horn blast, see the blinding high beams of a tractor trailer, and swerve to avoid the truck. As they emerge and the light level picks up, there is a crash; guests round a corner to witness a barrier crash test. Their own vehicles then accelerate toward the same barrier. Just when a collision seems imminent, doors open up and the vehicles emerge outside on an elevated track. A long straightaway feeds into a series of heavily banked (about 45-degree) turns and another straight shot that sends vehicles rocketing around the front of the pavilion at top speed (up to 65 miles per hour). Strobe lights add to the effect. (Displays in the vehicles register real-time data so guests know what tests are being conducted at any given time.) Upon re-entering the building, there's a final hurrah before guests disembark: thermal imaging screens that illuminate friction points in the vehicle, pointing to areas prone to excessive wear and tear. So ends a wild and wonderful trip that also happens to be the fastest and, at 5,200 feet, longest Disney ride.

In the post-show area, there is a demo of car technology and a multimedia presentation on auto assembly. General Motors' latest models and concept cars are also on display. A shop features General Motors merchandise, as well as a selection of items with a Test Track theme. Impulse buyers take note: There are no actual automobiles available for purchase here.

Note: Children under seven years old must be accompanied by an adult; guests under 40 inches tall are not permitted to ride; signs state that passengers must be free of back problems, heart conditions, motion sickness, and other physical limitations to ride this attraction.

On the Horizon

The future is looking bright for the pavilion that celebrates the future. Horizons, located in Future World's western hemisphere between the Test Track and Wonders of Life pavilions, is undergoing a massive refurbishment. Though the pavilion will remain closed through most of 1998, expect a dazzling new attraction to take its place in the near future.

Wonders of Life

The 72-foot-tall steel DNA molecule at the entrance to this popular pavilion beckons guests to humorous and informative experiences related to health. Housed in a 100,000-square-foot geodesic dome and two attached buildings, this pavilion allows guests to enjoy both a serious and an amusing look at health, fitness, and modern lifestyles. Wonders of Life also boasts Body Wars, Epcot's first authentic thrill ride—a fast and furious journey through the human body.

From outside the gold-topped dome, the Wonders of Life sign seems to rest on the flumes of water shot up by two fountains. Once inside the building, guests find themselves at the Fitness Fairgrounds.

At the Fairgrounds, a variety of shows and activities for both children and adults are offered. *Goofy About Health* is an eight-minute multiscreen montage that sees Goofy go from a sloppy-living guy to a health-conscious fellow. Using old Goofy cartoons that haven't been seen for many years, the show traces Goofy's ups and downs, and winds up with new footage of Goofy at his doctor's office. The film is shown in a 100-seat open theater where visitors can come and go as they please.

At the AnaComical Players Theater, a corny (but nonetheless informative) show is presented by an improvisational theater group. Audience members are asked to participate, and it's all a lot of fun. This theater seats 100 people. The third theater at the Fitness Fairgrounds is enclosed. The 14-minute film shown here, *The Making of Me*, is a story starring Martin Short as a man who wonders how he came into existence. To find out, he travels back in time to the birth of his parents, their first few years together, and their decision to have a child—him. Footage from an actual delivery is part of the film; it is sensitively presented and provides a tangible and touching view of childbirth. It was written and directed by Glenn Gordon Caron, who directed the TV show "Moonlighting" and the film *Clean and Sober*.

Parents should be aware, however, that the film is a bit graphic and so may not be suitable for some children. It also leaves a few key questions unanswered, thereby allowing parents to satiate their kids' appetite for knowledge on a case-by-case basis.

There are plenty of hands-on activities in areas surrounding the theaters. Guests can ride Wondercycles, computerized stationary bicycles that enable guests to pedal through a variety of locales including Disneyland and the Rose Bowl Parade. At Coach's Corner, golf, tennis, or baseball swings are analyzed, and a professional knowledgeable in each sport offers free, albeit taped, advice to help you on your way. The Sensory Funhouse offers hands-on activities for kids. It's the Disney version of a children's museum, where education and entertainment go hand in hand.

At the Met Lifestyle Revue, guests punch in such information as age, weight, height, exercise habits, whether they smoke, and perceived stress levels at an interactive computer terminal. The computer then processes the information and offers some advice on how to lead a healthier and less stressful existence.

Frontiers of Medicine, located toward the rear of the Fitness Fairgrounds, features the only completely serious segment of Wonders of Life. Here guests can see some scientific and educational exhibits of leading developments in medicine and health sciences. The exhibits change regularly.

Pure and Simple offers a variety of healthy snacks. Nearby, Well & Goods Limited offers a selection of athletic wear, most of which features Disney characters participating in a variety of sports, and some educational materials. Presented by MetLife.

and reacts. The other animated participant, General Knowledge, helps Buzzy learn which portion of the mind is required for a particular situation. The right and left sides of the brain, the stomach, the heart, and the adrenal gland are all represented by familiar celebrities. Our favorite is George Wendt (Norm from "Cheers"), operating the stomach. Other characters include Bobcat Goldthwait as the adrenal gland, Dana Carvey and Kevin Nealon (Hans and Franz of "Saturday Night Live" fame) as the heart, Charles Grodin as the left brain, and John Lovitz as the right brain.

Cranium Command is an altogether whimsical and entertaining show—one of the best at Epcot. This 17-minute show is fast-paced and packed with so many details that you'll notice new things even after seeing it many times.

CRANIUM COMMAND: This area of the Wonders of Life pavilion welcomes guests into the mind of a 12-year-old kid. The preshow sets the mood as an animated film explains what you are about to see. General Knowledge is recruiting pilots for an assortment of new brains. There are jokes aplenty, many of which go right over the heads of young kids. Buzzy, our star pilot, fumbles through basic training and gets assigned to the most volatile brain of all, that of an adolescent boy.

Inside a 200-seat theater, the enormously exaggerated head of our 12-year-old subject is piloted by Buzzy, a delightfully goofy Audio-Animatronics figure. The two large eyes are actually rear-projection video screens, and it is through them that the audience gets an idea of how a young boy thinks

BODY WARS: The same state-of-the-art technology that sends guests on a rollicking ride through space at the Star Tours attraction at the Disney-MGM Studios also exists at Wonders of Life in the form of this five-minute thrill ride. After boarding the vehicles, which are actually the same type of flight simulators employed by military and commercial airlines in pilot training, guests are whisked away on a bumpy, rocky, and exciting ride through the human body. (When instructed to fasten your seat belt, do so. This is a rough ride.) Movie buffs will think immediately of the film *Fantastic Voyage* and the more recent *Inner Space*. The queue area features exhibits from a fictional company specializing in the latest technology in the miniaturization of people. Guests pass through two special-effects portals and are declared ready to do a routine medical probe of the human body—from the inside.

During the course of this bumpy trip, a scientist is dispatched to remove a splinter that has made its way beneath the patient's skin. Guests go along for the ride, but end up on a rescue mission when the scientist is attacked by a white blood cell. Of course, there are some problems along the way, making this trip seem out of control.

Note: This is a rougher ride than Star Tours at the Disney-MGM Studios. Signs posted outside Body Wars warn that passengers must be free of back problems, heart conditions, motion sickness, and other such physical limitations. Pregnant women are not permitted to board. Kids must be at least three years old to ride. Those under seven must be accompanied by an adult. Finally, if the sight of blood makes you woozy, this attraction may not be for you.

Universe of Energy

Although it's easy to spot this pavilion's mirrored pyramid, the facade doesn't provide any clue at all to the 45 minutes of surprises in store. One of the most technologically complex experiences at Epcot, the show consists of several movies and a ride-through segment. None of these are exactly what guests might expect. This is especially true after the pavilion's 1996 renovation, which repackaged the attraction, placing its legendary Audio-Animatronics dinosaurs and lofty environmental message in a decidedly comedic, and much more personal context.

The show begins with a film featuring a few familiar faces. A character named Ellen is in her living room watching a game show on which her college roommate, Judy, is a contestant. Ellen tries to play along, but keeps striking out, particularly in the ENERGY category. As she watches, her neighbor Bill Nye, the Science Guy, comes over to borrow supplies for an experiment and is aghast at Ellen's ignorance. Bill leaves, and Ellen falls asleep. She dreams she is on the game show competing against her friend Judy and Albert Einstein. The topic is ENERGY, and, as Einstein ponders and Ellen fumbles, Judy is cleaning up. Ellen, who has a negative score ("this nightmare game is a lot harder than the home version"), decides to freeze her dream and ask Bill Nye for help.

The second segment leads guests into a theater where Bill Nye vows to educate Ellen about the importance of energy. He persuades her to travel back in time to see exactly where some of our energy sources came from. Suddenly, the whole seating area rotates, and then breaks up into six smaller sections that move slowly forward—prompting a chorus of oohs and aahs from startled members of the audience. The vehicles embark with Ellen upon an odyssey through the primeval world. Enormous prehistoric trees crowd the forest. Apatosauruses wallow in the lagoon out front. A lofty allosaurus battles with an armored stegosaurus a bit farther along, and an elasmosaurus bursts out of a tide pool with frightening suddenness—all under the vulturelike gaze of winged creatures known as pteranodons. Then an Audio-Animatronics Ellen becomes trapped by a snake-like dinosaur. She manages to free herself and departs, apologizing to the dinosaurs for the intrusion.

Next, guests move out of the forest and view a fast-paced montage of pictures capturing the history of human civilization, from cave dwellers to the present. (Keep your eyes peeled for the caveman who discovers fire—you just might recognize him.) The issue of alternative energy sources is raised, and the message communicated is that there is no save-all energy source, but rather many possibilities with promise. The attraction winds up with Ellen returning to the game show of her dreams. This time, she's beating her friend Judy, who is not at all happy about how much Ellen has learned during the commercial break. Ellen bets everything in the final round. In order to win, she must name the one energy source that will never be depleted. (We won't reveal the answer, but are not too proud to brag about getting it right!)

Almost as intriguing as the attraction is the technology behind it. The vehicles weigh about 30,000 pounds when fully loaded with passengers, yet are guided along the floor by a wire only *one-eighth inch* thick. Some of the pavilion's energy is generated by two acres of photovoltaic cells mounted on the roof. The cells generate enough energy to run six average homes. Presented by Exxon.

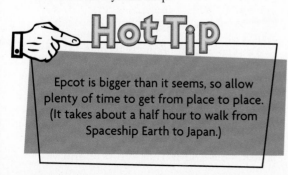

Epcot is bigger than it seems, so allow plenty of time to get from place to place. (It takes about a half hour to walk from Spaceship Earth to Japan.)

WORLD SHOWCASE

Noble sentiments about humanity and the fellowship of nations, which have motivated so many world's fairs in the past, also inhabit World Showcase. But make no mistake about it: This half of Epcot, located to the south of Future World, is unlike any previous international exposition.

The group of pavilions that encircle World Showcase Lagoon (a body of water that is about the size of 85 football fields) demonstrates Disney conceptions about participating countries in remarkably realistic, consistently entertaining styles. You won't find the real Germany here; rather, the country's essence, much as a traveler returning from a visit might remember what he or she saw. Shops, restaurants, and attractions are housed in a group of structures that is an artful pastiche of all the elements that give that nation's countryside and towns their distinctive flavor. Although occasional liberties have been taken when scale and proportion required, careful research governed the design of every nook and cranny.

In the shops, many of the wares on display represent the country in whose pavilion they are offered for sale. The food focuses on native cuisine, and the entertainment is as authentic as the Disney casting directors can make it, with native performers commonly featured and new festivities always in the works. Craftspeople are occasionally on hand to demonstrate their art in the appropriate shops. Thanks to special Epcot cultural exchange programs and the personnel department's efforts to recruit nationals, nearly all the World Showcase staff members in restaurants, shops, and attractions were born in the countries the pavilions represent (or at least spent many years living there) to contribute still more atmosphere.

Home gardeners should be sure to note the World Showcase landscaping: Each pavilion's plantings closely approximate what would be found in the featured nation. The 1.3-mile World Showcase Promenade, which links pavilions on the shores of World Showcase Lagoon, has its own interesting vegetation, beginning near Showcase Plaza with 75-foot Washingtonia fan palms, Arizona-California natives that were imported to Central Florida. Underneath them is a garden full of rosebushes. All told, there are more than 10,000 tree roses, grandifloras, teas, and miniature roses planted throughout World Showcase.

We recommend taking in as many shows, rides, and films as possible in the afternoon, and saving the shops for the pleasant evening hours.

Pavilions are described here in the order that they would be encountered while moving counterclockwise (from west to east) around the World Showcase Lagoon after crossing the bridge from Future World.

Canada

Celebrating the many beauties of America's neighbor to the north, the area devoted to the Western Hemisphere's largest nation is complete with its own mountain, waterfall, rushing stream, rocky canyon, mine, and splendid garden massed with colorful flowers. There's even a totem pole, a trading post, and an elaborate, mansard-roofed hotel similar to ones built by the Canadian railroads as they pushed west around the turn of the century. All this is imaginatively arranged somewhat like a split-level house, with the section representing French Canada on top, and another devoted to the mountains alongside it and below. From a distance, the Hôtel du Canada, the main building here, looks like little more than a bump on the landscape—as does Epcot's single Canadian Rocky Mountain. But up close they both seem to tower as high as the real thing, thanks to a technique known as forced perspective, which exaggerates the relative smallness of distant parts of a structure to make the totality appear much taller than it actually is.

The gardens were inspired by the Butchart Gardens in Victoria, British Columbia, a famous park created on the site of a limestone quarry. The hotel is modeled after Ottawa's Victorian-style Château Laurier.

Lively, engaging entertainment is provided by Canadian folk dancers and the Caledonia Bagpipe Band.

O CANADA!: This 17-minute motion picture, presented in Circle-Vision 360 inside Canada's mountain, portrays the Canadian confederation in all its coast-to-coast splendor—the prairies and plains, sparkling shorelines and rivers, and the untouched snowfields and rocky mountainsides. The Royal Canadian Mounted Police also put in an appearance. All the maritime provinces are pictured, with their covered bridges and sailing ships, as is Montreal, with its Old World cafés and churches; the scene in the Cathédrale de Notre Dame, with its organ booming and choirboys in attendance, is

Hot Tip

Don't try to fit all of the World Showcase movies into one day, especially if you are traveling with small children.

particularly stirring. The great outdoors gets equal play. In one scene, Canada snow geese take off all around the screen, and the beating of their wings is positively thunderous. Eagles, possums, mallards, bobcats, wolves, bears, deer, bison, and herds of reindeer were all filmed. Filmed too were steers being roped at a rodeo and the chuck wagon race that takes place every year at that great provincial fair known as the Calgary Stampede. Skiers in the vast and empty Bugaboos, dogsledders, and ice-skaters are featured in the winter scenes; in a hockey game, the sound system almost perfectly conveys the scratch of skates on ice and the sharp whack of sticks slamming against the puck. And throughout, the motion picture provides a you-are-there feeling that makes all of this spectacular scenery still more memorable. Note that there are no seats in this theater.

NORTHWEST MERCANTILE: The first shop to the left upon entering the pavilion's plaza on the way to the Hôtel du Canada features heavy lumberjack shirts, maple syrup, Royal Canadian Mounted Police merchandise, and other wares that trappers might have purchased back in pioneering days. Skeins of rope, tin scoops, lanterns, and a pair of antique ice skates hanging from the long beams overhead set the mood, together with the structure itself.

Located to the store's rear are Indian artifacts and souvenirs—items like fur vests and moccasins, and sleek-lined sculptures (some carved in soapstone by the Inuit). Notable are handcrafted Canadian items that are seldom seen elsewhere in the American market.

LA BOUTIQUE DES PROVINCES: This small shop, which features a variety of items with an Anne of Green Gables theme, also proffers jewelry, prints, ceramics, and giftware.

United Kingdom

In the space of only a few hundred feet, visitors to this pavilion stroll from an elegant London square to the edge of a canal in the rural countryside—via a bustling urban English street framed by buildings that constitute a veritable rhapsody of historic architectural styles. But one scene leads to the next so smoothly that nothing ever seems amiss. Here again, note the attention to detail: the half-timbered High Street structure that actually leans a bit, the hand-painted "smoke" stains that make the chimneys look as if they had been there for centuries. When a thatched roof is required, it's right where it should be—though the roof may be made of plastic broom bristles because fire regulations prohibit the real thing. Off to the side is a pair of scarlet phone booths identical to those that used to be found all around the U.K. And there are eight architectural styles characteristic of the streetscapes, from English Tudor to Georgian and English Victorian.

There is no major attraction in this pavilion; instead, it features half a dozen fine shops and a pub that serves a selection of beers and ales that would be the toast of any first-class "local" in London itself. There's also plenty of good entertainment, including a group of comedians called the World Showcase Players, who, when not engaged in general clowning on the World Showcase Promenade, coax audience members into participating in their farcical (if unsophisticated) playlets. In the pub, a pianist plays, sings just about any request, and interacts with guests late into the evening.

Characters, such as Mary Poppins and Winnie the Pooh, often appear in the garden courtyard. A traditional English hedge maze is found near Anne Hathaway's cottage.

THE TOY SOLDIER: This delightful shop presents a variety of British toys, as well as a rather extensive selection of merchandise starring Winnie the Pooh, Piglet, Eeyore, and Tigger, too. Outside, the shop resembles a stone manor built during the last half of the 16th century.

THE CROWN & CREST: This shop looks like a backdrop for a child's fantasy of the days of King Arthur, with its high rafters decked out with bright banners, vast fireplace (and crossed swords above), and immense wrought-iron chandelier. Dart boards, fragrance products, "pub mugs," glasses that serve yards of beer, limited-edition chess sets, and coin and stamp sets are the stock-in-trade at this emporium adjoining The Toy Soldier.

PRINGLE OF SCOTLAND: On a sweltering summer day in Central Florida, trying on lamb's wool and cashmere may not hold terrific appeal. But the huge selection of styles and colors in men's and women's sweaters, knitted by Scotland's most famous

Where to Eat in Epcot

A complete listing of all eateries—full-service restaurants, fast-food emporiums, and snack shops—can be found in the *Good Meals, Great Times* chapter. See the Epcot section beginning on page 219.

maker, may well prove enticing despite the temperature outside. Tam-o'-shanters, socks, hats, ties, mittens, and kilts are only some of the items offered. Don't miss the tartan map on the wall across from The Crown & Crest; it identifies plaids from Glen Burn and Gordon to Langtree and St. Lawrence.

THE QUEEN'S TABLE: Sponsored by the Royal Doulton, Ltd., china makers, this shop (opposite Pringle of Scotland) may be one of the loveliest in Epcot. This is particularly true of the store's elegant Adams Room, embellished with elaborate moldings, hung with a crystal chandelier, and painted in cream and robin's-egg blue. The setting is a perfect background for the selection of superbly crafted collector's statuettes. The prices range from $5 to $12,500. A selection of fragrances and Royal Doulton china dinnerware are also available.

Don't forget to inspect small, serene Britannia Square just outside the shop entrance farthest from World Showcase Promenade. But for its somewhat reduced scale and the distinctively Floridian climate, it feels almost like London itself.

THE MAGIC OF WALES: This small emporium offers pottery, jewelry, souvenirs, and handcrafted gifts from Wales. Despite its modest size, it does the highest volume of business among the United Kingdom shops.

THE TEA CADDY: Fitted out with heavy wooden beams and a broad fireplace to resemble the Stratford-upon-Avon cottage of William Shakespeare's wife, Anne Hathaway, this shop, presented by R. Twinings & Company, Ltd., stocks English teas, both loose and in bags, in a variety of flavors. Other items include teapots, biscuits, and candies.

International Gateway

GATEWAY GIFTS: Disney memorabilia, convenience items, and a package pickup depot are located at this spot near the France entrance.

WORLD TRAVELER: Disney fashions and character merchandise, plus film, video camera rentals, and a drop-off for two-hour film processing are conveniently located here.

STROLLER AND WHEELCHAIR RENTAL: Strollers and wheelchairs are available for rent at this location. Remember to keep your rental receipt; it can be used on the same day in the Magic Kingdom, at the Disney-MGM Studios, Animal Kingdom, or again in Epcot should you leave and return at a later hour.

France

The buildings here have mansard roofs and casement windows so Gallic in appearance that you expect to see some sad, bohemian poet looking down from above. A canal-like offshoot of the World Showcase Lagoon seems like the Seine itself; the footbridge that spans it recalls the old Pont des Arts. There's a kiosk nearby like those that punctuate the streets of Paris, a sidewalk café at which to sip a glass of wine and watch the crowds go by, and a bakery whose heavenly rich aromas announce its presence long before it's visible. Shops sell perfumes, jewelry, crystal, and other luxury items. Their roofs are of real copper or slate, and the cabinetry is crafted finely enough to dazzle

even the most skilled woodworker. Galerie des Halles—the iron-and-glass-ceilinged market that Paris once counted as one of its most beloved institutions—lives again (near the Palais du Cinéma exit). But perhaps most special of all are the people. Hosts and hostesses who hail from Paris and the French provinces answer questions in lyrically French-accented English. It's fun to time your visit to take in the shows put on by mimes and clowns (have you ever seen a clown with four legs?).

Some interesting background notes: The dusty rose–colored, lace-trimmed costumes that the hostesses wear were inspired by the dresses in *Le Bar aux Folies-Bergère* by the Impressionist painter Edouard Manet; and the main entrance to the pavilion recalls the architecture of Paris, most of which was built during the Belle Epoque ("beautiful age"), the last decades of the 19th century.

Don't miss the garden on the opposite side of this arcade. It is one of the most peaceful spots in World Showcase.

Birnbaum's Best

IMPRESSIONS DE FRANCE: Shown in the Palais du Cinéma, an intimate, elegant little theater that's not unlike the one at Fontainebleau. This enchanting 18-minute film takes viewers from one end of France to the other. The film shows off a beautiful tree-dotted estate, fields and vineyards at harvest time, a flower market and a luscious pastry shop, the ribbed tongue of a glacier, and a harbor full of squawking gulls. Viewers visit the Eiffel Tower; Versailles and its gilt Hall of Mirrors (just outside Paris); Mont St. Michel; the French Alps; and Cannes, the star-studded resort city on the Mediterranean coast. All this is even more appealing thanks to a superb sound track, consisting almost entirely of the music of French classical composers.

The exceptionally wide screen adds yet another dimension. This is not a Circle-Vision 360 film; it wasn't shot with the nine cameras needed for the movies shown at China and Canada. The France film used only five cameras, and it is shown on a screen made up of five large projection surfaces—200 degrees around. It's a beautiful film; one of the park's best. The wait here is generally not long, but it's best to see the film soon after World Showcase opens or in the early evening. Note that unlike its Circle-Vision 360 counterparts, this theater has seats.

PLUME ET PALETTE: This is one of World Showcase's loveliest shops. The best of the Art Nouveau style is reflected in the curves that embellish the wrought-iron balustrade edging the mezzanine and the moldings that decorate the cherry-wood cabinets and shelves.

The decor makes a fine backdrop for an array of merchandise that includes a number of collectible miniatures, small china boxes, and intricate tapestries. On the mezzanine level, a handful of fine oil paintings (by well-known French landscape artists) are for sale from $300 to $3,000 each, along with attractive prints of French countryside scenes.

LA SIGNATURE: Another beautiful spot, with a chandelier, wallpaper that resembles watered silk, brass-and-crystal sconces, and velvet curtains, this boutique carries Guerlain cosmetics, fragrances, and bath products.

GALERIE DES HALLES: Souvenirs—from Eiffel Tower statues to CDs with music by French composers to merchandise featuring the Hunchback of Notre Dame—are the stock-in-trade at this area located at the exit from the Palais du Cinéma. The area is based on Paris's now-demolished Les Halles, designed by the noted architect Victor Baltard (1805–74).

LA CASSEROLE: This shop presents a selection of gifts themed to the artwork of French artists, such as Monet and Renoir. Mugs, tote bags, umbrellas, and picture frames are among the offerings.

LA MAISON DU VIN: Selections in this lovely wine shop range from the inexpensive to the pricey, from *vin ordinaire* going for several dollars to upwards of $290 for a rare vintage. Wine tastings are held here to sample the offerings (a small charge is levied, but you get to make a souvenir of the glass). Those who don't want to carry their purchases may have them dispatched to Package Pickup for retrieval later in the day.

Morocco

Nine tons of tile were handmade, handcut, and shipped to Epcot to create this World Showcase pavilion. To capture the unique quality of this North African country's architecture, Moroccan artisans came to Epcot to practice the mosaic art that has been a part of their homeland for thousands of years. Koutoubia Minaret, a detailed replica of the famous prayer tower in Marrakesh, stands guard at the entrance. A courtyard with a fountain at the center leads to the Medina (Old City). Between the traditional alleyways and the more modern sections are the pointed arches and swirling patterns of the Bab Boujouloud gate, a replica of the one that stands in the city of Fez. An ancient working waterwheel irrigates the gardens, and the motifs repeated throughout the buildings include carved plaster and wood, tile, and brass. Festival Marrakesh takes over the courtyard, with belly dancing and Moroccan songs performed by native musicians.

GALLERY OF ARTS AND HISTORY: This museum houses ever-changing exhibits of Moroccan art, artifacts, and costumes.

MOROCCAN NATIONAL TOURIST OFFICE: An information center offers literature useful in planning a visit to Morocco, and the Royal Air Maroc desk makes it easy to book a trip if the mood strikes.

CASABLANCA CARPETS: Hand-knotted Berber carpets, Rabat carpets with brightly colored geometric designs, prayer rugs, wall hangings, and handloomed bedspreads and throw pillows are among the offerings here.

TANGIER TRADERS: This is the perfect place to buy a fez, plus woven belts, leather sandals, leather purses, and other traditional Moroccan clothing.

MARKETPLACE IN THE MEDINA: Handwoven baskets, sheepskin wallets and handbags, assorted straw hats, and split-bamboo furniture and lampshades are available.

THE BRASS BAZAAR: Brass, brass, and more brass—and it's all shiny. Discover pitchers, planters, pots, and serving sets.

BERBER OASIS: This shop on the promenade spills over with crafted brasswork. Baskets and leather goods abound.

MEDINA ARTS: Stop in this shop for merchandise featuring characters from the animated film *Aladdin*.

Japan

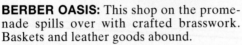

Serenity rules in Japan. Except, of course, when the pavilion resounds with traditional Japanese music performed by a drum-playing duo or group. A small gathering of extraordinary stilt walkers resembling colorful birds make appearances here as well.

The landscaping, designed in accordance with traditional symbolic and aesthetic values, also contributes to the pavilion's peaceful mood. Rocks, which in Japan represent the enduring nature of the earth, were brought from North Carolina and Georgia (since boulders are scarce in the Sunshine State). Water, symbolizing the sea (which the Japanese consider a life source), is abundant; the Japan pavilion garden has a little stream and a couple of pools inhabited (in good weather) by *koi* (specially bred fish). A small bamboo device at the edge of one of these rivulets regularly fills up with water falling from above,

and then, weighted by its contents, empties out, and in the process emanates regular, but somehow soothing, clacking noises. Evergreen trees, which in Japan are symbols of eternal life, are here in force.

Disney horticulturists created this very Japanese landscape using few plants and trees native to that country because the climate there is so different from that of Florida. The evergreens near the brilliant vermilion *torii* (gate) are native Florida slash pines. The curly-leaved trees by the stream are corkscrew willows. Among the few trees here actually native to Japan are the *sago* near the courtyard entrance to the Yakitori House; the two Japanese maple trees (identifiable by their small leaves) not far away (near the first stairway from the promenade on the left side of the courtyard as you face it); and the prickly monkey-puzzle trees near the walkway to the promenade, on The American Adventure side of the pagoda. Needle-sharp thorns make the latter the only species of tree that monkeys cannot climb.

Visitors who have been to Japan will be interested to observe that most of the structures inside the pavilion have their Japanese antecedents. The pagoda was modeled after an eighth-century structure located in the Horyuji Temple in Nara. The striking *torii* on the shore of World Showcase Lagoon derives from the design of the one at the Itsukushima shrine in Hiroshima Bay.

BIJUTSU-KAN GALLERY: A changing cultural display, this small art museum has offered, among other exhibitions, "Netsuke — Historic Carvings of Old Japan," a showcase of traditional Japanese art forms that features carved miniatures (from a private collection).

MITSUKOSHI DEPARTMENT STORE: There are kimonos in silk, cotton, and polyester; attractive T-shirts bearing Japanese characters; expensive, almost sculptural traditional headdresses; and an excellent selection of bowls and vases meant for flower arranging. But on the whole, no one would

ever apply the term *quaint* to this spacious store set up by Mitsukoshi—an immense, three-century-old retail firm that was once dubbed "Japan's Sears." Some of the china dinnerware is too often seen elsewhere in United States department stores to arouse more than passing interest. It's unfortunate

that this familiarity also makes it easy to dismiss some of the other merchandise that has considerable meaning in Japanese culture. One example is the dolls, of which there are literally rows and rows, priced from $3.50 to $3,000, clad in elaborate kimonos sashed with wide, stiff obis. These are traditionally given to female children on Girls' Day, a popular Japanese national holiday. The blank-eyed, egg-shaped papier-mâché scarlet masks, which come in a wide range of sizes from small to very large, are part of the traditional New Year celebration. The Japanese color in one eye when making a New Year's resolution, keep the one-eyed "face" in plain view throughout the next 364 days as a reminder of the holiday vow, and celebrate success when the year draws to its close by completing the face.

The structure housing the merchandise was inspired by the Gosho Imperial Palace, which was constructed in Kyoto in the year 794 A.D., and is widely recognized as a fine example of early Japanese architecture.

The American Adventure

When it came to creating The American Adventure, the centerpiece of World Showcase, Disney Imagineers were given relatively free rein. So the 110,000 bricks of the imposing Colonial-style structure that houses the show, a fast-food restaurant, and a shop are of real brick—made *by hand* from soft Georgia clay. The show inside stands out because of its wonderfully evocative settings, its detailed

sets, and the 35 superb Audio-Animatronics players, some of the most lifelike ever created by the Disney organization. The digital sound system is also one of the most advanced that Disney has ever used, and the show is also technically complex, involving the world's largest rear-projection screen (72 feet across) and a number of sophisticated sets that rise up from below the stage to the delight of the audience. A superb a cappella vocal group called The Voices of Liberty periodically serenades guests in the building's foyer.

Be sure to note the four luxuriant trees out front. They were originally planted in 1969 on Hotel Plaza Boulevard, and have been moved four times in the intervening years. The Disney characters often appear here. Presented by American Express.

THE AMERICAN ADVENTURE SHOW: One of the truly outstanding Epcot attractions, this 26-minute presentation celebrates the American spirit from our nation's earliest years right up to the present. Beginning with the arrival of the Pilgrims at Plymouth Rock and their hard first winter on the western shore of the Atlantic, the Audio-Animatronics narrators—an amazingly lifelike Ben Franklin and a convincing, cigar-puffing Mark Twain—recall certain key people and events in American history: the Boston Tea Party, George Washington and the grueling winter at Valley Forge, the influential black abolitionist Frederick Douglass, the celebrated 19th-century Nez Percé Chief Joseph, and many more. The Philadelphia Centennial Exposition is remembered, along with the contributions of women's rights campaigner Susan B. Anthony, telephone inventor Alexander Graham Bell, and the steel giant and philanthropist Andrew Carnegie. Naturalist John Muir converses on stage with Teddy Roosevelt. Charles Lindbergh, Rosie the Riveter, Jackie Robinson, Marilyn Monroe, and Walt Disney are represented. So are John Wayne, Lucille Ball, Margaret Mead, John F. Kennedy, Martin Luther King Jr., Muhammad Ali, and Billie Jean King.

The idea is to recall episodes in history, both negative and positive, which most contributed to the growth of the spirit of America, either by engendering "a new burst of creativity" (in the designers' words) "or a better understanding of ourselves as partners in the American experience." The presentation is hardly comprehensive; instead, it's "a hundred-yard dash capturing the spirit of the country at specific moments in time."

Throughout the show, the attention to historical detail is meticulous. Every one of the rear-projected illustrations was executed in the painting style of the era being described. The Chief Joseph and Susan B. Anthony figures are speaking their originals' own words. The precise dimensions of the cannon balls in another scene were carefully investigated—then reproduced. In the Philadelphia Centennial Exposition scene, Pittsburgh's name is spelled without the *h* that subsequent years have added.

For information about how each of the various historical figures actually spoke during his or her lifetime, researchers contacted about half a dozen historians and cultural institutions—the Philadelphia Historical Commission, Harvard's Carpenter Center of Visual Arts, the State Historical Society of Missouri, the Department of the Navy's Ships Historical Branch, and others. When recordings were not available, educated guesses were made: Bell's voice was created on the basis of contemporary comments about his voice's clarity, expressiveness, and crisp articulation, coupled with the fact that his father taught elocution. To select Will Rogers' speeches for the Depression scene, whole pages of quotes were collected, reviewed, edited, and re-edited; the voice is the humorist's own, from an actual broadcast, as is that of FDR, here heard over the radio in the roadside gasoline-stand scene. That particular scene was suggested by a *Life* magazine photograph; details are accurate down to the price for a gallon of gasoline (18 cents).

One of the most interesting aspects of the show is its inner workings. Underneath the entire theater is a movable carriage device that designers have dubbed "the war wagon." The basement that supports this mechanism is itself supported by pilings driven approximately 300 feet into the ground; it carries ten different sets, and during the presentation rolls forward or backward to position the appropriate set underneath the stage at the right time. Also, because the height of the space underneath the theater is relatively limited, the sets themselves were specially designed to allow certain sections to contract telescopically as proved necessary. These operations are computer controlled.

The 12 life-size statues on either side of the stage represent the Spirits of America. These are, on the left, from front to rear, Individualism, Innovation, Tomorrow, Independence, Compassion, and Discovery; and, on the right, from front to back, Freedom, Heritage, Pioneering, Knowledge, Self-Reliance, and Adventure. The 44 flags flanking the Hall of Flags corridor in the escalator area are those that have at some point flown over the United States. Revolutionary War flags, Colonial flags, and even flags representing the countries that had claims to American soil before Independence can be seen.

A special highlight of the show is the majestic music played throughout by the Philadelphia Symphony Orchestra. The Golden Dreams sequence includes notable figures such as Muppet creator Jim Henson, Ryan White—the young hemophiliac who succumbed to AIDS after a courageous battle with the disease—and basketball star Earvin "Magic" Johnson.

As one of the most compelling of all the World Showcase attractions, The American Adventure is often quite busy. Seats in the front of the house give the optimal view of the Audio-Animatronics figures (although all seats provide an acceptable view). Perhaps the best time to schedule a visit to the show is soon after World Showcase opens or in the early evening. Be sure to check your guidemap for exact showtimes and arrive early. If you have some time before the show, read the quotes on the walls—Wendell Willkie, Jane Addams, Charles Lindbergh, Ayn Rand, Archibald MacLeish, Herman Melville, Thomas Wolfe, and Walt Disney are all represented.

HERITAGE MANOR GIFTS: Visit this shop for a variety of nostalgic Americana. Gifts include American flag–colored men's and women's clothing, housewares, baseballs, coins, and books on American history.

AMERICA GARDENS THEATRE: An ever-changing slate of entertainment is presented several times a week in this lakeside amphitheater in front of The American Adventure pavilion. Check your guidemap for details and exact times. Showtimes are also posted on the promenade at the east and west entrances to the amphitheater.

Be sure to note the pruning of the western sycamores overhead; the old-fashioned pollarding method used, which involves trimming the treetops flat and allowing the lower branches to fill out and interlock, eventually produces a thick canopy. The flower beds outside are planted with appropriately red, white, and blue blossoms.

Italy

The arches and cut-out motifs that adorn the World Showcase reproduction of the Doge's Palace in Venice are just the more obvious examples of the attention to detail lavished on the individual structures in this relatively small pavilion. The angel atop the scaled-down campanile was sculpted on the model of the original right down to the curls on the back of its head—then covered with real gold leaf, despite the fact that it was destined to be set almost 100 feet in the air. The other statues in the complex, including the sea god Neptune presiding over the fountain in the rear of the piazza, are similarly exact. And the pavilion even has an island like Venice's own, its seawall appropriately stained with age, plus moorings that look like barber poles, with several distinctively Venetian gondolas tied to them. St. Mark the Evangelist is also remembered, together with the lion that is the saint's companion and Venice's guardian; these can be seen atop the two massive columns that flank the small arched footbridge that connects the landfall to the mainland. The only deviation from Venetian reality is the alteration of the site of the Doge's Palace in reference to the real St. Mark's Square.

The sounds of opera, accompanied by an accordion and guitar, frequently fill the courtyard. Some of most interesting entertainment at this pavilion is The Living Statues, amazing white-robed performers who stand motionless, and then suddenly change poses when you least expect it.

The pavilion is equally interesting from a horticultural point of view. The island boasts kumquat trees, citrus plants typical of the Mediterranean, and a couple of olive trees that can be seen on both sidewalls of the Delizie Italiane; originally located in a Sacramento, California, grove, they arrived in Florida via flatbed truck a bit slimmer than when they started out. (Arizona border inspectors decreed that the trees be trimmed

to the ten-foot width required by state law, and so, the ancient olives were shorn en route. The hardy trees survived, leaving only their scars to remind visitors of the ordeal; the darker bark is what remains of the original, while the lighter areas are new growth.) The tall, narrow trees that stand like dark columns in the pavilion are Italian cypress, which are extremely common in Italy.

DELIZIE ITALIANE: This open-air market on the western edge of the piazza is a good spot for a sweet snack of tasty Italian chocolates and other goodies.

IL BEL CRISTALLO: The production of fine glassware has been a tradition in Italy for centuries, so a shop like this one (just off the promenade on the Germany side of the piazza) was a must for the pavilion. On display are Venetian glass paperweights and other items, their bright colors trapped in smooth spheres of clear or milky glass; small porcelain figurines and flower bouquets so

finely crafted that they look almost real; pastel flowers made of beads; and lead crystal bowls and candlesticks. The name of the shop means "the beautiful crystal."

LA CUCINA ITALIANA: This gourmet shop tempts with an assortment of Italian pastries and desserts. Expect to find wines from some of the finest vineyards in Italy. Pasta, olive oils, vinegars, and coffee are just a few of the other provisions available. An eclectic blend of decorative ceramics, cookware, and cutlery rounds out the selection.

LA GEMMA ELEGANTE: Located to the rear of the piazza on its eastern edge, this small shop focuses on jewelry. There are gold and silver chains galore, and some are expensive, but it's possible to find lovely—and affordable—beads, earrings, and pendants made of Venetian glass; mosaic brooches and pillboxes bearing images of tiny bouquets; cameos; and coral necklaces.

Germany

There are no villages in Germany quite like this one. Inspired variously by towns in the Rhine region, Bavaria, and in the German north, it boasts structures reminiscent of those found in urban enclaves as diverse as Frankfurt, Freiburg, and Rothenburg. There are stair-stepped rooflines and towers, balconies and arcaded walkways, and so much overall charm that the scene seems to come straight out of a fairy tale. The beer hall to the rear is almost as lively as the one at Munich's famed Oktoberfest, especially during the later show. The shops, which offer a range of merchandise from wine and sweets to ceramics and cuckoo clocks, toys, and books—and even art—are so tempting that it's hard to leave the area empty-handed.

The various elements that constitute the Germany pavilion are described here as they would be encountered walking from west to east (counterclockwise) around the cobblestone-paved central plaza, which is formally known as the St. Georgsplatz, after the statue found at its center. Saint George, the patron saint of soldiers, is depicted with a dragon that legend says he slew during a pilgrimage to the Middle East.

Try to time your World Showcase peregrinations to bring you to Germany on the hour, when the handsome, specially designed glockenspiel at the plaza's rear can be heard chiming in a melody composed specifically for the pavilion. Check the guidemap to see if a German trio will be performing outside the Biergarten restaurant.

DER BUCHERWURM: This two-story structure, whose exterior is patterned after a merchants' hall known as the Kaufhaus (located in the German town of Freiburg in Breisgau), stocks prints and English books about Germany; handsome prints of German cities; and an assortment of souvenir items, including ashtrays, vases, and more. (Film and sundries are also available.)

VOLKSKUNST: Small and exceptionally appealing, this establishment is full of a burgher's bounty of German timekeepers, plus a smattering of other items made by hand in the rural corners of the nation. The latter include beer steins in all sizes, from the petite to the enormous and expensive; wood carvings made in the German town of Oberammergau; nutcrackers; and a whole collection of "smokers" (carved wooden dolls with a receptacle for incense and a hollow pipe for the smoke to escape). As for cuckoo clocks, some are small and unprepossessing, and some are so immense that they'd look appropriate only in some cathedral-ceilinged hunting lodge. A must.

DER TEDDYBAR: Located adjacent to Volkskunst, this toy shop would be a delight if only for the lively mechanized displays: Some of the stuffed lambs and the dolls wearing folk dresses (called dirndls) have been animated so that tails wag and skirts swirl in time to German folk tunes. The shop is also home to one of WDW's best selections of toys, including an assortment of expensive stuffed keepsakes from Steiff. Colorful wooden toys are tempting as well, along with all kinds of building blocks. Last but not least, the dolls are simply wonderful—you can even have one customized to your personal specifications.

WEINKELLER: The Germany pavilion's wine shop, situated between the cookie shop and the Biergarten toward the rear of St. Georgsplatz, offers about 250 varieties of German wines produced and bottled by H. Schmitt Söhne, one of Germany's oldest and largest vintners. Wine tastings are held here daily. The selection includes not only those vintages meant for everyday consumption, but also fine estate wines whose prices run into the hundreds of dollars per bottle. These are white (with a few exceptions), because white wine constitutes the bulk of Germany's vinicultural output. (Only 20% of all German bottlings are red.) The setting itself is quite attractive— low-ceilinged and cozy, and full of fir cabinets embellished with carvings of vines and bunches of grapes.

KUNSTARBEIT IN KRISTALL: This shop to the left of the Biergarten features Austrian and crystal jewelry, tall beer mugs, wineglasses in traditional German tints of green and amber, and crystal decanters. Guests can have glassware etched on the spot.

SUSSIGKEITEN: It's a mistake to visit this tiny confectionery shop on an empty stomach: Chocolate cookies, butter cookies, and almond biscuits mix with caramels, nuts, and pretzels on the shelves; and there are boxes upon boxes of *Lebkuchen*, the spicy crisp cookies traditionally baked in Germany at Christmas, not to mention Gummy Bears (which the packages announce as *Gummibaeren*). Be sure to note the attractive display of old Bahlsen cookie tins by the door.

DIE WEIHNACHTS ECKE: This is a shop that can set a visitor's mind to thoughts of Christmas—even in the dog days of summer. Ornaments, decorations, and gifts manufactured by various German companies line the shelves of this store.

GLAS UND PORZELLAN: Featuring glass and porcelain items made by the German firm of Goebel, this is an attractive establishment with rope-turned columns, curved moldings, delicate scrollwork, and tiny carved rosettes. But no matter how attractive the background, the stars of the show are the M. I. Hummel figurines that Goebel

makes. Cherubic, rosy-cheeked children, shown carrying baskets, trays, umbrellas, and other items—depicted as in the drawings of a young German nun named Berta Hummel—are favorites of collectors around the world. There is always an elaborate showpiece at the center of the shop, and a Goebel artist is here to demonstrate the process by which Hummel creations are painted and finished.

China

Dominated by the Disney equivalent of Beijing's Temple of Heaven, and announced by a pair of banners that offer good wishes to passersby (the Chinese characters translate: "May good fortune follow you on your path through life and May virtue be your neighbor"), this pavilion conveys a level of serenity that offers an appealing contrast to the hearty merriment of the bordering Germany and the gaiety of nearby Mexico. Part of this quiet environment is the by-product of the soothing traditional Chinese music that plays over the sound system. Live flute, zither, or dulcimer music is performed inside the Temple of Heaven, while agile acrobats do tricks in the courtyard. The gardens also make a major contribution. They are full of rosebushes native to China, and there is a century-old mulberry tree (to the left of the main walkway into the pavilion), with a pomegranate tree and a wiggly-looking

Village Traders

Located between Germany and China, this open-air shop, notable for its *Lion King* merchandise, also offers gifts from Africa, India, and Australia. Browse through such souvenirs as boomerangs, handbags, hats, and T-shirts.

Florida native known as a water oak nearby. In addition, a spacious emporium is devoted to Chinese wares, and two Chinese restaurants add to the overall atmosphere. However, all this is secondary to the motion picture shown inside the Temple of Heaven — a Circle-Vision 360 film that is one of the most diverting World Showcase attractions. Note that there are no seats in the theater.

WONDERS OF CHINA: LAND OF BEAUTY, LAND OF TIME: This 19-minute presentation shows the beauties of a land that few Epcot visitors have seen firsthand — and does it so vividly that it's possible to see the film over and over and still not fully absorb all the wonderful sights. The Disney crew was the first Western film group to shoot certain sites, and their remarkable effort includes such marvels as Beijing's Forbidden City; vast, wide-open Inner Mongolia and its stern-faced tribespeople; the 2,400-year-old Great Wall; the Great Buddha of Leshan, eight centuries old and dramatically imposing; the muddy Yangtze River and the 3,000-year-old city of Suzhou. Its location on the Grand Canal, which is believed to be the largest man-made waterway in the world, led Marco Polo to call it the Venice of the East.

The number of stones in the floor of the pavilion's main structure is not random; the center stone is surrounded by nine stones because nine is considered a lucky number in China. Around the edge of the outer room rise 12 columns — because 12 is the number of months in the year and the number of years in a full cycle of the Chinese calendar. Be sure to stand on the round stone in the center: Every whisper is amplified.

When exiting, pass by the House of the Whispering Willows, an exhibit of ancient Chinese art and artifacts. Changed about every six months, it invariably includes fine pieces from well-known collections.

YONG FENG SHANGDIAN: This vast Chinese emporium, located off the narrow, charming Street of Good Fortune at the exit to the film, offers a huge assortment of merchandise — silk robes, prints, paper umbrellas, embroidered items, and more. Trinkets, moderately priced items, and expensive antiques are available in an array that may be matched in few places in the United States. The calligraphy on the curtains wishes passersby good fortune, long life, prosperity, and happiness.

Norway

Set between the Mexico and China pavilions is Norway, the last pavilion added to the mix at World Showcase. Built in conjunction with many Norwegian companies, the pavilion celebrates the history, folklore, and culture of one of the Western world's oldest countries.

The cobblestone town square is an architectural showcase of the styles of such Norwegian towns as Bergen, Alesund, and Oslo. There's also a Norwegian castle fashioned after Akershus, a 14th-century fortress still standing in Oslo's harbor; the castle here houses the Akershus restaurant. Few can resist walking into the bakery for a taste of its treats. In a show of modernity, a statue of Norway's living legend, marathoner Grete Waitz, stands behind the bakery. Shops stock handicrafts and folk items: hand-knit woolens, wood carvings, and glass and metal artwork. The World Class Brass comic musicians put on a show in the courtyard.

MAELSTROM: Appropriately, visitors tour Norway by boat — 16-passenger, dragon-headed longboats inspired by those Eric the Red and other Vikings used a thousand years ago. The ten-minute voyage through time begins in a tenth-century Viking village where a ship is being readied to head out to sea. Seafarers then find themselves in a mythical Norwegian forest, populated by trolls who cause the boats to plummet backward, through a maelstrom to the majestic grandeur of the Geiranger fjord, where the vessel narrowly avoids spilling over a waterfall. Ultimately, after a plunge through a rocky passage, the boats wind up in the stormy North Sea. Lightning flashes reveal an enormous oil rig; as the boat passes the concrete platform legs, the storm calms and a coastal village appears on the horizon.

Survivors disembark and enter a movie theater, where the journey continues on-screen for five additional minutes, giving visitors a

sense of the scenic spectacles and unique personalities that make up modern Norway.

Maelstrom is one of World Showcase's more popular attractions. Try to visit in the late evening, when it is least crowded.

STAVE CHURCH GALLERY: Inside the wooden stave church, there is a small exhibit that explores Norwegian culture. It's interesting to note that only 30 stave churches remain in Norway today.

THE PUFFIN'S ROOST: A collection of Norwegian gifts, sweaters, activewear, jewelry, fine leather goods, pewter, candy, toys, and trolls are the wares for sale at this shop.

Mexico

The tangle of tropical vegetation surrounding the great pyramid that encloses this pavilion and the Mexican restaurant at the lagoon's edge on the promenade provide only the barest suggestion of the charming area inside. Dominated by a re-creation of a quaint plaza at dusk, this area is rimmed by balconied, tile-roofed, colonial-style structures. Crowding a pretty fountain area is a quartet of stands selling Mexican handicrafts, and to the left is a shop stocked with other handsome wares. The Mariachi Cobre band keeps things lively. To the rear, the San Angel Inn, a corporate cousin of the famous Mexico City restaurant, serves authentic Mexican fare. Behind it, the pavilion's main show chronicles Mexican culture from earliest times right up to the present. Take a look at the cultural exhibit inside the pyramid entrance on the way in. Note that the pyramid itself was inspired by Meso-American structures dating from the third century A.D.

EL RIO DEL TIEMPO: THE RIVER OF TIME: Over the course of this six-minute boat trip, sprinkled with vignettes of pre-Columbian, Spanish colonial, and modern Mexican life, visitors greet a Mayan high priest, watch dances by performers in vivid costumes, and are assailed by vendors at a market. A band dressed to look like skeletons entertains at one juncture (in a reference to the Day of the Dead, a holiday celebrated in Mexico with candies and sweets shaped like skulls and skeletons). The cheery montage of film, props, and Audio-Animatronics figures is reminiscent of the Magic Kingdom's It's A Small World. During peak seasons, long lines, which prevail from late morning on, usually thin out in the afternoon.

PLAZA DE LOS AMIGOS: Brightly colored paper flowers, sombreros, wooden trays and bowls, peasant blouses, baskets, and pottery make this *mercado* (shopping area) at the plaza's center as bright and almost as lively

as one in Mexico itself. The colorful papier-mâché piñatas that figure so strongly in the scenery here are so popular that Epcot has to buy them from suppliers by the truckload.

ARTESANIAS MEXICANAS: This shop carries Mexican-made home decor items. Among the featured items are candles, glasses, and pottery.

EL RANCHITO DEL NORTE: Gifts and souvenirs from northern Mexico are the featured items at this spot.

LA FAMILIA FASHIONS: Mexican fashions and accessories for women and kids, malachite, plus silver and turquoise jewelry are available.

Showcase Plaza

PORT OF ENTRY: A children's shop carrying infants' and kids' clothing, girls' character dresses, plush dolls, and toys.

DISNEY TRADERS: Merchandise combining the charms of Disney characters and World Showcase themes are the primary stock-in-trade. Sunglasses, film, cigarettes, and sundries are also available.

ENTERTAINMENT

pcot presents an intriguing array of live performances each day, making it important for guests to consult an entertainment schedule, which is incorporated in the current park guidemap. While the overall lineup is constantly changing, certain shows—the not-to-be-missed IllumiNations, for one—are fixtures. The following listing offers an indication of Epcot's crowd-pleasing potential. For information about special events at Epcot, see the "Holidays & Special Events" section of *Getting Ready to Go.* For up-to-the-minute schedules call 824-4321.

AMERICA GARDENS THEATRE: The venue alongside the lagoon at The American Adventure in World Showcase hosts high school choirs and international dance companies alike. Check a schedule for current offerings.

FOUNTAIN OF NATIONS: This dramatic fountain in Future World's Innoventions Plaza breaks into a computer-choreographed water ballet every 15 minutes.

FUTURE WORLD ENTERTAINMENT: Expect increased visibility for ever-changing performances designed to bring more fun to Future World. Future Corps, a drum-and-bugle corps, performs nearly every day. Try to catch a performance by the Jammitors, a unique group that uses trash cans as a drum set.

ILLUMINATIONS: A spectacular display of lasers, fireworks, and fountains to the accompaniment of symphonic music, this show is a sure highlight of any Epcot visit. The nightly extravaganza, visible from anywhere on the World Showcase Promenade, is scheduled at closing time year-round. To snare a prime viewing spot (we recommend the area between Italy and The American Adventure), claim it about 45 minutes before showtime.

KIDS' ZONES: There is a special play area in each of the 11 countries of World Showcase. These Kids' Zones give young guests the opportunity to play games and make crafts that are native to each country's culture, from painting totem poles in Canada to designing paper dolls in the United Kingdom.

WORLD SHOWCASE PERFORMERS: It's all but impossible to complete a circuit of World Showcase without catching a few performances en route. Keep an eye on the schedule to take in live entertainment at each pavilion, often performed by natives of the country represented. Among the possibilities: worldly comedians, a nomadic troupe of

Stilt Birds, French mimes, a Mexican mariachi band, Moroccan belly dancers, Chinese acrobats, Canadian bagpipers, African drummers, and more. A bus full of Caribbean songsters travels the promenade. For details, see descriptions in the "World Showcase" section of this chapter.

Holiday Happenings

During certain holidays, such as the Fourth of July, Christmas, and New Year's Eve, Epcot usually stays open extra late and presents added entertainment for the occasion.

Note, too, that World Showcase keeps an international holiday calendar. January visitors might celebrate Scottish Heritage Day or Chinese New Year. In February there's Mardi Gras and Carnaval de Quebec. May visitors cheer Cinco de Mayo in Mexico or Independence Day in Norway. July packs France's Bastille Day, Japan's Tanabata Festival, and Canada's Dominion Day in addition to the U.S.A.'s Fourth of July. Oktoberfest and Morocco's Independence Day also get their turn.

As always, precise entertainment plans are subject to change, so it's important to call 824-4321 to confirm schedules.

CHRISTMAS: Epcot celebrates the holiday in a big way, with a nightly tree-lighting ceremony, a wondrously lighted archway that hugs the pathway to Showcase Plaza, a candlelight choral processional, and a special edition of IllumiNations among the traditional elements of its Holidays Around the World festivities. The holiday IllumiNations features a special score, complete with Tchaikovsky's "Nutcracker Suite," a Chanukah medley, and a dramatic "Let There Be Peace on Earth" finale.

HOT TIPS

- Stop by Guest Relations for a guidemap. Consult the entertainment schedule to be sure you won't miss any of the special shows.
- The best time to visit World Showcase is as soon as it opens (usually at 11 A.M.). See Future World in the late afternoon until park closing. Remember that lines throughout Epcot are longest during midday, and shortest during the early evening.
- During peak seasons, preferred priority seating times at Epcot's full-service restaurants book quickly. So be sure to arrive at Epcot early to get a jump on the day and help ensure that you get the restaurant and seating time of your choice. Remember, too, that non-prime dining hours are often available to those making late arrangements, so adjusting your eating schedule may well help you to visit the restaurant of your choice. Most World Showcase restaurants seat guests until park closing. Guests can also make advance plans by calling WDW-DINE (939-3463).
- Check the Tip Board in Innoventions Plaza for current wait times for the most popular Epcot attractions, and adjust your plans accordingly.
- Save the shops in World Showcase for the afternoon, when just about everything else is very crowded.
- Guests staying at WDW resorts can have purchases delivered to their hotels for free.
- Although a *FriendShip* water taxi is unlikely to transport you across World Showcase Lagoon any faster than a brisk walk would, it is a peaceful foot-friendly way to make the half-mile-plus journey—especially at the end of a long day, or if you are traveling with small children.
- Be sure to allow extra time for Image Works at Journey Into Imagination, Innoventions, and Sea Base Alpha at The Living Seas.
- The jumping fountains outside Journey Into Imagination and on the path between Future World and World Showcase are a favorite with children of all ages.

Where to Find the Characters

In Future World, characters host each meal at The Land's Garden Grill restaurant (see *Good Meals, Great Times* for details). Also, find Goofy at Wonders of Life, and Dreamfinder and Figment at Journey Into Imagination. Mickey often appears at the Centorium. In World Showcase, characters favor the country of their literary origin. Discover *Snow White* characters in Germany, familiar faces from *Beauty and the Beast* and *The Hunchback of Notre Dame* in France, and friends from *Aladdin* in Morocco. The United Kingdom is home to Winnie the Pooh, Alice in Wonderland, Mary Poppins, and others. Check a guidemap for current locations.

Disney-MGM Studios

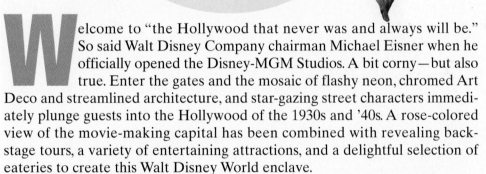

Welcome to "the Hollywood that never was and always will be." So said Walt Disney Company chairman Michael Eisner when he officially opened the Disney-MGM Studios. A bit corny—but also true. Enter the gates and the mosaic of flashy neon, chromed Art Deco and streamlined architecture, and star-gazing street characters immediately plunge guests into the Hollywood of the 1930s and '40s. A rose-colored view of the movie-making capital has been combined with revealing backstage tours, a variety of entertaining attractions, and a delightful selection of eateries to create this Walt Disney World enclave.

The Disney-MGM Studios is situated on a 110-acre site southwest of Epcot. The water tower, known to punsters (for obvious reasons) as the "Earffel Tower," is reminiscent of the structures looming over most Hollywood studios of the Golden Age. Here, however, it gets that special Disney touch—it's capped by a Mouseketeer-style hat.

What makes this area of Walt Disney World different from other Disney theme parks is the extent to which guests can participate in the attractions. Our best advice is to volunteer, wherever and whenever possible. It's fun, and it adds enormously to the experience.

The Studios is still expanding and evolving. If the Magic Kingdom is the home of the classics, this park is the place where Disney's latest animated hits debut as creative shows, parades, and attractions. It's also where the contemporary characters make their first live appearances.

Unless otherwise noted, all phone numbers are in area code 407.

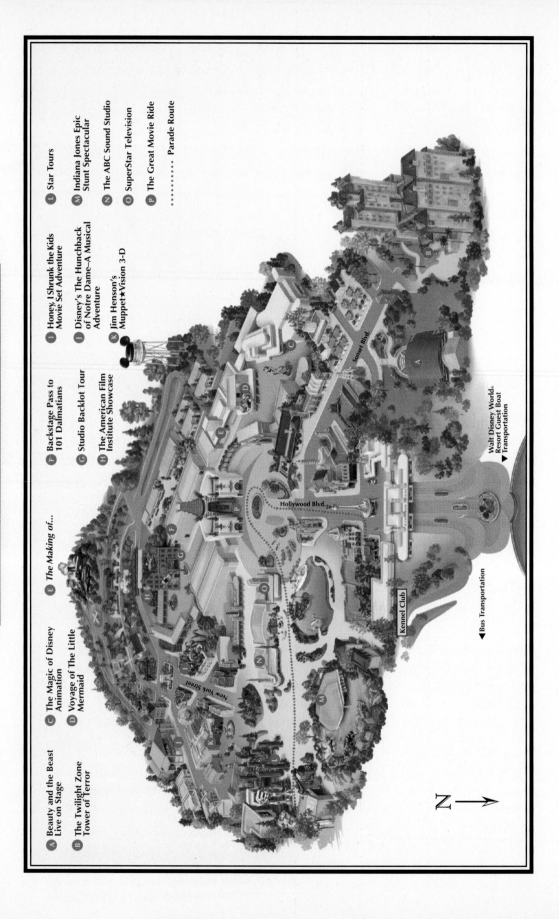

A — Beauty and the Beast Live on Stage

B — The Twilight Zone Tower of Terror

C — The Magic of Disney Animation

D — Voyage of The Little Mermaid

E — The Making of...

F — Backstage Pass to 101 Dalmatians

G — Studio Backlot Tour

H — The American Film Institute Showcase

I — Honey, I Shrunk the Kids Movie Set Adventure

J — Disney's The Hunchback of Notre Dame–A Musical Adventure

K — Jim Henson's Muppet★Vision 3-D

L — Star Tours

M — Indiana Jones Epic Stunt Spectacular

N — The ABC Sound Studio

O — SuperStar Television

P — The Great Movie Ride

••••••• Parade Route

Sunset Blvd.

Hollywood Blvd.

New York Street

Kennel Club

Walt Disney World® Resort Guest Boat
▼ Transportation

▼ Bus Transportation

N →

GETTING ORIENTED

While the Disney-MGM Studios is about half the size of Epcot, the park has a sprawling layout with no distinctive shape or main thoroughfare. Even so, the Studios is easily navigated, with just a handful of broad avenues veering off toward different attractions, restaurants, and shops.

The park entrance is at Hollywood Boulevard. This shop-lined avenue leads straight to Hollywood Plaza, address of the Studios' most central landmark, a replica of Mann's Chinese Theatre that doubles as the site of The Great Movie Ride. Walking along Hollywood Boulevard toward the plaza, you'll come to the first major intersection, Hollywood Junction. Here, a wide, palm-fringed thoroughfare known as Sunset Boulevard (the Studios' newest block) branches off to the right. Anchoring Sunset Boulevard's far end is The Hollywood Tower Hotel, home of The Twilight Zone Tower of Terror. The strip is also graced with several shops, the Sunset Ranch Market, and the Theatre of the Stars amphitheater, where Beauty and the Beast Live on Stage is performed.

Stand in Hollywood Plaza facing the Chinese Theater, and you'll notice an archway just off to your right; this leads to Mickey Avenue. A self-contained area with a backstage feel to it, Mickey Avenue entices with tours of working animation and television studios. If you make a left off Hollywood Boulevard and proceed clockwise past Echo Lake, you are on course for such participatory attractions as SuperStar Television, The ABC Sound Studio, Indiana Jones Epic Stunt Spectacular, and Star Tours. (The opposite side of the small lake is given mainly to dining spots.) Just beyond Star Tours there is one last entertainment zone. The highest-profile attractions here: Jim Henson's Muppet*Vision 3-D, Disney's The Hunchback of Notre Dame—A Musical Adventure, and New York Street. Walk left past the skyscraper end of New York Street, and you're on a quick track back to Hollywood Plaza and the Chinese Theater.

HOW TO GET THERE

Take Exit 26B or Exit 25 off I-4. Continue about a half mile to reach the parking area. Take a tram to the park entrance.

By WDW Transportation: From the Swan, Dolphin, Yacht Club, Beach Club, and BoardWalk: boats. From Fort Wilderness and Downtown Disney: bus to the Transportation and Ticket Center (TTC), then transfer to the Disney-MGM Studios bus. From the Magic Kingdom, Epcot, Animal Kingdom, all other WDW resorts, and the resorts on Hotel Plaza Blvd.: buses.

PARKING

All-day parking at the Studios is $5 for day visitors (free to WDW resort guests with presentation of resort ID). Trams circulate regularly, providing transportation from the parking area to the park entrance. Be sure to note the section and the aisle in which you park. Also be aware that the parking ticket received allows for reentry to the parking area throughout the day.

HOURS

The Disney-MGM Studios is usually open from 9 A.M. to 7 P.M. During certain holiday periods and the summer months, hours are extended. It's best to arrive at the park at least a half hour before the posted opening time, particularly during these busy seasons. Depending on the season, some attractions do not open until late in the morning.

Admission Prices

ONE-DAY TICKET

(Restricted to use only in the Disney-MGM Studios. Prices include sales tax and are subject to change.)

Adult..$42.14
Child*..$33.92

*3 to 9 years of age; children under 3 free

PARK PRIMER

BABY FACILITIES

Changing tables and facilities for nursing mothers can be found at the Baby Care Center, which is tucked inside the Guest Relations lobby near the park entrance. Disposable diapers are kept behind the counter at many Studios shops; just ask.

CAMERA NEEDS

The Darkroom on Hollywood Boulevard stocks film, batteries, and disposable cameras; it also rents camcorders ($30 per day with a $450 refundable deposit). Two-hour film processing is offered here and wherever you see a Photo Express sign. Film is sold in most Studios shops.

DISABILITY INFORMATION

Nearly all attractions, eateries, and shops are barrier-free. Convenient parking is reserved for guests with disabilities. Provisions have been made to enhance sight- and hearing-impaired guests' enjoyment. The *Walt Disney World Guidebook for Guests with Disabilities* is available at Guest Relations. For more information, see the "Travelers with Disabilities" section of *Getting Ready to Go*.

EARLY-ENTRY DAYS

On Wednesday and Sunday, guests staying at WDW resorts may enter the Disney-MGM Studios 1½ hours prior to the official opening time to enjoy such attractions as Tower of Terror, The Great Movie Ride, and Star Tours. Early-entry days and attractions are subject to change.

FIRST AID

Minor medical problems can be handled at the First Aid Center, located next to Guest Relations at the park entrance.

INFORMATION

Guest Relations, located just inside the park entrance, offers the requisite guidemaps and ever-resourceful staff. To make same-day dining arrangements for certain Studios eateries, go to the booth at the junction of Hollywood and Sunset boulevards.

LOCKERS

Attended lockers, found at Oscar's Super Service near the entrance, cost $3 per day (plus a $2 refundable deposit) for unlimited use.

LOST & FOUND

Located near the park entrance, past the turnstiles on the right. To report lost items after your visit, call 824-4245.

LOST CHILDREN

Report lost children at Guest Relations or alert a Disney employee to the problem.

MONEY MATTERS

There is an ATM located outside the park entrance, on the right. In addition to cash, credit cards (American Express, Visa, The Disney Credit Card, and MasterCard), traveler's checks, and WDW resort IDs are accepted for admission, merchandise, and also for meals at full-service restaurants and at all fast-food spots.

PACKAGE PICKUP

Shops can arrange for cumbersome purchases to be transported to package pickup at the Lost and Found (near the park entrance) where they can be picked up later. There is no charge for this service.

SAME-DAY REENTRY

Be sure to have your hand stamped upon exiting the park and to retain your ticket if you plan to return later in the same day.

STROLLERS & WHEELCHAIRS

Strollers, wheelchairs, and Electric Convenience Vehicles (ECVs) may be rented from Oscar's Super Service, located just inside the park entrance on the right. Cost for strollers and wheelchairs is $5, with a $1 refundable deposit. Remember to keep your receipt, which can be used on the same day for a replacement at the Magic Kingdom, Epcot, Animal Kingdom, or here at the Studios (at the In Character costume shop). Cost for ECVs is $30, with a $10 refundable deposit. Quantities are limited.

TIP BOARD

Check this board at the junction of Hollywood and Sunset boulevards to learn the current waiting times for the most popular attractions in the park. This is also the place to look for showtimes. Hosts and hostesses stand nearby to provide additional information.

THE MAIN ATTRACTIONS

The Disney-MGM Studios has a brand of attractions altogether unique. Some offer guests behind-the-scenes looks at the creative and technical processes that generate television, movies, and animation. Others go so far as to allow guests to gain a bit of showbiz experience along with the insight. Still others resurrect popular characters and stories in new forms—from stage shows to thrill rides.

Because many shows and attractions at the Studios are presented at scheduled times throughout the day, it's very important to consult a guidemap and the park's Tip Board for specific starting times. Attractions are described roughly in the order they might be visited in a sweep of the park's major sections: Sunset Boulevard, Mickey Avenue, the area stretching from Hollywood Boulevard to Star Tours, and the New York Street vicinity.

The Twilight Zone Tower of Terror

The Hollywood Tower Hotel is the decrepit home of the Studios' most exhilarating thrill ride. A relic of Hollywood's Golden Age, the hotel has clearly had some problems. On the facade of the 199-foot-tall building (the tallest attraction at any Disney theme park) hangs a sparking electric sign. As the legend goes, lightning struck the building during a violent storm on Halloween night in 1939. An entire guest wing disappeared, along with an elevator carrying five people. The disappearances remain a mystery.

The line for the ride winds through the once-glorious lobby, where dusty furniture, cobwebs, and newspapers circa 1939 add to the eerie atmosphere. As guests enter the library, they see a television set brought to life by a bolt of lightning. Rod Serling intones a typical monologue, inviting them to enter another part of the building—and The Twilight Zone. He introduces the one-time staff and guests of the hotel. During his spiel, Serling informs you that the maintenance elevator is the only working elevator in the hotel.

Visitors are led through an old hallway toward the boiler room to enter the ride elevator. (This is your only chance to change

your mind about riding. Guests who decide to skip the trip can take a real elevator to the exit.) Once inside, passengers are seated on benches equipped with safety bars. The doors close and the elevator begins its ascent. At the first stop, the elevator doors open and guests have a view down an endless hotel corridor. Among the many special effects is a ghostly visit by the hotel guests who vanished. Suddenly, the view of the hall disappears and is replaced by a sky full of stars. The doors close again and you continue your trip skyward.

At the next stop, you enter the Fifth Dimension, a combination of eerie sights and sounds reminiscent of "The Twilight Zone" TV series. In fact, Disney Imagineers watched each of the 156 original "Twilight Zone"

BIRNBAUM'S Best

episodes at least twice (over 174 hours) for inspiration. Notice the clock that ticks incessantly as it hangs in midair, and the giant eyeball (watch it closely and you may see your image floating inside). This part of the ride is a disorienting experience, in part because the elevator is actually moving horizontally.

What happens next depends upon the whim of Disney Imagineers, who have programmed the ride so that the drop sequence can easily be changed by computer. At press time the ride was taking an immediate plunge (of about eight stories) before traveling quickly back up to the 13th floor. When the elevator reaches the top (at a height of about 157 feet) passengers can look out at the Studios below. The flash of light you see is a camera capturing your look of horror, while the noises you hear may have you convinced the elevator cables are breaking. The doors shut again and you plummet 13 stories. The drop is over in about 2½ seconds, but it seems like longer.

Just when you think it's over, the vehicle launches skyward, barely stopping before it plunges 13 stories again. As you prepare to exit, Rod Serling offers a tip: Next time you enter an old hotel, use the stairs.

From the time you are seated in the service elevator, the trip takes about five minutes. Note that you must be at least 40 inches tall to go on the ride. It is not recommended for pregnant women, those with a heart condition, or people with back and neck problems.

On the way out, you'll pass through Tower Hotel Gifts, where key chains, T-shirts, and other Hollywood Tower Hotel merchandise is for sale. This is also the place to buy the photo taken at the top of the tower. A bit of trivia: The motors running the ride vehicles are three times as powerful as those that propel the elevators at New York City's 110-story World Trade Center.

Beauty and the Beast Live on Stage

Here's the show that gave birth to the hit Broadway musical. Five times each day, Belle, Gaston, Mrs. Potts, Lumière, and the rest of the cast of the Disney film *Beauty and the Beast* come to life at the 1,500-seat Theatre of the Stars amphitheater on Sunset Boulevard. The 20-minute show is as entertaining as they come. The staging is just right and the music simply addictive as it traces the classic tale—from Belle's dissatisfaction with her life in a small French town to the climactic battle between the staff of the Beast's castle and Gaston and the townspeople. Lumière and friends perform the song, "Be Our Guest," with a delightful display of giant dancing spoons and Jell-O

molds. The costumes are exceptional and the special effects that transform the Beast into a dashing prince are quite effective. A happy-ending finale, complete with a send-off of white doves, is a delight. Although showtimes vary, the first performance is usually in the early morning.

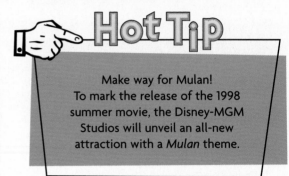

Make way for Mulan! To mark the release of the 1998 summer movie, the Disney-MGM Studios will unveil an all-new attraction with a *Mulan* theme.

The Magic of Disney Animation

Though this attraction will temporarily close in January, its grand reopening will coincide with the opening of a brand-new animation facility this spring. The sprawling new structure makes room for another 400-plus animation whizzes to work their Disney magic—on the screen and in the studio. Watching them work is a bona fide treat. The tour is one of the most interesting attractions at the Studios. In each 45-minute tour (which runs continuously), guests learn about the animation process and watch as Disney animators work on a forthcoming film. They generally work weekdays, quitting between 5 P.M. and 6 P.M. each night, so plan accordingly.

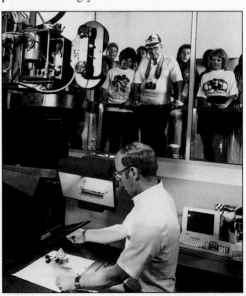

In the lobby, duplicates of 12 of the many Oscars won by the Disney Animation Team are on display, along with character drawings from famous films. Be sure to take note of the pictures—later in the tour you'll get to see how animators manage to bring simple drawings like these to life.

Next stop: the animation studio. During your visit, you may see animators at work on *Mulan*, *Tarzan*, *Fantasia 2000* or another soon-to-be classic film.

Once inside the studio, guests visit the story room, where plot lines are developed for animated features. Next, it's on to the drawing boards, where characters undergo the metamorphosis from pencil sketch to moving picture. Working at their desks in full view of visitors, animators are seen creating the drawings that will later appear in real films.

A tour guide describes what the artists are doing at any given moment. To learn even more, just look up: Video monitors allow guests to view snippets of the films the animators are working on and other works in progress. At one point, an animator takes time out to meet with guests on the tour.

Visitors also view the special camera that's used to transform drawings to digital images. To produce one full second of animation, it takes 24 drawings *per character*. To complete 80 minutes of film featuring 40 different characters it takes, well, *you* do the math! Of course, you can always try to stump your tour guide with the question—since guests are encouraged to ask questions before the tour is wrapped up.

Before moving on, spend some time browsing at the Animation Gallery, where Disney animation cels, exclusive limited-edition reproductions, books, figurines, and many other collectibles are for sale.

Voyage of The Little Mermaid

One of the Studios' most popular attractions, this 17-minute live musical production, adapted from the Disney animated classic, is presented in a theater with an underwater feel. Many of the film's characters, such as Flounder and Sebastian, are brought to life by puppeteers. The show opens with the lively song "Under the Sea"; then clips from the movie are shown as actors join the puppets on stage to help tell the tale.

The mermaid Ariel is the star of the show and performs songs from the film. Prince Eric makes an appearance, and an enormous Ursula glides across the stage to steal Ariel's voice. Of course, the happy ending prevails. The story line is a bit disjointed, and hops from scene to scene, but most viewers are familiar with the plot, so this doesn't detract from the show.

Some of the special effects in the Voyage of The Little Mermaid are best seen from the rear of the theater.

There are excellent special effects inside the theater, including cascading water, lasers, and a lightning storm that may be a bit intense for younger children. Expect to wait a while for this popular show.

The Making of ...

What happens *before* a movie director yells action and *after* he or she screams cut? How do the stars prepare for their roles? Who is responsible for the musical score? And where do all the props come from? The answers to these questions and many more are found here (at least as far as the latest live-action Disney films are concerned).

The Making of... begins with a walk through a working production facility, and leads to a movie screening that gives guests a behind-the-scenes glimpse of the intricacies of making a film. Typically, it introduces the actors and directors, as well as composers, lyricists, and other folks whose names and titles we see as movie credits roll by.

The film yields interesting, and perhaps surprising, bits of information. Consider an interview with Madonna, the star of *Evita*, a film recently featured in this attraction. Madonna admitted that she "dreaded" filming Eva Perón's famous balcony scene because it is so well-known. According to director Alan Parker, Madonna had nothing to worry about. As she stepped onto the balcony in Buenos

Aires and sang "Don't Cry for Me, Argentina," "the crowd went crazy, as did all of the crew," Parker said. "It wasn't just the illusion . . . it was strangely real." Most guests come away with a real appreciation for the work involved in producing a movie.

This attraction is updated periodically to keep up with new Disney releases. Depending on when you visit, you might see *The Making of Flubber* or get a look at the making of another Disney feature. The Walt Disney Theater entrance is on Mickey Avenue. The show, which runs continuously, lasts about 15 minutes.

Studio Backlot Tour

Guests go backstage to see—and experience—some little-known aspects of television and movie production on a tour of real sets and prop stations. Highlights of the 35-minute tour (which runs continuously) include two special-effects sequences in which guests learn how natural disasters and waterborne scenes are created on a studio set. Crowds seem to thin out during the late-afternoon hours, so if the line is long, your time will be better spent at one of the other attractions until then.

First stop is an outdoor special-effects area, where two guests are tapped to hit the high seas. The show demonstrates the effects required to reproduce battle scenes at sea in a water tank. Pyrotechnics, simulated depth charges, and torpedo blasts combine in an action-packed display.

Guests then wait in a queue area to board the trams that travel to the backlot area. This tour segment passes by television and movie production departments, where actual work is being done. The tram then winds through a tunnel, where guests can get a good look at the wardrobe department. More than 100 designers produce the costumes for all of Disney's movie, TV, and other entertainment projects—and with 2.25 million garments, Walt

Disney World has the world's largest working wardrobe. Famous costumes are on display.

The tram then passes through the camera, props, and lighting departments, where equipment is stored. Disney's camera equipment is so advanced that many visiting network TV crews often borrow it when they cover space shuttle launches at the Kennedy Space Center, about 70 miles to the east. A look into the scene shop reveals carpenters at work on sets that are later finished on the soundstages.

The tram turns into the backlot residential street, where empty, hollow facades give the

Hot Tip

Guests who sit on the left side of the tram sometimes get wet at Catastrophe Canyon, while those on the right stay dry. Choose accordingly.

outward appearance of a lovely neighborhood. Used mainly for exterior shots, the houses on this street include Vern's home from *Ernest Saves Christmas*. In addition, there's the facade of "The Golden Girls" home and the house from "Empty Nest."

As trams head for the highlight of the tour, the guide explains how landscapes can be created by set designers to fill a given need. He or she then asks, "Where in Central Florida can you find an active oil field in the middle of a dry, rocky, barren desert canyon prone to flash floods?" The answer is Catastrophe Canyon, which produces a spectacular set of special effects. As the guide will tell you, crews are filming a movie in which a backstage tram gets stuck in the canyon during a flash flood. But supposedly it's safe to go in because they're not filming today.

In an amazing series of special effects, a rainstorm begins; then there's an explosion, complete with flames that are so hot even riders on the right side of the tram feel them; followed by a flash flood that is so convincing it forces everyone to lean the other way. The road underneath the tram shifts and dips hydraulically, lending even more reality to the adventure. A later behind-the-scenes look reveals the tanks, capable of releasing enough water to fill ten Olympic-size swimming pools. Some of the water is blown out by air cannons, which can shoot 25,000 gallons of water over 100 feet. To put that in better perspective, if a basketball were stuck into one of the cannons, it could be shot over the top of the Empire State Building.

Nightmare on New York Street

Beware: a new set of characters has moved into town and they're so spooky they even stand out on New York Street! Each day, Curly the skeleton, Slappy the ventriloquist, Khor-Ru the dummy, and Amaz-O the magician bring the Goosebumps book series to life in a creepy magic show that goes mysteriously awry. After the show, guests may visit the Goosebumps Horrorland Funhouse. Enter the Funhouse through the abandoned ticket booth. It's a scream! Check a guidemap for showtimes.

From Catastrophe Canyon, the tram rides by New York Street, where meticulously reproduced facades line the urban streets. Though the brickwork looks authentic, these backless facades are constructed mostly of fiberglass and Styrofoam. The skyscrapers, including the Empire State Building and the Chrysler Building, are actually painted flats. Forced perspective (the same technique that makes Cinderella Castle appear much taller than it is) makes the 4-story Empire State Building appear as if it were the actual 104-story structure. Though clearly a New York reproduction, the facades can be altered to fit the role for Any City, USA. Tour groups often encounter film crews setting up or taking down equipment from shoots done on the lot. If crews are not filming, guests can explore New York Street on foot.

Backstage Pass to 101 Dalmatians

This 25-minute behind-the-scenes look at moviemaking is a walking tour that begins with a funny video clip about the process of casting dogs for roles in the featured live-action film. Guests are then led into a room called the Special Effects Creature Shop, where they see all kinds of props that were used to produce Disney's *101 Dalmatians*. The guide explains how certain props, such as Audio-Animatronics puppies, helped filmmakers create action scenes that otherwise would have been impossible to shoot.

Before the tour proceeds to the Special Effects Stage, a guest is randomly picked to participate as an actor. The crowd learns how film shot against a blue screen can be superimposed onto any background. Then the "actor" is filmed performing in front of the blue screen. The footage is quickly edited into a scene from the movie and shown to guests.

Then it's on to the soundstages, where specially designed, soundproof catwalks allow visitors to gawk and talk all they want. The tour takes in three soundstages, where filming may be in progress for movies or television shows. It is also possible, however, that nothing will be happening on the set. In this case, guests will view a short video about the challenges of orchestrating action scenes involving hundreds of puppies (each of which had its own trainer).

From this area, guests are led into a walkway, where they see a short film introducing the character Cruella de Vil (played by actress Glenn Close). At the film's conclusion, guests visit a large room overflowing with props and sets used to create Cruella's world, and the guide explains how these elements helped establish her lusciously villainous character. In addition to costumes and part of the set of the de Vil mansion, guests will get a close look at Cruella's car, built especially for the film.

American Film Institute Showcase

Costumes, props, and set pieces used in recent as well as classic movies and television shows are on display in this ever-changing exhibit. Although showcased items may be different when you visit, displays have included costumes from *Mary Poppins*, the police car from *Dick Tracy*, the caricature mural from *Three Men and a Baby*, concept artwork from *Toy Story*, and live-action sets and stop-motion puppets from *James and the Giant Peach*. Other props have come from *Evita*, *Crimson Tide*, *Flubber*, and *George of the Jungle*. An interactive area demonstrates the five phases of movie-making. Souvenirs sold here include movie memorabilia, as well as personalized directors' clapboards and film reel frames.

The Great Movie Ride

Housed in a full-scale reproduction of historic Mann's Chinese Theatre, this 22-minute attraction captivates guests' imaginations from the start. The queue area winds through the lobby and into the heart of filmmaking, where guests will see some famous movie scenes on a large screen. (Note that if the queue extends outside the building, you're in for a long wait. It takes about 25 minutes to reach the ride vehicles once you've entered the theater.)

The guided tour begins in an area reminiscent of the hills of Hollywood in its heyday (which, as the famous, now abbreviated sign indicates, was then known as Hollywoodland.) As a ride vehicle whisks guests under a vibrant marquee, they are transported to the celluloid world of yesteryear.

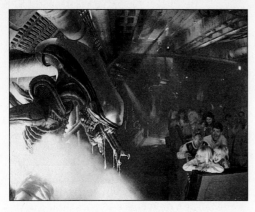

More than 60 dancing mannequins atop a large-tiered revolving cake greet guests in a replay of the "By a Waterfall" scene from the Busby Berkeley musical *Footlight Parade*. Gene Kelly's memorable performance from *Singin' in the Rain* is the next scene, in which rain seems to drench the soundstage, but doesn't dampen the spirits of the Audio-Animatronics representation of Mr. Kelly. Then Mary Poppins and Bert the chimney sweep entertain, as Mary floats from above via her magical umbrella and Bert sings the classic tune "Chim Chim Cher-ee" from a rooftop.

From the world of musical entertainment, guests segue to adventure. James Cagney re-creates his role from *Public Enemy* as the ride proceeds along Gangster Alley. A Prohibition-style mob shootout begins and puts guests in the midst of an ambush. An alternate route leads to a western town, where John Wayne can be seen on horseback eyeing some would-be bank robbers. When the thieves blow up the safe and flames pour from the building, heat can be felt from the trams.

As the ride vehicle glides into the spaceship from the film *Alien*, Officer Ripley guards the corridor while a slimy monster threatens riders from overhead. (Note that this and several other scenes are presented in a dark setting and may be upsetting to young children.)

The legendary farewell from *Casablanca* is also depicted, complete with a real airplane and lifelike Rick and Ilsa. (Ingrid Bergman's daughter Isabella Rossellini has taken her kids here to "see Grandma.") Guests are moved from the airfield to the swirling winds of Munchkinland, where a house has just fallen on the Wicked Witch of the East. Her sister, as portrayed by Margaret Hamilton, appears in a burst of smoke. This Audio-Animatronics figure is impressively lifelike (and scary). But happy endings prevail, and guests follow Dorothy and company along the Yellow Brick Road to the Emerald City of Oz. As the ride draws to a close, guests view a montage of memorable moments from classic films.

The 50 Audio-Animatronics figures created for this ride were crafted by many of the same artists who created the characters in

The Hall of Presidents in the Magic Kingdom. Their attention to detail is amazing. The costumes worn by the Julie Andrews and Dick Van Dyke Audio-Animatronics figures are modeled after the originals from the 1964 film *Mary Poppins*. And Gene Kelly personally inspected his likeness before it was shipped to Florida.

SuperStar Television

Do you fancy yourself the next Lucille Ball or think it's time to team up with Tim "the Tool Man" Taylor? Then you've come to the right place. Roles from famous shows are up for grabs at this remarkable attraction. In the outdoor pre-show area, a casting director chooses members of the audience to "star" in a variety of television scenes. Note: Most would-be actors are picked from the front of the area; a few more roles are filled inside the theater. So, if there's even a little ham in you, move up front and volunteer as enthusiastically as possible. (If you don't make the cut, try again later.)

Audience members are led into a 1,000-seat theater reminiscent of the days of live television broadcasting. At the same time, audience actors head backstage for costuming, makeup, and meetings with the directors.

The stage has several sets, and as the camera operators film the actors in their various roles, the audience watches on eight six-foot-wide projection screens suspended from the ceiling. The pictures on the screens vary significantly from the live events on stage because the use of "blue screen" electronic techniques allows backstage editors to merge the live action with historic clips from classic shows.

In one scene, a guest plays the part of Al Borlund opposite Tim Taylor in a segment from "Home Improvement." Applause signs flash when appropriate, and audience members respond enthusiastically for their fellow tourist-thespians. Be sure to smile, too—the

camera is known to pan the studio audience. Another scene is a classic from "Cheers," in which Woody, Norm, and Cliff star with four guests. Yet another gives several youngsters the chance to star in the opening moments of an episode of "Gilligan's Island."

There are no bad seats in the house, as the eight monitors can easily be seen by the entire audience. This attraction tends to be less crowded during the morning hours, so try it then, and if time permits, go again; each new cast brings a fresh flavor to the presentation. The entire show takes about 30 minutes, from the choosing of stars till the end. Presented by Sony. Note that although the lineup of TV shows may change, the attraction will continue to deliver the same interactive punch for starry-eyed guests.

The ABC Sound Studio

What would a cartoon be without the usual battery of boinks, booms, and in some cases, barks? Boring! Sound effects are the shining stars of every show—especially animated ones. Hear for yourself at this newly renovated attraction (formerly known as Monster Sound Show), which spotlights the important role of sound in animation. It does so by allowing guests to create the sound effects for a short animated film, with predictably funny results.

The pre-show begins outside the theater with a short video presentation featuring *101 Dalmatians*, a new member of ABC's Saturday morning lineup. Upon entering the 270-seat theater, the host chooses several "Foley" artists from the audience. (Foley is the Hollywood sound-effects system named for its creator, Jack Foley.) The audience is then treated to a 45-second clip based on the animated series *101 Dalmatians*. Volunteers are asked to step in when the sound effects go awry. As the film clip is shown again, the amateur crew does its best to match the proper sound effects to the action on the screen. The finished product features the new sound track created by the studio's newest Foley artists. Nothing ever creaks, bumps, or bonks when it's supposed to—but that's the point and it's all a lot of fun.

The 15-minute show features many original gadgets created by sound master Jimmy Macdonald. He invented more than 20,000 sound gadgets during his 45 years with the Walt Disney Studios in California, and also became the voice of Mickey Mouse during the 1940s. There are some special artifacts on display, including Tinker Bell's chimes, a door used in *Alice in Wonderland*, and the coconut shells used to produce the hoofbeats in the *Legend of Sleepy Hollow*. But most of the sounds guests hear are created by the ingenious use of barrels, nails, sandpaper, and other gadgets that go bonk, buzz, zip, or bump.

Don't miss SoundWorks, the post-show area—it's one of Walt Disney World's true hidden gems. SoundWorks offers some hands-on fun for the rest of the audience. Earie Encounters allows visitors to reproduce the flying-saucer sounds from the 1956 film *Forbidden Planet*. At Movie Mimics, guests can dub their voice over those of Clark Gable, Snow White, Roger Rabbit, and other beloved movie stars; and at Soundsations, our personal favorite, "3-D Audio" puts guests in a room filled with sound so realistic that the wind from a hair dryer can almost be felt.

Indiana Jones Epic Stunt Spectacular

Earthquakes, fiery explosions, and assorted other dramatic events give guests some insight into the science of movie stunts and special effects at this impressive 2,000-seat amphitheater. Stunt men and women re-create scenes from Indiana Jones films to demonstrate the skill required to keep audiences on the edge of their seats. Show director Glenn Randall, who served as stunt coordinator of such films as *Raiders of the Lost Ark*, *Poltergeist*, *Never Say Never Again*, *E.T.*, and *Jewel of the Nile*, calls the show "big visual excitement."

But the 30-minute show isn't all flying leaps. Guests also see how the elaborate stunts are pulled off—safely—while the crew and an assistant director explain what goes on both in front of and behind the camera.

In one segment, a scene from *Raiders of the Lost Ark* is staged. A 12-foot-tall rolling ball chases a Harrison Ford look-alike out of the temple. The steam and flames are so intense that the audience can feel the heat. The crew then dismantles the set, revealing the remarkable lightness of movie props, as two assistants roll the ball uphill for the next show.

In a scene at a busy Cairo street market, "extras" chosen from the audience play out the famous scene in which Indiana Jones pulls a gun while others are fighting with swords. The explosive action continues, and leads to a

sensational desert finale in which the hero and his sweetheart make a death-defying escape.

There are moments during this presentation when the audience might wonder if, just for a minute, something has gone wrong. But by revealing tricks of the trade, the directors and stars show that what appears to be very dangerous is actually a perfectly safe, controlled bit of movie magic. It's a great show.

Star Tours

Having witnessed the unyielding popularity of this attraction at Disneyland, California, Disney made the decision to open a counterpart here. The attraction, which was inspired by George Lucas' *Star Wars* film trilogy, offers guests the chance to board Star-Speeders that are actually the same type of flight simulator regularly employed by the military and commercial airlines to train pilots. By synchronizing a stunning film with the virtually limitless motion of the simulator, the ride allows guests to truly feel what they see. (Note that when instructed to put on your seat belt, you should do so. This is a very rough ride.)

Visitors enter an area where the famed *Star Wars* characters R2D2 and C-3PO are working for a galactic travel agency. They spend their time in a bustling hangar area servicing the Star Tours fleet of spacecraft. Riders board the 40-passenger craft for what is intended to be a leisurely trip to the Moon of Endor, but the five-minute ride quickly develops into a harrowing flight into deep space, including encounters with giant ice crystals and laser-blasting fighters. The flight is out of control from the start, as the rookie pilot comically proves that Murphy's Law applies to the entire universe.

Signs at Star Tours warn that passengers must be free of back problems, heart conditions, motion sickness, and other physical limitations. Pregnant women are not permitted to board. There is a minimum height requirement of 40 inches, and children under seven must be accompanied by an adult; children under three are not permitted to ride.

Jim Henson's Muppet*Vision 3-D

One of the most entertaining attractions at the Disney-MGM Studios, this spectacular 3-D movie is quite remarkable. As with so many other Disney attractions, much of the appeal is in the details. A funny 12-minute pre-show gives some clues about what's to come. Characters, including Scooter, Gonzo, and Sam Eagle, entertain on overhead screens.

Once inside the theater, many will notice that it looks just like the one from the television series "The Muppet Show." Even the two curmudgeonly fellows, Statler and Waldorf, are sitting in the balcony, bantering with each other and offering their typically critical commentary on the show. The production comes directly from Muppet Labs, presided over by Dr. Bunsen Honeydew—and his long-suffering assistant, Beaker—and introduces a new character, Waldo, the "Spirit of 3-D." The 3-D effects are convincing, and most viewers can't resist reaching out at least once. Among the highlights are Miss Piggy's solo, which Bean Bunny turns into quite a fiasco. Sam Eagle's grand finale leads to trouble as a veritable war breaks out, and with an appearance by everyone's favorite Swedish Chef, a cannon blasts the screen from the rear balcony.

Where to Eat at the Studios

A complete listing of eateries at the Studios—full-service restaurants, fast-food emporiums, and snack shops—can be found in the *Good Meals, Great Times* chapter. See the Disney-MGM Studios restaurant section, which begins on page 226.

The 3-D effects, spectacular as they may be, are only part of the show: There are appearances by live Muppet characters, fireworks, and lots of funny details built into the walls that surround the seating area of the huge theater. Carryings-on abound for most of the senses—sight, smell, and touch, among them—and it's hard to know where to look first. We're glad that they've put the show in such a large theater, to allow the crowds to enjoy it without too long a wait. Including the pre-show, expect to spend about 25 minutes with Kermit and company. Shows run continuously.

Disney's The Hunchback of Notre Dame— A Musical Adventure

The Studios' newest showpiece, a 32-minute musical based on Disney's animated feature *The Hunchback of Notre Dame*, is performed in the shaded comfort of the Backlot Theater—a canopied bleacher-style theater located just beyond New York Street. The show takes guests to the catacombs of 15th-century Paris, where gypsies reprise the age-old tale of the bell ringer Quasimodo and his struggle to find love and happiness.

Clopin, the King of the Gypsies, is the narrator. It is he who parts the curtains for this play within a play, inviting guests to watch as a troupe of gypsies re-enact the bittersweet story of Quasimodo and Esmeralda. While gypsy magic plays a part throughout, the show is characterized by an imaginative simplicity akin to street theater. Runway ramps that bring characters into the audience enhance the feeling of being part of the performance.

The curtain opens on a gypsy campsite beneath the city. Here, Clopin and the gypsies create a colorful set filled with such treasures as Persian rugs and jewels. The gypsies impart the details of Quasimodo's life in the cathedral's bell tower, telling the story through song, costumes, masks, puppets, and dance. As the show evolves, the gypsies' theatrics reveal Quasimodo's oppression at the hands of Judge Claude Frollo, his love for Esmeralda, and the kindness of Phoebus, the guard who helps the lonely bell ringer.

Lest there be too much sorrow, the set again transforms and a wonderfully lively scene steals away to the streets of Paris for a thoroughly rambunctious revival of the Festival of Fools. Comic relief is provided by the gargoyles, Victor, Hugo, and Laverne, who act as Quasimodo's collective conscience. A point of interest: The first two gargoyles' namesake is author Victor Hugo, while Laverne's is the Andrews Sister of the same name. The show features many of the film's memorable tunes, including "Topsy Turvy," "A Guy Like You," and, of course, "God Help the Outcasts." The first show of the day is usually in the late morning.

Honey, I Shrunk the Kids Movie Set Adventure

The set for the backyard scenes of the popular Disney movie has been re-created as an oversize playground for kids. Blades of grass soar 30 feet high and giant tree stumps and LEGO toys provide climbing opportunities. Kids love to crawl into the discarded film canister and slide out along an oversize reel of film. A hose with a small leak also provides entertainment as it squirts in a slightly different location each time. It's great fun, and the props make kids and adults look and feel very tiny indeed.

SHOPPING

Hollywood Boulevard

CELEBRITY 5 & 10: Modeled after a 1940s Woolworth's, this large shop carries Disney-MGM Studios logo merchandise, frames, clothing, and backpacks, as well as movie-themed items.

COVER STORY: Just through The Darkroom, this is where guests can have their images put on the front cover of a large selection of magazines. If you've had your picture taken by any of the park photographers, this is the place to pick it up. Costumes and appropriate accessories are also available.

CROSSROADS OF THE WORLD: In the middle of the entrance plaza, Mickey Mouse keeps watch from atop this Hollywood Boulevard landmark. The small kiosk deals in souvenirs, sunglasses, film, rain gear, sundries, and guidemaps.

THE DARKROOM: The Art Deco facade of this shop allows guests to enter through an aperture-like doorway. Here, video cameras are available for rent at $30 per day, with a refundable deposit of $450. Deposits can be charged on American Express, The Disney Credit Card, MasterCard, or Visa. Blank tapes must be purchased separately. Although no 35 mm cameras are available for rent, disposable cameras, film, and camera accessories are sold.

KEYSTONE CLOTHIERS: Women's fashions and accessories are the specialties of the house. A favorite item here is a Mickey Mouse umbrella that sprouts two ears when opened. There is also a large selection of character ties.

L.A. CINEMA STORAGE: A great source for kids' stuff, with a variety of clothing. (We love the denim shirts embroidered with characters.) Many items feature characters from recent animated films, but classic characters, especially Winnie the Pooh and friends, have a presence as well.

LAKESIDE NEWSSTAND: No newspapers—just one-stop shopping for Studios logo merchandise and other souvenirs.

MICKEY'S OF HOLLYWOOD: The place to find T-shirts, sweatshirts, hats, plush toys, watches, socks, wallets, tote bags, books, mugs, and sunglasses, plus items emblazoned with the Disney-MGM Studios logo or Walt Disney Studio logo.

MOVIELAND MEMORABILIA: Located just to the left of the main entrance, this kiosk stocks stuffed toys, hats, books, sunglasses, film, key chains, and other souvenirs.

OSCAR'S CLASSIC CAR SOUVENIRS & SUPER SERVICE: The 1949 Chevrolet Tow Truck parked out front gets plenty of attention. Automotive memorabilia, mugs, models, and key chains are for sale. (The truck, by the way, is not.) Services offered here include stroller and wheelchair rental, lockers, and infant products, plus a stamp machine.

SID CAHUENGA'S ONE-OF-A-KIND: Unique antiques and curios are the stock-in-trade here. Autographed photos, old movie magazines and posters, and assorted Hollywood memorabilia are among the many celebrity-oriented collectibles with which Sid is willing to part—for a price.

SWEET SUCCESS: Specialty candies and more traditional treats are available at this sweet-smelling shop.

Sunset Boulevard

LEGENDS OF HOLLYWOOD: A tribute to Disney's newest animated matinee idol, Mr. "Zero to Hero" himself—Hercules. Expect to find an abundance of shirts, hats, books, and other colorful merchandise featuring the flaxen-headed hero.

MOUSE ABOUT TOWN: The best source for casual men's apparel featuring the famed mouse subtly embroidered onto dark-colored sportswear, button-down shirts, polo shirts, and jackets. We particularly like the Tommy Hilfiger–inspired Mickey logo.

ONCE UPON A TIME: The exterior of this shop replicates the Carthay Circle Theatre in Hollywood, where *Snow White* premiered in 1937. The focus is on the classic Disney characters and of course, Snow White and the seven dwarfs. Look for unique collectible items, such as limited-edition porcelain characters. For $25, a Disney artist will customize a character sketch for you.

PLANET HOLLYWOOD SUPERSTORE: A star-studded tribute to Tinseltown, this new spot specializes in Planet Hollywood brand items such as housewares, shirts, caps, and jackets. It also features "Celebrity Edition" artwork and memorabilia.

SUNSET CLUB COUTURE: A sophisticated selection of mostly Mickey watches includes many limited-edition pieces and great pocket watches. A Disney artist can customize character watches on the spot. Jewelry highlights stylized Mickey designs.

SUNSET RANCH: This open-air shop carries a variety of character hats, totes, and apparel, plus sunscreen, film, and sundries.

Beyond the Boulevards

ANIMATION GALLERY: Don't overlook this shop in the Animation Building, where limited-edition figurines, Disney animation cels, and other collectibles ensure great browsing, even if buying isn't on your mind.

ELLEN'S BUY THE BOOK: This cozy nook next to Sci-Fi Dine-In Theater is patterned after its namesake from the TV show "Ellen"; it even has authentic props. "Ellen" logo items, specialty coffees, and, of course, books are also on hand; occasional book signings are held.

ENDOR VENDORS: The shop outside Star Tours offers intergalactic souvenirs tied to the *Star Wars* films and the Star Tours attraction, some of which are hard to find anywhere else.

FOTOTOONS: After the Studio Backlot Tour, visitors can have their photo combined with an image of a cartoon character.

GOLDEN AGE SOUVENIRS: Between The ABC Sound Studio and SuperStar Television, this shop stocks a variety of logo items from all four of the Disney theme parks.

IN CHARACTER: In front of Voyage of The Little Mermaid, this costume shop has everything a child needs to dress up like his or her favorite Disney character.

INDIANA JONES ADVENTURE OUTPOST: Right next to the attraction, discover an assortment of adventure clothing and memorabilia with the Indiana Jones insignia.

IT'S A WONDERFUL SHOP: Tucked away in a corner behind Muppet*Vision 3-D, this "snow-covered" shop—with Disney ornaments galore—feels like Christmas year-round.

THE LOONY BIN: A perfect stop after the Studio Backlot Tour. The shop carries a huge variety of Disney character items.

STAGE 1 COMPANY STORE: Near the exit of Muppet*Vision 3-D, guests can find merchandise with the likenesses of Muppets in addition to a variety of Disney character items.

THE STUDIO STORE: In the Animation Courtyard, expect to find T-shirts, sweatshirts, hats, and accessories inspired by *Hercules* and classic Disney films here.

Where to Find the Characters

You'll often find Disney characters—such as Hercules and Meg, Belle and the Beast, and Aladdin and Jasmine—strolling throughout the park. Look for Woody and Buzz on New York Street. Throughout the day, Mickey, Minnie, and the rest of the gang make appearances in the festive Animation Courtyard. Another good way to meet the characters is at the Soundstage restaurant. As always, check the park guidemap or with a cast member for current details.

ENTERTAINMENT

As you might expect from a park fashioned in the image of Hollywood's heyday, the Disney-MGM Studios knows how to put on a show. (The great movie music that's piped into the park when small bands aren't strolling through certainly sets the stage.) Celebrity appearances are a distinct possibility as well. Basically, in these parts, it's showtime all the time. So guests should be sure to pick up a guidemap at Guest Relations first thing, not only to check attraction starting times, but also to find out what other entertainment is on tap.

While specifics may change, the following listing is a good indication of the Studios' stage presence. As always, we advise calling 824-4321 for entertainment schedules. For information on special events at the Studios, see the "Holidays & Special Events" section of *Getting Ready to Go.*

HERCULES ZERO TO HERO VICTORY PARADE: This colorful 14-minute procession marches to the gospel-rock sounds of *Hercules,* Disney's 35th animated feature. The film's hero is joined by a cast of Greek gods and goddesses, mythological monsters, and the infamous Hades, god of the underworld and notorious hothead (real steam actually spews from his ears). The parade makes its way down Hollywood Boulevard at 2 P.M. daily (twice a day during busy seasons).

SORCERY IN THE SKY: During seasons when the park is open late, this top-notch fireworks display lights up the sky over the Chinese Theater. The impressive ten-minute show is set to music from *Fantasia* and other classic films. The best viewing spots are located along Hollywood Boulevard.

STREETMOSPHERE CHARACTERS: This troupe of performers infuses Hollywood Blvd. with old-time Tinseltown ambience. Would-be starlets searching for their big break, starry-eyed fans seeking guests' autographs, and gossip columnists chasing leads entertain daily.

Coming Attraction

Fantasmic!, a 25-minute nighttime spectacular, makes its WDW debut in late 1998. The eye-popping mix of magic, music, live performances, and special effects will take place on a lake behind Tower of Terror.

Holiday Happenings

Like Epcot and the Magic Kingdom, the Disney-MGM Studios usually stays open extra late to mark holidays such as New Year's Eve, the Fourth of July, and Christmas. During these times, special nighttime entertainment such as Sorcery in the Sky fireworks is often in store. Of course, entertainment plans are subject to change, so it's important to call 824-4321 for up-to-the-minute schedules.

CHRISTMAS: Spectacle of Lights is the Studios' brilliant, twinkling homage to the season. An extraordinary luminous holiday display featuring about four million lights (owned by Little Rock businessman Jennings Osborne and his family) sets the backlot area of the Studios aglow. The display is lit nightly throughout the season. Check a guidemap for exact times.

HOT TIPS

- Arrive at the Disney-MGM Studios before the posted opening time. The gates usually open at about 8:30 A.M.
- Check the Studios Tip Board often to get an idea of showtimes and crowds.
- See Muppet*Vision 3-D, Voyage of The Little Mermaid, and Star Tours early in the day, before the crowds build up.
- Tower of Terror is a popular attraction with very long lines. Ride it early in the day—and never right after a meal.
- For a full-service meal, make priority seating arrangements when you arrive at the park, at either Hollywood Junction at the corner of Sunset and Hollywood boulevards or the desired eatery: 50's Prime Time Café, Hollywood Brown Derby, Sci-Fi Dine-In Theater, or Mama Melrose's Ristorante Italiano. Or make advance plans by calling WDW-DINE (939-3463) up to 60 days ahead.
- Snag a spot along Hollywood Boulevard about 45 minutes before the parade.
- The shops on Hollywood Boulevard are open a half hour past park closing.

Disney's Animal Kingdom

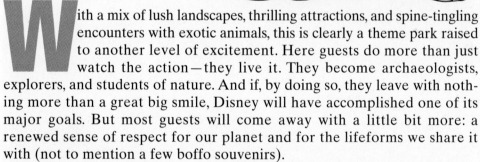

NEW FOR 1998 • NEW FOR 1998 • 1998

ANIMAL KINGDOM

With a mix of lush landscapes, thrilling attractions, and spine-tingling encounters with exotic animals, this is clearly a theme park raised to another level of excitement. Here guests do more than just watch the action—they live it. They become archaeologists, explorers, and students of nature. And if, by doing so, they leave with nothing more than a great big smile, Disney will have accomplished one of its major goals. But most guests will come away with a little bit more: a renewed sense of respect for our planet and for the lifeforms we share it with (not to mention a few boffo souvenirs).

The attractions at Disney's Animal Kingdom are meant to engage, entertain, and inspire. They immerse guests in a tropical landscape and introduce them to wondrous creatures from the past and present—as well as a few that exist only in our collective imagination.

The park, which opens in May, is home to more than 1,000 animals representing 200 different species. Most of the creatures are of the animate variety, as opposed to the Audio-Animatronics kind. Despite that, you won't see beasts behind bars at Animal Kingdom. Instead, you'll see a menagerie of wild critters living in spacious habitats, with virtually no separations visible to the naked (human) eye.

The following pages will help you get the most out of your first visit to Disney's Animal Kingdom. It is, after all, a jungle out there.

Unless otherwise noted, all phone numbers are in area code 407.

GETTING ORIENTED

Though Disney's Animal Kingdom encompasses about five times the area of its Magic counterpart, one need not be in training for the Olympics to tackle it. By all estimates, pedestrians rack up roughly the same amount of mileage in one day here as they do in a day at Epcot. (If you *want* to pack the hiking boots, by all means do—there are plenty of pretty trails to explore.) The park's layout is reminiscent of the Magic Kingdom's: a series of sections, or "lands," connected to a central hub. In this case, the hub is Safari Village, an island surrounded by Discovery River, and home to The Tree of Life, the giant icon that can be spotted from just about anywhere in the park. A set of bridges connect Safari Village with other lands: The Oasis, DinoLand U.S.A., Africa (via Harambe village), and the Disney character area. (Although a special zone had been reserved for characters, it had not been officially named at press time. However, rest assured that many of your favorite characters will be on hand to meet and greet upon your arrival.) By the end of this year, another land will be unveiled: Asia.

As you pass through Animal Kingdom's entrance plaza, you approach The Oasis. Feel free to meander at a leisurely pace, absorbing the soothing ambience of a thick, elaborate jungle, or to proceed more quickly, and plan to revisit this relaxing region later on. Each of several pathways deposits you at the foot of a bridge leading to Safari Village. As you emerge from The Oasis, you'll see the awe-inspiring Tree of Life, a 14-story Disney-made tree, looming ahead.

At the center of Safari Village stands The Tree of Life. Off to the southwest is the character area. You could stop and visit with some Disney characters now, or postpone your socializing until a less crowded time of day.

To the southeast lies DinoLand U.S.A., home of countless prehistoric animals, a fossil dig, and an attraction that's sure to induce a mammoth adrenaline surge: Countdown to Extinction. Behind Safari Village and to the northwest is Africa, where guests go on an African safari and experience a heart-pounding chase for ivory poachers, explore a nature trail, and take a train to Conservation Station, the park's research and education center. Note that Animal Kingdom's two biggest thrill rides, Countdown to Extinction and the Kilimanjaro Safaris, are at opposite ends of the park.

HOW TO GET THERE

Take Exit 26B off I-4. Then follow the signs to Animal Kingdom. Trams run continually between the parking lot and the main entrance.

By WDW Transportation: From the All-Star Sports and All-Star Music resorts: direct buses. Bus transportation from all other Disney resorts may include a stop at Blizzard Beach. From Downtown Disney: bus to the Transportation and Ticket Center (TTC), then transfer to the Animal Kingdom bus. From Magic Kingdom, Epcot, the Disney-MGM Studios, and the resorts on Hotel Plaza Blvd.: buses.

PARKING

All-day parking at Animal Kingdom is $5 for day visitors (free to WDW resort guests with presentation of resort ID). Trams circulate regularly, providing transportation from the parking area to the park entrance. Be sure to note the section and aisle in which you park. Also, be aware that the parking ticket allows for reentry to the parking area throughout the day.

HOURS

Although park hours are subject to change, Animal Kingdom is expected to be open daily from 7:30 A.M. until about one hour after dusk. During certain holiday periods and the summer months, hours may change. It's best to arrive at the park at least a half hour before the opening time. Call 824-4321 for schedules.

Admission Prices

While Animal Kingdom admission prices were undetermined at press time, they are expected to be comparable to those at other Walt Disney World theme parks. For up-to-the-minute information, call (824-4321) or contact your travel agent.

BABY FACILITIES

Changing tables and facilities for nursing mothers can be found at the Baby Care Center in Safari Village, behind Creature Comforts. Also, disposable diapers are kept behind the counter at many Animal Kingdom shops; just ask.

CAMERA NEEDS

Film may be dropped off for processing at Garden Gate Gifts near The Oasis, Disney Outfitters in Safari Village, Mombasa Marketplace in Harambe, and Chester and Hester's in DinoLand U.S.A. The photo pickup location is at Disney Outfitters. Video cameras may be rented at Garden Gate Gifts near the The Oasis ($25 per day with a $300 refundable deposit). Film is sold in most shops.

DISABILITY INFORMATION

Nearly all of the Animal Kingdom attractions, shops, and restaurants are barrier-free. Parking is available for guests with disabilities. Provisions have been made to enhance sight- and hearing-impaired guests' enjoyment of the park. The *Walt Disney World Guide for Guests with Disabilities* is available at many Guest Relations locations. (For additional information, refer to page 30.)

FIRST AID

Minor medical problems can be handled at the First Aid Center, located in Safari Village on the northwest side of The Tree of Life, near Creature Comforts.

INFORMATION

Guest Relations, located just inside the entrance in The Oasis is equipped with guidemaps and a helpful staff.

LOCKERS

Attended lockers are found on the opposite side of the main entrance area, near Garden Gate Gifts and Guest Relations. Cost is $3 plus a $2 refundable deposit for unlimited use all day.

LOST & FOUND

The department is located at the main entrance to Animal Kingdom, near Guest Relations in The Oasis. To report lost items after your visit call 824-4245.

LOST CHILDREN

Report lost children at Guest Relations, near the park entrance, or alert a Disney employee to the problem.

MONEY MATTERS

There is an ATM at the entrance to the park. It's just outside the turnstiles and to the right, next to kennel. Currency exchange can be handled at Guest Relations. Disney Dollars, in $1, $5, and $10 denominations, are also available at Guest Relations. (The bills feature Mickey, Goofy, and Minnie, respectively.) In addition to cash, credit cards (American Express, Visa, MasterCard, and The Disney Credit Card), traveler's checks, and WDW resort IDs are accepted for admission and merchandise, and for meals at all full-service restaurants and fast-food spots. Snack carts accept cash only.

PACKAGE PICKUP

Animal Kingdom shops can arrange for bulky purchases to be transported to Garden Gate Gifts for later pickup (purchases will be ready for pickup three hours after purchase). There is no charge for this service. WDW resort guests can arrange for packages to be delivered to their resort at no extra charge.

SAME-DAY REENTRY

Be sure to have your hand stamped upon exiting the park and to retain your ticket if you plan to return later the same day.

STROLLERS & WHEELCHAIRS

Strollers, wheelchairs, and Electric Convenience Vehicles (ECVs) may be rented at Garden Gate Gifts (the first shop on the right inside the park entrance, near the entrance to The Oasis). The cost is $5 for strollers, with a $1 refundable deposit; $5 for wheelchairs, with a $1 refundable deposit; and $30 for ECVs, with a $20 refundable deposit. Quantities are limited. Keep your rental receipt; it can be used that same day to obtain a replacement at the Magic Kingdom, Epcot, the Disney-MGM Studios, or here at Animal Kingdom.

TIP BOARD

Check this board in Safari Village throughout the day to learn the current wait times for the most popular attractions at Animal Kingdom.

THE OASIS

Traditionally, one has to travel across a long, sunbaked stretch of desert in order to experience the soothing atmosphere of a tropical oasis. With that in mind, think of the Animal Kingdom parking lot as a concrete version of the Sahara. Once you've trekked across it, your journey takes you through the park's front gate and entrance plaza. What's that up ahead? Could it be the towering figure of an enormous banyan tree? Here in central Florida? It must be a mirage.

But no. Within seconds you arrive at The Oasis, a thriving tropical garden filled with waterfalls, running streams, and lush vegetation. The transition is by no means a subtle one. You are immediately enveloped in a world of nature and animals. The atmosphere is idyllic.

The Oasis is basically a big jungle. It is thick and elaborate and teeming with critters. As visitors walk along the pathways, they will catch glimpses of all kinds of wildlife, from deer and iguanas to anteaters and wallabies. As in the rest of the park, there is the illusion that guests are walking among the wildlife. The Oasis is at once an exciting and calming experience. It sets the stage for what's to come.

Guests have several options once they've entered The Oasis. They can continue on a northerly path, making tracks toward The Tree of Life and across a bridge to Safari Village. They can proceed at a more snail-friendly pace, keeping a tally of the various lifeforms that slither by. Or they can simply take time to stop and smell the flowers.

Where to Find the Characters

What would a theme park be without a gregarious cast of handshaking characters? You'll find the patented Disney character experience in all of its animated glory in a small enchanted "land" across a bridge from Safari Village. This garden-like setting with a *Lion King* theme is home to a bevy of beloved characters, including those from *The Lion King*, *The Jungle Book*, and other Disney classics.

Though the area is not limited to the stars of *The Lion King*, they certainly dominate. Different characters make appearances throughout the day. In addition to meeting, greeting, and rustling up grubs, the cast of *The Lion King* periodically performs. Their lively outdoor show is presented several times daily. Keep in mind that this is the *only* place in Animal Kingdom where you can shmooze with the characters. Therefore, if you are traveling with small children, this area is not to be missed. Due to its proximity to the park entrance, this heavily trafficked spot is likely to see its biggest crowds at opening and closing times. Plan your visits accordingly.

SAFARI VILLAGE

Once you've passed through The Oasis, you will come to a bridge spanning Discovery River. The bridge leads to Safari Village, an island at the center of Animal Kingdom and the hub from which all other realms of the park may be reached.

Safari Village is defined by the brilliant colors, tropical surroundings, and equatorial architecture of Africa and the South Pacific. The facades of the buildings are all carved and painted, based on the art of native peoples from around the world. Don't fail to notice all of the bright, whimsical folk-art images representing various members of the animal kingdom.

This island is the shopping and dining center of Animal Kingdom. Many of the park's popular fast-food restaurants can be found here, including Pizzafari and Flame Tree Barbecue.

By far the most striking element in Safari Village is The Tree of Life. It is on the map, but chances are you'll have no trouble finding it. Rising from the center of the island and as tall as a 14-story building, The Tree of Life is hard to miss.

The Tree of Life

The majestic Tree of Life is the dramatic 140-foot icon of Animal Kingdom. The imposing banyan-like tree, with its swaying limbs and gnarled trunk, looks an awful lot like the real thing—from a distance. Up close, it's apparent that this is a most unusual bit of greenery. Completely covered with more than 300 animal images, it is a swirling tapestry of carved figures, painstakingly assembled by a team of Disney artisans. The tree, though inorganic, stands as a symbol of the connected nature of life on Earth. Joyce Kilmer would be proud.

Inside the trunk of the tree is a 450-seat auditorium, featuring a six-minute 3-D film about the some of world's smallest, yet most

> "I have learned from the animal world. And what everyone will learn who studies it is a renewed sense of kinship with the earth and all of its inhabitants."
>
> —Walt Disney

abundant inhabitants—insects. Lots and lots of insects. They creep, crawl, and demonstrate why, someday, they just might inherit the earth. It's a bugs-eye view of the trials and tribulations of their multi-legged world. The line for "It's Tough to Be a Bug" forms on the north side, or back, of the tree.

A walkway snakes around The Tree of Life, allowing guests to get a close-up view of the trunk and perhaps even play a game of "spot the animals." (The spiraling animal images go all the way to the top of the tree. You'll need a pair of binoculars if you hope to see them all.)

Scattered about the tree's base and throughout Safari Village are a variety of animal exhibits. The animals can be seen in a very open, somewhat traditional parklike setting, with lush grass, trees, and vegetation. Among the creatures you may recognize are kangaroos, otters, and storks. Others to which you may be introduced for the very first time as you meander through the exhibits include capybaras (humongous rodents with an affinity for swimming) and ring-tailed lemurs (not quite monkeys' uncles, but more like cousins).

Discovery River Boats

Safari Village is surrounded by the free-flowing Discovery River. Guests can cruise along it by boarding a Discovery River Boat at one of two docks: The first is located along the banks of Safari Village and can be accessed on the right as you cross the bridge from The Oasis to Safari Village; the second, called Upcountry Landing, is located across Discovery River to the east, or right, as you face Africa. Launches are dispatched, on average, every ten minutes.

Discovery River launches are themed to an open-air, cargolike vessel. Each 62-passenger boat has its own skipper. The river cruise offers a great orientation to the park, passing along the edge of each land. It also includes a close-up view of waterfowl and other animals along the riverbanks. Expect a few entertaining surprises, including an encounter with a water dinosaur near DinoLand U.S.A. and a steaming geyser pit by Africa. River cruisers also experience a run-in with a fire-breathing dragon and other interesting diversions along the way.

Theater in the Wild

To the southeast of Safari Village on the edge of DinoLand U.S.A. is one of the two entertainment venues in Animal Kingdom. Theater in the Wild is an impressive amphitheater, seating 1,500 guests at a time. Here, audience members are treated to a variety of live Disney stage shows.

Caravan Stage

The 700-seat Caravan Stage is located behind Safari Village, in an area that will one day be a part of Asia. The Caravan features live shows daily. One show focuses on live birds, enveloping guests in a high-flying celebration of the winged wonders of the world. Note that the performers may still be in rehearsal when Animal Kingdom first opens. If so, the Caravan Stage curtain will be raised soon after.

Coming Attractions

Just as a tiger cub is prone to dramatic growth spurts, so is Animal Kingdom, Disney's youngest theme park. Expect a big one late this year, when the park will expand to include a whole new continent: Asia. In addition to the Caravan Stage, Asia will be home to Tiger Rapids Run, a thrilling, high-speed white-water rafting expedition. Located northeast of Safari Village, across Discovery River, Asia begins welcoming visitors in December.

DINOLAND U.S.A.

If the look and feel of DinoLand U.S.A. seems familiar, there's a reason: It was designed to capture the flavor of roadside America. It is a delightful mixture of culture and kitsch—the likes of which you might stumble upon during a cross-country road trip. Here you'll come face-to-face with fossil fanatics, jump into gigantic sidewalk footprints, and browse through a typically tacky roadside souvenir stand, where you can pick up dinosaur mementos for the folks back home.

There is no separate admission fee to enter DinoLand U.S.A., yet it feels as if there should be. This self-contained corner of Animal Kingdom is a park within a park, complete with its own dramatic entrance: a 50-foot skeleton of a brachiosaurus.

As guests stroll beneath the giant bones, they find themselves smack in the middle of a remote archaeological dig. Here, guests of all ages have the opportunity to play archaeologist and dig through a fossil-packed pocket of dinosaur discovery.

While the dinos that dwell in DinoLand U.S.A. are all of the Audio-Animatronics

variety, keep your eyes peeled for the prehistoric life forms scurrying about the land. That is, for real creatures that exist in the here and now, but whose ancestors kept company with the likes of the carnotaurus and its dinosaur cousins from the Cretaceous era: frogs, turtles, lizards, Gila monsters, and more.

The Boneyard

The Boneyard gives guests—especially younger ones—an opportunity to dig for fossils in a discovery-oriented playground. They will excavate woolly mammoth bones in this imaginative re-creation of an archaeological dig. They'll also unearth clues that will help them solve the mystery of how and when the animal died.

For serious "boneheads" who just aren't satisfied with simple digging, there are plenty of other bone-related activities. You can play music on a boney xylophone, zip down prehistoric slides, and work your way through a fossil-filled maze. While exploring, watch your step: if you accidentally wander into a giant dinosaur footprint, you'll be greeted with a tremendous roar. Be sure to check out the Olden Gate Bridge, too. It's a gateway structure made from the giant skeleton of a dinosaur. The bridge links one end of The Boneyard with the other.

Countdown to Extinction

This thrilling attraction is dramatic with a capital *D*. The dizzying adventure begins with guests being strapped into high-speed vehicles and catapulted back in time to complete a dangerous, albeit noble, mission: to save the last of the iguanodons—a 16-foot plant-eating dinosaur. The iguanodon lived more than 65 million years ago, during earth's Cretaceous period. Just what caused the demise of the iguanodon? Possibly a violent meteor shower that pummeled the planet and destroyed much of its life in the process.

Throughout the frenetic quest to save the iguanodon, you cling to an out-of-control vehicle while dodging meteors and a mix of friendly and ferocious dinosaurs. At one point, you will encounter the carnotaurus— a fearsome, carnivorous dinosaur. The carnotaurus, which has horns like a bull, a face like a toad, and squirrelly little arms, is an especially ugly specimen. (Incidentally, its appearance in Disney's Countdown to Extinction marks the carnotaurus's theatrical debut.)

All of the dinosaurs, both friend and foe, are especially fierce-looking and move as though they were alive. Even their nostrils move as they "breathe."

This attraction offers much more than a thrill a minute. You rocket through time, get pelted by asteroids, and narrowly escape becoming dinner as a dinosaur turns the tables and chases after *you*.

Guests access the Countdown to Extinction attraction through the Dino Institute, a museumlike building inside DinoLand U.S.A. The entire adventure takes about five minutes. We won't reveal the details of the ending, but there hasn't been an iguanodon sighting in about 65 million years.

Note: This is an extremely intense attraction. You must be at least 46 inches tall and seven years old to experience it. The attraction is not recommended for pregnant women, those with a heart condition, or people with back and neck problems.

Cretaceous Trail

Looking for something totally different from the high drama of the Countdown to Extinction? We recommend a leisurely stroll on the decidedly calmer Cretaceous Trail. This simple, shaded walking path is filled with living plants and animals that have survived from the Cretaceous period, a time when dinosaurs ruled the land. Along the way, you will come across several dig sites that are at various stages of exploration, providing a firsthand look at their evolution.

Many of the land plants of the Cretaceous period were much like those that lived in the Jurassic period, the time that immediately preceded it, with a notable exception: the presence of angiosperms, or flowering plants. These and many other prehistoric flora evolved into the plants we see today.

DID YOU KNOW...

The napkins in Disney's Animal Kingdom might look dirty even before you use them. Fear not. Their sandy color is a natural one—no bleach was used in the manufacturing process. It's a much more environment-friendly approach to cleaning up all those sticky faces and fingers.

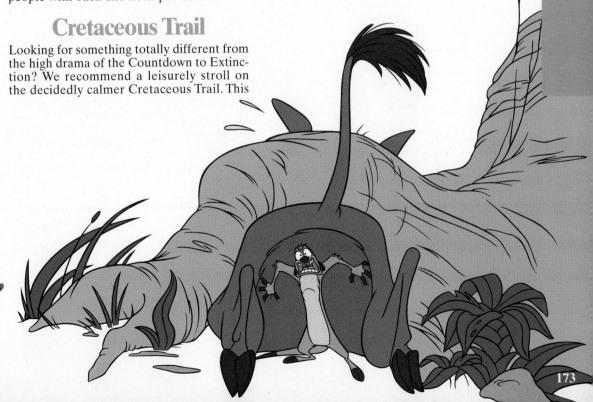

AFRICA

The largest section of Animal Kingdom, Africa is bigger than the Magic Kingdom all by itself. This 100-acre, truer-than-life replica of an African savanna is packed with pachyderms, giraffes, hippos, and other jungle beasts. Guests enter Africa through Harambe, a village based on an East African coastal town. Harambe, the dining and shopping center of Animal Kingdom's Africa, is located to the northeast of Safari Village.

The instant you cross the bridge to Harambe, you are transported to Africa. Everything is authentic, from the architecture to the landscaping to the merchandise in the marketplace. The result was achieved after Disney Imagineers made countless trips to the continent. After seven years of observing, filming, and photographing the real thing, they re-created it here in North America.

The animals, however, are not re-creations. They are quite real, most varied, and extremely abundant. In fact, this chunk of land puts the *animal* in Animal Kingdom.

Kilimanjaro Safaris

The Kilimanjaro Safaris, Africa's big attraction, has something for everyone: breathtaking landscapes, free-roaming animals, and a white-knuckle thrill-ride adventure. It's everything you'd expect from a trip to Africa, and more.

The 25-minute adventure begins with a brief introduction from a safari guide. (The guide does double duty as the driver of the safari vehicle.) The brown, camouflaged vehicle, which seats 32 people, has a roof but no windows. Once you've boarded, look at the plates on the back of the seat in front of you. They'll help you identify the animals you're about to see.

As the open-air safari vehicle travels along dirt roads, you'll spot large herds of exotic animals: zebras, gazelles, hippos, elephants, lions, warthogs, rhinos, and more. Some of the animals wander near your vehicle, and others cross its path. (Relax. Only the harmless creatures approach. Others, such as lions and cheetahs, only *appear* to invade your personal space.)

The calm majesty of the Serengeti may lull you into a state of serenity, but rest assured it's a temporary calm before the storm. You'll soon be jostled and jolted as the vehicle crosses rough, pothole-filled terrain and rickety old bridges—one of which puts you perilously close to a horde of hungry crocodiles.

The ride takes a sudden, even more dramatic, turn when a band of renegade ivory poachers are discovered searching for elephants. Your guide abandons the prepared itinerary and chooses to chase the outlaws, taking you along for what promises to be an especially wild ride. The mad pursuit that follows is a speedy adventure over hills, through valleys, and into one water-filled canyon. It culminates at Ranger Station, a site far removed from the safari boarding area. Any guests hoping to return to civilization are advised to take a hike—literally—on the Gorilla Falls Exploration Trail.

Gorilla Falls Exploration Trail

This self-guided walking trail winds past communities of gorillas and other rare African animals. It can be reached at the end of the Kilimanjaro Safaris or by a separate entrance located in the village of Harambe.

The first stop on the trail, which is as dense and lush as any other area of Animal Kingdom, is the Research Station. The station contains several exhibits, including naked mole rats, a free-flight aviary, and an aquarium teeming with exotic fish. Not far away is the hippo exhibit, which provides close-up views of hippopotomuses both in and out of water. Further along the Exploration Trail there is a spectacular scenic overlook point, where you can get an unobstructed view of the African savanna. Afterward, you can swing by the "Pumbaa and Timon" exhibit, featuring warthogs and meerkats. As you come to the end of the suspension bridge, you will find yourself in a beautiful green valley. Congratulations! You've finally reached the gorilla area—an experience well worth the wait. Visit the gorilla research station and the gorilla valley, where you will be completely surrounded by these magnificent animals.

Wildlife Express to Conservation Station

On the east side of Harambe, bordering what will one day be Asia, is the Harambe Train Station. Here you can climb aboard the Wildlife Express and enjoy a scenic tour of Africa, as well as a rare behind-the-scenes-look at a Disney theme park. As part of the tour, you'll glide past the buildings where elephants and

rhinos sleep at night. You will also see animal care facilities at Conservation Station and get a backstage view of the Kilimanjaro Safaris. A guide narrates throughout the journey.

Conservation Station

While many of Animal Kingdom's themes and stories carry a conservation message, this part of the park really brings that message home. A functioning veterinary lab, Conservation Station is the conservation headquarters for Disney's Animal Kingdom. The huge facility is also the park's research and education hub. Here guests go backstage for an insider look at how all of the animals are cared for.

"Much of the world's wildlife is in imminent danger," says Judson Greene, Walt Disney Attractions president. "Disney is working directly to save endangered animals, but we also hope to motivate our guests to support wildlife programs that are in urgent need of support." After visiting Conservation Station, they just might have the motivation they need. Games and other hands-on exhibits are geared to spark curiosity and wonder about wildlife and conservation efforts around the world. Here are a few highlights of this area.

The Affection Section: A large animal encounter area with accessible, friendly animals to see and touch. A not-to-be-missed experience for kids.

Animal Cams: Guest-operated video monitors that observe animals in their "back-of-house" or nighttime enclosures.

Animal Health & Care: A tour of veterinary labs and research facilities.

Eco Heroes: A set of touch-sensitive video kiosks that allow guests to interact with world-famous biologists and conservationists.

EcoWeb: A computer link to conservation organizations around the world.

Planet Watch: An interactive video that connects guests to information about endangered animals.

Song of the Rainforest: A not-to-be-missed "3-D" audio show that surrounds guests with the sounds of the rain forest.

Get Involved!

When it comes to conservation efforts, the folks at the Walt Disney Company want you to do as they say—*and* as they do: The Disney Wildlife Conservation Fund helps nonprofit groups protect and study endangered and threatened animals and their habitats. Among those groups are the ASPCA, African Wildlife Foundation, International Rhino Foundation, and the Wildlife Conservation Society. To date, Disney has contributed more than $3 million to programs in 24 countries.

Of course, as a trip to Animal Kingdom makes clear, there are many ways to help make the world a better place for its wild inhabitants. Be sure and stop by Conservation Station during your visit. There you can get information about conservation efforts in your neck of the woods. Don't leave your enthusiasm behind when you leave the park!

SHOPPING

Entrance Area

OUTPOST: This small shop, located just outside the park entrance, features a variety of character merchandise and Animal Kingdom souvenirs.

GARDEN GATE GIFTS: Located near the entrance to The Oasis, this is where guests can rent strollers, wheelchairs, and video cameras. Film and disposable cameras are for sale, as is a sizable selection of hats and other merchandise.

Safari Village

ISLAND MERCANTILE: This sprawling shop is themed as a shipping company that celebrates working animals—camels, elephants, beavers, and others. Here you'll find a variety of character merchandise, clothing, candy, and Disney paraphernalia, similar to that sold at the Magic Kingdom's Emporium.

BEASTLY BAZAAR: Look for merchandise relating to fish, turtles, alligators, and other beasts prone to make a splash—this airy shop celebrates aquatic animals.

CREATURE COMFORTS: This open-air shop offers items for kids—toys, clothes, costumes, hats, and more.

DISNEY OUTFITTERS: This shop pays tribute to "Animals of the Six Directions"— north, south, east, west, above, and below. It features men's and women's apparel, jewelry, and hats. Make a point of checking out the carved animal totem poles in the center room.

Africa

MOMBASA MARKETPLACE: An African marketplace and trading company, this shop features animal toys and puzzles, safari clothing and gear, T-shirts, sweatshirts, books, and other Africa-themed gifts.

DinoLand U.S.A.

CHESTER AND HESTER'S: Themed as an American roadside souvenir stand, this shop represents all reptiles and prehistoric animals. Its dinosaur focus is reflected in an assortment of wacky dino-inspired items.

Where to Eat in Animal Kingdom

A complete listing of eateries at Disney's Animal Kingdom—full-service restaurants, fast-food shops, and snack stops—can be found in the *Good Meals, Great Times* chapter of this book. See the Animal Kingdom restaurant section, which begins on page 229.

Everything Else in the World

While the total turf of the World comprises 45 square miles, the theme parks cover less than 1,000 acres. Much of the remaining Walt Disney World terrain is crammed with irresistible activities of a variety and quality seldom found anywhere else.

There's superb golf and tennis, beaches for sunbathing, lakes for speedboating and sailing, canoes for rent and winding streams to paddle along, bicycles for hire, campfire sites, nature trails, and picnic grounds. The recreation options continue with River Country, Disney's old-fashioned swimming hole; Typhoon Lagoon, a state-of-the-art water park complete with surfing lagoon; and Blizzard Beach, a thrilling watery wonderland that translates the hallmarks of a ski resort to the realm of swimming.

Add to all that Downtown Disney, a dining, shopping, and amusement district encompassing Pleasure Island, an after-dark entertainment complex; the Downtown Disney Marketplace, a colorful assortment of shops and restaurants; and Downtown Disney West Side, a new cluster of themed eateries, unique shops, and interactive entertainment experiences. A host of programs invite guests to slip behind the scenes and learn about the workings of the World. Finally, the Disney Institute gives guests a different way to vacation in the World. A resort geared to discovery, it offers the opportunity to dabble in animation, the culinary arts, and many other areas. As Michael Eisner said at the 1996 dedication, "It's like putting the cherry on top of the cake at Walt Disney World."

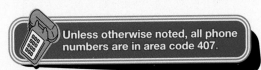

Unless otherwise noted, all phone numbers are in area code 407.

DISNEY INSTITUTE

center of all activity. Facilities include a state-of-the-art cinema, outdoor amphitheater, performance center, closed-circuit TV and radio station, 29 program studios, and a youth center. Note the inscriptions surrounding signs at the Disney Institute, which offer inspirational quotes.

Sports & Fitness Center: This 38,000-square-foot center boasts an indoor exercise pool, a basketball court, two large aerobics rooms, and a wealth of state-of-the-art Cybex weight-training equipment and cardiovascular machines. (Use of the center is complimentary to those participating in programs.) The Disney Institute also encompasses four clay tennis courts, six swimming pools, and the Lake Buena Vista golf course. Within the fitness center, a full-service spa invites guests to indulge in an extensive array of facials, massage, aromatherapy, body therapies, and hand and foot treatments (all of which are priced à la carte). Locker rooms include a steam room, sauna, and whirlpool.

The Programs

Here's the fun part. Guests get to design their own vacation by choosing from a menu of fascinating programs. Instructors are experts in their field, and the small student–instructor ratio ensures plenty of personal attention. The idea is that participants get to try something different, taking home with them newfound skills, creations, and insights. Our advice: Bring a large suitcase. On a recent trip we came home with a topiary, rosemary-infused oil, a best-seller, a dried floral arrangement, and new perspective.

Animation: Discover the techniques behind Disney's animated hits from the artists themselves. No drawing skills are necessary to sketch a Disney character and create its voice, or learn about computer and clay animation.

U nlike its contemporaries that also include *institute* in their monikers, the Disney Institute does not impart wisdom in the traditional higher-ed style. True, there's a lot of learning going on here, but it doesn't happen inside a stuffy classroom. Instead, this resort actively engages guests in a variety of innovative programs ranging from animation and wilderness exploration to topiary gardening, rock climbing, and the culinary arts.

Guests choose from a variety of different program areas, including one designed for youths, to create a customized vacation. The Disney Institute provides a creative environment that inspires guests to try something new. While some are cooking up a healthy feast, others are scrambling up a rock face. As one member of the family is hosting a radio show, another is making a topiary. While some guests hone their photography skills, others are learning self-defense, improving their golf game, or taking a stab at computer animation. Contributing to the environment of experimentation are artists-in-residence, who bring their expertise to workshops during the day and then perform at night.

Getting Oriented

Guests stay in the surrounding villas as part of an intimate lakeside community. The architecture is reminiscent of a quaint American village, with a town green as the

EVERYTHING ELSE IN THE WORLD

Communication Arts and Entertainment: Learn production secrets from experts in the media, such as broadcasting, photography, desktop publishing, and the Internet. Participants may get to become a news anchor for the Disney Institute television station, learn how to shoot better home videos and photographs, or act as a deejay for the Disney Institute radio station.

Culinary Arts: In these popular programs, guests can try preparing regional cuisine, party planning, pairing food and wine, or executing new techniques, all at individual cooking stations with chefs leading the way. A bonus: At the end of the program, participants can eat their creations (and take home the recipes).

Disney Discoveries: For those who can't get enough Disney, these programs explain the creative processes behind the magic. Learn the Disney art of telling a great story or tap into your inventive side as an "Imagineer."

Home, Gardens, and the Great Outdoors: These programs celebrate nature and homes, with a focus on gardens. Some workshops explore the principles of design used in WDW's architecture and landscaping. Guests might try painting a faux finish, taking a canoe adventure, or creating a container garden or topiary.

Performing Arts and Film: A changing roster of artists-in-residence offer interactive workshops in music, film, theater arts, dance, and the spoken word. Guests may see an open rehearsal, film screening, or noted speaker.

Sports and Fitness: Extensive programming is available, including sports clinics, aerobics, golf, tennis, dance, relaxation techniques, rock climbing, self-defense, strength training, and water exercise. Many sessions do not require pre-registration, so allow time to take advantage of facilities and join scheduled classes.

Camp Disney: Kids 7 to 15 have special courses geared just for them in many of the different program areas, plus behind-the-scenes theme park tours. Examples of the fun experiences offered include wildlife adventures, radio broadcasting, rock climbing, and comic strip illustration.

Entertainment

Through the artist-in-residence program, guests have the opportunity to witness the creative process. Accomplished musicians, dancers, writers, and filmmakers stay at the Disney Institute for a few days, holding workshops (and taking programs themselves) during the day, and entertaining in the evening. Seeing one of their performances is the perfect ending to any day, particularly in the intimate Performance Center, so be sure to check the program and events board (in the town green) to see what's on tap. Whatever is planned, trust us when we say it is not to be missed.

Essentials

Disney Institute guests stay in Bungalows and Town Houses at The Villas at the Disney Institute. For room configurations, see page 65 of *Transportation & Accommodations*.

Where to Eat: Seasons Dining Room offers full breakfast, lunch, and dinner menus for the convenience of guests. See *Good Meals, Great Times* for details.

Shopping: Dabblers, in the Welcome Center, has items related to programs.

Rates: Accommodations are based on double occupancy; rates also cover unlimited programs, use of facilities including the Sports & Fitness Center (but excluding spa treatments), taxes, and baggage gratuities, plus a one-day theme park ticket. Single rates are available. An optional meal plan is offered. Spa packages are also available.

Bungalows start at $499 for three nights, $653 for four nights, and $1,111 for seven nights. One-bedroom Town Houses start at $573 for three nights, $750 for four nights, and $1,282 for seven nights. Two-bedroom Town Houses start at $678 for three nights, $890 for four nights, and $1,527 for seven nights. Cost per additional person sharing the same accommodation is $275 for three nights, $353 for four nights, and $587 for seven nights. Rates are higher during peak seasons. All prices are subject to change.

Reservations: It's wise to pre-register for Disney Institute programs up to 90 days in advance; however, changes can be made upon arrival (based on availability). For additional information, call 800-496-6337. To make reservations, call 800-282-9282.

Day Programs at the Disney Institute

If you can't spend a week, then at least come for the day. Full-day programs designed to offer a "day in the life" allow guests to sample two programs, use the Sports & Fitness Center, and catch the extraordinary evening performance for $79. Half-day programs are available for $49. Reservations are necessary; call 827- 4800 up to 14 days in advance.

Another package offers a more literal taste of the Disney Institute, with dinner at Seasons Dining Room plus evening entertainment. The cost is about $27 per person; call 939-3463 for reservations.

DOWNTOWN DISNEY
Downtown Disney Marketplace

The Marketplace (formerly known as the Disney Village Marketplace) teams up with Pleasure Island and the West Side to form the bustling area collectively known as Downtown Disney. (All three sections are linked by walking paths and ferry service.) Located on the shores of Buena Vista Lagoon, the Marketplace is a relaxing setting for shopping, dining, and much more.

The waterside enclave is sprinkled with gardens, including whimsical topiaries (keep an eye out for Lumière). Kids enjoy seeking out the interactive fountains and Hidden Mickeys scattered throughout the area. A particular favorite is the big fountain whose jets shoot up in the (drenching) shape of Mickey's head. Younger kids can be let loose at the sand play area near Cap'ns Tower. And adults may want to enjoy a drink in one of the atmospheric lounges. While some guests eat lunch in one of the themed restaurants, others may grab a bite at the Gourmet Pantry and eat at one of many waterfront tables. Some gravitate toward the marina for boating or fishing. Refer to the *Good Meals, Great Times* chapter for lounge and restaurant information.

Despite all there is to do here, the pace is more leisurely than that of the parks. The best way to take it all in is to wander at will. Note that weekends are busy in these parts.

Shopping

The boutiques in the Downtown Disney Marketplace stock everything from toys and books to fashions for the whole family. The descriptions below suggest the types of wares each store has to offer. Most shops are open daily from 9:30 A.M. to 11 P.M., and later during certain seasons. Note that delivery of purchases to a Walt Disney World resort is complimentary.

THE ART OF DISNEY: Disney animation cels, porcelain figures, ceramics, and collectibles are the goods available at this gallery next to 2R's Reading and Riting.

CAP'NS TOWER: This shop boasts a broad selection of Disney merchandise, which changes several times a year.

CHRISTMAS CHALET: Here's the place to deck the halls Disney-style. In addition to Disney character items, the shop boasts a large assortment of handcrafted ornaments from the United States and Europe. Many items can be personalized.

EUROSPAIN: This shop sells handcrafted items from Spanish artisans and designers (similar to the merchandise at Main Street's Crystal Arts in the Magic Kingdom). Large cut-glass bowls and vases are available, along with mugs, sculptures, and other items, all of which can be engraved. If you bring a photo, it can be reproduced on a plate or other item. Presented by Arribas Brothers.

GOURMET PANTRY: Though escargots and smoked oysters can be found here, there are also breads and pastries, meats and cheeses, cereals, beer, wine, soft drinks, and many more items—both mundane and exotic. Unusual teas and specially blended, freshly ground coffees are available, as are chocolates, sandwiches, and salads. Occasional free tastes are offered to lucky passersby. Guests staying at

Downtown Disney Essentials

GUEST SERVICES: Located next to Cap'n Jack's Oyster Bar in the Downtown Disney Marketplace, this information center is also the place to go for priority seating assistance, Lost and Found, an ATM (there is an ATM at Pleasure Island and at the West Side, too), stroller and wheelchair rental, theme park ticket purchase, and more.

HOW TO GET THERE: Downtown Disney (including the Marketplace, Pleasure Island, and the West Side) is easily accessible from Exit 26B off I-4.

By WDW Transportation: From The Villas at the Disney Institute: walkway or bus. From Port Orleans, Dixie Landings, and Old Key West: boats or buses. From the Magic Kingdom, Epcot, the Grand Floridian, Contemporary, and Polynesian resorts: monorail to the Transportation and Ticket Center (TTC), then transfer to a Downtown Disney bus. From the Disney-MGM Studios, Animal Kingdom, the Wilderness Lodge, and Fort Wilderness: bus to the TTC, then switch for a Downtown Disney bus. From all other Walt Disney World resorts: buses. For additional information, turn to the *Transportation & Accommodations* chapter.

the nearby villas, take note: Purchases can be delivered to your villa; if you aren't going to be there, the delivery person will even stash perishables in your refrigerator. The Gourmet Pantry is open daily from 8:30 A.M. until 11 P.M. To order by phone, call 828-3886.

HARRINGTON BAY CLOTHIERS: Designed to have the appearance of a Bermuda plantation home, this shop has a sizable stock of traditional and casual men's clothing from designers such as Nautica, Ralph Lauren, and Tommy Hilfiger. It is located near the Cap'ns Tower, close to the parking lot.

LEGO IMAGINATION CENTER: World of Disney's next-door neighbor, this shop is a dynamic showcase for larger-than-life LEGO models, including dinosaurs and aliens. It also invites guests to flaunt their creativity in a spacious play area that's chock full of LEGO bricks. The store stocks a variety of LEGO products and educational toys.

RESORTWEAR UNLIMITED: This shop features bright and classy fashions for women. An assortment of sportswear and swimwear is enhanced by bold jewelry, hats, and bags. Lancôme cosmetics are available.

STUDIO M: Here guests can have a professional protrait taken with Mickey Mouse, have their image "magically" added to photos of Disney characters, and watch as robotic artists decorate colorful apparel.

SUMMER SANDS: A beach lover's delight, this shop stocks swimwear, Florida clothing and souvenirs, jewelry, sun care products, straw hats, and bags.

TEAM MICKEY'S ATHLETIC CLUB: This store, which recently doubled in size, has a locker-room decor that offers the perfect setting for sports clothing, activewear, and sports equipment. You'll find items with Disney University logos, as well as Mickey and Goofy in sporting poses emblazoned on shirts. There is also a large selection of athletic footwear.

TOYS FANTASTIC: This fun spot stocks a wide variety of Mattel toys and games, including the newest playthings featuring Disney characters, a full line of Hot Wheels action toys, and Barbie fashions.

2R'S READING AND RITING: A large selection of hardcover and paperback books on many subjects can be found here. Located near the WDW bus drop-off, the shop also stocks greeting cards and stationery. In keeping with the nationwide bookstore trend, you can sip cappuccino while browsing.

WORLD OF DISNEY: With more than 38,000 square feet of space stuffed with Disney merchandise, this is the place for one-stop shopping. In fact, it's the largest Disney character shopping experience in the World. Twelve themed rooms provide the backdrop for the huge array of goods. The enchanted dining room from *Beauty and the Beast* was the inspiration for the culinary section; famous Disney villains are celebrated in a room that's filled with items such as clocks, watches, candles, and frames; and fairies from *Cinderella* and *Sleeping Beauty* can be seen floating through the intimate apparel department. Disney characters are available on everything from hats and shirts to blankets and bags.

The vast space not only makes for comfortable shopping; it also inspired Disney to provide entertainment. Upon entering, look up at the colorful airships overhead, each one piloted by a different Disney character. Check out the video screen for movie showings and the 24-foot wall of stuffed animals. Engraving and personalization services are available for many items. A concierge can help locate any item in the store, then make arrangements for delivery home or to a WDW resort.

Lakeside Activities

Buena Vista Lagoon, the 35-acre expanse that borders this community of cedar-shingled shops, gives the Marketplace much of its atmosphere: When the sidewalks radiate heat, the water looks cool and inviting; in the slanting rays of the late-afternoon sun, it glistens like a sheet of silver.

There's always something going on. Little Water Sprites zip to and fro, speeding across the lake, while more laid-back folks float gently along in pontoon or canopy boats, and still others fish off the dock.

It's pleasant to sit and watch all this activity from waterside benches and tables over cool, chocolaty refreshments from Ghirardelli's Soda Fountain and Chocolate Shop on the lake's west shore, or over Maryland crab cakes and strawberry margaritas at Cap'n Jack's Oyster Bar.

Those who would rather participate need walk only a few steps to the marina, where several types of boats can be rented from morning until dusk. Opening and closing hours change from season to season. Call 828-2204 for details. No swimming is permitted. For more information on sporting activities here, see the *Sports* chapter.

Where to Eat at Downtown Disney

A complete listing of restaurants, bars, and snack spots can be found in the *Good Meals, Great Times* chapter. See the Downtown Disney restaurant listing, including the Marketplace, Pleasure Island, and the West Side, beginning on page 236. Most restaurants here are open from about 11:30 A.M. to midnight. Planet Hollywood serves until 1 A.M.

Pleasure Island

A six-acre water-bound nighttime entertainment complex, Pleasure Island
delivers a wealth of options that nicely
top off a day in the parks. In addition to
clubs, there are several restaurants, and a
variety of unusual shops.

Pleasure Island, the central area of Downtown Disney, is connected to the Marketplace
and the West Side by various footbridges. The
island's clubs open at 7 P.M. or 8 P.M. and don't
close until 2 A.M. There is no fee to explore
Pleasure Island before the clubs open or to eat
at its restaurants. A single admission of $19.03
(including tax) allows access to all clubs and
the nightly street party. Length of Stay Passes
and Five-Day World Hopper Passes include
Pleasure Island admission. An annual pass
costs $54.01 ($43.31 for a renewal). Guests
under age 18 must be accompanied by a parent
or legal guardian. Valet parking is available for
$5. Guidemaps provide showtime information.

Specialty drinks, beer, wine, and soft
drinks are available at all of the clubs. The
drinking age in Florida is 21. Guests who are
18 and over will be admitted to the clubs
(except Mannequins), but will not be served
alcohol. A valid U.S., foreign, or international driver's license with a photo, an active
U.S. military identification card, or a passport must be presented as proof of age.

Clubs

ADVENTURERS CLUB: "Explore the unknown,
discover the impossible," states the credo
posted at the entrance. The place is modeled
on the paneled libraries and elegant salons
of similar clubs of the 19th century, and is
jam-packed with memorabilia. Just about all
the items on display were collected at garage
sales, antiques shows, and shops all around
the world by Disney Imagineers. The
recesses hide rooms where the masks on the
walls come to life; current club members,
including an inept pilot, mingle—with most
amusing results.

The two-story club is littered with "stuff," so
stroll around and snoop all you like. If you
have a seat at the bar, ask the bartender to
work some magic; your stool may slowly sink
toward the floor. In the library, a haunted
organ sets the scene for outrageous storytellers.
The show is a little corny, but entertaining.

BET SOUNDSTAGE CLUB: The space
previously occupied by the Neon Armadillo
Music Saloon now features jazz,
rhythm and blues, soul, and hip-
hop. The club is operated by BET
Holdings, Inc., which owns Black
Entertainment Television.

COMEDY WAREHOUSE: A comedy troupe
performs five times each evening from 7 P.M.
to 1 A.M. There are five comedians and one
musician. It's a funny, entertaining show that
features improvisational comedy based on
audience suggestions. Every seat offers a good
view, even if the stools are a little tough on
bad backs. Popcorn is the snack of choice.

8TRAX: Got a penchant for the Partridge Family? Do the Bee Gees have a special place in
your heart? If so, make tracks for 8Trax. Music
from the early seventies and the disco era fills
this dance spot. To keep things in a 1970s mode,
the staff dresses in polyester. The club also has
eighties nights for the seventies-challenged.

MANNEQUINS: This is the place to head to
dance the night away. Guests enter through
an elevator that rises to the third floor.
Lights, contemporary dance music, and an
overall exuberant atmosphere dominate the
scene. The name of the club comes from the
many mannequins serving as props. Each of
the figures is tied to dance in some way. There
are several "cats" from the musical of the
same name, and re-creations of Deborah
Kerr and Yul Brynner dressed as Anna and
the King of Siam in the "Shall We Dance?"
scene from the film *The King and I.*

The main dance floor is actually a big
turntable, and the music is provided by a
deejay. The lighting is a major attraction,
with 60 robotically controlled lighting instruments and a matrix of lights behind the stage
that has been dubbed "the toaster oven" by
Disney Imagineers (because it warms the
entire room when lit). There are also
machines that can create bubbles, hurl confetti, and even make it snow. Note that Mannequins is restricted to guests 21 and older.

PLEASURE ISLAND JAZZ COMPANY: Reminiscent of jazz clubs from the 1930s, the interior
of this one resembles an old warehouse. There

Shopping at the Crossroads

Constructed by the WDW folks, the Crossroads of Lake Buena Vista shopping center, located adjacent to the resorts on Hotel Plaza Blvd., is a convenient dining and shopping area. The retail center is anchored by a Gooding's supermarket, which is open 24 hours a day and has a full-service pharmacy (open 10 A.M. to 6 P.M. weekdays). Guests at the nearby villas will find this an especially convenient stop. In addition to the many shops and services, there's Pirate's Cove Adventure Golf, a miniature golf course with a swashbuckling motif.

is live entertainment nightly, featuring jazz from the 1930s to the present. Guests sit at cocktail tables. The music is not too loud, so conversation is possible. Tapas-style appetizers are served. To snag a good table, arrive about 20 minutes before showtime.

ROCK 'N' ROLL BEACH CLUB: A combination of dancing, noshing, and surfer-style decor awaits guests here. The dance floor is on the lowest level of the building, and there are billiard tables and games on the other two floors.

Live bands perform hits from the 1960s to the present. The band plays 45 to 50 minutes each hour, and a deejay takes over during the breaks. The atmosphere is a little frenetic but nonetheless exciting. There is an ATM outside.

Entertainment

In addition to the many clubs, Pleasure Island offers even more evening diversions.

LATE-NIGHT STREET PARTY: Every night at Pleasure Island is like New Year's Eve. There is a fireworks show with special-effects lighting and confetti, and a talented troupe of dancers entertains on the streets.

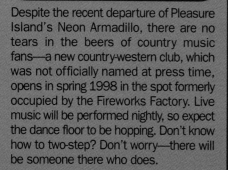

Country Club Countdown

Despite the recent departure of Pleasure Island's Neon Armadillo, there are no tears in the beers of country music fans—a new country-western club, which was not officially named at press time, opens in spring 1998 in the spot formerly occupied by the Fireworks Factory. Live music will be performed nightly, so expect the dance floor to be hopping. Don't know how to two-step? Don't worry—there will be someone there who does.

WEST END STAGE: Bands, including some top-name groups, perform here nightly. The Island Explosion, Pleasure Island's own dance troupe, also entertains.

Shopping

The variety of merchandise at Pleasure Island's shops is a little more eclectic than that found at the other WDW emporiums. Shops are open from 11 A.M. to 1 A.M.

AVIGATOR'S SUPPLY: The latest in men's and women's casual attire is featured here.

CHANGING ATTITUDES: This shop reveals its hip young style with an assortment of shirts, accessories, jewelry, bags, and other goods.

DTV: A collection of fun and colorful contemporary fashions featuring Mickey Mouse and his friends is available here.

ISLAND DEPOT: The shop features surfwear and activewear, including shirts, shorts, backpacks, and hats, plus watches and jewelry. The No Fear and Mossimo collections are here.

MUSIC LEGENDS: Compact discs, T-shirts, and memorabilia from the early days of rock 'n' roll to heavy metal and hip-hop are available at this location. There are three sections, highlighting different types of music.

REEL FINDS: Movie- and television-themed memorabilia constitute the stock at this star-studded spot. Items once owned by celebrities are on display.

SUPERSTAR STUDIOS: Ready to make your big musical debut? Now's your chance to star in your own music video. Guests lip-sync to favorite songs for video recordings. A particular favorite with teens.

SUSPENDED ANIMATION: Posters, prints, lithographs, cels, and original Disney animation art are sold here. It's a pleasant place to browse.

Downtown Disney West Side

When Disney's shopping and entertainment district underwent its recent growth spurt, it did so in true American style: It went west. The West Side, which made its debut in late 1997, boasts a wide variety of restaurants, shops, movies, and clubs. The area that makes up the westernmost neighborhood of the Downtown Disney region is adjacent to Pleasure Island. Although it does not have an admission fee, some venues may charge a cover.

Clubs

BONGOS CUBAN CAFE: Situated behind the AMC Theatres on the edge of the Buena Vista Lagoon, Bongos echoes the style of clubs in Miami's sizzling South Beach. Created by Gloria Estefan and her husband, Emilio, it features the flavors and rhythms of Cuba and other Latin American entertainment centers. The bold design is dramatic, yet whimsical. Guests dine and, if the mood strikes, even dance amid the colorful, tropical decor (and one remarkably oversize pineapple).

There is entertainment nightly. The food here moves to a Latin beat as well, with its slate of traditional and nouvelle Cuban dishes. (For more information on this and other West Side dining spots, refer to *Good Meals, Great Times*.)

HOUSE OF BLUES: A combination restaurant-music hall with seating for 2,000, House of Blues was inspired by one of America's most celebrated musical traditions. Lest too much of the blues bring you down, there is a lively dose of jazz and country, plus a little bit of R & B and some rock 'n' roll thrown into the music mix. The site is also a working television production facility, multimedia development site, and radio broadcasting center. As such, it will be the home of many original programs. Tickets can be purchased through TicketMaster (839-3900) or the House of Blues box office (394-2583). Prices range from about $5 to $30, depending on the performer.

Moved to buy some official "House" merchandise? Take It Easy Baby–that's the name of the shop stocking everthing from House of Blues baseball caps to the latest CDs from the blues world. The House of Blues restaurant features an interesting melange of Delta-inspired cuisine, including jambalaya, étouffée, and homemade bread pudding. (Refer to the *Good Meals, Great Times* chapter for additional information.)

Entertainment

AMC THEATRES: The most popular multi-screen theater complex in the state of Florida is now the largest. The 24 screens show an impressive selection of current movie releases. The seats are roomy and comfortable, and the sound system is first-rate. (It was developed by George Lucas, the creative force behind the trilogy of *Star Wars* blockbusters.)

DISNEYQUEST: This wildly imaginative, state-of-the-art entertainment complex features high-tech activities that engage kids and grown-ups alike. The interactive attractions here combine the Disney experience with cutting-edge technology. Although pricing information for this pay-for-play environment had not been determined at press time, it will be available at the entrance to DisneyQuest.

Note: This Downtown Disney venue makes its official debut in summer 1998.

Coming Attraction

The building that towers over all the others at Downtown Disney West Side is actually a tent—a circus tent. It will be the home of a most extraordinary circus experience: Cirque du Soleil. Known for its high energy and artistic performances, Cirque features a unique mix of acrobatics and modern dance combined with outrageous costumes, magical lighting, and dramatic original music.

The eclectic show premieres for Walt Disney World resort guests in fall 1998. A cast of more than 70 international performers will showcase their talent in this 70,000 square-foot, 1,650-seat theater.

Shopping

AUTHENTIC ALL STAR: This shop specializes in sports gear, hats, sweatshirts, and other items stamped with the logo of the Official All Star Café.

CANDY CAULDRON: Stop here for some homemade southern-style sweets in an open candy kitchen.

CELEBRITY EYEWORKS: Are you looking to change your eyeglass image? Slip into some shades that have been sported by the stars—or at least convincing replicas of them. Celebrity Eyeworks has a huge collection of designer styles worn by celebrities in recent films.

FORTY THIRST STREET: The perfect place for a java jolt, this spot specializes in cappuccino, espresso, and fine imported coffees. Fresh-squeezed juices, smoothies, and desserts round out the selection.

GUITAR GALLERY: Whether you prefer it plugged or unplugged, this spot can satisfy your guitar needs. An informed staff can help you make the right selection. A vintage guitar display entices buyers and browsers alike.

MAGNETZ: Your refrigerator will never be the same once you've visited this specialty magnet shop with its eclectic assortment of collector-quality magnets.

SOSA FAMILY CIGARS: In addition to offering a selection of premium cigars, this shop showcases the art of hand-rolling.

STARTIFACTS: The spotlight here is on memorabilia—music, television, movie, political, and historical—allowing you to bring a piece of Hollywood to the folks back home.

VIRGIN MEGASTORE: This store stocks an enormous variety of music, from classical to contemporary. Much of the musical fare can be sampled with headphones at its 300 CD listening stations. Giant photos of celebrities adorn the walls of the three-story, circular structure. In addition to musical fare, the shelves of this emporium are lined with current video and book titles. Outside, an elevated stage is used for live performances.

It's a Celebration!

What happens when a little bit of Disney magic spills into the real world? A town called Celebration, Florida. Founded in 1996, by a subsidiary of the Walt Disney Company, Celebration was designed to be a friendly place to live, work, and play. The cozy town is surrounded by 4,700 acres of protected green land. The homes, with their front porches and picket fences, hark back to a much simpler time. Yet the area is really more of an experimental prototype community of tomorrow, or E.P.C.O.T.— realizing one of Walt Disney's dreams.

In addition to residential neighborhoods, the community boasts a thriving downtown area. The old-fashioned retail and business district was modeled after those found in small American towns. It invites visitors to celebrate good times and family fun at a variety of dining, shopping, and entertainment spots including a bookstore, antique shop, an old-fashioned ice cream parlor, 1950s-style diner, and movie theater.

Built along a scenic lakeside promenade, Downtown Celebration is a pleasant place to relax outdoors. Guests may shop, stroll, skate, rent pedal boats, or simply enjoy a picnic by the lake. There are several village parks, miles of nature trails, and an 18-hole public golf course (rates range from $45 to $95). Near the par-72 course is a three-hole youth course where the Tiger Woods of tomorrow can practice their golf swings.

Located south of the intersection of U.S. 192 and I-4, Celebration, Florida, is about a ten-minute drive from Walt Disney World. For information, call 939-TOWN (939-8666), or write: Celebration Information, 200 Celebration Place; Celebration; FL, 34747-4600.

BOARDWALK ✓

A stroll at Disney's BoardWalk is a journey back in time. Inspired by the Middle-Atlantic seaside attractions of the early 1900s, BoardWalk recaptures the carefree atmosphere of that bygone era. The resort is surrounded by restaurants, clubs, and amusements similar to those enjoyed by beachgoers of yesteryear. It's bordered by a wood-planked walkway, which hugs the shore of Crescent Lake. By day, BoardWalk is a peaceful place to soak up sun, enjoy lunch, or simply walk the boards. After dark, the place turns into a twinkling center of nighttime activity—some of it elegant, some of it downright raucous.

The Wyland Galleries, which features the world's foremost marine environmental art, is one of the more calming diversions. Wild-Wood Landing challenges onlookers to test their luck and skill at a collection of classic carnival games. And strolling performers enchant passersby of all ages with magic shows, balloon tricks, and more.

BoardWalk is open to everyone. Although there is no admission price, individual venues may charge a cover. There is a $5 charge for valet parking after 5 P.M. for guests who are not staying at a Walt Disney World resort. Self-parking is free.

Clubs

ATLANTIC DANCE: Elegant and nostalgic, this is a delightful place to socialize, sip champagne, and dance the night away. The multilevel nightclub, which anchors the boardwalk on the side bordering the Swan resort, recently underwent some refurbishment. It now boasts a much improved sound system and better acoustics, as well as a whole new musical concept—turning away from mainstream popular music and focusing on "retro-swing." Think of it as 1940s music with a '90s spin.

While retro-swing encompasses many styles of music, Atlantic Dance focuses on contemporary swing, a form made popular by artists such as Harry Connick Jr. and the Brian Setzer Orchestra. Live bands—some big, some small—perform each night.

You can swing and sway here from 8 P.M. until 2 A.M. nightly, and admission is usually $3 weekdays, $5 weekends (the cover charge sometimes varies, depending on the acts scheduled to perform). Guests must be 21 or older, with a legal ID, to enter.

ESPN CLUB: This club aims to please sports enthusiasts of all kinds, from the casual armchair quarterback to the most rabid fanatic. It includes a multimedia center, complete with Internet connection, broadcasting facility, arcade, and full-service restaurant and bar.

More than 70 televisions broadcast live sports events, so guests always know the score. (Need to make a pit stop at a crucial moment of the game? Don't sweat it—there are even TVs in the bathrooms.)

The ESPN Club has three sections. As you enter, you're on the 50-yard line at The Sidelines. You can catch a game on a monitor above the "penalty box" bar or sit at a nearby table (from which you can pick up the sound of any TV in the room). Beer, wine, and soft drinks are available, as is sports-pub fare.

Sports Central, the main dining area, has a big screen, showing—what else—the big game. The kitchen is open until 11:30 P.M. for meals, 1 A.M. for snacks and appetizers. For more information, turn to page 230 of the *Good Meals, Great Times* chapter.

The Yard Arcade, a gameroom with an "urban playground" motif, lets you play the latest sports-themed video games while listening to the big game of the moment.

JELLYROLLS: You might want to warm up your vocal chords before crossing the threshold. They don't call it a sing-along bar for nothing: Guests are expected to sing, clap, and join in the fun at this rollicking warehouse–home of Disney's dueling pianos. You'll hear everything from Garth Brooks to *Grease!* The piano players take requests, so plan ahead. Write your request—a cocktail napkin will do—and slip it onto the piano. (Although it's not required, we recommend slipping a tip along, too. It'll increase the odds of your hearing the request *and* help the musicians pay their rent.)

Jellyrolls is open from 7 P.M. until 2 A.M. nightly. There is a $3 cover charge on weekends, none on weekdays. To get in, you must be at least 21 and willing to prove it.

WATER PARKS
Typhoon Lagoon

A furious storm once roared 'cross the sea,
Catching ships in its path, helpless to flee,
Instead of a certain and watery doom,
The winds swept them here to Typhoon Lagoon!

So reads the legend that guests see as they approach Typhoon Lagoon, a 56-acre aquatic park. The watery playground was inspired by an imagined legend: A typhoon hit a tiny resort village many years ago, and the storm—plus an ensuing earthquake and volcanic eruption—left the village in ruins. The locals, however, were resourceful and rebuilt their town as best they could.

The centerpiece of Typhoon Lagoon is a huge watershed mountain known as Mt. Mayday. Perched atop its peak is the *Miss Tilly*, a marooned shrimp boat originally from Safen Sound, Florida. *Miss Tilly*'s smokestack erupts every half hour, shooting a 50-foot flume of water into the air.

The surf lagoon is huge; thrilling slides snake through caves; tamer ones offer twisting journeys; and tiny slides entertain small kids. What follows is a description of Typhoon Lagoon activities.

TYPHOON LAGOON: The main swimming area contains nearly three million gallons of water, making it one of the world's largest wave pools. The Caribbean-blue lagoon is surrounded by a white-sand beach, and its main attraction is the waves that come crashing to the shore. The less adventurous can loll about in two relatively calm tide pools, Whitecap Cove and Blustery Bay.

CASTAWAY CREEK: This 2,100-foot circular river that winds through the park offers a lazy, relaxing orientation to Typhoon Lagoon.

Tubes are free and are the most enjoyable way to make the trip along the three-foot-deep waterway. The ride takes guests through a rain forest, where they are cooled by mists and spray; through caves and grottoes that provide welcome shade on hot summer days; and through an area known as Water Works, where "broken" pipes from a water tower unleash showers on helpless passersby. The current is calm, and aside from a few floating props, the journey is unimpeded. There are exits along the way, where guests can hop out for a while and do something else, or just dry off a bit and then jump right back into the water. It takes 25 to 35 minutes to ride around the park without taking a break.

Hot Tip

Modest maidens beware! A one-piece suit is far safer than a two-piece on many of the more adventurous water slides—especially Typhoon Lagoon's Humunga Kowabunga and Blizzard Beach's Summit Plummet.

GANGPLANK FALLS, KEELHAUL FALLS, AND MAYDAY FALLS: These three white-water rides offer guests a variety of slippery trips, two of them in inner tubes. All of the slides course through caves and waterfalls, and past intricate rockwork, making the scenery an attraction in itself. Gangplank Falls gives families a chance to ride together in a three- to five-passenger craft.

HUMUNGA KOWABUNGA: These two speed slides, reported to have been carved into the landscape by the historic earthquake, will send guests zooming through caverns at speeds of 30 miles per hour. The 214-foot slides offer a 51-foot drop, and the view from the top is a little scary. But it's over before you know it, and once-wary guests hurry back for another try. Guests are also warned that they should be free of back trouble, heart conditions, and other physical limitations to take the trip. Pregnant women are not permitted to ride.

STORM SLIDES: The Jib Jammer, Rudder Buster, and Stern Burner body slides send guests off at about 20 miles per hour down winding fiberglass slides, in and out of rock formations and caves, and through waterfalls. It's a somewhat tamer ride than Humunga Kowabunga, but still offers a speedy descent. The slides run about 300 feet, and each offers a different view and experience.

SHARK REEF: Guests obtain free snorkel equipment for a swim through an artificial coral reef, where they come face-to-face with sharks and fish. The reef is built around a sunken tanker (where guests who don't care to swim among the fish can get a close look from the portholes). The sharks, by the way, are leopard, nurse, and bonnethead sharks, all passive members of the species. Guests must shower before entering the reef's depths.

KETCHAKIDDEE CREEK: Open only to those four feet tall or under (unless accompanied by a small child), this kiddie area offers comparable rides scaled down for pint-size visitors. Children *must* be accompanied by an adult. There are slides, fountains, waterfalls, squirting whales and seals, a mini rapid ride, and a grotto with a thin veil of water that kids love to run through.

Essentials

WHEN TO GO: Typhoon Lagoon gets very crowded early in the day. Once it reaches a certain capacity, only guests using WDW transportation will be admitted. When the park reaches peak capacity, no one will be admitted until crowds subside (usually after 3 P.M.). Hours vary seasonally, but the park is generally open from 10 A.M. to 5 P.M. with extended hours in the summer months. All of the pools are heated in the winter. Note that Typhoon Lagoon is usually closed for refurbishment during certain winter months, typically November and December. The park may also close due to inclement weather. Call 824-4321 for schedules.

HOW TO GET THERE: Buses are available from the TTC and all WDW resorts, except the Grand Floridian, Contemporary, Polynesian, Wilderness Lodge, and Fort Wilderness (which require transfers at the TTC).

LOCKER ROOMS: Restrooms with showers and lockers are located near the entrance. Other restrooms are available farther into the park. These are labeled "Buoys" and "Gulls." Small lockers cost $3 plus a $2 deposit to rent for the day, while large lockers cost $5 plus a $2 deposit. Towels rent for $1, and life jackets are available with a $25 refundable deposit.

WHERE TO EAT: There are two restaurants at Typhoon Lagoon, both offering similar fare and outdoor seating at tables with colorful umbrellas. Leaning Palms, which was known as Placid Palms before the typhoon hit, was renamed to fit its somewhat unorthodox architecture. Burgers, hot dogs, salads, ice cream, and assorted snacks are sold here. Typhoon Tilly's offers a similar menu and has a separate area just for ice cream and frozen yogurt. Let's Go Slurpin offers frozen drink specialties and spirits. Also on hand are picnic areas, where guests can bring their own food or enjoy a sampling from the restaurants. Note that no alcoholic beverages or glass containers can be brought into the park.

FIRST AID: A first-aid station capable of handling minor medical problems is located just to the left of Leaning Palms.

BEACH SHOP: Singapore Sal's, located to the right of the park's main entrance, is set in a ramshackle building left a bit battered by the typhoon. Bathing suits, sunglasses, hats, towels, sunscreen, souvenirs, thong sandals, and beach chairs are among the wares for sale here.

Admission Prices

ONE-DAY TICKET
(Prices include sales tax and are subject to change.)

Adult	$26.45
Child*	$20.67

ANNUAL PASS

Adult	$93.45
Child*	$74.73

Note: Admission is included with a Length of Stay Pass or a Five-Day World Hopper Pass.

*3 to 9 years of age; children under 3 free

Blizzard Beach

A wintery, watery wonderland, Blizzard Beach is said to be the result of a freak storm that dropped a mountain of snow onto Walt Disney World, prompting the quick construction of Florida's first ski resort. When temperatures soared and the snow began to melt, designers prepared to close the resort. But when they spotted an alligator sliding down the slopes they realized that they had created an exhilarating water adventure park! The slalom and bobsled runs became downhill water slides. The ski jump is now the world's tallest (120 feet), fastest (60 miles per hour), free-fall speed slide.

The centerpiece of Blizzard Beach is the snow-capped Mt. Gushmore and its Summit Plummet. Most of the more thrilling runs are found on the slopes of this mountain, which tops out at 90 feet. At the summit, swimmers have a choice of speed slides, flumes, a white-water raft ride, and an inner-tube run. There is also an observation tower that offers a spectacular view. Guests reach the top of Mt. Gushmore via chairlift. The lift is equipped with a gondola for guests with disabilities. There are also three sets of stairs for those who prefer to scale the mountain on foot.

This is the most action-packed Disney water park yet, with enough activities for the entire family to fill at least a day. Note that kids under ten must be accompanied by an adult.

MELT-AWAY BAY: This one-acre pool at the base of Mt. Gushmore is equipped with its own wave machine. No tsunamis here, however, just a pleasant bobbing wave.

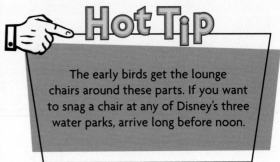

Hot Tip

The early birds get the lounge chairs around these parts. If you want to snag a chair at any of Disney's three water parks, arrive long before noon.

CROSS COUNTRY CREEK: This meandering 3,000-foot waterway circles the entire park. A slow current keeps visitors moving along. Inner tubes, which are free, are the most pleasant way to travel. The ride includes a trip through a bone-chilling ice cave, where guests are splashed with the "melting ice" from overhead.

SUMMIT PLUMMET: The big thrill ride begins 120 feet in the air on a platform built 30 feet above the top of Mt. Gushmore. (In other words, it's high! If you suffer from vertigo, pass on this plummet.) Brave souls travel about 60 miles per hour down a 350-foot slide. Near the top, guests pass through a ski chalet. To those watching from below, riders seem to disappear into an explosion of mist.

SLUSH GUSHER: This tame, double-humped water slide offers a brisk journey through a snow-banked mountain gully. Topping out at 90 feet, Slush Gusher is the tallest slide of its kind. You'll find it on Mt. Gushmore, next to Summit Plummet.

TEAMBOAT SPRINGS: The longest family white-water raft ride in the world takes five-passenger rafts down a twisting, 1,400-foot series of rushing waterfalls.

TOBOGGAN RACERS: An eight-lane water slide sends guests racing over a number of dips. They lie on their stomachs on a mat and travel headfirst down the 250-foot route.

SNOW STORMERS: A trio of flumes descends from the top of the mountain. Guests race down on a switchback course that includes ski-type slalom gates.

RUNOFF RAPIDS: On this inner-tube run, guests careen down three different twisting, turning flumes, one completely in the dark.

DOWNHILL DOUBLE DIPPER: Guests travel down these two parallel 230-foot-long racing slides at speeds of up to 25 miles per hour. The partially enclosed water runs feature ski-racing graphics, flags, and time clocks.

SKI PATROL TRAINING CAMP: An area designed specifically for preteens. Frozen Pipe Springs looks like an old pipe and drops sliders into eight feet of water. The Thin Ice Training Course tests agility skills as kids try to walk along broken "icebergs" without falling into the water. Snow Falls' "wide" slides allow a parent and child to ride together. At the Ski Patrol Shelter, guests grab on to a T-bar for an airborne trip. At any point in the ride they can drop into the water below. Ski patrol participants also experience Cool Runners, where riders can bank on hurtling and whirling over lots of moguls on twin inner-tube slides. No bunny slopes for these brave daredevils.

TIKE'S PEAK: A kid-size variation of Blizzard Beach, this attraction features miniature versions of Mt. Gushmore's slides and a snow-castle fountain play area.

Essentials

WHEN TO GO: As the World's newest water park, Blizzard Beach becomes very crowded early in the day. Once the park reaches a certain capacity, only guests using Walt Disney World transportation will be admitted, so plan accordingly. When the park reaches peak capacity, no one is admitted until crowds subside (usually after 3 P.M.). Hours vary seasonally, but the park is generally open from 10 A.M. to 5 P.M., with extended hours in summer. All pools are heated in winter. Blizzard Beach is often closed for refurbishment during certain winter months, typically January and February. It may also close due to inclement weather. For schedules, call 824-4321.

HOW TO GET THERE: Direct buses are available from the TTC and all WDW resorts.

LOCKER ROOMS: Restrooms with showers are located near the main entrance. Other restrooms and dressing rooms are located around the park. Small lockers cost $3 plus a $2 deposit to rent for the day, while large lockers cost $5 plus a $2 deposit. Towels rent for $1, and life jackets are available with a $25 refundable deposit.

WHERE TO EAT: Burgers, hot dogs, fruit salads, and drinks are available at Lottawatta Lodge, a fast-food restaurant located in the main village area. Two other snack stands with limited offerings are located in more remote areas: Avalunch, Frostbite Freddie's Frozen Frosty Freshments, and The Warming Hut offer snacks and soft drinks. There are also picnic areas for those who prefer to pack their own. Note that no alcoholic beverages or glass containers are permitted in the park.

FIRST AID: Minor medical problems are handled at this station near the main entrance.

BEACH SHOP: The Beach Haus, near the main entrance, stocks bathing suits, T-shirts, shorts, sunglasses, hats, suntan lotion, beach towels, and all the other accoutrements needed for a day in the park. Logo merchandise is in large supply.

Admission Prices

ONE-DAY TICKET
(Prices include sales tax and are subject to change.)

Adult	$26.45
Child*	$20.67

ANNUAL PASS

Adult	$93.23
Child*	$74.73

Note: Admission is included with a Length of Stay Pass or a Five-Day World Hopper Pass.

*3 to 9 years of age; children under 3 free

River Country

It's next to impossible to go through childhood reading such classic books as *The Adventures of Tom Sawyer* and *The Adventures of Huckleberry Finn* (and other great tales of growing up) without developing a few fantasies about what it would be like to swim in the perfect swimming hole. A group of Disney Imagineers concocted a Disney version on a somewhat larger scale at River Country, a water-oriented playground that occupies a corner of Bay Lake near Fort Wilderness campground.

Fred Joerger—the same Disney rock builder who created Big Thunder Mountain, Schweitzer Falls at the Jungle Cruise, and the caves of Tom Sawyer Island in the Magic Kingdom—also helped design the rocks used to landscape one of the largest swimming pools in the state. The rocks, scattered with real pebbles acquired from streambeds in Georgia and the Carolinas, look so real that it's hard to believe they aren't.

More to the point, the place is great fun. Slipping and sliding down the curvy water chutes at top speed, floating along White Water Rapids, and slamming into the water from the swimming pool's high slides make even careworn grown-ups smile, grin, giggle, chortle, and roar with delight. People who climb to the top of the Raft Rider water slide ridge with trepidation may be surprised to find themselves rushing back for more. Line-haters queue up—over and over again. Those who associate lakes with muck and weeds get ecstatic over the way the soft sand on the River Country bottom squishes between their toes.

WHAT TO DO: There are several sections to River Country—the 330,000-gallon swimming pool; Bay Cove (a.k.a. the Ol' Swimmin' Hole), the big walled-off section of Bay Lake that most people consider the main (and best) part of River Country; Kiddie Cove, an adjoining junior version of the above for small children, with its own beach; and the grassy grounds, with picnic tables and Indian Springs, a squirting fountain in which to play. On the edge of the lake there's also Cypress Point, a boardwalk nature trail through a lovely cypress swamp, and a wide (if not terribly long) white-sand beach.

The large swimming pool that's known as Upstream Plunge is heated in winter. It has a pair of Slippery Slide Falls water slides that begin high enough above the water to make an acrophobe climb right down again. They plunge at such an angle that it's impossible to see the bottom of the slide from the top. Daredevils who don't chicken out are shot into the water from a height of about

seven feet—hard enough, as one commentator observed, to "slap your stomach up against the roof of your mouth." Gutsy kids adore the experience; those who like their thrills a bit tamer might prefer to watch.

The heart of River Country, Bay Cove, is actually a part of Bay Lake (and quite chilly during cooler months). It's fitted out with a rope climb, a ship's boom for swooping and plunging, and other constructions designed to put hearts into throats as swimmers plunge from air to water. The big deals, however, are the two flume rides—one 260 feet long (accessible by a bridge and stairway to the far right of the swimming hole as you face it) and a smaller one, 100 feet shorter (accessible by a stairway to the left)—and a white-water raft ride called White Water Rapids.

The flumes, which are steep-sided water slides, corkscrew through the greenery at the top of the ridge, sending even the most stalwart shooting into the water, usually like greased lightning. White Water Rapids involves a more leisurely trip through a series of chutes and pools in an inner tube from the crest of Raft Rider Ridge (adjoining Whoop-'N-Holler Hollow) into Bay Cove. It's not a high-speed affair like the flumes, but some people like it better.

Essentials

WHEN TO GO: Daytime temperatures in Central Florida are such that it's possible to enjoy River Country almost all year round, though it is perhaps most pleasant in spring, when the weather is getting hot but the water is still on the cool side.

In summer, the place can be very busy indeed. Ticket windows close as the crowd approaches a certain capacity. During the busiest seasons, that may happen as early as 11 A.M. It's worth noting, however, that those who already have tickets will be admitted anyway, until the park has reached peak capacity. Things usually quiet down after 3 P.M. Although hours vary, River Country often opens its gates at 10 A.M. It generally closes at 5 P.M. during the summer months. Call 824-4321 for up-to-the-minute schedules. River Country is usually closed for refurbishment during certain off-peak months, typically September and October. Note that the park may also close due to inclement weather.

HOW TO GET THERE: From the Transportation and Ticket Center, buses drop off passengers within walking distance of River Country. It's also possible to go by boat. Launches leave regularly from the dock near the gates of the Magic Kingdom. Guests arriving at River Country by car may take a bus from the Fort Wilderness visitor parking lot to the entrance.

LOCKER ROOMS: Men's and women's dressing rooms with showers and lockers are available. Small lockers cost $3 plus a $2 deposit to rent for the day; large lockers cost $5 plus a $2 deposit. Towels are available for rent at $1 each at the concession window, but they're small, so you'll probably want to bring at least one beach towel.

WHERE TO EAT: Pop's Place has barbecued and fried chicken, baked beans, brownies, ice cream, and peanut butter and jelly sandwiches. The Waterin' Hole offers a limited selection during peak seasons. Picnicking is permitted (but no alcohol or glass containers can be brought into the park). Eat on the beach or seek out one of the shaded tables.

FIRST AID: A first-aid station capable of handling minor medical problems is located near the locker rooms.

BEACH SHOP: Film, towels, sand pails, sunscreen, and other beach essentials are available at the River Relics stand.

Admission Prices

ONE-DAY TICKET
(Prices include sales tax and are subject to change.)

Adult	$17.95
Child*	$14.50

ANNUAL PASS

Adult	$59.31
Child*	$47.17

Note: Admission is included with a Length of Stay Pass or a Five-Day World Hopper Pass.

*3 to 9 years of age; children under 3 free

FORT WILDERNESS

In a part of the state where campgrounds tend to look like pastures—barren and very hot—the Fort Wilderness campground, located almost due east of the Contemporary resort, is an anomaly—a forested 700-acre wonder of tall slash pines, white-flowering bay trees, and ancient cypress hung with streamers of Spanish moss. Seminole Indians once hunted and fished here.

There are more than a thousand campsites arranged in several campground loops; among them, Fleetwood units and cabins are available for rent, completely furnished and fitted with all the comforts of home. For information about lodging options, see *Transportation & Accommodations*.

Scattered throughout the campground loops are sporting facilities, including two tennis courts, and many tetherball, basketball, and volleyball courts. Fort Wilderness has riding stables, two swimming pools, a marina full of boats, a canoe livery, a beach, bikes and golf carts for rent, and a nature trail. Some facilities are available to campground guests only; some are open to guests at WDW-owned resort hotels and villas as well; some can also be enjoyed by guests lodging at the establishments at the resorts on Hotel Plaza Blvd. as well as off the property.

There's also a petting farm and a barn that's home to the horses that pull the Magic Kingdom's Main Street trolleys. The barn houses a small museum that celebrates horses and the role they've played in Disney history.

Two stores—the Settlement Trading Post and the Meadow Trading Post—stock campers' necessities, groceries, and souvenirs. And then there's Pioneer Hall, widely known as the home of the Hoop-Dee-Doo Musical Revue dinner show (described in *Good Meals, Great Times*). This rustic structure (made of western white pine shipped all the way from Montana) also has a buffet-style restaurant and a lounge.

Last but not least in the Fort Wilderness neighborhood is River Country. The eight-acre expanse of water-oriented recreation embodies everyone's idea of a perfect old-fashioned swimming hole. It's a separate attraction, with its own hours and admission fee.

BEACHES AND SWIMMING: The clear waters of Bay Lake, which lap the 315-foot white-sand beach at the north end of the campground, are delightful. Wading is allowed inside the roped-off areas, and there are also two pools for campers' use. Note that beaches and pools are open to Fort Wilderness guests only.

BIKE RENTALS: Tandems and other bikes can be rented at the Bike Barn for trips along the bike paths and roadways of Fort Wilderness—or just for getting around. Bikes cost $3 per hour or $12 per day. Tandems cost $6 per hour or $13 per day; $19 overnight.

BLACKSMITH SHOP: The pleasant fellow who shoes the draft horses that pull trolleys in the Magic Kingdom is on hand at some time every day to answer questions and talk about his job; occasionally guests can watch him at work, fitting the big animals with the special polyurethane-covered, steel-cored horseshoes that are used to protect the horses' hooves. This shop is located at the Tri-Circle-D Ranch.

BOATING: Fort Wilderness is ribboned with tranquil canals that make for delightful canoe trips of one to three hours—or longer if you take fishing gear and elect to wet your line. Canoe rentals are available at the Bike Barn for $6 per hour or $10 per day. Pedal boats ($6 per half hour or $10 per hour) can also be rented here for use in the canals. For a trip around Bay Lake, zippy little Water Sprites, Ocean Kayaks, sailboats, and pontoon boats are available for rent at the marina, at the north end of the campground. (See the *Sports* chapter for details and fees.)

CAMPFIRE PROGRAM: Held nightly near the Meadow Trading Post at the center of the campground, this evening entertainment program features Disney movies, a sing-along, and cartoons. It's open to WDW resort guests only (no charge). Also, Chip 'n' Dale always put in an appearance.

ELECTRIC CART RENTALS: Available at the Bike Barn ($35.51 for 24 hours) for sightseeing or transportation. Renters must be 18 years old and have a valid driver's license. Reservations are necessary; call 824-2742.

ELECTRICAL WATER PAGEANT: This twinkling cavalcade of lights (described in more detail in the *Good Meals, Great Times* chapter) can be seen from the beach here nightly at 9:45 P.M.

FISHING EXCURSIONS ON BAY LAKE: Walt Disney World's restrictive fishing policy means plenty of angling action—largemouth bass weighing two to eight pounds, mainly—for those who sign up for the special 8 A.M., 11:30 A.M., and 3 P.M. fishing excursions. The fee is about $150 for up to five people for a two-hour excursion (one additional hour is $50) and includes gear, a guide, and refreshments; no license is required. Note that all fishing is strictly catch-and-release. Call 824-2621 for reservations.

FISHING IN THE CANALS: In addition to largemouth bass, catfish and panfish can be caught here as well. Those without their own gear will find cane poles and lures for sale at the trading posts; equipment is also available for rent at the Bike Barn. Cane poles are $2 per hour or $4 for the whole day. Rods and reels are $4 per hour or $8 per day. Bait costs about $3.50. No license is required. Fort Wilderness resort guests may toss their lines in right from the shore.

HAYRIDES: The hay wagon departs from Pioneer Hall at 7 P.M. and 9:30 P.M., and carries guests on a trip through wooded areas near Bay Lake. Each ride lasts about an hour and concludes at Pioneer Hall. Purchase tickets from the hayride host: $6 for adults; $4 for children three to nine. Children under ten must be accompanied by an adult.

LAWN MOWER TREE: The tree that somehow, mysteriously, grew around a lawn mower is a Fort Wilderness point of interest worth hunting down. It's just off the sidewalk leading to the marina.

PETTING FARM: This fenced-in enclave just behind Pioneer Hall is home to some friendly goats, sheep, rabbits, chickens, and other assorted barnyard critters. (A colony of prairie dogs didn't work out because its members persisted in burrowing out of their compound; no sooner would their Disney caretakers try to thwart them—by digging a bigger hole and installing a below-ground-level wire fence—than the little creatures would gnaw through it.) Pony rides are available between 9 A.M. and 5 P.M. for $2. Note that the pony-ride weight limit is 80 pounds. Though designed with youngsters in mind, the Petting Farm is also fun for adults, and a good place to pass the time while waiting for seating at the Hoop-Dee-Doo Musical Revue.

TENNIS: Two tennis courts are available; play is on a first-come, first-served basis.

TRAIL RIDES: Horseback trips depart four times daily from the Trail Blaze Corral and take riders on a leisurely, meandering ride through the Florida wilderness, where it is not uncommon to see birds, deer, and even an occasional alligator. Galloping is not part of

Hoop-Dee-Doo Musical Revue

Sturdy, porch-rimmed Pioneer Hall is best known Worldwide as the home of the Pioneer Hall Players, an energetic troupe of singing, dancing, wisecracking entertainers who keep audiences chuckling, grinning, and whooping it up for two hours during a procession of barbecued ribs, fried chicken, corn-on-the-cob, strawberry shortcake, and other stomach-stretching vittles. If you have time for only one of the Disney dinner shows, make it this one (for more details see *Good Meals, Great Times*). Reservations are hard to come by. See the reservation chart on pages 16 and 17 for details.

the ride, so you don't need riding know-how to sign up. Cost is $17 per person for both day visitors and for guests at WDW-owned properties. No children under nine are allowed to ride. There is a weight limit of 250 pounds. Reservations are necessary; phone 824-2621 up to two weeks in advance.

TRI-CIRCLE-D RANCH: This corner of Fort Wilderness is the place that the world champion Percherons and the draft horses that pull trolleys down Main Street in the Magic Kingdom call home. You can watch them chomping placidly on their food, and occasionally see young colts and fillies as well. The Tri-Circle-D insignia above the barn door—two small circles, Mouse-ears style, atop a large one with the letter *D* inside—is the WDW brand. The barn is also the site of a museum that pays tribute to horses and their role in Disney history.

VOLLEYBALL, TETHERBALL, AND BASKETBALL COURTS: Open only to guests at WDW-owned properties, these are scattered throughout the camping loops. No charge.

WATERSKI TRIPS: Ski boats with drivers and equipment can be hired (including instruction) for $82 an hour at the marina. There is a minimum of two people and a maximum of five. Reservations are necessary and can be made up to two weeks in advance. Call 824-2621.

WILDERNESS SWAMP TRAIL: A three-quarter-mile trail, this smooth footpath into the woods skirts the marshes along the shore of Bay Lake, then plunges into a forest full of tall, straight-standing cypress trees. It is near Marshmallow Marsh, at the northern end of the campground.

Essentials

HOW TO GET THERE: From outside the World, take Magic Kingdom Exit 25 off I-4 onto U.S. 192, go through the Magic Kingdom Auto Plaza, and, bearing to your right, follow the Fort Wilderness or River Country signs. This is the most expeditious way to go, even for WDW resort guests.

By WDW Transportation: There is a direct bus (or bicycle path) from the Wilderness Lodge to Fort Wilderness. From Epcot, the Contemporary, Polynesian, and Grand Floridian resorts, take the monorail to the Transportation and Ticket Center (TTC), and transfer for the bus to Fort Wilderness. From Disney-MGM Studios, Animal Kingdom, Downtown Disney, and the resorts on Hotel Plaza Blvd., take a bus to the TTC. Change there to the bus to Fort Wilderness. From all other WDW resorts take a bus to Downtown Disney, switch for the bus to the TTC, then take the Fort Wilderness bus. Allow yourself plenty of time to make transfers.

Boats are also available from Magic Kingdom marinas (about a 30-minute ride) and from the Contemporary and Wilderness Lodge resorts (about a 25-minute ride). For details about WDW Transportation, see the *Transportation & Accommodations* chapter.

WHERE TO EAT: For a description of the restaurant at the Fort Wilderness campground, see pages 231 to 232 in the *Good Meals, Great Times* chapter. The Settlement Trading Post, located not far from the beach at the north end of the campground, and the Meadow Trading Post, located near the center of Fort Wilderness, also offer food staples.

DISCOVERY ISLAND

This 12-acre zoological park (an accredited member of the American Zoological Association) is a delightful place to go for a change of pace. Its lush scenery and Bay Lake island location create a mood different from anywhere else in the World. The sweet-smelling flowers that dot the landscape, the trees that canopy the footpaths, the butterflies, the dense thickets of bamboo, and the graceful palms, not to mention the animals themselves, provide all the distraction needed. Don't forget to bring a camera because there are many wonderful photographic possibilities here.

Though the paths and boardwalks can be traversed in 45 minutes or so, spending several hours here is a far better idea, since there is so much to see that it warrants more than just a rushed look. Each season offers its own rewards on the island. In the summer you'll find the flowers in full bloom. On a fall day, you might discover a vibrant peacock feather abandoned on a path, since these magnificent birds lose their long tail feathers every autumn. Come in winter and you'll get to see their new coats growing in. Spring is an especially nice time to visit because it's breeding season and the birds put on all of their courting displays.

Discovery Island has always been known for its tropical birds, but the addition of many more mammals and reptiles has added to the diversity of the population here. Along your journey you'll find two Asian fishing cats, several kinds of South American primates, and large rabbitlike animals called Patagonian cavies. The Galápagos turtles on **Tortoise Beach** are always a treat to see, as are the native Florida gators in the **Alligator Swamp**. At **Crane's Roost** you'll find small demoiselle cranes, white-crested hornbills, and Asian muntjac deer. **Trumpeter Springs** offers trumpeter swans—the largest members of the waterfowl family. You'll encounter lemurs, endangered primates from Madagascar, at **Primate Point**. The **South American Aviary**, one of the largest walk-through aviaries in the world, houses the United States' most extensive breeding colonies of scarlet ibis. You'll also find some ibis speckled among the Caribbean flamingos in **Flamingo Lagoon**. **Pelican Bay** is the home of several brown pelicans that suffered at birth from DDT poisoning and, though healthy now, would not be able to survive in the wild.

Discovery Island KidVenture offers kids age seven to ten a chance to explore Marshmallow Marsh and Discovery Island. **Discovery Island Explorers**, for kids 11 to 15, focuses

on animal care. Each of the 3½-hour programs features hands-on nature activities and costs $49. For information, call 800-282-9282.

Essentials

WHEN TO GO: Discovery Island is open daily from 10 A.M. to 6 P.M. (to 7 P.M. during the summer). The last boat to the island leaves 1¼ hours before closing.

HOW TO GET THERE: The island can be reached from the Magic Kingdom, the Contemporary, Fort Wilderness, and River Country by watercraft. Show an admission ticket or a WDW resort ID to ride.

WHERE TO EAT: Thirsty Perch snack bar and gift shop near the main entrance, and The Outback, next to the aviary, both offer snacking options, but it's also fun to pack a picnic lunch to eat on the beach near the handsome old wreck (which is still aging gracefully along the Bay Lake shore), just don't forget that swimming isn't allowed.

Admission Prices

ONE-DAY TICKET
(Prices include sales tax and are subject to change.)

Adult	$11.40
Child*	$6.20

Note: Admission is included with a Length of Stay Pass, a Five-Day World Hopper Pass, or a Water Park Hopper Annual Pass.

*3 to 9 years of age; children under 3 free

BEHIND-THE-SCENES TOURS

Adult Discoveries programs offer you the opportunity to experience Walt Disney World from the inside out. These behind-the-scenes guided tours give visitors 16 and older a glimpse of the magic, and a few of the logistics, that make up many of Disney's greatest creations. You can venture backstage at the theme parks, tour the topiary gardens with a Disney expert, or even get a hands-on introduction to animation.

The programs last from two to seven hours, only run on certain days, and are very popular, so we recommend that you plan ahead. The following are some of our favorite tours. They are subject to change without notice, so for current information and to make reservations call WDW-TOUR (939-8687).

Backstage Magic (Monday, Wednesday, Thursday, Friday): This is Walt Disney World's most popular program. Highlighting this seven-hour exploration is an underground tour of the Magic Kingdom's Utilidors—Disney's hidden tunnel system. As you tour the backstages of Epcot, you'll get a glimpse of the computer systems that control Body Wars and the special care needed to maintain The Living Seas. Try your hand at animation in the Disney-MGM Studios and the cel that you paint is yours to keep. Lunch is included in the program, plus a few other surprises along the way. Cost is $160 per person, and theme park admission is not required.

Keys to the Kingdom (daily): This four-hour tour offers an on-site orientation to the history and workings of the Magic Kingdom. Guests visit several attractions (waiting in regular attraction lines) and take a peek at the Production Center and the Utilidors. The tour departs at 10 A.M. from City Hall. The cost is $45, plus theme park admission, for each person.

Gardens of the World (Tuesday, Thursday): Hosted by a Disney horticulturist, this three-hour program is especially popular among gardeners. It guides guests through a study of the plants, flowers, and trees of Epcot's World Showcase. Cost is $25, plus theme park admission, per person.

Inside Animation (Tuesday and Thursday): A 2½-hour program that takes place at the Disney-MGM Studios. Participants learn about the art of animation, discover how the classics are brought to life, and create their own Mickey Mouse cel. Cost is $45, plus theme park admission, per person.

Hidden Treasures of World Showcase: There are three programs to choose from. Hidden Treasures–East (Tuesday) takes you through Mexico, Norway, China, Germany, Italy, and The American Adventure. Uncover the mysteries of Canada, United Kingdom, France, Morocco, Japan, and The American Adventure on Hidden Treasures–West (Saturday). Each program costs $25 per person, plus theme park admission, and lasts two hours. Hidden Treasures (Wednesday) is a comprehensive five-hour journey through all 11 pavilions and includes lunch at Restaurant Marrakesh in Morocco. Cost is $65 per person, and theme park admission is not required.

DiveQuest (daily): This program takes you down into the depths of The Living Seas. The highlight of the 2½-hour program is the 30-minute underwater adventure in one of the world's largest aquariums. Visitors wishing to participate must present proof of current scuba "open water" adult certification. Cost per person is $140 plus tax, theme park admission is not required, and all gear is provided.

A dolphin exploration program offers guests the chance to learn about dolphin behavior as they interact with the animals and observe researchers and trainers working with them. For more information, call 939-8687.

Just for Kids

There is also a selection of behind-the-scenes tours and programs designed especially for kids. They are offered by Camp Disney at the Disney Institute and cost $49 for a half-day program or $79 for a full-day program. For more information, call 800-496-6337.

Sports

SPORTS

Many first-time visitors don't realize that Walt Disney World comprises much more than just the theme parks. Within WDW's 27,000-plus acres there are more tennis courts than at most tennis resorts, more holes of championship-caliber golf than at most golf centers, and so many other diversions—from fishing and bicycling to boating, swimming, and parasailing—that the quantity and variety are matched by few other vacation destinations.

So while the family golfers are pursuing a perfect swing on one of five first-rate 18-hole courses, tennis buffs can be wearing themselves out on the courts, sailors can be sailing, waterskiers can be skimming back and forth across powerboat wakes, and anglers can be dangling a cane pole in hopes of hooking a big bream. Those who prefer to spectate rather than participate can visit a virtual sports mecca at Disney's Wide World of Sports, an enormous state-of-the-art facility that hosts a staggering array of sporting events, both amateur and professional.

Instruction, as well as guides, drivers, and assorted supervisors, makes every sport as much fun for beginners as for hard-core aficionados. Moreover, the ready accessibility of WDW sporting activities—via an excellent system of public transportation (see *Transportation & Accommodations*)—means that no visiting family or group member need curtail play time to chauffeur others around.

Note: Prices are subject to change, and do not include applicable state tax.

Unless otherwise noted, all phone numbers are in area code 407.

A MATTER OF COURSES

Most people don't immediately think of Walt Disney World when they contemplate a golf vacation. Yet there are six superb courses here: The Magnolia, the Palm, and the Oak Trail are situated across from the Polynesian resort and extend nearly to the borders of the Magic Kingdom. Just a short drive away is the Lake Buena Vista course, whose fairways are framed by the Disney Institute and Old Key West resort. Osprey Ridge and Eagle Pines play from the Bonnet Creek Golf Club near Fort Wilderness.

While the original Joe Lee–designed courses (the Palm, Magnolia, and Lake Buena Vista) won't set anyone's knees to knocking in terror from the regular tees, all three are demanding enough to merit the status of an annual stop on the PGA Tour tournament trail. And the annual LPGA Health-South Inaugural is contested on the Lake Buena Vista course.

Tom Fazio designed Osprey Ridge to offer a reasonable challenge for beginners as well as more advanced players. Eagle Pines, designed by Pete Dye, is a low-profile layout built level with, or lower than, the surrounding land.

Depending on the tee from which a golfer opts to play, the Disney courses will prove challenging and/or fun, and all are constructed to be especially forgiving for the mid-handicap player.

PALM & MAGNOLIA: The wide-open, tree-dotted Magnolia measures 5,232 yards from the front tees, 6,642 from the middle, and 7,190 from the back. The Palm is tighter, with more wooded fairways and nine water hazards; it measures 5,398 yards from the front, 6,461 from the middle, and 6,957 from the back. Both courses have received a four-star ("outstanding") rating from *Golf Digest* magazine. Together with the Lake Buena Vista course, the pair hosts the Walt Disney World/Oldsmobile Golf Classic every year. The Magnolia and Palm share two driving ranges and two putting greens.

Oak Trail: This nine-hole 2,913-yard layout, a walking course tucked in a corner of the Magnolia, was designed for beginners; but it has some tough holes, including two par 5s.

OSPREY RIDGE & EAGLE PINES: These two par-72 courses play from the Bonnet Creek Golf Club. The Tom Fazio–designed Osprey Ridge measures 5,402 yards from the front tees, 6,680 from the middle, and 7,101 from the back. It takes guests through remote areas of WDW property as it winds through wooded landscape near Fort Wilderness. Dramatic contouring puts some tees 20 to 25 feet above the basic grade. In contrast, the Pete Dye–designed Eagle Pines is a low-profile layout. It plays 4,838 yards from the front tees, 6,309 from the middle, and 6,772 from the pro tees. Many of the fairways are bordered by scrub and pine needles; water comes into play as well. Osprey Ridge and Eagle Pines share a driving range and a putting green.

LAKE BUENA VISTA COURSE: This Joe Lee design measures 5,176 yards from the front tees, 6,268 from the middle, and 6,829 from the rearmost markers. Among the shortest of the 18-hole, par-72 courses, it has a fair amount of water, and its tree-lined fairways are the World's narrowest. The course is well suited for beginners but equipped to challenge experienced players. A driving range and putting green are available. This is the location for the Disney Institute's extensive golf programs.

Essentials

WHEN TO GO: January through April is peak golfing season. To beat the crowds, play on a Monday or Tuesday, tee off in the late afternoon, or take advantage of low summer rates. WDW resort guests pay just $45 after 9 A.M. (after 10 A.M. for day visitors) from May 24 through August 31. From May 1 through October 31, season badges ($50) net steep discounts.

RESERVATIONS: Call WDW-GOLF (939-4653) to confirm rates and to secure tee-off times. From January through April, morning and early afternoon tee times should be reserved well in advance; starting times after 3 P.M. are often available at the last minute. Those buying a golf package can reserve tee times up to 90 days prior to their check-in date. Guests with confirmed reservations at a WDW resort or at one of the resorts on Hotel Plaza Blvd. can reserve 60 days ahead. Others can book tee times 30 days ahead with a credit card, 7 days in advance without a credit card.

FEES: At the 18-hole courses, greens fees (including the required cart) vary with the course and season. Rates range from $90 to $120 for guests at WDW resorts and the resorts on Hotel Plaza Blvd., and from $100 to $135 for day visitors. Twilight rates, usually in effect beginning at 3 P.M., are $45 to $68. Cost for adults to play Oak Trail is $24 for 9 holes, $32 for 18 holes; juniors (17 and under) pay $12 for 9 holes, $16 for 18 holes. Prices are subject to change.

INSTRUCTION: At the Walt Disney World Golf Studio at the Palm and Magnolia, private lessons cost $50 per half hour for adults; $30 for juniors. Pros offer 45-minute video sessions;

cost is $75. Nine-hole playing lessons in which a pro gives instruction in club selection, strategy, and more, cost $150 for adults or $100 for juniors. Reservations are necessary for lessons; call 939-4653. The Bonnet Creek Golf Club offers the Callaway Golf Experience: a system that lets golfers evaluate their swings, and compare various clubs and balls. The 45-minute session is free. For information, call 888-223-7842. Note, too, that the Disney Institute offers a first-rate golf instruction program at the Lake Buena Vista course (see page 178 for details on the Disney Institute).

DRESS: Proper golf attire is required. Shirts must have collars and any shorts must be Bermuda length.

EQUIPMENT RENTAL: Equipment can be rented at all courses; Callaway Golf Clubs ($40 for graphite shaft; $30 for steel), shoes ($6), and range balls ($5 per basket) are among the items available.

Tournaments

The Walt Disney World/Oldsmobile Golf Classic is among the biggest spectator events on WDW's sports calendar. It features most of the pro tour's top players, and takes place October 22–25. Guests who plan to golf during their WDW vacation are advised not to visit during tournament week. You can, however, play with the pros if you are willing to pay for it: Members of the Classic Club, whose annual dues start at about $5,150, count this privilege among their perks.

The LPGA HealthSouth Inaugural, a relative newcomer to Disney turf, is contested in January. It's exciting to behold, but again, be advised that tee times can be rather hard to come by. The World Putting Championship, by Dave Pelz, has also become an annual WDW event. For details on these and other special events, call WDW-GOLF (939-4653). Private tournaments may be arranged at no charge beyond the normal greens fees by calling the same number.

TENNIS EVERYONE

N̲o one comes to Walt Disney World strictly for a tennis vacation; it just doesn't exude the country-club ambience of a tennis resort where everyone is totally immersed in the game. But the facilities and instruction programs here are extensive enough that such holidays are certainly possible. The addition of Disney's Wide World of Sports, with its 11 clay courts and full-blown tennis stadium, has expanded the WDW spectator tennis scene considerably (see page 206 for details on this new sports facility). Certainly, playing a couple of sets of tennis on one of the World's 25 resort courts is a good way to unwind after a mad morning in the parks.

With six courts and a professional shop, Disney's Racquet Club at the Contemporary resort is Walt Disney World's major tennis facility for guest use. Located just beyond the hotel's north wing, the club features state-of-the-art hydrogrid clay courts. Elsewhere on-property, The Villas at the Disney Institute merits attention, though its four hydrogrid clay courts are available almost exclusively to guests participating in the Disney Institute's tennis programs. The Grand Floridian and BoardWalk each boast a pair of clay courts. All other WDW tennis is played on hard courts. Fort Wilderness has two, the Yacht Club and Beach Club share a pair, Old Key West has three, and the Swan and Dolphin have a four-court facility.

Essentials

WHEN TO GO: Courts are generally open from 8 A.M. to 8 P.M. daily (hours may vary during winter); lighted courts are available at each of the above-mentioned resorts. In February, March, April, June, and July the courts endure fairly heavy use, but there is usually a lull between noon and 3 P.M., and again from dinnertime until 9 P.M. January, October, and November are considered prime months for tennis enthusiasts.

RESERVATIONS: Courts may be reserved up to one year in advance for play at Disney's Racquet Club at the Contemporary and at the Grand Floridian courts (824-3578), and as far ahead as desired for courts at the Swan and Dolphin (934-4396). Other courts are available on a first-come, first-served basis. Solo players seeking partners can find them through the "Tennis, Anyone?" program at Disney's Racquet Club. The amount of time a single group of players can occupy a court is restricted only during very busy periods — to two hours on any morning, afternoon, and evening.

FEES: Play is $15 per hour at the Contemporary, Grand Floridian, Swan, and Dolphin. Courts at the Disney Institute are tough to get, but available with a $15 one-day health club pass. All other courts are free.

INSTRUCTION: The tennis program at the Contemporary resort offers clinics for $40. Nobody will try to change your game radically; the idea is to help you play better with what you have. Private lessons with a United States Tennis Association–certified professional run $50 per hour. Or you can skip the lesson and simply hit with a pro for $45 per hour. Lessons at the Grand Floridian are $40 per 45-minute session.

For information about Walt Disney World tennis opportunities or to make reservations, call 824-3578. Consider, too, that the Disney Institute has an extensive tennis program. (For details on the Disney Institute, see page 178 of the *Everything Else in the World* chapter.)

TOURNAMENTS: Private tourneys may be arranged by calling 824-3578 ($50 per hour). For information on upcoming tournaments at Disney's Wide World of Sports, call 363-6600.

DRESS: Tennis whites are appropriate, but not required, for play on Disney's courts.

EQUIPMENT RENTAL: Ball machine rental is $12.50 per half hour; good-quality (adult or child) racquets may be rented for $5. New balls sell for about $5 per can, and used balls are rented for $4 per basket.

LOCKERS: Lockers are available at the Contemporary and Grand Floridian resorts.

WATERS OF THE WORLD

Boating

Walt Disney World is the home of the country's largest fleet of pleasure boats. Cruising on Bay Lake and the Seven Seas Lagoon can be excellent sport, and a variety of boats are available for rent at WDW resort marinas. Bay Lake excursions originate from the Contemporary, on the lake's western shore; Wilderness Lodge, on the southern shore; and Fort Wilderness, which occupies the lake's southeastern shore. The Polynesian and Grand Floridian resorts send boaters out from their marinas on the southern shore of Seven Seas Lagoon. The Caribbean Beach resort leases watercraft for use on its own 45-acre Barefoot Bay. The Yacht Club, Beach Club, BoardWalk, Swan, and Dolphin share a boating haven in 25-acre Crescent Lake. And marinas at Dixie Landings, Port Orleans, Old Key West, and the Downtown Disney Marketplace set guests up to cruise the waterways adjoining the 35-acre Buena Vista Lagoon. Guests at Coronado Springs may rent watercraft for use on the 15-acre Lago Dorado.

To rent, day visitors and resort guests alike must show a resort ID, a driver's license, or a valid passport. Rental of certain craft may carry other special requirements (described below). Note that no privately owned boats are permitted on any of the WDW waters. Also, all prices are subject to change.

CANOEING: A long paddle down the smooth, wooded Fort Wilderness canals is such a tranquil way to pass a misty morning that it's hard to remember that the bustle of the Magic Kingdom is just a launch ride away. Canoes are available for rent at the Bike Barn at Fort Wilderness ($6 per hour, $10 per day). Most trips last one to three hours; those with fishing gear can easily stay out longer. Canoes may also be rented at the Caribbean Beach, Port Orleans, The Villas at the Disney Institute, and Dixie Landings marinas. Ocean Kayaks (open-top kayaks) may be rented at La Marina at Coronado Springs and at the Bike Barn at Fort Wilderness ($6 per half hour, $10 per hour).

CANOPY BOATS: These 16-foot, V-hulled motorized boats with canopies are a good choice for relaxing cruises. They accommodate up to eight adults, and can be rented for about $20 per half hour at the Downtown Disney Marketplace, Polynesian, Contemporary, Grand Floridian, Wilderness Lodge, Yacht Club and Beach Club, Old Key West, Port Orleans, Caribbean Beach, and Dixie Landings marinas.

PARASAILING: Excursions are offered at the Contemporary marina, where the man who invented the sport supervises seven- to ten-minute flights over Bay Lake. Cost is $60 per person or $35 to ride along; reservations are necessary (call 824-1000, ext. 3586).

PEDAL BOATS: These craft rent for $6 per half hour or $10 per hour at most WDW resort marinas. They're available for rent (to resort guests only) at the Caribbean Beach, Port Orleans, Dixie Landings, Coronado Springs, Yacht Club and Beach Club, and Swan and Dolphin marinas. Watercraft are available to all guests at the Downtown Disney Marketplace and at the Fort Wilderness Bike Barn. For pedaling of a different sort, Hydro Bikes (boats resembling bicycles affixed to pontoons) may be rented at the Yacht Club and Beach Club and the Swan and Dolphin when it's not too windy; single-bike units cost $8 per half hour at each location; doubles, $13 per half hour at the Swan and Dolphin, $16 per half hour at the Yacht Club and Beach Club.

PONTOON BOATS: Flotebotes—motorized, canopied platforms on pontoons—are perfect for families, for inexperienced sailors, and for visitors more interested in serenity than in thrills. Available at most resort marinas, the 20-foot craft hold up to ten adults and cost about $22 per half hour; $44 per hour.

SAILBOATS: The running room and usually reliable winds of Bay Lake and the adjoining Seven Seas Lagoon make for good sailing, and the Grand Floridian, Polynesian, Contemporary, Wilderness Lodge, and Fort Wilderness resort marinas rent a variety of craft so that guests might get a little wind in their sails on the 650-acre expanse. Various types of sailboats are available; models accommodate two to six people and rent for $11 to $19 per hour. Experience is required for rental of catamarans, available at the Contemporary, Polynesian, and Grand Floridian.

Sailing conditions are usually best in March and April, and before the inevitable late-afternoon thundershowers in the summer—and that's when demand is greatest. So don't tarry. Head for the marina as soon as the urge to sail strikes.

SPEEDBOATS: Particularly when the weather is warm, there are always dozens of small boats zipping back and forth across Bay Lake, Seven Seas Lagoon, and the lakes at the Downtown Disney Marketplace and the Caribbean Beach resort. These are called Water Sprites, and they are just as much fun as they look. Though they don't go very fast, they're so small that a rider feels every bit of speed, and they zip around quickly enough so that a lot of watery terrain can be covered in a half-hour rental period (about $16).

Water Sprites can be rented at the Grand Floridian, Polynesian, Wilderness Lodge, Contemporary, Yacht Club and Beach Club, Fort Wilderness, Caribbean Beach, and Downtown Disney Marketplace marinas. When the weather is warm, lines usually form at about 11 A.M. and remain fairly constant until about 4 P.M. The minimum rental age is 12, except at the Marketplace, where the minimum age is 14. Children under the minimum age may ride as passengers, but are not allowed to drive.

At the Contemporary marina, even zippier little boats called Seariders may be rented for $30 per hour. Accommodating up to three people, Seariders can attain speeds up to 30 miles per hour; riders must be 18 to drive. Spincraft speedboats (slightly slower than Water Sprites) may be rented at Coronado Springs ($10 per half hour, $16 per hour). The minimum age to rent is 12.

WATERSKIING: Ski boats with driver and equipment ($82 an hour, with a minimum of two guests and a maximum of five) are available for rent at the Contemporary, Polynesian, Grand Floridian, Wilderness Lodge, and Fort Wilderness resort marinas. Reservations must be made at least 48 hours in advance; call 824-2621 up to two weeks ahead.

Fishing

The 70,000 bass with which Bay Lake was stocked in the mid-1960s have grown and multiplied as a result of WDW's restrictive fishing policy. (It's strictly catch-and-release.) No angling is permitted on Bay Lake or the Seven Seas Lagoon, except on the guided two-hour Fort Wilderness fishing expeditions. Large-mouth bass weighing two to eight pounds are the most common catch. Excursions depart from the campground marina daily at around 8 A.M., 11:30 A.M., and 3 P.M.; five people can be accommodated on a trip. The fee per boatload is $148.40 for two hours ($50 for one additional hour) and includes guide, gear, and refreshments (coffee and pastries in the morning, soft drinks in the afternoon). Reservations must be made at least 24 hours in advance and may be secured up to two weeks ahead; call 824-2621. Guides will pick up guests at the Contemporary, Polynesian, Grand Floridian, and Wilderness Lodge resort marinas.

Other trips depart from the Downtown Disney Marketplace marina at 6:30 A.M. and 9 A.M. for fishing on Buena Vista Lagoon and adjoining waterways. Reservations must be made at least 24 hours in advance and can be made up to two weeks ahead; call 828-2204 or 828-2461. Cost for up to five people, including guide, gear, and refreshments, is $137 for two hours per boat or $68.50 per person ($50 for one additional hour).

At Dixie Landings, a two-hour fishing trip tours the Sassagoula River and the Buena Vista Lagoon. The daily 6:30 A.M. excursion can accommodate five people; includes guide, gear, artificial bait, and soft drinks; and costs $50 per person. Reservations must be made 24 hours in advance and can be made up to two weeks ahead by calling 934-5409. Children under ten must be accompanied by an adult.

Anglers might also consider the two-hour trips that leave the Yacht Club and Beach Club marina at 7 A.M. and 10 A.M. daily for fishing on Crescent Lake and the adjoining

SPORTS

waterways. The cost for up to five people, including guide, gear, and refreshments, is $140. Reservations must be made 24 hours in advance and can be made as far ahead as 30 days; call 824-2621.

Fishing on your own—again, strictly catch-and-release—is permitted off the dock at the Downtown Disney Marketplace; in the canals near The Villas at the Disney Institute, Fort Wilderness, and BoardWalk; and at the stocked fishing hole at Dixie Landings. Fort Wilderness guests may toss in lines from any campground shore. Licenses are not required. Canoes, rods and reels, and cane poles are available for rent at the Fort Wilderness Bike Barn. Bait (in the form of worms) can be purchased for $3.50. Poles may also be rented at Dixie Landings, BoardWalk, and the Downtown Disney Marketplace.

Swimming

Between Bay Lake and Seven Seas Lagoon, Walt Disney World resort guests have five miles of powdery white-sand beach at their disposal. Although the lakes are strictly for wading, serious swimmers can get down to business in one of the many pools in every shape and size imaginable. River Country, Typhoon Lagoon, and Blizzard Beach (see *Everything Else in the World*) only add to the fun.

BEACHES: When Walt Disney World was under construction during the mid-1960s, Bay Lake had an eight-foot layer of muck on its bottom. It was drained and cleaned, and below the muck, engineers unearthed the pure, white sand that now edges WDW resort shorefronts, most notably at the Contemporary, Grand Floridian, Caribbean Beach, and Fort Wilderness. These four sections of beach, plus the ones at the Polynesian, Wilderness Lodge, Yacht Club and Beach Club, and Swan and Dolphin, make up WDW's sandy areas. They aren't walk-forever strands, but they are long enough that most people don't bother to go to the end. Note that all Walt Disney World resort beaches are open only to those guests staying at the respective hotels.

POOLS: WDW resorts have at least one pool apiece. With the exception of the sister resorts (Yacht Club and Beach Club, Dixie Landings and Port Orleans, All-Star Sports and All-Star Music, and Swan and Dolphin), which share some of their recreational facilities, WDW hotel pools are open only to guests staying at those resorts. This policy was initiated to prevent overcrowding. Note that most of the pools are heated in winter.

Featuring one pool apiece are the Grand Floridian, Wilderness Lodge, and Port Orleans. The Contemporary, Polynesian, Fort Wilderness, All-Star Sports, and All-Star Music resorts have two pools each. BoardWalk features three pools; Coronado Springs and Old Key West have four swimming holes each, Dixie Landings and The Villas at the Disney Institute have six apiece, and Caribbean Beach has seven. The Yacht Club and Beach Club resorts have between them two quiet pools plus a small water park, called Stormalong Bay, that features slides, jets, and a sand-bottomed wading area. The Swan and Dolphin share a themed grotto pool with a slide, one huge rectangular pool, and a third smaller pool. For descriptions of the delightfully themed pools at WDW resorts, consult hotel listings in *Transportation & Accommodations*.

There are no diving boards at any of the pools; swimmers in search of a big splash should head for River Country, Blizzard Beach, or Typhoon Lagoon. Lifeguards are on duty during most daylight hours. In addition, each of the resorts on Hotel Plaza Blvd. has its own pool.

DISNEY'S WIDE WORLD OF SPORTS

Variety is the name of the game at Disney's Wide World of Sports. The brand-new, multi-million-dollar complex invites athletes and spectators alike to dive into more than 30 types of sporting experiences. It's truly a grand-slam experience for die-hard sports fans.

The 200-acre state-of-the-art facility hosts amateur and professional events in everything from archery to wrestling. The new home of the Amateur Athletic Union (AAU) is also the training site for Major League Baseball's Atlanta Braves and basketball's Harlem Globetrotters. Designed as a modern vision of old-time Floridian building styles, the architecture harks back to the days when sports facilities were extensions of their neighborhoods; to this end there is even a town commons.

The complex includes a 7,500-seat baseball stadium; a 5,000-seat field house that accommodates basketball, wrestling, and volleyball; a track-and-field complex; 11 clay tennis courts; four multipurpose fields fit for football, soccer, lacrosse, and more. Given the possibilities, sports-loving spectators have a world of choices on their hands.

A general admission ticket for Disney's Wide World of Sports costs $8 for adults and $6.75 for children ages three to nine. Tickets can be purchased at the gate and allow guests to spend the day watching a variety of "nonpremium" events.

Tickets to premium events such as Atlanta Braves games (beginning February 1), the U.S. Men's Clay Court Championships (beginning April 14), and the NFL Quarterback Challenge, may be purchased through TicketMaster (839-3900) and include admission to the complex and the right to roam, relax, and root for any team at any given moment. Premium tickets are also available at Disney's Wide World of Sports ticketing office on the day of an event. Prices vary, depending on event.

Essentials

HOW TO GET THERE: Walt Disney World resort guests can take a bus to Blizzard Beach and transfer to a bus headed for Disney's Wide World of Sports. If you are driving, take the Magic Kingdom exit (25) off I-4. The complex is between U.S. 192 and Osceola Parkway. Parking is free.

WHERE TO EAT: The big-ticket eatery here is the Official All-Star Café. The colorful sports-themed restaurant is owned by a team of high-profile athletes, including Wayne Gretzky, Monica Seles, and Ken Griffey Jr.

There are more than 30 concessions for those seeking a lighter (or quicker) bite. They offer the standard stadium fare of hot dogs, popcorn, and beer (not to mention peanuts and Cracker Jack) as well as a few slightly more substantial, yet just as portable, snacks.

WHERE TO SHOP: D-Sports Shop, located just outside the baseball stadium (on the third-base line), features a powerful lineup of NBA, NFL, and NHL merchandise, as well as other sporting items. Disney's Clubhouse, which is inside the stadium, is a hit with the baseball-loving crowd.

Touch Base

Do you have any questions about Disney's Wide World of Sports? Get the scoop on all the action by calling 363-6600. This information line covers the following areas:
- Ticket information
- Weekly calendar of events
- General information (directions, hours, admission, special activities)
- Volunteer opportunities
- Event registration
- Walt Disney World resort information
- Dining information
- Resort accommodations

MORE FUN STUFF

BIKING: Pedaling along the rustic pathways and lightly trafficked roads at Fort Wilderness and The Villas at the Disney Institute can be a pleasant way to spend a couple of hours. Both areas are sufficiently spread out so that bicycles are a practical means of getting around. Bikes are available for rent at Fort Wilderness, Old Key West, Wilderness Lodge, Port Orleans, Caribbean Beach, Dixie Landings, Board-Walk, The Villas at the Disney Institute, and Coronado Springs. The cost is about $3 an hour or $12 per day; tandem bicycles are offered at some locations.

HEALTH CLUBS: While some of the fitness centers located within WDW hotels are reserved for guests staying at the resort that houses them, several have open-door policies. The Contemporary Fitness Center, Grand Floridian Spa & Health Club, Muscles & Bustles at BoardWalk, and the Sports & Fitness Center at The Villas at the Disney Institute are accessible to all WDW resort guests; Body By Jake at the Dolphin is open to anyone.

The basic facility at the Swan is free to the hotel's guests. The Contemporary Fitness Center features Nautilus, a variety of cardiovascular machines, a sauna, and massage; rates are $8.50 per day or $20 per family for length of stay. Directly comparable to the Contemporary Fitness Center are R.E.S.T. at Old Key West (free to guests staying at the resort), Muscles & Bustles at BoardWalk ($7 per day, $20 per family for length of stay for resort guests; otherwise $10 per day, $35 per family for length of stay), and La Vida health club at Coronado Springs (about $6 per day, $12 for length of stay). Ship Shape at the Yacht Club and Beach Club ($7.50 per day or $21.50 per family for length of stay) has more extensive equipment, a whirlpool, a steam room, and personal trainers. The Grand Floridian Spa & Health Club ($6 per day, $12 per length of stay) has all that, plus a luxurious ambience. The Dolphin's first-rate Body By Jake ($8 per day or $16 for length of stay) offers aerobics. The huge Sports & Fitness Center at The Villas at the Disney Institute (free to Disney Institute guests; otherwise $15 per day, $35 for length of stay) has aerobics, a gymnasium, and a state-of-the-art facility with the best lineup of Cybex machines anywhere.

HORSEBACK RIDING: Trail rides into pine woods and scrubby palmetto country set off from the front of Fort Wilderness four times daily. This trip is not meant for seasoned gallopers—you can't ride off on your own.

The horses have been culled for gentleness, so the trips are suitable for novices. Cost is $17 per person. Kids under nine are not allowed to ride, and there's a weight limit of 250 pounds. Reservations are necessary, and can be made up to two weeks ahead by calling 824-2621.

JOGGING: Except from late fall to early spring, the weather is usually too steamy in Central Florida for comfortable jogging. If you run very early in the morning in warm seasons, the heat is somewhat less daunting. The 1.4-mile promenade around the Caribbean Beach resort's lake is ideal for jogging, as is the three-quarter-mile promenade surrounding Crescent Lake, the peaceful waterway that's bordered by the Swan and Dolphin, Yacht Club and Beach Club, and BoardWalk resorts. Fort Wilderness and the Wilderness Lodge share a three-quarter-mile path with exercise stations. Dixie Landings and Old Key West also have scenic routes. Courses range from one mile to about three.

MINIATURE GOLF: The Fantasia Gardens Miniature Golf complex, located near the Swan, Dolphin, and BoardWalk resorts, offers players two 18-hole courses themed to the classic Disney film. Fantasia Fairways offers a difficult layout sure to tantalize serious golfers. It features traditional golf obstacles, such as sand traps, water hazards, doglegs, and roughs. Don't be fooled by the

small size of the course—the challenges here are big. At this writing, only one golfer had ever made par!

Fantasia Gardens, on the other hand, is all in fun, with clever things (a dancing hippo, xylophone stairs, brooms dumping buckets of water) at every hole. The degree of difficulty varies from hole to hole, but overall this is an easy course to conquer. There are a few challenges out there, however. Hole 15, for example, is one of the trickier ones. Here golfers aim through four mini-geysers that randomly squirt water into the air.

Soft drinks and chips are sold at the Fantasia Gardens snack bar. There is a small video arcade available to golfers and spectators alike. A round on either course costs $9 for adults, $8 for children ages three to nine. Typical playing time is about an hour. Hours are generally 10 A.M. to midnight, but vary seasonally. For information, call 560-8760.

SKATING: In-line skating enthusiasts who bring their own gear (including the appropriate array of safety equipment and pads) will find the paths and roadways of Old Key West, Fort Wilderness, and The Villas at the Disney Institute especially appealing. Beginners may find the wooded trails at Fort Wilderness tough going.

STOCK CAR RACING: The Richard Petty Driving Experience (RPDE) takes motorsports fans out of the grandstands and into a scene that most can only dream about: behind the wheel of a speeding stock car. The RPDE, located at the Walt Disney World Speedway, near the Magic Kingdom guest parking lot, is a training ground for racer wannabes. It offers two levels of actual driving experience: "Rookie Experience" and "Experience of a Lifetime." For the less "driven," there is the "Riding Experience," which sends guests zooming around the track at blazing speeds while still maintaining their passenger status. No reservations are required for the Riding Experience. The cost is $99.

The Rookie Experience includes instruction, eight high-speed (up to 145 miles per hour) laps around the one-mile oval track, as well as a warm-up and a cool-down lap. The three-hour program costs about $400. Reservations are required.

The Experience of a Lifetime is a 30-lap program completed over three separate sessions. Participants work on building speed and establishing a comfortable driving line. The program costs about $1,300. Reservations are a must.

The RPDE operates on a daily schedule year-round, with the exception of dates on which actual races are held at the Walt Disney World Speedway. Call 800-237-3889 for more information or to make reservations. Prices are subject to change.

VOLLEYBALL & BASKETBALL: Except for the volleyball courts at River Country and Typhoon Lagoon, all courts are reserved for WDW resort guests. The Grand Floridian, Contemporary, Yacht Club and Beach Club, Fort Wilderness, Wilderness Lodge, Swan and Dolphin, Coronado Springs, and The Villas at the Disney Institute have volleyball courts. Contemporary, Fort Wilderness, and Old Key West have basketball hoops.

GoodMeals, Great Times

Although fast food is in great supply, it is hardly the entire Walt Disney World dining story. Epcot adds international flavors to the WDW menu. Tempting options at the Disney-MGM Studios, the Magic Kingdom, BoardWalk, and Downtown Disney—not to mention new dining frontiers in the ever-growing brood of WDW resorts—make deciding where to eat a mouthwatering dilemma. And Disney's ongoing effort to expand its culinary horizons has been successful, producing prominent palate pleasers such as California Grill and Artist Point.

Because the number and variety of eateries around the World are so large, this chapter presents dining information in three formats. First, to help guests find a specific eating spot or watering hole, we've provided an alphabetized directory of all restaurants and lounges on the property with their exact locations. Second, we've included an area-by-area rundown—a comprehensive section whose precise descriptions of food purveyors, including sample menu options, will prove most helpful to guests who are getting hungry in a particular part of the World. Third, we've set forth a meal-by-meal primer that highlights restaurants by breakfast, lunch, and dinner specialties. We've even indicated entrées for which we think it's worth going a bit out of your way.

Finally, in the chapter's last section, we offer a guide to the varied lounges of Walt Disney World, along with a briefing on special nighttime entertainment options in the World—and assurance that great times are destined to follow.

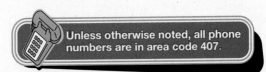

Unless otherwise noted, all phone numbers are in area code 407.

WDW RESTAURANT & LOUNGE INDEX

The list below includes the names and locations of all restaurants, lounges, and snack spots currently operating in Walt Disney World—not only at the theme parks, but also at the water parks, the hotels, Fort Wilderness, Discovery Island, and Downtown Disney. In the sections following this listing, the restaurants and lounges are described in detail.

Note: The Walt Disney World dining landscape is ever evolving, and while this inventory was correct at press time, changes will inevitably occur. We advise guests to call WDW Information (824-4321) or WDW-DINE (939-3463) shortly before their visit to confirm restaurant information.

ABC Commissary: Disney-MGM Studios; near The Great Movie Ride

Akershus: Epcot; in the Norway pavilion in World Showcase

Ale and Compass: Yacht Club resort; in the lobby

Aloha Isle: Magic Kingdom; in Adventureland, near the Swiss Family Treehouse

Artist Point: Wilderness Lodge resort; in the main lodge building

Atlantic Dance: BoardWalk resort; on the farthest end of the boardwalk (to the left)

Auntie Gravity's Galactic Goodies: Magic Kingdom; near Merchant of Venus in Tomorrowland

Aunt Polly's Dockside Inn: Magic Kingdom; in Frontierland, on Tom Sawyer Island

Avalunch: Blizzard Beach; near Ski Patrol Training Camp

Backlot Express: Disney-MGM Studios; near the Epic Stunt Theater

Banana Cabana: Caribbean Beach resort; near the pool

Barefoot Bar: Polynesian resort; near the Swimming Pool Lagoon

Beaches & Cream Soda Shop: Yacht Club and Beach Club resorts; in the central area between the two hotels

Belle Vue Room: BoardWalk resort; near the lobby

Biergarten: Epcot; to the rear of the St. Georgsplatz area in the Germany pavilion in World Showcase

Big River Grille & Brewing Works: Board-Walk resort; on the boardwalk's left side, near Jellyrolls

BoardWalk Bakery: BoardWalk resort; on the boardwalk's right side

Boatwright's Dining Hall: Dixie Landings resort; adjacent to the Cotton Co-Op lounge

Bonfamille's Café: Port Orleans resort; off the main lobby, across from the front desk

Bongos Cuban Café: Downtown Disney West Side; across from the AMC Theatres

Boulangerie Pâtisserie: Epcot; France pavilion, around the corner from Chefs de France, in World Showcase

Bridgetown Broiler: Caribbean Beach resort; at Old Port Royale food court

Cabana Bar & Grill: Dolphin resort; by the pool

California Grill: Contemporary resort; on the 15th floor

California Grill Lounge: Contemporary resort; on the 15th floor

Cantina de San Angel: Epcot; on the promenade opposite the Mexico pavilion's pyramid in World Showcase

Cape May Café: Beach Club resort; adjacent to the lobby

Cap'n Jack's Oyster Bar: Downtown Disney Marketplace; on the edge of Buena Vista Lagoon

Captain Cook's Snack Company: Polynesian resort; on the lobby level of the Great Ceremonial House

Captain's Tavern: Caribbean Beach resort; at Old Port Royale

Casey's Corner: Magic Kingdom; on the west side of Main Street

Catwalk Bar: Disney-MGM Studios; above the Soundstage restaurant

Chef Mickey's: Contemporary resort; on the fourth floor

Chefs de France: Epcot; in the France pavilion in World Showcase

Cinderella's Royal Table: Magic Kingdom; in Cinderella Castle

Cinnamon Bay Bakery: Caribbean Beach resort; at Old Port Royale food court

Cítricos: Grand Floridian resort; on the second floor of the main building

Coke Cool Zone: Animal Kingdom; at the gateway to Asia, along Discovery River

Columbia Harbour House: Magic Kingdom; in Liberty Square, near the entrance to Fantasyland

Concourse Steakhouse: Contemporary resort; on the fourth-floor concourse

Copa Banana: Dolphin resort; lobby level

Coral Café: Dolphin resort; lower level

Coral Isle Café: Polynesian resort; on the second floor of the Great Ceremonial House, around the corner from 'Ohana

Coral Reef: Epcot; in Future World's The Living Seas

Cosmic Ray's Starlight Café: Magic Kingdom; at the Fantasyland edge of Tomorrowland, across from Tomorrowland Speedway

Cotton Co-Op: Dixie Landings resort; in the main reception area

Crew's Cup: Yacht Club resort; next to the Yachtsman Steakhouse

Crockett's Tavern: Fort Wilderness campground; in Pioneer Hall

Crystal Palace: Magic Kingdom; at the north end of Main Street, near the Adventureland bridge

Diamond Horseshoe Saloon Revue: Magic Kingdom; in Frontierland, at the edge of Liberty Square

Dinosaur Gertie's Ice Cream of Extinction: Disney-MGM Studios; on Echo Lake

Dolphin Fountain: Dolphin resort; on the lower level

D-Zertz: Pleasure Island; near Pleasure Island Jazz Company

Electric Umbrella: Epcot; in Future World's Innoventions Plaza

El Pirata Y el Perico: Magic Kingdom; in Adventureland, opposite Pirates of the Caribbean

Enchanted Grove: Magic Kingdom; on the east side of Fantasyland, opposite Cosmic Ray's Starlight Café

End Zone: All-Star Sports resort; in Stadium Hall

ESPN Club: BoardWalk resort; on the farthest end of the boardwalk (to the right)

50's Prime Time Café: Disney-MGM Studios; on the south side of Echo Lake

Flame Tree Barbecue: Animal Kingdom; in Safari Village, near The Tree of Life

Flying Fish Café: BoardWalk resort; on the boardwalk, near the transportation dock

Food and Fun Center: Contemporary resort; first floor

Fountain View Espresso and Bakery: Epcot; next to Innoventions

Francisco's: Coronado Springs resort; main building

Frostbite Freddie's Frozen Frosty Freshments: Blizzard Beach

Fulton's Crab House: Between Pleasure Island and Downtown Disney Marketplace

Garden Grill: Epcot; on the second floor of The Land in Future World

Garden Grove Café: Swan resort; first floor

Garden View: Grand Floridian resort; on the Windsor Level

Gasparilla Grill & Games: Grand Floridian resort; first floor of the main building

Ghirardelli's Soda Fountain and Chocolate Shop: Downtown Disney Marketplace; near World of Disney

Good's Food to Go: Old Key West resort; on the boardwalk

Gourmet Pantry: Downtown Disney Marketplace; near the Christmas Chalet

Grand Floridian Café: Grand Floridian resort; first floor of the main building

Gurgling Suitcase: Old Key West resort; on the boardwalk

Harry's Safari Bar & Grille: Dolphin resort; on the third floor

Hollywood & Vine: Disney-MGM Studios; on Hollywood Boulevard

Hollywood Brown Derby: Disney-MGM Studios; on Hollywood Boulevard

Hook's Tavern: Magic Kingdom; in Fantasyland, next to Peter Pan's Flight

House of Blues: Downtown Disney West Side; next to Wolfgang Puck Café

Hurricane Hanna's Grill: Yacht Club and Beach Club resorts; near Stormalong Bay

Intermission: All-Star Music resort; in Melody Hall

Jellyrolls: BoardWalk resort; on the left side of the boardwalk, near Atlantic Dance

Juan & Only's: Dolphin resort; lower level

Kimono's: Swan resort; on the first floor

Kingston Pasta Shop: Caribbean Beach resort; at Old Port Royale food court

Kringla Bakeri og Kafé: Epcot; in the Norway pavilion in World Showcase

Leaning Palms: Typhoon Lagoon; near the main entrance

Leaping Horse Libations: BoardWalk resort; near the Luna Park pool

Liberty Inn: Epcot; alongside The American Adventure pavilion in World Showcase

Liberty Square Market: Magic Kingdom; in Liberty Square

Liberty Tree Tavern: Magic Kingdom; in Liberty Square

Little Big Top: Magic Kingdom; in Fantasyland, near Legend of the Lion King

Lobby Court: Swan resort; in the lobby

L'Originale Alfredo di Roma Ristorante: Epcot; on the east side of the piazza in the Italy pavilion, in World Showcase

Lottawatta Lodge: Blizzard Beach; near the main entrance

Lotus Blossom Café: Epcot; in the China pavilion in World Showcase

Lumière's Kitchen: Magic Kingdom; in Fantasyland, near Dumbo, the Flying Elephant

Lunching Pad at Rockettower Plaza: Magic Kingdom; at the base of the Astro Orbiter in the center of Tomorrowland

Main Street Bake Shop: Magic Kingdom; on the east side of Main Street, halfway between the Hub and Town Square

Mama Melrose's Ristorante Italiano: Disney-MGM Studios; on New York Street

Mardi Grogs: Port Orleans resort; near the pool

Marrakesh: Epcot; in the Morocco pavilion in World Showcase

Martha's Vineyard: Beach Club resort; on the first floor

Matsu No Ma: Epcot; in the Mitsukoshi building in World Showcase's Japan pavilion

Maya Grill: Coronado Springs resort; near Pepper Market food court

McDonald's: Downtown Disney Marketplace; near the LEGO Imagination Center

Meadow Trading Post: Fort Wilderness; near the playing fields

Min and Bill's Dockside Diner: Disney-MGM Studios; on Echo Lake

Missing Link Sausage Co.: Pleasure Island; near 8 Trax

Mitsukoshi: Epcot; in the Japan pavilion in World Showcase

Mizner's: Grand Floridian resort; on the second floor of the main building

Montego's Deli: Caribbean Beach resort; at Old Port Royale food court

Mrs. Potts' Cupboard: Magic Kingdom; in Fantasyland near Cinderella's Golden Carrousel

Muddy Rivers: Dixie Landings resort; near Ol' Man Island

Narcoossee's: Grand Floridian resort; at the end of the dock near the marina

Nine Dragons: Epcot; in the China pavilion in World Showcase

1900 Park Fare: Grand Floridian resort; on the first floor of the main building

Oasis: Magic Kingdom; in Adventureland, near the Jungle Cruise

'Ohana: Polynesian resort; second floor of the Great Ceremonial House

Official All-Star Café: Disney's Wide World of Sports; near the main entrance

Olivia's Café: Old Key West resort; on the boardwalk

Only's Bar & Jail: Dolphin resort; adjacent to Juan & Only's

Outback: Discovery Island; next to the avairy

Outer Rim: Contemporary resort; on the fourth floor

Palio: Swan resort; on the first floor

Pasta Piazza Ristorante: Epcot; in Future World's Innoventions Plaza

Pecos Bill Café: Magic Kingdom; near the Walt Disney World Railroad Frontierland depot

Pepper Market: Coronado Springs resort; in the main building

Pinocchio Village Haus: Magic Kingdom; in Fantasyland, adjoining It's A Small World

Pizzafari: Animal Kingdom; in Safari Village

Planet Hollywood: Pleasure Island; near the AMC Theatres

Plaza: Magic Kingdom; on Main Street around the corner from the Plaza Ice Cream Parlor

Plaza Ice Cream Parlor: Magic Kingdom; on the east side of Main Street

Plaza Pavilion: Magic Kingdom; east of the Plaza restaurant, on Tomorrowland's border

Pop's Place: River Country

Portobello Yacht Club: Pleasure Island; near Fulton's Crab House

Port Royale Hamburger Shop: Caribbean Beach resort; at Old Port Royale food court

Pure and Simple: Epcot; in Future World's Wonders of Life pavilion

Rainforest Café: One location is at Downtown Disney Marketplace, near Cap'n Jack's Oyster Bar; the other is at Animal Kingdom, near the main entrance

Reflections Coffee & Pastries: Disney Institute; near Willow Lake

Refreshment Outpost: Epcot; between the China and Germany pavilions in World Showcase

Refreshment Port: Epcot; next to the Canada pavilion in World Showcase

Restaurantosaurus: Animal Kingdom; in DinoLand U.S.A., near Countdown to Extinction

Rip Tide: Beach Club resort; in the lobby

Roaring Fork Snacks: Wilderness Lodge resort; in the main lodge building

Rose & Crown Pub and Dining Room: Epcot; in the United Kingdom pavilion in World Showcase

Royale Pizza Shop: Caribbean Beach resort; at Old Port Royale food court

San Angel Inn: Epcot; inside the Mexico pavilion's pyramid, in World Showcase

Sand Bar: Contemporary resort; right near the beach

Sand Trap Bar & Grill: Bonnet Creek Golf Club; Osprey Ridge and Eagle Pines

Sassagoula Floatworks & Food Factory: Port Orleans resort; off the main lobby

Scat Cat's Club: Port Orleans resort; next to Bonfamille's Café

Sci-Fi Dine-In Theater: Disney-MGM Studios; near Star Tours

Seashore Sweets': BoardWalk resort; across from the transportation dock

Seasons Dining Room: The Villas at the Disney Institute; next to the Welcome Center

Seasons Terrace Lounge: The Villas at the Disney Institute; near the Welcome Center

Settlement Trading Post: Fort Wilderness; near the marina

Siesta's: Coronado Springs; near the Dig Site

Singing Spirits: All-Star Music resort; near the pool and the Intermission food court

Sleepy Hollow: Magic Kingdom; in Liberty Square, near the Liberty Square bridge

Sommerfest: Epcot; in the Germany pavilion in World Showcase

Soundstage: Disney-MGM Studios; near the Animation Building

Splash Grill: Swan resort; near the pool

Spoodles: BoardWalk resort; on the right side of the boardwalk, near the bakery

Starring Rolls Bakery: Disney-MGM Studios; on Hollywood Boulevard

Studio Catering Co.: Disney-MGM Studios; near The Loony Bin

Summerhouse: Grand Floridian resort; near the beach

Sunset Ranch Market: Disney-MGM Studios; on Sunset Boulevard

Sunshine Season Food Fair: Epcot; on the first floor of Future World's The Land

Sunshine Tree Terrace: Magic Kingdom; in Adventureland, adjoining The Enchanted Tiki Birds

Tambu: Polynesian resort; on the second floor of the Great Ceremonial House

Tamu Tamu Yogurt Shop: Animal Kingdom; in Harambe village in Africa

Team Spirits: All-Star Music resort; near the pool and the End Zone food court

Tempura Kiku: Epcot; on the second floor of the Mitsukoshi building in World Showcase's Japan pavilion

Teppanyaki Dining Rooms: Epcot; on the second floor of the Mitsukoshi building in World Showcase's Japan pavilion

Territory: Wilderness Lodge resort; in the main lodge building

Thirsty Perch: Discovery Island; near the main entrance

Tony's Town Square: Magic Kingdom; on the east side of Town Square

Toy Story Pizza Planet: Disney-MGM Studios; in the arcade near Muppet*Vision 3-D

Trail's End Buffet: Fort Wilderness resort; in Pioneer Hall

Trout Pass: Wilderness Lodge resort; near the beach and the pool

Tubbi's: Dolphin resort; on the lower level

Tune-In Lounge: Disney-MGM Studios; adjacent to the 50's Prime Time Café

Turtle Shack: Old Key West resort; near Turtle Pond Road

Tuskers: Animal Kingdom; in Harambe village in Africa

Typhoon Tilly's: Typhoon Lagoon; near Shark Reef

Victoria & Albert's: Grand Floridian resort; on the second floor of the main building

The Warming Hut: Blizzard Beach; near Summit Plummet

Westward Ho: Magic Kingdom; in Frontierland, near Pecos Bill Café

Whispering Canyon Café: Wilderness Lodge resort; in the main lodge building

Wolfgang Puck Café: Downtown Disney West Side; between House of Blues and Bongos Cuban Café

Wolfgang Puck Express: One location is at Downtown Disney Marketplace, near the Gourmet Pantry; the other is at Downtown Disney West Side, inside Wolfgang Puck Café

Yacht Club Galley: Yacht Club resort; off the lobby

Yachtsman Steakhouse: Yacht Club resort; overlooking Stormalong Bay

Yakitori House: Epcot; on the east side of the Japan pavilion in World Showcase

Special Requests

Full-service eateries can accommodate special dietary needs, providing kosher, low-sodium, lactose-free, and other selections with 24 hours' notice. Make your request when booking your table by calling WDW-DINE (939-3463).

RESTAURANTS OF WDW
In the Magic Kingdom

The lion's share of eateries here in Walt Disney World's first theme park are fast-food spots. These establishments' colorful facades and costumed servers are natural extensions of the fantasy surrounding the park's seven distinct "lands." The healthy variety of food available on the fly is a testament to Magic Kingdom visitors' typical preference for a quick bite with no need for firm plans. For those who prefer an all-out meal, the park's small handful of full-service restaurants offer fine mealtime escapes in magical settings that only Disney could create. Visitors interested in character meals have breakfast, lunch, and dinner options here (see page 244 for details).

First Things First

- As Disney chefs tweak their menus to keep abreast of trends and new concepts are unveiled, the inventory of dining options changes. We advise guests to call WDW-DINE (939-3463) to confirm restaurant information.

- The letters that conclude each entry are a key to meals served there: breakfast (B), lunch (L), dinner (D), or snacks (S).

- As an indication of what you should expect to spend for a meal, we've classified restaurants, based on dinner prices, as very expensive ($30 and up); expensive ($18 to $30); moderate ($8 to $18); or inexpensive (under $8). These prices are based on an average meal for one adult, not including drinks, tax, or tips. Note that lunch generally costs less.

- All Walt Disney World restaurants and fast-food spots (except those with outside seating or at the Swan and Dolphin resorts) are nonsmoking only.

- Priority seating arrangements for most full-service restaurants should be made in advance by calling WDW-DINE (939-3463). For complete details, see page 245 of this chapter.

Adventureland
FAST FOOD & SNACKS

Aloha Isle: This refreshment stand located near the Swiss Family Treehouse often sells pineapple spears and juice, along with other tropical offerings, including the especially refreshing Dole Whip pineapple soft serve. Inexpensive. S.

El Pirata Y el Perico: The Spanish name of this snack stand, directly across from Pirates of the Caribbean, means "The Pirate and the Parrot." The offerings feature Mexican items, such as tacos, taco salads, and nachos, as well as hot dogs. Open during busy seasons. Inexpensive. L, S.

Oasis: Tucked away near the Jungle Cruise, this is the perfect spot for a soft drink. Inexpensive. S.

Sunshine Tree Terrace: So close to The Enchanted Tiki Birds that you can hear José, the Audio-Animatronics parrot, squawking his spiel. Offerings here are some of the tastiest in the Magic Kingdom: orange slushes, nonfat frozen yogurt shakes, frozen yogurt, and the citrus swirl—soft-serve nonfat frozen yogurt swirled through with frozen orange-juice concentrate. Cappuccino, espresso, and soft drinks are also available. Inexpensive. S.

Fantasyland
FULL SERVICE

Cinderella's Royal Table: Hostesses at this festive establishment wear 13th-century-style French headdresses and long medieval gowns, while hosts sport puffy shirts, pants, and long vests. The hall itself is high-ceilinged and as majestic as the old mead hall it is designed to represent. The delightful salads and sandwiches on the midday menu make lunch here pleasant indeed. Dinner includes prime rib, seafood, and chicken. There's also a children's menu, and Cinderella is usually on hand to greet kids and grown-ups alike.

The "Once Upon A Time" character breakfast is held here every morning. This all-you-care-to-eat breakfast is $14.95 for adults and $7.95 for children ages 3 to 11. Priority seating is necessary. Expensive. B, L, D.

FAST FOOD & SNACKS

Enchanted Grove: A small stand that's the perfect spot for a lemonade, lemonade slush, or soft-serve swirl. Inexpensive. S.

Hook's Tavern: Soft drinks and chips are available at this small refreshment stand just west of Cinderella's Golden Carrousel. Inexpensive. S.

Little Big Top: Soft drinks and shaved ice are the big draw here. Open seasonally. Inexpensive. S.

Lumière's Kitchen: Located near Dumbo, the Flying Elephant, this spot caters to kids with a variety of selections, including corn dog nuggets and chili dogs, to please even finicky eaters. Adult menus are available. Operated seasonally. Inexpensive. L, D, S.

Mrs. Potts' Cupboard: Ice cream gets top billing at this restaurant just west of the Mad Tea Party. There are soft-serve cones in chocolate, vanilla, and chocolate-vanilla swirl; hot fudge sundaes; shakes; and root beer floats. Inexpensive. S.

Pinocchio Village Haus: Located near It's A Small World (some tables offer a peek at the attraction via sizable picture windows), this is another one of those Magic Kingdom restaurants that seem a lot smaller from the outside than they really are, thanks to a labyrinthine arrangement of a half-dozen rooms decorated with antique cuckoo clocks, oak peasant chairs, and murals depicting characters from Pinocchio's story—Figaro the Cat, Cleo the Goldfish, Monstro the Whale, and Geppetto, the puppet's creator. The menu offers hot dogs, burgers, turkey sandwiches, and pasta salad. Inexpensive. L, D, S.

Frontierland

FAST FOOD & SNACKS

Aunt Polly's Dockside Inn: The much trumpeted sense of getting away from it all that islands always convey can also be found out on Frontierland's Tom Sawyer Island. Though only a couple of minutes' ride across the Rivers of America via the Tom Sawyer Island rafts, this landfall manages to seem remote even when there are dozens of youngsters clambering through its caves, over its hills, and across its rickety barrel bridges. Therein lies the charm of Aunt Polly's. While the adults in a party get some well-needed rest and relaxation sipping lemonade in the shade of the old-fashioned porch and watching the gleaming white riverboats docking or chugging by, the kids can go out exploring. And at nearby Fort Longhorn, kids can ping the toy rifles perched on the gun holes.

It doesn't even matter that Aunt Polly's offers a selection barely wider than the fare that the lady might have served young Tom

Sawyer himself—peanut-butter-and-jelly and ham-and-cheese sandwiches, chilled fried chicken, apple pie, soft-serve ice cream, cookies, iced tea, lemonade, and soda. Inexpensive. L, S.

Diamond Horseshoe Saloon Revue: From about 10 A.M. until early evening, a troupe of singers and dancers presents a sometimes corny, occasionally sidesplitting, always entertaining show in this Wild West dancehall saloon. Stop by anytime for sandwiches, potato chips, and cookies. Inexpensive. L, S.

Pecos Bill Café: This is not one of those Magic Kingdom eateries so tucked away that only those who hunt will find it. Sooner or later, almost every guest passing from Adventureland into Frontierland—ambling by the Frontierland depot of the Walt Disney World Railroad on their way to Splash Mountain—walks by Pecos Bill. And as a sidewalk café, this establishment—fitted out with leather-seated chairs, ceilings made of twigs, and red-tile floors—has few peers.

There are tables indoors (in air-conditioned rooms) and outdoors under umbrellas and in an open courtyard. Burgers, barbecued chicken sandwiches, salads, and hot dogs are the staples. Inside, three shaggy animal heads hang on the walls in keeping with the Wild West theme. Guests who stand around long enough will see one animal turn to another and wink, for these are Buff, Melvin, and Max—Audio-Animatronics figures, just like the ones on the wall inside the Country Bear Jamboree. Inexpensive. L, D, S.

Liberty Square

FULL SERVICE

Liberty Tree Tavern: At this pillared and porticoed eatery opposite the riverboat landing, the floors are wide oak planks, the wallpaper looks as if it might have come from Williamsburg, the curtains hang from cloth loops, and the venetian blinds are made of wood. The rooms reflect mementos that might have been found in the homes of Thomas Jefferson, George Washington, and Ben Franklin. The window glass was made using 18th-century casting methods, but most of the tables and chairs were mass-produced (for sturdiness' sake). So the Liberty Tree Tavern's charm is not of a random type.

Lunch, served à la carte, includes fresh fish, pot roast, turkey, salads, and sandwiches, including the Minuteman Club, (a ham, cheese, lettuce, and tomato sandwich).

Dinner, served family-style, is hosted by Disney characters; menu items include roasted turkey, flank steak, honey mustard ham, tossed garden greens, homemade mashed potatoes, fresh vegetables, and rolls. The Patriot's Platter character dinner costs $19.50 for adults and $9.95 for children ages 3 to 11. Priority seating suggested. Expensive. L, D.

FAST FOOD & SNACKS

Columbia Harbour House: A fast-food fish house with some class. Fried fish, fried chicken fingers, clam chowder, salads, and assorted sandwiches are available. There are enough antiques and other knickknacks decking the halls to raise this place, located near the Liberty Square entrance to Fantasyland, above the ordinary. Model ships, copper measures, harpoons, nautical instruments, little lace tie-back curtains, small-print wallpaper, and low-beamed ceilings give the restaurant a cozy air. Operated seasonally. Inexpensive. L, D, S.

Sleepy Hollow: Light snacks, including ice cream sandwiches, chocolate chip cookies, and a special Legendary Punch (fruity and not half bad) are for sale at this snack stand located in the The Hall of Presidents neighborhood, near the Liberty Square bridge. Eat on the secluded brick patio outside. Inexpensive. L, D, S.

Healthier Options

Health-conscious folks need not abandon all restraint for want of suitable foodstuff. Most restaurants offer low-fat, low-cholesterol, low-salt, and vegetarian entrées. Most restaurants, including fast-food stands, now feature fresh salads, grilled chicken sandwiches, fresh fruit, turkey burgers, and nonfat frozen yogurt.

Main Street

FULL SERVICE

Crystal Palace: One of the Magic Kingdom's landmarks, this restaurant takes its architectural cues from a similar structure that once stood in New York, and from San Francisco's Conservatory of Flowers, which still graces that city's Golden Gate Park. The place is huge but not overwhelming, because the tables are scattered among a host of nooks and crannies. Guests dine amid a Victorian-style garden, complete with fresh flowers and hanging greenery. Tables in the front look out on flower beds, while those at the east end have views of a secluded courtyard. The restaurant is located on a pathway at the end of Main Street, U.S.A., heading west toward Adventureland.

Three topiaries—Winnie the Pooh, Tigger, and Eeyore—greet guests at the entrance, an indication of the character presence here. After decades as a cafeteria, the restaurant is now offering all-day buffet dining, with none other than Winnie the Pooh visiting guests.

Menu items vary according to season and available produce. The buffet features a full variety of traditional breakfast items every morning; a salad bar, deli bar, pasta dishes, chicken, and fish for lunch; and spit-roasted beef, paella, chicken, shrimp, and carved meats for dinner. Kids particularly like the sundae bar offered at lunch and dinner. Priority seating suggested. Expensive. B, L, D.

Plaza: This airy, many-windowed establishment, around the corner from the Plaza Ice Cream Parlor, is done up in mirrors with sinuous Art Nouveau frames. The menu offers fresh salads, hamburgers, turkey burgers, and hot and cold sandwiches—plus milk shakes, ice cream, floats, and the biggest sundaes in the Magic Kingdom. Café mocha, which combines chocolate and coffee, is another specialty. Priority seating suggested. Moderate. L, D, S.

Tony's Town Square: One of the best bets for Magic Kingdom full-service meals. The decor comes straight out of Walt Disney's film *Lady and the Tramp*. It is genteelly Victorian, with plenty of polished brass and curlicued, beautifully painted woodwork. The terrazzo-style patio offers a fine view of Town Square.

Breakfast options include eggs, *Lady and the Tramp* character waffles, cold cereals (with low-fat milk on request), and freshly baked pull-apart sweet rolls. The lunch menu offers Italian specialties, steaks, and seafood. Pizzas with selected toppings are perennial favorites. Other specialties include Caesar salad, sandwiches, and freshly prepared daily specials. At dinner select from grilled fish, steaks, and spaghetti with meatballs, along with a variety of daily specials. For dessert, Italian pastries and spumoni complement a cup of freshly brewed espresso or cappuccino. Children's menus are available. Priority seating suggested. Expensive. B, L, D.

FAST FOOD & SNACKS

Casey's Corner: The small round tables at this spacious, old-fashioned red-and-white stop on the west side of Main Street, (located adjacent to the Crystal Palace) spill out onto the sidewalk. Except when the weather is terrifically hot, it's a delightful spot for fast food—hot dogs in jumbo sizes, french fries, brownies, soft drinks, and coffee. During busy periods a pianist plinks away on the restaurant's white upright. Inexpensive. L, D, S.

Main Street Bake Shop: If the sight of this old-fashioned storefront doesn't lure you in, the heavenly aroma most certainly will. A genteel little tearoom, with prim white tables and cane chairs, the Main Street Bake Shop is a pleasant place for a light breakfast, midmorning coffee break, or midafternoon rest stop. Assorted pastries, cakes, and pies are the main temptations. Also offered are fresh cookies: chocolate chunk, oatmeal raisin, Snickerdoodle, sugar, and Nestlé's Original Toll House recipe. Cinnamon rolls are baked on the premises. Inexpensive. B, S.

Plaza Ice Cream Parlor: Ice cream lovers from all over the country converge on this corner of the park, which boasts the Magic Kingdom's largest variety of ice cream flavors. Ice cream cookie sandwiches are "built to order." Inexpensive. S.

Tomorrowland

FAST FOOD & SNACKS

Auntie Gravity's Galactic Goodies: This small spot located across from the Tomorrowland Speedway (between Merchant of Venus and Mickey's Star Traders) serves natural foods, fruit smoothies, soft-serve frozen yogurt, soft drinks, and fresh fruit. Inexpensive. S.

Cosmic Ray's Starlight Café: The largest fast-food spot in the Magic Kingdom, located directly across from the Tomorrowland Speedway. Three distinctive menus are offered at different sections along the counter. Cosmic Chicken serves rotisserie chicken; Blast-off Burgers has cheeseburgers (single and double), vegetarian burgers, and hot dogs; and Starlight Soup, Salad, Sandwich offers soups, Caesar salad, chef's salad, grilled chicken sandwiches, and cheese steak sandwiches. A child's menu and soft drinks are available. Inexpensive. L, D, S.

Lunching Pad at Rockettower Plaza: Located at the base of the Astro Orbiter in the center of Tomorrowland's vast concrete plaza, this small spot offers smoked turkey legs, potato chips, assorted desserts, and soft drinks. Inexpensive. S. (While you're in the area, take some time to investigate the video phone booths—one is near Take Flight, the other is by Astro Orbiter.)

Plaza Pavilion: Just east of the Plaza restaurant on Main Street, this sleek spot on the edge of Tomorrowland serves pan pizzas, fried chicken strips, Italian specialty sandwiches, and salads. Some particularly pleasant tables look past the graceful willow trees nearby, toward the Hub Waterways and a very impressive topiary sea serpent. Inexpensive. L, D, S.

Magic Kingdom Mealtime Tips

- The hours from 11 A.M. to 2 P.M., and again from about 5 P.M. to 7 P.M., are the mealtime rush hours in Magic Kingdom restaurants. Try to eat earlier or later whenever possible.
- When a restaurant has more than one food-service window, don't just amble into the nearest queue. Instead, inspect them all, because the one farthest from a doorway occasionally will be almost wait-free.
- Sit-down restaurants offering full-scale meals are usually less crowded at lunch than they are at dinner.
- To avoid queues, eat lunch or dinner at a restaurant that offers priority seating—Tony's Town Square, Crystal Palace, or the Plaza restaurant on Main Street; Liberty Tree Tavern in Liberty Square; or Cinderella's Royal Table in the castle. Priority seating arrangements can be made in advance by calling WDW-DINE (939-3463). Check for same-day seating at the individual restaurant or City Hall. Refer to page 245 for further details.
- Consider taking the monorail to the Contemporary, Polynesian, or Grand Floridian to have lunch or dinner in a resort restaurant, and then return to the Magic Kingdom later. (Remember to have your hand stamped and keep your ticket for reentry to the park.)

In Epcot

The two worlds that make up Epcot offer a spectrum of eating options that extends from the usual burgers and fries to mouthwatering international specialties. Future World counts a please-all food court among its fast-food spots, plus two full-service restaurants whose menus and atmosphere innovatively reflect the themes of the pavilions they inhabit. World Showcase, on the other hand, is characterized by international flavors. Here, the cuisine of each country is served in settings that strive to transport visitors, if just for the duration of their meal. While the abundance of appealing full-service restaurants makes World Showcase a very popular dining destination, the promenade is also ringed with fast-food spots, most of which feature international fare. Priority seating is an important part of the Epcot dining equation (for complete details, turn to page 245). Character meals are options for breakfast, lunch, and dinner in Future World (for specifics, see page 244).

Future World

FULL SERVICE

Coral Reef: Decorated in cool greens and blues to complement its surroundings, this restaurant in The Living Seas offers diners a panoramic view of the coral reef through large windows. The acrylic windows are eight feet high and more than eight inches thick. The dining room is constructed on several tiers, so all guests have an unobstructed view. The menu features fresh fish and shellfish,

including marinated red snapper; clams; Mediterranean shrimp baked with tomatoes, leeks, and onions; and Maine lobster with

crabmeat stuffing. Landlubber selections are also available. The menu varies seasonally. Priority seating suggested. Expensive. L, D.

Garden Grill: Sleek upholstered wood-trimmed booths illuminated with handsome brass lamps help to make this an exceptionally attractive eatery. The restaurant itself revolves, past a mural of giant sunflowers and above scenes of the thunderstorm, sandstorm, prairie, and rain forest featured in the Celebrate the Land boat ride below. The scenes were designed with diners in mind, and provide them with a peek into a farmhouse window that's out of viewing range of the waterborne passengers.

Mickey and Minnie join Chip 'n' Dale to host three character meals here each day.

The all-you-can-eat country breakfast is $14.95 for adults and $8.25 for children ages 3 to 11. Lunch and dinner menus feature rotisserie chicken, hickory-smoked steaks, and fish, with a separate menu for children. The character lunch costs $16.95 for adults and $9.95 for children. Dinner is $17.50 for adults and $9.95 for children. Priority seating suggested. Moderate to expensive. B, L, D.

FAST FOOD & SNACKS

Electric Umbrella: This large fast-food establishment, located in Innoventions, is decorated in shades of blue, mauve, and magenta. It's a particularly good bet when the weather is temperate enough to allow dining at the tables on the terrace outside—or when bound for World Showcase with finicky eaters in tow. Offerings include chicken sandwiches, grilled ham-and-cheese sandwiches, grilled vegetable pita sandwiches, hot dogs, burgers, fruit salad, and chef's salad. Inexpensive. L, D, S.

Fountain View Espresso and Bakery: Delicious baked goods and desserts—croissants, cheesecake, tiramisu, and éclairs—can be found at this spot located in Innoventions Plaza, across from the Fountain of Nations. Espresso, cappuccino, wine, and beer are among the assorted beverages available here. Inexpensive. B, S.

Pasta Piazza Ristorante: Pizza, pasta, and antipasto salad are among the specialties at this eatery located in Innoventions, opposite the Electric Umbrella restaurant. The decor is traditional Italian, accented by some unusual neon lights. Inexpensive. B, L, D, S.

Pure and Simple: Located in the Wonders of Life pavilion, this snack spot offers a variety of healthy treats, including salads, oat bran waffles with fruit toppings, sandwiches, frozen yogurt, yogurt shakes, muffins, fruit juices, and more. Inexpensive. B, L, S.

Sunshine Season Food Fair: One of the most interesting of the Epcot eateries, and a wrinkle on the Walt Disney World fast-food scene, this handful of diverse counter-service stands is on the lower level of The Land pavilion. Each of these stands boasts a unique menu. Soup & Salad offers Florida seafood chowder, fruit salad, and rotini pasta salad. The Bakery Shop's morning offerings include fresh fruit, bagels with cream cheese, jumbo cinnamon rolls, Danish pastries, apricot crumb cake, and muffins. After 11 A.M., apple pies appear, along with cheesecake and chocolate cake, strawberry shortcake, rich double-chocolate brownies, hermit cookies with cinnamon—plus chocolate chip cookies baked on the premises. (The latter are so delicious that some Disney employees have been known to make special trips to The Land just to nibble on them.)

The Barbecue stand sells barbecued chicken and ribs smoked on the premises; barbecued beef, pork, or chicken breast sandwiches; and sides of beans, corn-on-the-cob, and corn bread muffins. The Cheese and Pasta stand offers baked macaroni with ham and cheese, tortellini or fettuccine with meat sauce, noodles with Asian-style chicken, and vegetable lasagne. The Sandwich Shop regales the hungry with several types of hefty combinations, including the Handwich (a sandwich you can eat with one hand), while an ice cream stand tempts guests with cooling cones and cups, frozen yogurt, and sundaes. The Potato

Store serves steaming baked potatoes stuffed with Asian-style chicken and vegetables, cheddar cheese and bacon, and other fillings. Even the Beverage House here proffers something special—not just an array of soft drinks, beer, and wine, but also frozen drinks.

Each stand has a farm-style facade done in bright colors, not unlike those that might be found in agricultural exhibit buildings at a midwestern state fair. With bright, umbrella-topped tables nearby, the effect is cheery. Because of the wide variety of foods available here, this is one of the best bets in Epcot for a family that can't agree on what to eat. It's also a good spot for weight watchers. Inexpensive. B, L, D, S.

World Showcase

FULL SERVICE

Akershus (Norway): The Norwegian castle of Akershus dominates Oslo's harbor, and is the most impressive of Norway's medieval fortresses. It is actually half fortress and half palace, and many of its grand halls continue to be used for elaborate state banquets. At Epcot's castle-like Akershus, guests are treated to an authentic royal Norwegian buffet called the *koldtbord*, literally "cold table." The diverse mix of offerings includes both hot and cold meats and seafood, and a selection of salads, cheeses, and breads. Traditional Norwegian desserts are also served, as are cocktails and Norwegian beer. Hosts and hostesses are on hand to answer any questions about the menu that guests may have. Priority seating suggested. Moderate to expensive. L, D.

Biergarten (Germany): Located at the rear of the St. Georgsplatz in the Germany pavilion, this huge tiered restaurant is set in a courtyard rimmed with geranium-studded balconies and punctuated by an old mill. It's every bit as jolly as Alfredo's restaurant in the Italy pavilion. This is partly because of the long tables that encourage a certain togetherness among guests—and partly because Beck's beer is served in 33-ounce steins. But equal credit for the *gemütlich* atmosphere must go to the restaurant's lively entertainment. A German trio performs during lunch. At dinner, yodelers, dancers, and other traditional Bavarian musicians—each clad in lederhosen or dirndl—play accordions, cowbells, a musical saw, and a harplike stringed instrument known as the "wooden laughter." The entertaining dinner shows take place every hour on the half hour. Diners are usually invited to join the fun on stage.

The food is hearty and presented as an all-you-can-eat buffet, featuring assorted sausages (grilled bratwurst, *Debrizinger*, *Bauernwurst*), frankfurters, rotisserie chicken, homemade spaetzle, assorted cold dishes, potato salad, cucumber salad, and many more German specialties. Because entertainment is intermittent, there's plenty of time to enjoy the pleasant setting, with the big mill waterwheel slowly turning and the sound of water splashing into the millstream blending with the rousing oompah music. Priority seating suggested, particularly during peak seasons. Moderate to expensive. L, D.

Chefs de France (France): There's good news for the fans of one of the most savory spots on World Showcase Lagoon—Chefs de France is bigger and better than ever before. Having undergone extensive refurbishment and expansion in late 1997, this popular eatery has reopened with a new look and

a new menu, while retaining its old-world charm and team of internationally acclaimed chefs. Paul Bocuse operates a restaurant outside Lyons, France, and Roger Vergé runs one just north of the French Riviera. Together with Gaston Lenôtre (widely recognized as France's premier preparer of pastries and other delicious dessert delicacies), they form a most unusual, and absolutely formidable, gastronomic trio. Bocuse, Vergé, and Lenôtre have designed a menu that features fresh ingredients readily available from Florida purveyors. In addition, the restaurant imports as many key ingredients from France as possible. The French chefs make regular visits to WDW to supervise and adjust certain items on the menu, though there is rarely any need to tinker.

As you might expect, the fare here is fiercely French, but the foundation of the menu is nouvelle cuisine, which involves lighter sauces using much less cream and butter than in classic French cooking. The lunch and dinner menus vary, with lunch featuring more salads and lighter items, such as sandwiches, quiches, and onion tarts.

The newly expanded 450-seat restaurant (which took over the space formerly occupied by Bistro de Paris and Au Petit Café), has a bright, airy feel, with yellow and creme-colored walls drenched in natural light. It boasts a glass-enclosed "outside" dining area with a conservatory motif, as well as a more intimate second-floor dining room.

Although wine and pastries are available exclusively to restaurant patrons during lunch and dinner, a wine and pastry bar is open to walk-in snackers from about 3:30 P.M. until

5 P.M. each day. Guests may sample an enhanced selection of French wines as a chef displays pastry-making panache.

Note that this can be one of the most expensive of all World Showcase restaurants. (There's a separate menu "for the little gourmet"—kids under 12—that features reduced prices.) Priority seating suggested. Expensive. L, D, S.

L'Originale Alfredo di Roma Ristorante (Italy): This restaurant's trompe l'oeil ("trick the eye") perspective paintings make diners believe they're seeing real scenes rather than mere murals, and lend character to the decor of this popular establishment. As in the famous Roman restaurant of the same name, the house specialty is fettuccine Alfredo—wide, flat noodles tossed in a sauce made of butter and imported Parmesan cheese. But many other sizes and shapes of pasta, all of it made right on the premises, are also available; they are significantly enhanced by tomato, meat, pesto (basil, garlic, and Parmesan), or carbonara (egg, bacon, cream, and pecorino cheese) sauces. There are also a number of less familiar Italian preparations involving chicken, eggplant, seafood, sausage, and veal, all of which are very good. For dessert, choose from a number of specialties such as ricotta cheesecake, spumoni, tortoni, or gelato. Even if you don't eat here, it's fun to stop and just peer through the glass kitchen windows to watch the cooks cranking out the rigatoni, ziti, linguine, lasagne, fettuccine, and spaghetti (which, the eminently readable menu reminds guests, were brought from Europe to America by Thomas Jefferson in 1786). Priority seating suggested. Expensive. L, D.

Marrakesh (Morocco): The most savory part of the Morocco pavilion features a variety of examples of traditional and modern Moroccan cuisine. Waiters are dressed in traditional Moroccan costumes. Menu specialties include roast lamb, chicken brochette, and couscous (steamed semolina served with your choice of lamb, chicken, or vegetables). Sampler platters are also available. The beautiful tilework was done by Moroccan craftsmen. Belly dancers and musicians entertain diners at both lunch and dinner. A children's menu is available. Priority seating suggested. Expensive. L, D.

Mitsukoshi (Japan): This complex of dining and drinking spots, all operated by the Japanese firm for which it is named, occupies the second level of the large structure on the west side of the Japan pavilion. There are two options. *Tempura Kiku* occupies a small corner of the Mitsukoshi restaurant that's devoted to the batter-dipped, deep-fried chicken, beef, seafood, and fresh vegetables that are collectively known as tempura. The individual tidbits are crisp and delicious. Priority seating not available. Expensive. L, D.

Teppanyaki Dining Rooms is composed of five rooms not unlike those popularized by the Benihana chain all around America. Guests sit counter-style around large flat grills while white-hatted chefs chop vegetables, meat, and fish at lightning speed and then stir-fry it all just as quickly. Whether the chopping and cooking accompany a mildly comic routine depends on the chef, but in any case the establishment is quite convivial. The seating arrangements make it quite natural to strike up a conversation with fellow diners; in fact, it's almost impossible to keep to yourself. Priority seating suggested. Expensive. L, D.

Nine Dragons (China): This stop on Epcot's varied international restaurant tour offers meals prepared in provincial Chinese cooking styles, including Mandarin, Cantonese, Hunan, Szechuan, and Kiangche. Entrées include braised duck (served Cantonese style), Kang Bao chicken (stir-fried chicken, peanuts, and dried hot peppers), and beef and jade tree (Chinese broccoli and sliced steak). Appetizers range from Chinese pickled cabbage to pan-fried dumplings and hot-and-sour soup. A selection of Chinese teas, beers, and wines is available. The varied dessert menu features red-bean ice cream, toffee apples, and assorted Chinese pastries. Priority seating suggested. Moderate to expensive. L, D.

Rose & Crown Pub and Dining Room (United Kingdom): The fare here runs to pub grub—that is, fish-and-chips and traditional meat pies. For lunch, however, it's possible to order hot roast beef with gravy and mashed potatoes, roast lamb, and a truly delicious fresh vegetable platter served with cheese and walnut dressing. At dinner the standard offerings are supplemented by roast prime rib with horseradish sauce. For dessert there's traditional sherry trifle, a confection of layered whipped cream, custard, strawberries, and sherry wine; apple-blackberry crumble; and chocolate cake. Bass India Pale Ale from England, Tennent's lager from Scotland, and Harp lager and Guinness stout, both from Ireland, are on tap. (They're served cold, in the American fashion, not at room temperature, as Britons prefer.)

The decor is beautiful, mainly polished woods, etched glass, and brass accents. In fine weather it's pleasant to lunch under the sunny yellow umbrellas on the terrace outside and watch the *FriendShip* water taxis cruising across World Showcase Lagoon. On the little island just to the east, the wind ruffles the leaves of the Lombardy poplars, a species of tree that is found along roadsides all over Europe.

Horticulturally speaking, it's interesting to note the vines on the pub's northwest wall. These Virginia creepers grow amazingly fast and, when Epcot opened, showed only a few tentative tendrils close to the ground. The spreading tree nearby is a laurel oak, distinguished from the southern live oaks more widely seen at Epcot by its upright growth and its leaves, which are shiny on both sides instead of just one.

As for the pub's architecture, it incorporates three distinct styles. The wall facing the World Showcase Promenade is reminiscent of urban establishments popular in Britain since the 1890s, while that on the south side evokes London's 17th-century Cheshire Cheese pub, with its brick-walled flagstone terrace, slate roof, and half-timbered exterior. The canal facade, with its stone wall and clay-tile roof, reminds visitors of the charming pubs so common in the English countryside.

The pub section of the Rose & Crown serves such snacks as cheese and fresh fruit platters, and mini chicken-and-leek pies—along with all the brews noted above and traditional British mixed drinks, such as shandies (Bass ale and ginger beer), lager with lime juice, black velvets (Guinness stout and champagne), and black and tans (Bass ale and Guinness stout). This drinking and snacking spot is quite popular, so it's often necessary to queue up at the door. But the wait is seldom very long, since few guests linger over their drinks. Priority seating is not available in the pub area, but suggested for the adjacent dining room. Moderate to expensive. L, D, S.

San Angel Inn (Mexico): The food at this establishment located to the rear of the plaza inside the Mexico pyramid (a corporate cousin of the famous Mexico City restaurant of the same name) may come as a surprise to most visitors. Although the tacos and tortillas and other specialties that usually fall under the broad umbrella of Mexican food are available, the menu also offers a wide variety of more subtly flavored fish, poultry, and meat dishes. To start, there's *queso fundido* for two (melted cheese and Mexican pork sausage with corn or flour tortillas). As entrées, the menu offers *sopes de pollo* (fried corn dough shells topped with refried beans, chicken with green tomatillo sauce, and cheese); grilled tenderloin of beef served with a chicken enchilada, guacamole, and refried beans; *mole*

poblano (chicken simmered with spices and a small amount of chocolate); *huachinango a la Veracruzana* (fresh fillet of red snapper poached in wine with onions, tomatoes, and peppers); and much more that is good and tasty. Mexican desserts are largely unfamiliar to North Americans, with the possible exceptions of the custard known as flan, and *arroz con leche*, best known in the United States as rice pudding. Still, such desserts as chocolate Kahlúa mousse pie and *helado con cajeta* (vanilla ice cream with milk-caramel topping) are well worth trying. Dos Equis brand beer, tart lemon-flavored water, and delicious margaritas make good accompaniments. Priority seating suggested. Expensive. L, D.

CAFETERIA SERVICE

Le Cellier (Canada): Tucked away on the lowest level of the pavilion near Victoria Gardens, this low-ceilinged, stone-walled establishment looks a little like the ancient wine cellars for which it is named. It offers a full menu of Canadian foods, with hearty sandwiches also available for lunch, and roast prime rib added to the offerings at dinner. The savory, Quebec-born pork-and-potato-filled pie known as *tourtièrre* is dished out in enormous slices, each one fully three inches high and covered with a tempting golden crust. Tangy Canadian cheddar cheese serves as the base of a rich soup and adds zip to some appetizing fruit platters. Chicken and meatball stew, poached fresh salmon in spinach velouté sauce, and carved Canadian bacon—all served with a choice of potatoes or rice, and vegetables—can round out the selection of entrées. Canada's own Molson and Labatt's beers are served in bottles. Children's selections include macaroni and cheese. This tempting combination makes Le Cellier a prime destination for those who haven't been able to book a table at one of the full-service World Showcase restaurants but still want something more substantial than what the fast-food eateries are offering. Operates seasonally. Inexpensive to moderate. L, D, S.

FAST FOOD & SNACKS

Boulangerie Pâtisserie (France): This bakery and pastry shop in the France pavilion is not hard to find: Just follow the wonderful aroma, then watch the crowds line up to consume the establishment's flaky croissants, éclairs, fruit tarts, and chocolate mousse. The treats are served under the management of the stellar trio of chefs who operate the popular Chefs de France restaurant not far away—Paul Bocuse, Roger Vergé, and Gaston Lenôtre. Hint for those who hate to wait: This has become a favorite snacking stop among Epcot veterans; your best bet is to stop here as soon as World Showcase opens at 11 A.M. or half an hour before park closing. Inexpensive. S.

Cantina de San Angel (Mexico): Located along the World Showcase Promenade, just outside the entrance to Mexico's pyramid, this fast-food stand serves beef-filled soft tortillas; *tacos al carbón*, flour tortillas filled with grilled chicken breast strips, onions, and peppers, served with refried beans and salsa; and *churros*, a sort of fried dough rolled in cinnamon and sugar. The Cantina is first-rate for a tasty rest stop, and even more so for its outdoor lagoonside seating. Dos Equis beer, margaritas, and watermelon juice are available, and the establishment's plant-edged terrace makes a fine grandstand for people-watching. Inexpensive. L, D, S.

Kringla Bakeri og Kafé (Norway): Tucked between the Norway pavilion's wooden church and a cluster of shops, this eating spot serves *kringles*, sweet candied pretzels eaten on special occasions in Norway; *vaflers*, heart-shaped waffles topped with powdered sugar and jam; *kransekake*, almond-pastry rings; and *smørbrøds*, open-face sandwiches of smoked salmon, roast beef, or turkey. Ringnes beer, brewed in Norway, is also available. There is also a pleasant, shaded outdoor eating area. Inexpensive. L, S.

Liberty Inn (The American Adventure): To many foreigners, American food means burgers, hot dogs, and french fries, and these are the staples at the Liberty Inn, located alongside the entrance to The American Adventure show on the far end of the World Showcase Lagoon. Salads, grilled chicken sandwiches, ice cream, apple pastries, and chocolate chip cookies round out the selections. As a result, the place is a delight for small children, and also quite a pleasant spot for their parents. There is veranda seating, a fountain, and an impressive array of antique-looking decoys and chests. Inexpensive. L, D, S.

Lotus Blossom Café (China): Adjacent to Yong Feng Shangdian shopping gallery in the China pavilion, this fast-food counter offers sweet-and-sour pork, egg rolls, and soup. There is a covered outdoor seating area nearby. Inexpensive. L, D.

Refreshment Outpost (between Germany and China): This is a perfect spot for a refreshing cold drink. Frozen yogurt and ice cream are also served. Inexpensive. S.

Refreshment Port (Canada): Another good spot for a quick thirst quencher, next to the Canada pavilion. Canadian beer and wine are served. Fresh fruit, frozen yogurt, and cookies are also available. Inexpensive. S.

Sommerfest (Germany): Bratwurst sandwiches, soft pretzels, Black Forest cake, apple strudel, Beck's beer, and wine are offered at this outdoor establishment, located at the rear of the Germany pavilion; seating is nearby. Inexpensive. L, D, S.

Yakitori House (Japan): The nature of the food offered at this establishment on a hillock in the Japan pavilion is representative of the pace of life in that country. The average Japanese spends about seven minutes consuming his or her *guydon*, a stewlike concoction flavored with soy sauce, spices, and the Japanese rice wine known as sake—all served over rice. That staple, together with skewered chicken known as *yakitori* (it is basted with soy sauce and sesame oil as it broils), teriyaki chicken sandwiches, and Japanese sweets and beverages, typifies the offerings here.

Located in the Japanese gardens to the left of the plaza, the restaurant occupies a scaled-down version of the 16th-century Katsura Imperial Summer Palace in Kyoto; sliding screens, lanterns, and kimono-clad hosts and hostesses add to the atmosphere. Inexpensive. L, D, S.

Epcot Mealtime Tips

• The international restaurants of World Showcase offer some of the best dining on the property. Since many of them are very popular, it's a good idea to arrange advance priority seating for any full-service restaurants by calling WDW-DINE (939-3463) long before arriving. However, many tables are left available for same-day seating. To make arrangements, head straight for a WorldKey Information Service terminal or Guest Relations first thing in the morning. Lunch can also be booked at the individual restaurants. Refer to page 245 for more details.

• If you aren't able to secure priority seating for dinner, don't despair. There are tasty alternatives to a table-service meal. Stop in Canada at the cafeteria-style Le Cellier for a quick but hearty meal. Japan has Tempura Kiku, a full-service spot with batter-dipped, deep-fried meats and vegetables, and Yakitori House, good for skewered bits of barbecued beef and chicken. Sample Mexican specialties at Cantina de San Angel (whose lagoonside tables provide a fine view of the sun setting behind Epcot). Also try the openface sandwiches at Kringla Bakeri og Kafé in Norway, or the sweet-and-sour pork at China's Lotus Blossom Café.

• Cravings for more conventional fast foods will be satisfied at the Electric Umbrella in Innoventions and at the Liberty Inn in The American Adventure. The Pasta Piazza Ristorante in Innoventions serves Italian fare. The Sunshine Season Food Fair in The Land pavilion offers a little bit of everything.

• Each of the restaurants has something special about it, and there's always a good menu selection even for unadventurous eaters—even in the more exotic restaurants of World Showcase. If you're undecided, ask at Guest Relations to see a book of menus.

• Don't dismiss the idea of an early seating if you can get it: If you have lunch at 11 A.M., a 5 P.M. dinner will not only be welcome, but more important, it will provide the opportunity to spend the most pleasant and uncrowded evening hours enjoying the Epcot attractions.

• Lunch provides guests with another chance to enjoy the most popular Epcot restaurants. It also has another important appeal: With a priority seating for 1 P.M., it's possible to spend some of the most crowded hours in the park consuming a pleasant meal while less fortunate visitors are waiting in some of the longest lines of the day.

In the Disney-MGM Studios

The eateries at the Disney-MGM Studios are a breed apart. Some feature decor that returns guests to a bygone era; others recapture memorable moments from the big or small screen. All reprise a beloved part of Hollywood's star-studded heritage. The Studios has five full-service restaurants, whose atmospheres and menus are so distinct they sate altogether different moods and whims. Priority seating is available for these dining rooms (for details, turn to page 245). Soundstage restaurant offers character meals (see page 244 for specifics). A solid—and fairly diverse—ensemble of fast-food places hits the spot for eaters on the move.

FULL SERVICE

50's Prime Time Café: The setting is straight out of your favorite sitcoms of the 1950s. Each of the plastic-laminate kitchen tables is set under a pull-down lamp, evoking a suburban kitchenette. Video screens around the room broadcast black-and-white clips (all related to food) from favorite fifties comedies; these nostalgic bits are visible from every seat. Meals are served on either Fiesta Ware plates or TV dinner–style compartment trays. The waitresses play "Mom" with considerable enthusiasm, making recommendations and encouraging guests to clean their plates (*or no dessert!*).

The menu is packed with "comfort foods." For openers there's a choice of chicken noodle soup, chili, or the French Fry Feast, served either plain or with chili and cheese. Specialties of the house include Magnificent Meat Loaf, served with mashed potatoes and mushroom gravy; fried chicken; and Granny's Pot Roast. There are also burgers with various toppings, Caesar salads, club sandwiches, and Aunt Selma's Chicken Salad. Milk shakes, ice cream sodas, and root beer floats are filling accompaniments. And when you've finished

everything on your plate, "Mom" will ask if you'd like dessert. Standouts include s'mores, a graham cracker topped with chocolate and toasted marshmallows (you'll feel like you're back at summer camp); sundaes; banana

splits; and apple pie à la mode. A full bar is available. Kids love this place, and a children's menu is available. Priority seating suggested. Moderate. L, D, S.

Hollywood Brown Derby: The home of the famous Cobb salad is alive and well. This re-creation of the former Vine Street mainstay is quite faithful, right down to the caricatures (reproduced from the original Derby collection) that cover the walls. Arch gossip queen rivals Louella Parsons and Hedda Hopper (portrayed by convincing actresses) still reign over the restaurant from reserved tables, just as they did in the heyday of the real Brown Derby.

The 235-seat restaurant is decorated predominantly in teak and mahogany, and the elegant chandeliers and perimeter lamps (shaped like miniature derbies) are reminiscent of those in the original eatery. The only nonauthentic element in the atmosphere is the theme park clientele who show up in shorts and tennis shoes.

The menu features the famed Cobb salad, created by owner Bob Cobb in the 1930s. It's a mixture of finely chopped fresh salad greens, tomato, bacon, turkey, egg, blue cheese, and avocado. It's tossed tableside and served with old-fashioned french dressing. A modern incarnation of the salad is also available with shrimp or chicken. Other menu selections of note include shrimp tortelloni, crab and roast corn quesadilla, blackened rib-eye steak, and sautéed grouper. The dessert tray is tempting—particularly the grapefruit cake, a Brown Derby institution. A children's menu is available, although the slightly formal atmosphere is not likely to enchant most kids. Priority seating suggested. Expensive. L, D.

Mama Melrose's Ristorante Italiano: This quirky pizzeria is located in a warehouse that has been converted into a dining room. Pizzas are prepared in a wood-burning oven; fresh fish and steaks are grilled over a hardwood charbroiler. The menu also features lasagne, chicken, risotto, and pasta—including "Grandma Grace's Bottomless Pasta Bowl." (All-you-can-eat pasta that comes with bread and Caesar salad. It costs $11.25 for lunch, $13.75 for dinner.) Priority seating suggested. Moderate to expensive. L, D (during busy seasons).

Sci-Fi Dine-In Theater: This 250-seat eatery re-creates a 1950s drive-in theater. The tables are actually flashy, 1950s-era cars, complete with fins and whitewalls. Fiber-optic stars twinkle overhead in the "night sky," and real drive-in theater speakers are mounted beside each car. All the tables face a large screen, where a 45-minute compilation of the best (and worst) of science fiction

Coming Attraction

1998 NEW FOR 1998 • NEW FOR 1998

Opening in fall 1998, Copperfield Magic Underground offers a truly magical dining experience. As guests chow down on American and international dishes, grand illusions are performed in a setting reflecting the history and mystery of magic. Part of a new chain of eateries to which master illusionist David Copperfield has given his name, this spot is accessible from both inside and outside the park. Admission to the Disney-MGM Studios is not necessary to enter the restaurant. Moderate. L, D, S.

trailers and cartoons plays in a continuous loop. Meals include the Monster Mash—actually roast turkey with dressing and mashed potatoes. Tossed in Space is a (huge) chef's salad, and Towering Terror is a platter of smoked chicken with orange barbecue sauce, seasonal vegetables, and oven-roasted potatoes. There are also hot and cold sandwiches and a unique slate of tempting desserts, including the Cheesecake That Ate New York; Twin Terrors, a banana-split cake; Science Gone Mad, Dutch apple pie served warm; and The Black Hole, a chocolate layer cake. There is a children's menu. Priority seating suggested. Moderate to expensive. L, D.

Soundstage: This cavernous restaurant in the Animation Courtyard has been transformed into a character buffet, featuring stars from animated classics. Characters from such films as *Beauty and the Beast*, *Hercules*, and *Pocahontas* gather at this restaurant all day long. Music from the films plays in the background. The buffet offers a salad bar, pasta, herb-baked chicken, beef stew, baked fish, roast pork, and various accompaniments. A kid's buffet includes chicken tenders, macaroni and cheese, and Mexican hot dogs. Priority seating suggested. Moderate to expensive. B, L.

CAFETERIA SERVICE

Hollywood & Vine: The distinctive Art Deco facade ushers guests into a contemporary version of a 1950s diner—all stainless steel with pink accents. An elaborate 42- by 8-foot wall mural depicts notable Hollywood landmarks, including the Disney Studios, Columbia Ranch, and Warner Brothers (back when they were the only studios in the San Fernando Valley). At the center of the mural is the Carthay Circle Theatre, where *Snow White* premiered in 1937.

The 368-seat cafeteria presents a varied menu. At breakfast, there's the Hollywood Scramble, two eggs served with bacon or sausage and a choice of potatoes or grits and a breakfast biscuit; french toast; pancakes; omelettes; assorted hot and cold cereals; and fresh fruit. Muffins, pastries, and croissants are also served. Lunch features a variety of salads. Baby-back ribs, roast chicken, and spaghetti and meatballs are offered. Pies head the dessert list. Beer and wine are available, and a children's menu is posted. Inexpensive to moderate. B, L, D, S.

FAST FOOD & SNACKS

ABC Commissary: The 550-seat restaurant located between the Chinese Theater and SuperStar Television features chicken breast sandwiches, chicken nuggets, burgers, deli subs, and milk shakes. There is a children's menu. Several times a day, the staff bursts into song, performing the theme song from the TV show "Happy Days." Inexpensive. L, D.

Backlot Express: This fast-food spot looks like the old crafts shops on a studio backlot. There's a paint shop, stunt hall, sculpture shop, and model shop. The paint shop has paint-speckled floors, chairs, and tables; the prop shop is decked out in car engines, bumpers, and fan belts. There is outdoor seating amid stored streetlights, plants, and trees. Menu offerings include burgers, hot dogs, chicken Caesar salad, grilled chicken sandwiches, tuna subs, and chili. For dessert, there's chocolate-chip cheesecake, brownies, apple pie, and fresh fruit. Beer is available. Inexpensive. L, D, S.

Dinosaur Gertie's: "Ice Cream of Extinction," claims the sign at this giant dinosaur set on Echo Lake. And indeed, ice cream has in fact been replaced with frozen slush drinks in a variety of flavors. Inexpensive. S.

Min & Bill's Dockside Diner: "There's good eats in our galley," proclaims the welcoming sign posted on the *S.S. Down the Hatch*, a bit of "California crazy" 1950s architecture. The little tramp steamer, complete with a cartoonlike smokestack, mast, and booms, never sets sail. Min & Bill's offerings include the Portside Sandwich (turkey ham and turkey salami, lettuce, and tomato rolled in a soft tortilla), tacos, and fruit. Soft-serve ice cream is available in cups or cones with a variety of toppings. Inexpensive. L, D, S.

Starring Rolls Bakery: Freshly baked rolls, pastries, muffins, croissants, and sugar-free desserts are sold at this sweet-smelling shop. Coffee, tea, and soft drinks are also served, making this a good place for an eat-and-run breakfast. For lunch, ready-made croissant sandwiches with ham and cheese or tuna salad are available. Inexpensive. B, L, S.

Studio Catering Co.: Guests on the Studio Backlot Tour come across this spot at the end of the tram ride. Situated just behind The Loony Bin, the eatery offers desserts and snacks. Beer is available. Inexpensive. S.

Sunset Ranch Market: Three food stands on Sunset Boulevard offer good snacking opportunities. Rosie's Red Hot Dogs specializes in the obvious, serving a curious assortment of hot dogs, including foot-long options. Catalina Eddie's offers frozen yogurt and fruit drinks, plus turkey legs. Popcorn, fresh fruit and vegetables, fruit juices, and soft drinks are also available at Anaheim Produce. Inexpensive. L, D, S.

Toy Story Pizza Planet: This arcade looks as if it were plucked out of the film *Toy Story*. The centerpiece is a Space Crane, complete with aliens and mechanical grabber. A limited menu includes individual pizzas, salads, pasta salad, Italian ices, and juice. Cappuccino and espresso are available. Inexpensive. L, D, S.

Studios Mealtime Tips

- To avoid traffic jams at fast-food spots, consider eating lunch or dinner at one of the restaurants that offer priority seating—Hollywood Brown Derby, 50's Prime Time Café, Sci-Fi Dine-In Theater, Soundstage (lunch only), or Mama Melrose's Ristorante Italiano. To arrange for priority seating in advance, call WDW-DINE (939-3463). To obtain same-day seating, go to the kiosk at Hollywood Junction (on the corner of Hollywood and Sunset, before 1 P.M.) or to the restaurant itself. Refer to page 245 for details.
- The many indoor and outdoor nooks within Backlot Express' seating area are nicely removed from the beaten path; relative quiet can frequently be enjoyed here even during prime mealtimes.
- Characters appear at the Soundstage restaurant during breakfast and lunch, so it's one of the best places to meet them at the Disney-MGM Studios.

In Animal Kingdom

Whether you eat like a bird or more like a horse, you'll have no trouble finding something to sink your teeth into at one of Animal Kingdom's many eateries. The emphasis at Disney's newest theme park—which opens in May 1998—is on fast food, with Rainforest Café as the only full-service establishment (only limited priority seating is accepted). The menagerie of quick-service options cater to carnivores and herbivores alike, featuring everything from freshly tossed Caesar salad to chicken roasted in a 16-foot "wall of flames." To avoid the inevitable feeding frenzy, consider eating meals a little before or after the usual times.

FULL SERVICE

Rainforest Café: Like The Oasis, the region of Animal Kingdom that it borders, the café is a lush, soothing tropical wonderland. Unlike The Oasis, any quiet moment here is merely a calm before the storm—as brief, dramatic thunderstorms occur throughout the day *inside* the café. Gushing waterfalls, twisting tree trunks, and colorful fish add to the ambience. The environmentally conscious cuisine includes items like Planet Earth Pasta and the Plant Sandwich. (The Calypso Dip appetizer—fresh salmon, artichoke hearts, onions, spices, and cheese served with warm pita—is especially tantalizing.) There's no net-caught fish on the menu, nor beef from countries that destroy rain forest land to raise cattle. An equally elaborate shop proffers logo merchandise, animal puppets and prints, and glow-in-the-dark toys.

Note: The restaurant and shop are accessible from both inside and outside Animal Kingdom—admission to the park is not necessary to come in here. It is located at the park entrance. Limited priority seating available. Moderate to expensive. B, L, D, S.

FAST FOOD & SNACKS

Coke Cool Zone: Relax along the Discovery River while sipping a soft drink at this refreshment spot located near the gateway to Asia. Inexpensive. S.

Flame Tree Barbecue: You will probably start licking your chops before you even arrive here, as the aroma of barbecue wafts not-so-subtly by. This outdoor fast-food establishment serves up a savory selection of American-style barbecue sandwiches and platters, all wood-roasted and fresh from the smoker. (The wood comes from farm-raised natural hardwoods.) Located in Safari Village, across from The Tree of Life. Inexpensive. L, D.

Pizzafari: Watch as gourmet pizzas are prepared before your eyes and served fresh from hearth ovens. In addition to the cheese-laden bill of fare, the specialty here is a freshly tossed Caesar salad with wood-roasted chicken. This counter-service restaurant is in Safari Village, on a walkway across from The Tree of Life. Inexpensive. L, D.

Restaurantosaurus: Located in the heart of DinoLand U.S.A., this spot is right in the midst of a summer campsite for student paleontologists. As such, the rooms are filled with fossils, bones, tools, and other artifacts from the dinosaur era. This eatery specializes in "dino-mite" fast-food favorites: hamburgers, cheeseburgers, hot dogs, salads, and snacks—and McDonald's french fries. It's next door to Countdown to Extinction. Inexpensive. L, D, S.

Tamu Tamu Yogurt Shop: Got a hankering for something cool and creamy? Stop by this snack spot in Africa's Harambe (across from Tuskers). Here you can indulge a sweet tooth with soft-serve yogurt and ice cream floats and sundaes. Inexpensive. S.

Tuskers: Harambe village sets the stage for a dining adventure at this fast-food restaurant. The menu features rotisserie chicken, cooked in a 16-foot "wall of flames." Grilled and fried chicken are also available, as are sandwiches. The signature salad, complete with warm chicken, is tossed to order. The on-site bakery provides a steady stream of fresh-from-the-oven breakfast treats and other desserts. Inexpensive. B, L, D, S.

GOOD MEALS, GREAT TIMES

229

In the Resorts

Among the more pleasant surprises at Walt Disney World is the delightful theming of the Disney hotels. Each resort sports a fanciful setting quite foreign to Central Florida, reminiscent of such places as the Pacific Northwest; the more regional-minded offer a tasty sampling of the native cuisine to complete the picture. Whereas the deluxe properties provide a variety of dining options, including at least one full-service restaurant, moderate resorts feature a sprawling food court plus an informal dining room, and the value-oriented All-Star resorts keep guests' appetites in check with huge food courts.

Suffice it to say that the possibilities range from hearty dinners served family-style on lazy susans to innovative cuisine you might not expect from Disney, presented in settings worthy of special occasions. Priority seating is an important part of the resorts' full-service dining circuit (for complete details turn to page 245). Character meals are an option for breakfast, Sunday brunch, and dinner (for specifics see page 244).

All-Star Sports & All-Star Music

Each of these resorts features a themed central food court. The **End Zone** food court in Stadium Hall at the All-Star Sports resort and the **Intermission** food court in Melody Hall at the All-Star Music resort have similar food stands. The selections include pasta, hand-tossed pizza, chicken, ribs, burgers, hot dogs, sandwiches, salads, frozen yogurt, and a wide variety of baked goods. Inexpensive. B, L, D, S.

BoardWalk

Big River Grille & Brewing Works: Guests observe (and later sample) as the brewmaster creates three flagship ales and two seasonal brews at this working brewpub. The menu features a variety of sandwiches, salads, and entrées. Moderate. L, D, S.

BoardWalk Bakery: The aromas wafting from Spoodles' next-door neighbor on the boardwalk reveal the fresh-baked goods therein. Display windows allow guests to watch bakers at work. "Bun rises" are held each morning. Inexpensive. B, S.

ESPN Club: A sports bar–family restaurant one-two punch, ESPN Club surrounds guests with no fewer than 70 TV monitors, so no one misses a play. The fare includes burgers, sandwiches, and a variety of salads and entrées. Moderate. L, D, S.

Flying Fish Café: This upbeat eatery delivers creative seasonal menus with an emphasis on seafood and healthy options. As an example of the entrées created in the open "onstage" kitchen, consider the potato-wrapped yellowtail snapper. Steaks are also served. Save room for the chocolate lava cake. Priority seating is suggested. Seating is available at the chef's counter. Expensive. D.

Seashore Sweets': Located next to the Flying Fish Café, this old-fashioned spot sates sweet tooths with candies, saltwater taffy, and ice cream and frozen yogurt. Specialty coffees are also offered. Inexpensive. S.

Spoodles: This family-oriented restaurant with butcher-block tables and Mediterranean tastes is on the boardwalk between Seashore Sweets' and the BoardWalk Bakery. The lunch and dinner menus highlight specialties from Greece, Spain, Northern Africa, and Italy, and

encourage diners to share dishes and try new foods. Offerings range from pizzas baked in wood-burning ovens to such creations as yogurt-marinated chicken kebabs served with corn risotto. The breakfast buffet features eggs, meats, fish, cereal, and french toast. A take-out window allows passersby to buy pizza by the slice. Priority seating suggested. Moderate to expensive. B, L, D.

Caribbean Beach

Captain's Tavern: Prime rib, chicken, and crab legs are on the menu at this cozy 200-seat restaurant located within Old Port Royale. Tropical drinks, beer, wine, and cocktails are also served. Priority seating is suggested. Moderate. D, S.

Old Port Royale: The food court in Old Port Royale features a 500-seat dining area and the following fast-food eateries. *Bridgetown Broiler* offers spit-roasted chicken and home-style meals. *Cinnamon Bay Bakery* serves croissants, freshly baked rolls, pastries, ice cream, and other high-calorie treats. Italian specialties are the order at the **Kingston Pasta Shop**. Soups, salads, and hot and cold sandwiches make up the selections at **Montego's Deli**. Burgers and grilled chicken sandwiches are among the offerings at **Port Royale Hamburger Shop**. And pizza is available by the slice or the pie at **Royale Pizza Shop**. Inexpensive. B, L, D, S.

Contemporary

California Grill: Perched on the hotel's 15th floor, with terrific views of sunsets and Magic Kingdom fireworks, this acclaimed restaurant offers the best in West Coast cuisine in a stylish, relaxing atmosphere. (It was recently named "restaurant of choice" by *Orlando Magazine*.) The ever-changing

menu is defined by sophisticated use of fresh produce. Wood-fired California pizzas, alderwood-smoked salmon, sushi, spit-roasted chicken, and jumbo soufflés are made to order in an open kitchen. Maui onion and artichoke soup, and oak-fired quail with zinfandel risotto suggest the culinary prowess. The excellent wine list is updated daily. Priority seating suggested. Expensive. D.

Chef Mickey's: As Chef Mickey and pals cook up a buffet-style feast, a glass window affords views of the passing monorail. Colorful life-size illustrations of Disney characters decorate the room. The changing menu takes advantage of seasonal offerings; a sundae bar provides a sweet finish. Priority seating suggested. Moderate to expensive. B, D.

Concourse Steakhouse: On the fourth-floor concourse, this spot offers omelettes, pancakes, and fresh fruit for breakfast. At lunch there are salads, soups, burgers, and sandwiches. Dinner adds prime rib and steaks to the menu. Priority seating suggested. Moderate to expensive. B, L, D.

Food and Fun Center: On the first floor adjacent to the arcade, this casual spot serves light fare 24 hours a day. Inexpensive. B, L, D, S.

Coronado Springs

Maya Grill: The only full-service restaurant at Disney's newest resort, it features Latin American dishes. Signature items include duck tamales with *chipotle* pepper sauce, snapper filet crusted with pumpkin seed and broiled tenderloin with garlic parsley sauce. Many items are cooked over an open-pit wood-fired grill. Maya Grill is located off the rotunda lobby, next to the Pepper Market food court. Priority seating suggested. Moderate. B, D.

Pepper Market: This food court, modeled after an open-air market, has a large seating area and lots of stands where vendors sell pizza, sandwiches, salads, burgers, regional specialties, baked goods, margaritas, and more. Inexpensive to moderate. B, L, D, S.

Disney's Old Key West

Good's Food to Go: Hamburgers, cheeseburgers, grilled chicken sandwiches, salads, ice cream, and frozen yogurt are among the offerings. Inexpensive. L, D, S.

Olivia's Café: An assortment of Key West favorites, including Key lime pie and conch fritters, are featured alongside more traditional fare, such as crab cakes. The menu changes seasonally. A Winnie the Pooh character breakfast is held Wednesday and Sunday. Priority seating suggested. Moderate. B, L, D.

Dixie Landings

Boatwright's Dining Hall: Be sure to notice the boat that's being built in this 200-seat full-service eatery. The specialties of the house include Cajun dishes as well as American home-style favorites. Priority seating suggested. Moderate. B, D.

Colonel's Cotton Mill: This high-ceilinged food court styled in the image of a working cotton mill offers half a dozen different counters and a sprawling seating area. Collectively, the stands offer pizza; pasta; fried, grilled, and spit-roasted chicken; burgers; barbecued ribs; salads; sandwiches; and fresh baked goods, including pies and sticky cinnamon buns. For guests on the go, the food court's deli doubles as a convenience store, stocking sandwiches, beer, wine, snack items, and prepared salads. Inexpensive. B, L, D, S.

Fort Wilderness

Most people cook their own meals here; ample supplies are available at both the Meadow Trading Post and the Settlement Trading Post (open from 8 A.M. to 10 P.M. in winter, to 11 P.M. in summer).

Trail's End Buffet: This informal log-walled restaurant offers standard breakfasts, plus grits, biscuits, gravy, and a seven-inch "breakfast pizza" that vaguely resembles an omelette. Hearty lunches and dinners feature barbecued chicken, fish, chicken pot pie, and spare ribs. There are sandwiches and a taco bar at lunch. Specially priced children's portions are available. Pizza is served every night from 9:30 P.M. until 11 P.M. (until midnight on weekends). Beer and wine are served by the glass or by the pitcher. Inexpensive to moderate. B, L, D, S.

Grand Floridian

Cítricos: The newest addition to the Grand Floridian's impressive restaurant lineup specializes in market-fresh, Floridian-Mediterranean cooking. The fare, which is presented with stylish simplicity, varies seasonally. The stunning view of the Seven Seas Lagoon is a year-round staple. Priority seating suggested. Expensive. D.

Gasparilla Grill & Games: Grilled chicken, hamburgers, pizza, hot dogs, and soft-serve ice cream are the mainstays at this 24-hour take-out, self-service restaurant near the pool. Continental breakfast is also available. Inexpensive. B, L, D, S.

Grand Floridian Café: Southern cooking is the specialty at this picturesque spot. Selections include honey-dipped fried chicken and filet mignon with braised mushrooms and potatoes. There are also salads and an assortment of more traditional entrées. Priority seating available. Moderate. B, L, D.

Narcoossee's: The open kitchen is the focal point at this casual, airy octagonal dining spot on the shores of the Grand Floridian beach. Specialties of the house include seafood nachos; grilled swordfish with mashed plantains; grilled steaks; rack of lamb; veal chops; and grilled jerk capon breast with sweet potato gnocchi. Priority seating suggested. Expensive. L, D.

1900 Park Fare: The all-American menu takes a backseat to the decor in this 248-seat buffet restaurant. Big Bertha, a band organ built in Paris nearly a century ago, sits 15 feet above the floor in a proscenium. The bellows-powered instrument simultaneously plays pipes, drums, bells, cymbals, and xylophone. Mary Poppins, Alice in Wonderland, and other

characters mingle with guests during breakfast. The dinner buffet features seafood, salads, vegetables, breads, and prime rib. Mickey and Minnie entertain at dinner. The offerings change weekly. Priority seating suggested. Expensive. B, D.

Victoria & Albert's: The premier restaurant of not only the Grand Floridian, but probably the entire Walt Disney World complex. The intimate dining room seats only 65, and elegant touches include Royal Doulton china, Sambonet silver, and Schott-Zweisel crystal. The menu is customized daily. Each night there are fish, fowl, red meat, veal, and lamb selections, which depend on the best ingredients in the market and are described in detail by your waiter. The chef may even make a personal appearance to accommodate special requests from patrons, or guests may choose to dine at the chef's table in the kitchen. There are also choices of two soups, two salads, and desserts, including specialty soufflés of fresh berries, chocolate, or Grand Marnier. There is an extensive wine list, and wine pairings are available with each course.

Once guests have made their selections, they are presented a personalized souvenir menu. At the completion of the meal, women receive a long-stemmed rose. Jackets

are required. One oddity of note: Every host and hostess at the restaurant is named Victoria or Albert. Priority seating necessary. Very expensive. D.

Polynesian

Captain Cook's Snack Company: A good spot for continental breakfast, hamburgers, hot dogs, fruit salad, and snacks; cans of beer are also available. Open 24 hours. Inexpensive. B, L, D, S.

Coral Isle Café: Located on the second floor of the Great Ceremonial House, just around the corner from 'Ohana. This standard coffee shop with a faintly South Seas decor serves the usual assortment of eggs every morning, plus granola and other cereals, and wonderful banana-stuffed french toast, one of the many unique Walt Disney World dishes. At lunch, the house does a booming business in burgers and a variety of sandwiches. At dinnertime, 20-ounce New York strip steaks, ribs, and tempting desserts are among the offerings. All things considered, it's a good choice when you want a no-fuss meal. Priority seating available. Moderate. B, L, D, S.

'Ohana: On the second floor of the Great Ceremonial House, this restaurant features a 16-foot-long open fire pit. Dinner choices in the all-you-can-eat family-style feast include shrimp, poultry, pork, and beef, all roasted on skewers up to three feet long. Meats are marinated in original combinations of soy, ginger, lemongrass, or garlic, and are served family-style with an assortment of fresh vegetables, salads, and homemade bread. The dessert offerings include passion fruit crème brûlée. The room itself is large and open and offers fine views across the Seven Seas Lagoon all the way to Cinderella Castle. Minnie's Menehune character

breakfast is held daily. Polynesian singers and dancers entertain at dinner. Priority seating suggested. Expensive. B, D.

Port Orleans

Bonfamille's Café: The name of this full-service restaurant derives from the Disney movie *The Aristocats*. Steaks, seafood, and Creole cooking highlight the menu. Breakfast is also served. Priority seating suggested. Moderate. B, D.

Sassagoula Floatworks & Food Factory: The stands at this festive food court feature pizza, pasta, gumbo, burgers, sandwiches, soups, salads, spit-roasted chicken, barbecued ribs, ice cream, and a full selection of fresh bakery products, including beignets. Inexpensive. B, L, D, S.

Swan & Dolphin

Cabana Bar & Grill: Burgers, grilled chicken sandwiches, fresh fruit, and yogurt are offered at this full-service poolside eatery. Inexpensive. L, S.

Coral Café: Buffets are offered for breakfast and dinner in this bright and casual restaurant. An à la carte menu is also available, offering turkey burgers, chicken, club sandwiches, pasta, and cheese steaks. Located at the Dolphin. Moderate. B, L, D, S.

Dolphin Fountain: Homemade ice cream is the highlight here. Flavors include dark chocolate, cappuccino, and mint chocolate chip. Oreo and Heath Bar mixes are available in waffle cones, cups, or as part of super sundaes. Burgers, shakes, and malts are also available. The old-time 1950s atmosphere is enhanced by an energetic staff that breaks into song and dance several times a day. Inexpensive to moderate. L, D, S.

Garden Grove Café: Situated in a five-story greenhouse, this Swan dining spot offers a full breakfast menu, and fresh fish and shellfish at lunch. At dinner, the restaurant is transformed into Gulliver's Grill, where you can order Blushklooshen (red snapper) and drink Caff Dupooshpoosh (double espresso) from oversize cups. Desserts are baked fresh daily in an open pastry kitchen. As you approach the restaurant, take a look through the glass windows to see the chefs at work. Character breakfasts and dinners are held here on certain days. Reservations suggested for dinner. Expensive. B, L, D, S.

Harry's Safari Bar & Grille: Grilled steaks, seafood, and chicken seasoned with herbs bought by "Harry" during his world travels mark the adventurous menu. On Sunday there is a character brunch. Reservations suggested for dinner, necessary for brunch. Located at the Dolphin resort. Expensive. D, Sunday brunch.

Juan & Only's: This festive Dolphin restaurant features authentic Mexican food. Specialties include fresh *pico de gallo* served with blue corn and spicy red chips; grilled beef, chicken, shrimp, and meatless fajitas

from the fajita bar; chimichangas; burritos; taco salads; and other Mexican fare. Reservations suggested. Moderate to expensive. D.

Palio: This Italian bistro gets high marks for its bruschetta, foccacia, pasta, and pizza. Other specialties include veal and fish dishes. A strolling musician adds to the ambience. Reservations suggested. Located at the Swan. Expensive. D.

Splash Grill: Burgers and other grilled fare join ice cream and frozen yogurt on the menu at this Swan poolside spot. Beer and frozen drinks are served. Prepackaged snacks are also on hand. Inexpensive. B, L, S.

Tubbi's: Checkerboard decor and a jukebox raise this cafeteria above the norm. The food, including meatball subs and pizza, is fresh, and the lines are seldom long. The adjoining convenience store (open 24 hours) at the Dolphin resort stocks snacks, sundries, and lots of baby items. Inexpensive. B, L, D, S.

Wilderness Lodge

Artist Point: Decorated with artwork representing the painters who first chronicled the Northwest landscape, this fine dining spot offers a creative menu that incorporates wild game as well as more traditional items

such as steaks, salmon, and other Pacific seafood. The solid wine list spotlights wines from the Pacific Northwest. A character breakfast hosted by Pocahontas and friends is served every morning. Priority seating suggested. Expensive. B, D.

Roaring Fork Snacks: Light snacks, salads, and yogurt are available 24 hours a day at this simple nook adjacent to the hotel's arcade. Inexpensive. B, L, D, S.

Whispering Canyon Café: A traditional family-style restaurant that's open for all-day dining. Hearty all-you-can-eat fare includes oven-roasted and wood-smoked meats with a variety of sides and salads plus

Par for the Course

The pleasant **Sand Trap Bar & Grill** in the Bonnet Creek Golf Club is a convenient dining option for golfers playing the adjacent Eagle Pines and Osprey Ridge courses. It's also close to the Magic Kingdom resorts. In addition to a variety of appetizers, burgers, Reuben sandwiches, barbecued pork, and grilled chicken sandwiches are served. There is a full bar; ice cream and milk shakes are also available. Moderate. L, D, S.

homemade desserts. Assorted sandwiches are available during lunch. Priority seating suggested. Moderate. B, L, D.

The Villas at the Disney Institute

Seasons Dining Room: Even the setup of this restaurant is seasonally driven. Four dining rooms are decorated to reflect the distinct seasons. The new lunch menu takes on a Floridian twist, featuring the freshest seasonal items the state has to offer, such as Gulf bouillabaisse. Dinner offerings include pan-seared chicken breast served with a potato-tomato relish, orangewood smoked beef tenderloin served with corn-on-the-cob, mashed potatoes, orange chili pepper seared shrimp in carmelized orange sauce dusted with red chili flakes, citrus cilantro pasta in cream, roasted pork tenderloin, Florida and California sushi rolls, lemon jerk chicken, and Key West conch chowder. Community tables are available for all three meals. Priority seating suggested. Expensive. B, L, D.

Yacht Club & Beach Club

Beaches & Cream Soda Shop: This restaurant straddles the Yacht Club and the Beach Club. Patterned after a turn-of-the-century ice cream parlor, it features over-size sundaes, cones, floats, shakes, and sodas, as well as the Fenway Park Burger—which can be ordered as a single, double, triple, or home run. Breakfast items are available as well. Inexpensive to moderate. B, L, D, S.

Cape May Café: An all-you-can-eat New England clambake is held each evening at the Beach Club. A cooking pit used for steaming is in full view of diners, and menu items include clams, mussels, chicken, shrimp, corn, red-skin potatoes, and chowder. Lobster is available for an extra charge. There is a character breakfast buffet each morning. Priority seating suggested. Moderate to expensive. B, D.

Hurricane Hanna's Grill: Located in the Stormalong Bay area. Hot dogs, burgers, sandwiches, french fries, and ice cream are on the menu. There is also a full bar. Inexpensive. L, S.

Yacht Club Galley: Vivid ceramic-tile tabletops help emphasize the yachting theme here at the Yacht Club. Breakfast features a buffet and a full menu; lunch and dinner are à la carte only. Priority seating suggested. Moderate. B, L, D.

Yachtsman Steakhouse: As its name implies, beef is the specialty of the house. Guests can see the butcher choosing cuts of meat in the glassed-in shop, and watch meals being prepared in the display kitchen. Fresh seafood and chicken are available. Located at the Yacht Club. Priority seating suggested. Expensive. D.

In Downtown Disney

The vast region known as Downtown Disney encompasses Pleasure Island, Downtown Disney Marketplace, and Downtown Disney West Side. While an admission fee applies after 7 P.M. for Pleasure Island club-goers, there is no charge simply to dine at any of Pleasure Island's full-service restaurants. (There is never a fee to roam the West Side or Marketplace.) In general, Downtown Disney restaurants operate from 11:30 A.M. to midnight; most of the snack spots are open from 11 A.M. to 2 A.M. For up-to-the-minute details on hours call 824-4321. It's worth noting that while the restaurants really hop at dinnertime, none are terribly crowded at lunch, with the exception of weekends.

Bongos Cuban Café (Downtown Disney West Side): This sizzling creation of Gloria Estefan and her husband spices up the Downtown Disney dining repertoire with a menu driven by Cuban and Latin American flavors. Like its big sister in Miami Beach, the spot is destined to tantalize taste buds with its slate of traditional and nouvelle Cuban dishes. Priority seating for parties of ten or more. Moderate to expensive. L, D, S.

Cap'n Jack's Oyster Bar (Downtown Disney Marketplace): This pier house juts right out over Buena Vista Lagoon, providing diners with water views. The menu is so full of good things—seafood marinara, peel-and-eat shrimp, crab specialties, garlic oysters, clam chowder, lobster, prime rib, and other "land lubber" specials—that it's as good for a light lunch or dinner as it is for a snack. There is a tempting variety of wines, microbrew beers, and other cocktails—and the house's special frozen margaritas are as tasty as they are beautiful. Cap'n Jack's is a terrific place to be, especially in late afternoon, as the sun streams through the narrow-slatted blinds and glints on the polished tables and the copper above the bar. Moderate. L, D, S.

D-Zertz (Pleasure Island): Pastries, chocolates, candy, frozen yogurt, and other such sweet treats are the mouth-watering fare available here. Coffee and cappuccino are also served, making it a pleasant spot for a quick snack. Inexpensive. S.

Fulton's Crab House (Pleasure Island): This traditional seafood house, operated by Levy Restaurants, occupies the three-deck riverboat formerly known as the *Empress Lilly*. Permanently docked on the western edge of Buena Vista Lagoon, it is a tribute to

Robert Fulton, who invented the steamboat. The place is so serious about seafood that it has hooked up with fishermen worldwide to ensure that the truckloads of fish and shellfish arriving daily at Fulton's back door are at their freshest.

The menu changes each day to reflect new arrivals, but is always brimming with several types of crabs, oysters, and fish, plus lobster, steaks, roast chicken, grilled vegetables, and combination platters. Signature dishes include cioppino, a savory San Francisco–style seafood stew with a tomato broth base. Accompaniments extend to corn-whipped potatoes and sugar snap peas. Desserts, coffee, and specialty drinks are also served. The children's menu runs from fish-and-chips to spaghetti.

Fulton's handsome polished-wood interior is awash in nautical knickknacks and nostalgia. Seating on the deck is sometimes available. The adjoining Stone Crab lounge has a mouthwatering raw bar—excellent for lunch or snacks. A grand character breakfast with Captain Mickey and friends is held twice daily (seatings are at 8 A.M. and 10 A.M.). The meal features scrambled eggs, chicken-apple sausage, hash browns, apple pastry, fruit, and mini muffins. Priority seating suggested for breakfast and dinner. Expensive. B, L, D, S.

Ghirardelli's Soda Fountain and Chocolate Shop (Downtown Disney Marketplace): San Francisco's famous sweet-maker finally comes East with a soda fountain extraordinaire. Stop in for a chocolaty treat, a root beer float, or a refreshing malt. Antique chocolate-making equipment demonstrates how the famous Ghirardelli chocolate got its start. It's hard to find a better place to please a sweet tooth. Inexpensive. S.

Gourmet Pantry (Downtown Disney Marketplace): Though it's technically a shop, this food-oriented establishment is positively brimming with sweet and savory possibilities. Among the delectables standing by for snackers and impromptu picnickers are specialty salads and sandwiches, tasty heroes sold by the inch, fresh baked cookies and desserts, Godiva chocolates, nuts, beer, wine, spirits, and gourmet coffees. Seating is available right outside and also along the waterfront on the Buena Vista Lagoon. Inexpensive. B, L, D, S.

House of Blues (Downtown Disney West Side): The nightclub that Blues Brother Dan Aykroyd helped launch doubles as a Mississippi Delta–inspired dining spot. House gives Downtown Disney a culinary boost from the Bayou—namely home-style Cajun and Creole cooking. Finally, Walt Disney World has a haven for diners desperately seeking to have their fill of such savory things as jambalaya, étouffée, and homemade bread pudding. A gospel brunch is presented on Sundays. Moderate. L, D, S.

McDonald's (Downtown Disney Marketplace): The Golden Arches and all of its Mc-specialties are showcased in this new installation of the familiar fast-food establishment located on the west side of Buena Vista Lagoon. Inexpensive. B, L, D, S.

Missing Link Sausage Co. (Pleasure Island): Hot dogs, bratwurst, kielbasa, and sausages (including a chicken-apple variety, and both mild and hot Italian links) dominate the menu of this snack spot across from 8Trax. Cheese steaks are also available. Inexpensive. L, D, S.

Planet Hollywood (Pleasure Island): This branch of the international restaurant chain is a standout for its spherical silhouette. Co-owned by Arnold Schwarzenegger, Sylvester Stallone, Bruce Willis, and

The lines for Planet Hollywood are usually shortest between 1 P.M. and 5 P.M.

Demi Moore, this globe is built on three levels. Classic movie and television memorabilia abound.

The creative, wide-ranging menu features first-rate salads, sandwiches, pasta dishes, burgers, appetizer pizzas, fajitas, and dessert specialties. Be sure to consider sampling the blackened shrimp, Far East chicken salad, vegetable burger, or pasta primavera. Cap off the meal with a piece of butter rum cake or a generous helping of Arnold Schwarzenegger's mother's apple strudel. No reservations are accepted. Smoking is permitted. Moderate. L, D, S.

Portobello Yacht Club (Pleasure Island): The elegant Bermuda-style house combines high gables and beamed ceilings, bright Mediterranean colors and earthy tones. This was the first dining spot opened by the Levy Restaurants of Chicago, and is one of our favorites on WDW property. The 326-seat establishment is divided into several informal dining rooms, each of which displays a collection of maritime memorabilia.

But food is definitely the highlight of the Portobello Yacht Club experience. The bustling open kitchen turns out grilled meat and fish and absolutely delicious small gourmet pizzas baked in the wood-burning oven. Try the *quattro formaggi*, a four-cheese pie that's a true taste treat and a great appetizer or snack. Pasta offerings include *spaghettini alla Portobello*—pasta with shrimp, scallops, clams, mussels, crab legs, tomatoes, garlic, olive oil, wine, and herbs— and *bucatini all'amatriciana*, long pasta tubes with plum tomatoes, Italian bacon,

garlic, and fresh basil. Be sure to save room for desserts such as *crema brucciata*, Italian custard with a caramelized sugar glaze or *cioccolato paradiso*, a layer cake with chocolate ganache frosting, chocolate toffee crunch filling, and warm caramel sauce. Portobello also offers a selection of specialty coffees and an impressive wine list. A children's menu is available. No reservations are accepted. Expensive. L, D, S.

Rainforest Café (Downtown Disney Marketplace): There's no mistaking the environmental orientation of this Amazon-emulating eatery near Cap'n Jack's Oyster Bar. The incredible dining environs transport guests to a makeshift rain forest, complete with banyan trees, tropical fish, gushing waterfalls, and a friendly population of hand-raised parrots. A talking tree offers a constant stream of ecological insights, and animal experts are on hand to field questions. Sophisticated special effects envelop guests in tropical storms, complete with lightning and thunder. Menu items include Planet Earth Pasta, Island Hopper Chicken, and the Plant Sandwich (portobello mushrooms, zucchini, roasted red peppers, and fresh spinach). The eatery, part of a national chain, is equally environment-conscious behind the scenes: All paper and plastic goods are recycled after use. No net-caught fish are served. And proceeds from the restaurant's wishing well are donated to selected environmental groups. A merchandise shop stocks a variety of logo clothing. Moderate to expensive. L, D, S.

Wolfgang Puck Café (Downtown Disney West Side): Wolfgang Puck's choice of Walt Disney World for his Florida debut is sure to spur a surge in cravings for his trademark California cuisine. Among his specialties are pizzas, pastas, chicken salad, and rotisserie chicken. The menu is equal parts sophisticated and straightforward—and ever so fresh. Priority seating suggested. Moderate to expensive. L, D, S.

Wolfgang Puck Express (Downtown Disney Marketplace and West Side): Renowned chef Wolfgang Puck turns his talents to fast service and signature treats, including pizza, focaccia sandwiches, soup, and fresh salads—for those with a lot of taste and little time. Inexpensive. L, D, S.

Crossroads of Lake Buena Vista

Walt Disney World visitors also have several restaurants from which to choose at the Crossroads of Lake Buena Vista shopping center, near the resorts on Hotel Plaza Blvd. These include Pebbles (the best bet here), T.G.I. Friday's, Red Lobster, McDonald's, Taco Bell, Jungle Jim's, Pacino's, Chevy's Mexican Restaurant, and Pizzeria Uno.

Resorts on Hotel Plaza Boulevard

Within the resorts on Hotel Plaza Blvd., you can dine in casual cafés, in an upscale dining room with a Tinker Bell's–eye view or Florida Keys ambience, or in an evocative restaurant with a Down Under or Sherlock Holmes theme. The larger properties offer more dining choices, of course, but even the smaller hotels have a family-style eatery on the premises. And if you go to a late movie or dance way past midnight at Pleasure Island, you can always count on a late-night bite at one of the round-the-clock cafés.

BUENA VISTA PALACE: Arthur's 27 has an international menu, and boasts a dramatic view over Downtown Disney. Very expensive. D. The lively **Outback** (not part of the chain of the same name), with Australia-inspired decor and a multilevel waterfall, serves dinner with an accent on steaks and fish. Moderate. D. The garden-like **Watercress Café & Pastry Shop** offers full meals and snacks, as well as a Sunday character breakfast. The bakery section of the café serves pastries, sandwiches, and fruit, and is open 24 hours a day. Moderate to expensive. B, L, D, S.

COURTYARD BY MARRIOTT: Courtyard Café & Grille serves an eclectic menu ranging from salads and sandwiches to seafood. There is a breakfast buffet, but guests may also order from an à la carte menu. Moderate. B, L, D. **Village Deli** features muffins, sandwiches, Pizza Hut pizza, and TCBY yogurt. Inexpensive. B, L, D, S. The **2 Go** breakfast bar and take-out facility is adjacent to an open seating area in the atrium lobby. Inexpensive. B.

DOUBLETREE GUEST SUITES: Streamers offers classic American dishes as well as shrimp tortellini and filet mignon. There is a breakfast buffet. Moderate. B, L, D, S. **Streamers Market** can provide snack items and groceries. Inexpensive. S.

GROSVENOR: This high-rise hotel's casual **Baskervilles** restaurant has a not-so-casual Sherlock Holmes theme. Prime-rib dinner buffets are popular. There is a Mystery Show on Saturday night. A Wednesday character dinner supplements the character breakfasts, held Tuesday, Thursday, and Saturday. Moderate. B, L, D. **Crumpets** lobby café, open 24 hours, serves continental breakfast and lighter fare. Inexpensive. B, L, S.

HILTON: Finn's Grill specializes in fresh seafood, steaks, and pasta served in an old Key West atmosphere. Expensive. D. At the **Benihana** Japanese steak house, chefs put on a tableside show; there's also a sushi bar. Moderate. D. **County Fair** serves a full breakfast (characters make rounds on Sunday); salads, sandwiches, and pasta are available for lunch and dinner. Moderate. B, L, D. **County Fair Terrace** offers outdoor seating as well as continental breakfast and menu items from the adjacent County Fair restaurant. Inexpensive to moderate. B, L, S. Note that both County Fair and County Fair Terrace are expected to be overhauled in 1998. The **Old-Fashioned Soda Shoppe** menu spans from ice cream to pizza. Inexpensive. L, D, S. **John T's Plantation Bar** serves light fare and cocktails. Inexpensive to moderate. L, S. **Rum Largo Pool Bar & Café** serves salads, sandwiches, and burgers alfresco. Inexpensive. L, D, S.

ROYAL PLAZA: Plaza Diner serves full-service, buffet, and family-style meals. Inexpensive to moderate. B, L, D, S. A deli provides yogurt, espresso, and take-out items.

TRAVELODGE: Traders has a buffet and à la carte breakfast; the à la carte dinner features fresh seafood and steaks. Moderate. B, D. **Parakeet Café** offers pizza, salads, sandwiches, and snacks. Inexpensive. B, L, D, S.

MEAL BY MEAL

When you're looking for something special in the way of a meal, and you're willing to go a bit out of your way to find it, the descriptions below should provide sufficient suggestions to sate your appetite. What follows are the highlights of WDW breakfasts, lunches, and dinners, as well as some suggestions for avoiding meal-time crowds at the eatery of your choice. This is a selective, not comprehensive, list; for complete information see the preceding listings under "Restaurants of WDW."

Breakfast

Most people opt for eggs and bacon or something similar at their own hotel. But those who decide to venture farther afield will be amazed at the choices available. For instance, the french toast served at the Polynesian resort's Coral Isle Café restaurant is made with thick slices of sourdough bread stuffed with bananas, deep-fried, and then rolled in cinnamon and sugar—and is one of the best breakfast concoctions ever.

At most hotel breakfast spots, there are likely to be lines between 8 A.M. and 10 A.M., the morning rush hour. So allow plenty of time at these hours, eat earlier or later, or stop at a snack shop for something light to stave off hunger until it's possible to have a no-wait breakfast (or an early lunch). At many of the Walt Disney World resorts, it's also possible to order breakfast from room service the night before.

The Magic Kingdom has no shortage of options for quick morning meals. During busy seasons, however, even early birds might wait for a table. Consider stopping by the Main Street Bakery or a fast-food spot—since many serve coffee and pastries from park opening until about 11 A.M. For a hearty breakfast, try Tony's Town Square, the Crystal Palace, or Cinderella's Royal Table.

In Epcot, the Sunshine Season Food Fair in The Land offers bagels and cream cheese, as well as delicious pastries. Fountain View Espresso and Bakery next to Innoventions has a great selection of pastries and specialty coffees to enjoy in the morning.

At the Disney-MGM Studios, try a home-cooked breakfast at the Hollywood & Vine cafeteria or coffee and a croissant at the Starring Rolls Bakery. If you are looking for breakfast at Animal Kingdom, consider Tuskers for a quick bite, or Rainforest Café for a more substantial meal.

Lunch

Breaking up a day in the theme parks with lunch at one of the resorts can provide the energy needed to keep you going until closing time. (However, a few of the eating spots do get crowded around midday. It's always a good idea to eat a little before or after the usual mealtime rush.)

Choice lunch spots in the Downtown Disney Marketplace are Wolfgang Puck Express and Cap'n Jack's Oyster Bar. At Pleasure Island, the Portobello Yacht Club's terrific individual pizzas hit the spot; ditto the seafood chowder and raw bar at Fulton's Crab House. Burgers, unique salads, pastas, and desserts are good at Planet Hollywood. Or for something lighter, try the frozen yogurt at D-Zertz.

If you can't tear yourself away from the Magic Kingdom to go elsewhere for lunch, there's still no lack of selection. Burgers and fries are for sale at practically every turn, but better yet are the salads, sandwiches, and pizza at Tony's Town Square restaurant; the sandwiches and seafood salads served (seasonally) at Columbia Harbour House in Liberty Square; turkey dinners, sandwiches, fish, and salads served at the Liberty Tree Tavern, also in Liberty Square; the pizza at the Plaza Pavilion in Tomorrowland; and the salads at Cinderella's Royal Table in Cinderella Castle.

As at breakfast, crowds can be a problem; the three hours between 11 A.M. and 2 P.M. are the busiest. To avoid the rush, eat a light breakfast and a big early lunch—or have a late breakfast and a late lunch. If necessary, snatch a midmorning snack to tide you over until things get less hectic.

In Epcot, lunch is a prime opportunity to sample the full-service restaurants offering ethnic specialties. Linger over their culinary delights, out of the heat of the midday sun, while hordes of other guests are lining up for attractions. Try not to miss the quiche at Chefs de France, and the *queso fundido* at Mexico's San Angel Inn restaurant. Germany's Biergarten has lively entertainment and a hearty buffet throughout the day. In World Showcase, meat pies and Epcot's best salad (the fresh vegetable platter) may be found at the Rose & Crown Pub and Dining Room; stir-fried meats and vegetables are the prime fare in the Mitsukoshi restaurants; Moroccan sampler platters are offered at Marrakesh; Chinese specialties are served at the Nine Dragons restaurant; hearty German food is offered in Germany's Biergarten; and fairly authentic Mexican fare fills the menu in Mexico's San Angel Inn restaurant. An enormous buffet is served at Akershus in Norway. Tempura Kiku in Japan is the only full-service restaurant that does not require priority seating. The most elaborate cooking is done at Italy's Alfredo's and at France's Chefs de France. Among full-service eateries in Future World, the Garden Grill is special for its family-style rotisserie chicken and hickory-smoked steaks.

Ethnic fast food is available at Japan's Yakitori House, China's Lotus Blossom Café, Norway's Kringla Bakeri og Kafé, and Mexico's Cantina de San Angel. But for burgers and other standard fast-food fare, try the Electric Umbrella restaurant in Innoventions or Liberty Inn at The American Adventure. The Sunshine Season Food Fair in The Land offers a cornucopia of choices, from baked potatoes, soups, and salads to barbecued sandwiches and more—and is therefore an ideal place for a family that can't arrive at a consensus. The chocolate chip cookies from the bakery make a good dessert.

At the Disney-MGM Studios, consider the famous Cobb salad at the Hollywood Brown Derby; a good home-cooked meal served by "Mom" at the 50's Prime Time Café; the character buffet at the Soundstage; salads, ribs, grilled chicken, and fruit at the Hollywood & Vine cafeteria; chili, charbroiled chicken, and burgers at Backlot

Express; or huge sandwiches, salads, and pastas at the Sci-Fi Dine-In Theater restaurant. When the lunchtime hunger pangs strike at Animal Kingdom, consider stopping for a meal at Flame Tree Barbecue.

Dinner

There's an awesome choice, from the humblest snack center to Victoria & Albert's. Walt Disney World has never exactly been a bastion of haute cuisine, but that doesn't mean that dinner experiences are anything less than pleasant. In fact, new restaurants popping up all over the World are continually changing the face of the dining scene. Service is almost unfailingly good (slipping just slightly during the busiest seasons), and the best of Walt Disney World's dinners are sure to impress. The fact that the famed L.A. chef Wolfgang Puck opened a full-service restaurant and quick-service café here is a testament to the World's upwardly mobile culinary consciousness.

Factor this kitchen can-do into the unique only-at-WDW atmosphere, and it's obvious why we like to make time on each trip for a dinner-as-event (when the only point of the evening is to savor a relaxing meal). For a night on the World, good choices abound. Of course, we certainly have our favorites.

The WDW resorts are particularly good places to find an exceptional meal. At the top of the list for special occasions is Victoria & Albert's at the Grand Floridian, one of the more extravagant meals money can buy. Try the wine pairings with each course for an extra treat. Narcoossee's, also at the Grand Floridian, is another favorite, and don't overlook the new Cítricos. At the Polynesian, 'Ohana delivers a South Sea feast (grilled meats that keep coming until you say when). The Yachtsman Steakhouse at the Yacht Club is good for a hearty meal. Combine it with a pre-dinner drink in the adjoining lounge, and you've got yourself some enchanted evening. Artist Point at the Wilderness Lodge is a culinary addition that keeps us coming back for more tastes of the Pacific Northwest (and that heavenly berry cobbler). California Grill at the Contemporary is another find, where the scents from the open kitchen and the panorama of the Magic Kingdom would warrant a visit even if the cuisine (paired with a wide selection of California wines) weren't excellent. Spoodles at the BoardWalk is a good place to try flavorful Mediterranean dishes, while the BoardWalk's Flying Fish Café sates with fresh seafood.

Elsewhere in the World, the Hollywood Brown Derby at the Disney-MGM Studios is the most elegant theme park meal around. Animal Kingdom's Rainforest Café serves up tasty meals in a tropical wonderland. And some of our old-time favorites, as well as notable newcomers, are at Pleasure Island.

Combine a meal at one of these restaurants with a night of dancing on Pleasure Island, and you just might not make it to the parks the next day. Portobello Yacht Club is an old standby that's worth getting to early (it's first-come seating, and lines develop quickly). We could recommend any number of the Italian specialties on the menu (and we've tried quite a few, including all of the desserts). Fulton's Crab House is the best bet on-property for fresh

seafood that seems to arrive hourly, served in a knockout setting (the former *Empress Lilly* riverboat has had quite a face-lift).

Of course, most of the aforementioned suggestions require a baby-sitter, since not a kid in the world (especially not *this* World) would sit still through such a meal. Refer to the *Getting Ready to Go* chapter's "Traveling with Children" section if that's what you have in mind. On the other hand, there are plenty of great meals to be had with kids in tow. Refer to the box below for our recommendations, many of which are suitable dinner options for kids and adults alike. Keep in mind that all Disney restaurants have a special menu just for children. Note that nearly all of the restaurants we list have been tested by the kids who help create *Birnbaum's Walt Disney World For Kids, By Kids.*

WDW restaurants outside the Magic Kingdom are busiest in the evening between 7 P.M. and 9 P.M. Those in the Magic Kingdom are busiest between 5 P.M. and 7 P.M.

During busy seasons, guests visiting the Magic Kingdom will do well to eat a late lunch and have dinner after 8 P.M. in order to catch the second, less crowded, showing of SpectroMagic. Those traveling with young children should plan to eat their meals on the early side and take in the first show.

Best Bets for Family Fare

Children are welcome at every Walt Disney World restaurant, but the leisurely pace of service at some places can make kids fidget. Still, there are plenty of choices that are well suited to dining *en famille*. Resort restaurants that are especially good for families include Chef Mickey's at the Contemporary resort, Whispering Canyon Café at the Wilderness Lodge, Boatwright's Dining Hall at Dixie Landings, and Bonfamille's Café at Port Orleans. The buffet-style clambake held at Cape May Café in the Beach Club resort is a hit with kids, (as is any other buffet-style meal where they can serve themselves). The food courts at the Caribbean Beach, Coronado Springs, Port Orleans, Dixie Landings, All-Star Sports, and All-Star Music resorts are other options for finicky eaters.

Most of the restaurants at the Magic Kingdom cater to kids, but Pecos Bill Café (for burgers and fries) and Tony's Town Square (for pizza) get particularly high marks. The character meals at the Crystal Palace offer a welcome compromise for kids and parents alike (the meals suit both tastes, and characters keep kids entertained).

At Epcot, Pasta Piazza Ristorante and Liberty Inn are top picks for kids who love fast food. Garden Grill in The Land pavilion provides a meal that kids and adults appreciate: Characters come to the table during the family-style meal, with a separate "bottomless skillet" menu for kids and adults (served all day). Sunshine Season Food Fair, also in The Land, is a huge food court with myriad choices—a good option for family members with differing tastes.

At the Disney-MGM Studios, kids enjoy the Sci-Fi Dine-In Theater and 50's Prime Time Café. The character buffet at Soundstage is also a top choice for breakfast or lunch. Other options include a quicker meal at Hollywood & Vine, ABC Commissary, or Backlot Express.

One of the best places to dine out with kids is Planet Hollywood at Pleasure Island. The movie memorabilia hanging from the ceiling and the great food are always a hit. Also try the Rainforest Café at either the Downtown Disney Marketplace or Animal Kingdom. Each is a themed restaurant with environmental (and kid) appeal.

Dinner Shows

The fact that the Disney organization is the expert in family entertainment is nowhere more strongly apparent than amid the whooping and hollering troupe of singers and dancers who race toward the stage at Fort Wilderness resort's Pioneer Hall. As guests plow through barbecued ribs, fried chicken, corn-on-the-cob, and strawberry shortcake, these enthusiastic performers sing, dance, and joke up a storm. It's all in the course of an evening at the Hoop-Dee-Doo Musical Revue, presented nightly at 5 P.M., 7:15 P.M., and 9:30 P.M. Cost is $37 per adult and $19.50 for children (3 to 11). Also presented at Fort Wilderness is the All-American Backyard Barbecue. The seasonal dinner show costs $35 per adult and $25 for kids.

Mickey's Tropical Luau, presented daily at 4:30 P.M. at the Polynesian resort, is a Polynesian show geared toward the younger set. Disney characters, dressed in traditional costumes, dance alongside the Polynesian performers. A full dinner complete with dessert is served. Cost is $30 for adults and $14 for children.

The Polynesian Luau at the Polynesian resort, presented nightly at 6:45 P.M. and 9:30 P.M., also has its moments. The performers' dancing is some of the most authentic this side of Hawaii. Many of the Walt Disney World dancers have studied at the well-respected Polynesian Cultural Center in Hawaii. A full Polynesian-style meal, including roasted chicken, spareribs, and a fruity dessert is served. Cost is $37 for adults and $18 for children.

The Biergarten at Epcot's Germany pavilion entertains diners with a musical trio during lunch and throughout the evening with intermittent shows featuring traditional German musicians, yodelers, and dancers. A hefty buffet is served. Lunch is $10.95 for adults, $5.50 for children; dinner is $14.75 for adults, $6.99 for children.

Plan to arrive 15 minutes or so before starting time, and allow enough time for transportation and parking. (Note that prices, which do not include tax or gratuity, are subject to change.)

Reservations for all these shows (priority seating suggested for Biergarten) can be made by calling WDW-DINE (939-3463). Reservations are required well in advance and are generally hard to come by. Groups of eight or more should call 939-7707.

Dining with Disney Characters

At some sites, food takes second place to Mickey Mouse, Donald Duck, Minnie Mouse, Goofy, and the rest of the Disney gang, who take turns making special appearances at these especially delightful affairs. Options abound, as the characters host meals throughout the day all over the World. Unless otherwise noted, character meals below are offered daily, and priority seating arrangements can generally be made up to 60 days in advance by calling WDW-DINE (939-3463). We strongly suggest making these arrangements prior to your visit, especially during busy seasons. Also, be sure to arrive at least 15 minutes before your seating time. Walk-ins are possible, but highly unlikely for any except the Swan's first-come, first-served character breakfast (held Saturday at the hotel's Garden Grove Café). Bottomless buffets and all-you-can-eat family-style dining are the rule, particularly for breakfast, but specific offerings vary from place to place. Finally, as you make note of the following menu of character affairs—organized by meal—keep in mind that the lineup is subject to change.

Character Restaurants: Meals with the Disney characters have become so popular that there are now several restaurants dedicated to providing them all day long. Winnie the Pooh entertains during the buffet-style meals at Crystal Palace in the Magic Kingdom. Epcot has its family-style Garden Grill restaurant, with homey fare and Chip 'n' Dale appearances. In the Disney-MGM Studios, characters from the most recent animated films preside over buffet-style breakfast and lunch at the Soundstage restaurant. At the Contemporary resort, Chef Mickey and friends cook up a buffet-style breakfast and dinner (at Chef Mickey's restaurant, of course). Breakfast costs $13.95 for adults and $7.95 for children ages 3 to 11. For other meals, cost ranges from $14.95 to $19.95 for adults, and from $7.95 to $9.95 for children.

Breakfast: Fulton's Crab House (between Pleasure Island and the Downtown Disney Marketplace) is the site of the biggest character shindig around, hosted by Captain Mickey and crew. There are two seatings every morning. Guests may also have breakfast with characters at 1900 Park Fare in the Grand Floridian resort (Mary Poppins drops in); at Cape May Café in the Beach Club resort (Admiral Goofy runs the show); at Olivia's Café at Old Key West (Winnie the Pooh and friends hold court on Wednesday and Sunday); at Artist Point in the Wilderness Lodge (Pocahontas, John Smith, and Meeko host a rustic affair); and at 'Ohana in the Polynesian resort (where Minnie's Menehune breakfast carries the South Seas theme). Character breakfasts are also served in the theme parks. Among the more popular is the "Once Upon A Time" breakfast at Cinderella's Royal Table in the Magic Kingdom. Prices are $14.95 for adults, $7.95 for children 3 to 11.

Sunday Brunch: Disney favorites host brunch at Harry's Safari Bar & Grille in the Dolphin resort (call 934-4884 in advance for reservations). Prices are about $15.50 for adults and $9.25 for children ages 3 to 11.

Dinners: The Liberty Tree Tavern in the Magic Kingdom hosts a character supper. Character dinners are also held at 1900 Park Fare in the Grand Floridian resort. Gulliver's Grill at Garden Grove in the Swan holds a character dinner each Monday, Thursday, and Friday (on certain nights *The Lion King* characters pay a visit); call 934-1609 to make reservations. Prices are about $19.50 for adults, $9.95 for children ages 3 to 11; the à la carte meal at the Swan may run higher.

All About Priority Seating

Priority seating has replaced reservations at almost all WDW full-service restaurants. Disney initiated the policy to provide the assurance of a reservation without the delays caused by no-shows and latecomers. Ideally, the system ensures that guests are not left waiting if a table is available. Here's how it works: You call ahead to request a priority seating time; then you arrive at the assigned time, check in at the podium, and receive the next available table that can accommodate your party. The priority seating system works very much like reservations, so you will always be seated before any walk-ins.

We strongly recommend making advance arrangements and arriving about 15 minutes early. Priority seating times can be secured up to 60 days ahead by calling WDW-DINE (939-3463). The number of tables available in advance varies. If you are unable to book a table ahead of time, try to make same-day arrangements (for details about how to do this in the theme parks, see the listings below).

While priority seating is the prevalent policy at WDW restaurants, there are several exceptions in which tables may be booked solely via traditional reservations. Most notably, reservations are necessary for certain dinner shows—the Hoop-Dee-Doo Musical Revue, Mickey's Tropical Luau, and the Polynesian Luau; they can be made up to two years ahead through WDW-DINE (939-3463). If you can't get a table for an early performance, try for a later one (usually less heavily booked). Also falling outside the priority seating domain are Harry's Safari Bar & Grille and Juan & Only's at the Dolphin resort (call 934-4884); and Palio and Garden Grove Café at the Swan resort (call 934-1609).

A concise guide to WDW restaurants that offer priority seating is provided below. For at-a-glance advice about the necessity of priority seating arrangements (or reservations) at specific restaurants, consult the chart on pages 16 and 17 of the *Getting Ready to Go* chapter.

Note: Because the dining scene at Walt Disney World is tremendously dynamic and procedures have changed more than a few times over the years, we advise calling WDW-DINE (939-3463) to confirm current policies.

MAGIC KINGDOM: Priority seating is suggested at Tony's Town Square, Plaza, Crystal Palace, and Liberty Tree Tavern; necessary at Cinderella's Royal Table. For same-day seating, go to the restaurant or City Hall.

EPCOT: Advance priority seating arrangements are strongly recommended for nearly all full-service restaurants at Epcot, particularly for dinner. However, on the day of your visit, it is possible to book lunch or dinner tables via WorldKey Information System screens. Look for the screens at Guest Relations on the east side of the pathway between Future World and World Showcase, and in Germany. Same-day lunch tables can also be booked in person at the chosen restaurant. Never bypass an eatery for which you have a sudden appetite; occasionally, you can walk right in. **Note:** Priority seating is not available for Tempura Kiku.

DISNEY-MGM STUDIOS: Priority seating is suggested for 50's Prime Time Café, Hollywood Brown Derby, Mama Melrose's Ristorante Italiano, Sci-Fi Dine-In Theater, and Soundstage. Go to Hollywood Junction or the chosen restaurant for same-day seating.

DOWNTOWN DISNEY: Priority seating is suggested at Fulton's Crab House and Wolfgang Puck Café.

WDW RESORTS: Priority seating is suggested for full-service resort restaurants, with a few exceptions (where it's necessary or offered only for dinner); a complete lineup follows. *Beach Club:* Cape May Café. *BoardWalk:* Flying Fish Café, Spoodles. *Dixie Landings:* Boatwright's Dining Hall. *Caribbean Beach:* Captain's Tavern. *Contemporary:* California Grill, Chef Mickey's, Concourse Steakhouse. *Coronado Springs:* Maya Grill. *Disney Institute:* Seasons Dining Room. *Dixie Landings:* Boatwright's Dining Hall. *Grand Floridian:* Citricos, Grand Floridian Café, Narcoossee's, 1900 Park Fare, Victoria & Albert's. *Old Key West:* Olivia's Café. *Polynesian:* Coral Isle Cafe, 'Ohana. *Port Orleans:* Bonfamille's Café. *Wilderness Lodge:* Artist Point, Whispering Canyon Café. *Yacht Club:* Yacht Club Galley, Yachtsman Steakhouse.

LOUNGES OF WDW

No one ever said the Magic Kingdom's no-liquor policy means that everyone in the World is a teetotaler. Actually, some of WDW's tastiest offerings are liquid (and decidedly alcoholic), and some of its most entertaining places are its bars and lounges.

Hours vary depending on the locale, but generally watering holes at Epcot and the Disney-MGM Studios shut their doors at park closing. Pool bars at the resorts generally keep daytime pool hours. Last call at lounges in the resorts is anywhere from 10 P.M. to midnight. Downtown Disney Marketplace spots stay open until the shops close, usually 11 P.M. The clubs at Pleasure Island and the West Side keep things going until 2 A.M. Note that specialty drinks sans alcohol are available at all establishments.

ALL-STAR SPORTS & ALL-STAR MUSIC

Singing Spirits: Beer, wine, and mixed drinks are served by the pool.

Team Spirits: Specialty drinks, wines, and beer are available at this poolside spot.

BEACH CLUB

Hurricane Hanna's Grill: This refreshment spot, located near Stormalong Bay between the Yacht Club and the Beach Club, offers specialty drinks and beer as well as a selection of fast-food items.

Martha's Vineyard: A light and airy atmosphere prevails at this cozy retreat. Wines from a real Martha's Vineyard winery, as well as selections from California, Long Island, and European vineyards, are on the extensive list. While wine is the house specialty, this is a full bar. Hors d'oeuvres and desserts are served.

Rip Tide: This lobby bar features California wines, wine coolers, and frosty drinks that are consistent with the hotel's beachside theme.

BOARDWALK

Atlantic Dance: This classic dance hall showcases a live band, hors d'oeuvres, desserts, a full bar, premium cigars, and champagne.

Big River Grille & Brewing Works: A working brewpub, where patrons can order appetizers at the bar while watching (and later sampling) as the brewmaster creates three flagship ales and two specialty beers.

Belle Vue Room: Snacks and a full bar accompany old-time tunes from antique radios in this lobby cocktail lounge.

ESPN Club: The ultimate sports bar provides live radio and television broadcasts along with a menu of ballpark favorites.

Jellyrolls: Dueling pianos and lively sing-alongs are the draw at this unique club, serving beer and other drinks.

Leaping Horse Libations: The pool bar at Luna Park offers cocktails, as well as tuna sandwiches, fruit salad, and garden salads in a carnival setting.

BONNET CREEK GOLF CLUB

Sand Trap Bar & Grill: Appetizers and sandwiches supplement the array of libations offered at this fully stocked bar.

CARIBBEAN BEACH

Banana Cabana: All types of drinks and fast-food items are served at this poolside bar.

Captain's Tavern: Tropical drinks, beer, wine, and cocktails are served at this restaurant lounge in Old Port Royale. Chicken, crab legs, and specialty items from the restaurant are available during dinner hours.

CONTEMPORARY

California Grill Lounge: Prime 15th-story digs eye-level to the Magic Kingdom fireworks. A large selection of California wine by the glass, all manner of other drinks, and appetizers are offered in this atmospheric spot adjoining the California Grill.

Outer Rim: This lounge overlooking Bay Lake serves beer (including a special microbrew called Monorail Ale), wine, cocktails, appetizers, and desserts.

Sand Bar: Beer, frozen drinks, and fast-food items are offered poolside. Seasonal.

CORONADO SPRINGS

Francisco's: Located in the main building, this lounge serves specialty drinks, beer, wine, and light snacks, accompanied by live music.

Siesta's: Swimmers and archaeologists alike take time out for cocktails, burgers, sandwiches, and tacos at this lounge near the pool in the Dig Site area.

DISNEY-MGM STUDIOS

Catwalk Bar: Above the Soundstage restaurant sits this cocktail lounge resembling a movie prop storage area. Appetizers, specialty drinks, beer, and wine are served.

Tune-In Lounge: A sitcom living room setting, with couches, chairs, and TV dinner–tray tables, characterizes this lounge next to the 50's Prime Time Café. Waiters in V-neck sweaters play the roles of sitcom "Dads," and old TV sets play scenes from beloved sitcoms. Appetizers, mixed drinks, beer, and wine are served.

DISNEY'S OLD KEY WEST

Gurgling Suitcase: This pocket-size lounge on the Turtle Krawl boardwalk serves an assortment of Key West specialties along with traditional cocktails, beer, and wine.

Turtle Shack: Refreshments at this poolside spot include beer, specialty drinks, and fast-food items.

DOWNTOWN DISNEY

All clubs have bars serving specialty drinks (with and without alcohol), beer, wine, and cocktails. The **Stone Crab** lounge at **Fulton's Crab House** (Pleasure Island) and **Bongos Cuban Café** (Downtown Disney West Side) are notable for exotic cocktails and outdoor seating. Pleasure Island's **Portobello Yacht Club** also has a pleasant lounge. The **Rainforest Café** is the site of the whimsical Mushroom Bar.

Cap'n Jack's Oyster Bar (Downtown Disney Marketplace): Agleam with copper and right on the water, this bar's specialty is its delicious strawberry margaritas. The nibbles of garlic oysters, clam chowder, shrimp, and seafood marinara are great for a snack, but also substantial enough for a light lunch or dinner.

DIXIE LANDINGS

Cotton Co-Op: Situated in a room designed as a cotton exchange, this lounge features specialty drinks as well as some light hors d'oeuvres. There is entertainment here five nights a week.

Muddy Rivers: The poolside bar serves beer, specialty concoctions, and selected fast-food items.

EPCOT

All restaurants, including some of the fast-food spots, serve alcoholic beverages. Restaurants such as the San Angel Inn have a small lounge at which patrons may wait for tables. Then there are a few other places that specialize in spirituous liquid refreshments:

Matsu No Ma: In addition to exotic sake-based specialty drinks, this Japan pavilion establishment offers a fine panoramic view over the whole of Epcot—including the World Showcase Lagoon, with Spaceship Earth as a backdrop—one of the best vistas of the property available. Japanese beer, green tea, and sushi are also served.

Rose & Crown Pub: This watering hole—a veritable symphony of polished woods, brass, and etched glass—adjoins the Rose & Crown Dining Room in the United Kingdom pavilion. British, Irish, and Scottish beers are available, along with a score of specialty drinks and appetizing snacks imported from the other side of the Atlantic. An entertaining pianist plays and sings just about any request well into the evening.

Sommerfest: Just outside the Biergarten restaurant in Germany, there's a small shaded terrace where soft pretzels, bratwurst, Black Forest cake, steins of Beck's beer, and German wine are available.

FORT WILDERNESS

Crockett's Tavern: Cocktails, beer, wine, and appetizers are served here. Afterward, for a change of pace, take a blue-flagged watercraft to the Contemporary resort.

GRAND FLORIDIAN

Garden View: A view of the lushly landscaped pool and garden area makes this lounge a pleasant place to meet for a drink or dessert. Afternoon tea is also served here.

Mizner's: Named after the eccentric architect who defined much of the flavor of southeastern Florida's Gold Coast, this handsome retreat is on the second floor of the main building. Ports, brandies, and appetizers are featured.

Narcoossee's: An unusual manner of service in this lagoonside bar-within-a-restaurant allows guests to choose from a mug, a half-yard, or a yard of beer. And they mean a yard.

Summerhouse: This bar between the pool and the beach stands by with beer, frozen drinks, and fast-food items.

POLYNESIAN

Barefoot Bar: This oasis adjoining the swimming pool lagoon serves beer, frozen tropical drinks, and fast food. Seasonal.

Tambu: This bar adjoining 'Ohana restaurant offers Polynesian-style appetizers and specialty drinks in a tropical setting.

PORT ORLEANS

Mardi Grogs: Beer, specialty drinks, popcorn, hot dogs, and hot pretzels are among the offerings at this poolside spot.

Scat Cat's Club: Traditional offerings from the bar join New Orleans specialties and hors d'oeuvres at this comfy little lounge. There is musical entertainment here five nights a week.

SWAN & DOLPHIN

Cabana Bar & Grill: Beer, frozen drinks, and fast-food selections are the main offerings at this Dolphin poolside spot.

Copa Banana: Tabletops designed to resemble slices of fruit, and giant pineapples and palm trees offer a fitting backdrop for tropical libations. There is a large-screen TV, and deejay music and karaoke are featured in the evenings. Located at the Dolphin.

Harry's Safari Bar: Join the peripatetic "Harry" for a drink and maybe a story or two in this Dolphin restaurant bar. Appetizers, a house microbrew, and unique specialty drinks are featured.

Kimono's: This Swan spot, attractively decorated in Japanese style, has a full bar, as well as sushi, and a variety of oriental specialties.

Lobby Court: The winding corridors of the Swan lobby have comfortable couches and chairs, punctuated by pianos where able musicians often perform. Specialty coffees,

desserts, and wines by the glass are featured. A special menu with ports, cognacs, and cigars is offered seasonally.

Only's Bar & Jail: Rare tequilas, an array of margaritas, sangria, and beers from every region of Mexico join Mexican-style appetizers on the menu here at the Dolphin. The small, atmospheric lounge, adjacent to Juan & Only's restaurant, resembles a jail.

Splash Grill: Beer, frozen drinks, and fast-food items are served at this poolside café at the Swan.

THE VILLAS AT THE DISNEY INSTITUTE

Seasons Terrace Lounge: A comfortable and inviting setting adjoining the Seasons Dining Room, this lounge serves specialty drinks, cocktails, beer, and wine. Entertainment is sometimes offered in the nearby lobby in the evening.

WILDERNESS LODGE

Territory: Located between Artist Point and the Whispering Canyon Café, this homage to the Old West is a nice spot for a light lunch or pre-dinner treat. Appetizers, microbrew beer, and specialty coffees are served.

Trout Pass: This poolside bar serves beer, frozen drinks, and fast-food selections.

YACHT CLUB

Ale and Compass: The lobby watering hole proffers a specialty drink menu complete with coffee and ale.

Crew's Cup: Styled after a New England waterfront pub, this lounge has a masculine feel to it. It's right next door to the Yachtsman Steakhouse, has almost 40 beers on hand, and is a choice spot for a drink before dinner.

Hurricane Hanna's Grill: Fast-food items, beer, and frozen drinks are offered at this poolside refreshment station, located near Stormalong Bay between the Yacht Club and the Beach Club.

More Special Nighttime Fun

The Magic Kingdom takes on additional dazzle after dark. SpectroMagic is a procession so amazing that it alone is worth the trip to Walt Disney World. Epcot is particularly lovely at night, when the lights sparkle on the lagoon, Spaceship Earth is aglow, and IllumiNations lights up the sky. And the Disney-MGM Studios is home to the terrific Sorcery in the Sky fireworks. But there are always a dozen or so other special happenings and events going on after dark throughout the World. Call 824-4321 to find out what's in store for your next visit.

CAMPFIRE PROGRAM: This event at Fort Wilderness, held nightly near Meadow Trading Post at the center of the campground, features a sing-along, Disney movies, and cartoons. Open only to WDW resort guests.

ELECTRICAL WATER PAGEANT: Best seen from a beach on Bay Lake, this show is a 1,000-foot-long string of illuminated floating creatures. Guest Services or City Hall can tell you when and where it can be seen—usually it's visible at 9 P.M. from the Polynesian, 9:20 P.M. from the Grand Floridian, 9:35 P.M. from the Wilderness Lodge, 9:45 P.M. from Fort Wilderness, and 10:05 P.M. from the Contemporary.

FANTASMIC!: Premiering in late 1998, this extravaganza takes guests inside the dreams of Mickey Mouse—into a world where his magic creates dancing waters, animated fountains, balls of fire, and more. The action will occur in an ampitheater behind Tower of Terror.

FANTASY IN THE SKY: When the Magic Kingdom is open late, it features nightly fireworks. The show lasts six minutes, and outshines displays many times its length.

ILLUMINATIONS: This nightly show is an absolutely spectacular display of music, laser lights, fireworks, and fountains that can be seen from any point on the World Showcase Promenade at Epcot, usually at closing time. Check at Guest Relations for the exact time.

SORCERY IN THE SKY: Every night during busy seasons, this ten-minute pyrotechnical production outshines the stars over the Chinese Theater at the Disney-MGM Studios. It features music from the silver screen and stands out as one of Disney's best fireworks shows.

SPECTROMAGIC: The Magic Kingdom's biggest extravaganza, this parade makes its way down Main Street on select nights throughout the year, twice a night during busy seasons. The advanced technology incorporates holograms, special lighting techniques, and a state-of-the-art sound system.

TENNIS: Courts at the Contemporary, Grand Floridian, Fort Wilderness, Yacht Club and Beach Club, Old Key West, BoardWalk, and The Villas at the Disney Institute are usually open until 8 P.M. Those at the Swan and Dolphin are open 24 hours a day.

INDEX

Dining at **Epcot**®

10% discount off dinner at

- Liberty Inn (at The American Adventure, World Showcase)
- Electric Umbrella (Innoventions Plaza, Future World)

50% off Accommodations at

Vacation Club Resorts

- Buy two nights accommodations at Disney's Vero Beach Resort and get the third night at 50% off.
- Buy three nights accommodations at Disney's Hilton Head Island Resort and get the fourth night at 50% off.

28% off

Your guide to all that's new, classic, and magic at Disney.

CALL 800-333-8734 and receive 8 issues (2 years) for $16.95—it's like getting 2 issues FREE!

Dining at the

10% discount off dinner at

- Tony's Town Square
- Crystal Palace

10% discount off any meal at

at the Disney Institute

Featuring Classic Floridian cuisine with a new twist.

ONE CAR CLASS UPGRADE

Present this certificate at a National rental counter in the U.S. or National Tilden in Canada for a one car class upgrade on a Compact through Full-size 4-door car. Valid at participating National Tilden locations in Canada.

Reservations recommended. Contact your travel consultant or National today at 1-800-CAR-RENT.
Subject to terms and conditions on reverse side.

PC# 013912-3
Valid Through: December 31, 1998

The Official Car Rental Company of Walt Disney World
©1997 National Car Rental System, Inc.

One Free Bucket of Golf Range Balls (per person) at

- Palm/Magnolia Golf Courses
- Bonnet Creek Golf Club
- Lake Buena Vista Club

Free Half Hour of Tennis Ball Machine Use at

Disney's Racquet Club
(Contemporary Resort)
Purchase one half hour and receive the second half hour free.